YOU DECIDE!
2008
Current Debates in American Politics

JOHN T. ROURKE
University of Connecticut

PEARSON
Longman

New York   San Francisco   Boston
London   Toronto   Sydney   Tokyo   Singapore   Madrid
Mexico City   Munich   Paris   Cape Town   Hong Kong   Montreal

Editor in Chief: Eric Stano
Executive Marketing Manager: Ann Stypuloski
Production Coordinator: Scarlett Lindsay
Project Coordination and Electronic Page Makeup: Lorraine Patsco
Cover Design Manager: John Callahan
Manufacturing Buyer: Roy L. Pickering, Jr.
Cover image courtesy of Getty Images, Inc.
Printer and Binder: R.R. Donnelley/Crawfordsville
Cover Printer: R.R. Donnelley/Crawfordsville

Library of Congress Cataloging-in-Publication Data

Rourke, John T., 1945–
  You decide! 2008 : current debates in American politics / John T. Rourke.
  — 4th ed.
      p. cm.
  1. Political planning—United States. 2. United States—Politics and government. I.
Title.
  JK468.P64R67 2007
  320.60973—dc22

                                                                    2006035192

For permission to use copyrighted material, grateful acknowledgment is made to the
copyright holders on pp. 283–285, which are hereby made part of this copyright page.

Visit us at www.ablongman.com

ISBN-13: 978-0-205-60596-5
ISBN-10:   0-205-60596-6

2 3 4 5 6 7 8 9 10–DOC–10 09 08

CONTENTS

Children's Access to Violence on Television: Leave to Parental Oversight

ADVOCATE: Laurence H. Tribe, Carl M. Loeb University Professor, Harvard
University and Professor of Constitutional Law, Harvard Law School

SOURCE: Testimony during hearings on "The Effects of Television Violence on
Children" before the U.S. Senate, Committee on Commerce, Science,
and Transportation, June 26, 2007

Also suitable for chapters on Civil Liberties, Social Policy

THE OIL INDUSTRY AND ENERGY PRICES:
PROFITEERING *OR* RESPONDING TO MARKET FORCES?

The Oil Industry and Energy Prices: Profiteering

ADVOCATE: Tyson Slocum, Director, Public Citizen's Energy Program

SOURCE: Testimony during hearings on "Prices at the Pump: Market Failure and
the Oil Industry" before the U.S. House of Representatives, Committee
on the Judiciary, Antitrust Task Force, May 16, 2007

The Oil Industry and Energy Prices: Responding to Market Forces

ADVOCATE: John Felmy, Chief Economist, American Petroleum Institute

SOURCE: Testimony during hearings on "Prices at the Pump: Market Failure and
the Oil Industry" before the U.S. House of Representatives, Committee
on the Judiciary, Antitrust Task Force, May 16, 2007

Also suitable for chapters on Energy Policy, Economic Policy

HILLARY CLINTON AND THE 2008 PRESIDENTIAL ELECTION:
THE DEMOCRATS' BEST BET *OR* A PROBLEMATIC CANDIDATE?

Hillary Clinton and the 2008 Presidential Election: The Democrats' Best Bet

ADVOCATE: Carl Cannon, White House correspondent for the *National Journal*

SOURCE: "She Can Win the White House," *Washington Monthly*, July/August 2005

Hillary Clinton and the 2008 Presidential Election: A Problematic Candidate

ADVOCATE: Amy Sullivan, editor, *Washington Monthly*

SOURCE: "Not So Fast," *Washington Monthly*, July/August 2005

Also suitable for chapters on Elections

THE ELECTORAL COLLEGE:
ABOLISH *OR* PRESERVE?

EXTENDED CONTENTS

WEB ISSUES

The following topics are available on the Web at:
http://www.ablongman.com/YouDecide/

23. TORTURING TERRORISTS

SOMETIMES JUSTIFIED *OR* ALWAYS ABHORRENT?

Torturing Terrorists: Sometimes Justified

ADVOCATE: Robert G. Kennedy, Professor of Management, University of St. Thomas

SOURCE: "Can Interrogatory Torture Be Morally Legitimate?" paper presented at the Joint Services Conference on Professional Ethics, U.S. Air Force Academy, January 2003

Torturing Terrorists: Always Abhorrent

ADVOCATE: Lisa Hajjar, Professor of Sociology, Law and Society Program, University of California–Santa Barbara

SOURCE: "Torture and the Future," *Middle East Report Online*, May 2004

Suitable for chapters on Civil Liberties, Criminal Justice, National Security Policy

24. THE SURGE OF U.S. TROOPS INTO IRAQ

SOUND STRATEGY *OR* WISHFUL THINKING?

The Surge of U.S. Troops into Iraq: Sound Strategy

ADVOCATE: Max Boot, Senior Fellow in National Security Studies, Council on Foreign Relations

SOURCE: Testimony during hearings on "A Third Way: Alternatives for Iraq's Future" before the U.S. House of Representatives, Committee on Armed Services, Subcommittee on Oversight and Investigations, July 12, 2007

The Surge of U.S. Troops into Iraq: Wishful Thinking

ADVOCATE: Wesley K. Clark, General (retired) U.S. Army and former NATO Supreme Allied Commander, Europe

SOURCE: Testimony during hearings on "A Third Way: Alternatives for Iraq's Future" before the U.S. House of Representatives, Committee on Armed Services, Subcommittee on Oversight and Investigations, July 12, 2007

Suitable for chapters on Foreign Policy, National Security Policy

PREFACE

To the Students

This book is founded on two firm convictions. The first is that each of you who reads this book is profoundly affected by politics, probably in more ways than you know. The second "truth" is that it is important that everyone be attentive to and active in politics.

POLITICS AFFECTS YOU

The outcome of many of the 18 debates in this printed volume and the six supplemental debates on the Web will impact your life directly. If you are a woman, for example, the controversy over gender pay equity laws in **Debate 21** has and will help determine whether your pay will be equal to that of men doing the same work with the same experience. College-age students are most likely to be sent to and to die in wars. There has not been a military draft since the Vietnam War era, and U.S. casualties in wars have been relatively light since then. But in that war, 61 percent of the more than 58,000 Americans killed were between the ages of 17 and 21. Now, after many years, there is renewed talk about a draft, featured in **Debate 24**, in part because the U.S. military is having trouble meeting its recruitment goals amid its ongoing involvement in Iraq.

Freedom of religion is one of Americans' most cherished rights and is protected by the First Amendment. But the application of the First Amendment is something of a double-edged sword. There is widespread agreement that people should have the right to whatever religious belief they may hold. What is controversial and presented in **Debate 3** is whether even such traditional references to God, such as the words "under God" in the Pledge of Allegiance violate the separation of church and state principle in the First Amendment.

YOU CAN AND SHOULD AFFECT POLITICS

The second thing this volume strongly suggests is that you can and should take part in politics. But there are limits to a good thing. **Debate 4** takes up the case of a student punished by his school for what it said was advocating illegal drug use. **Debate 6** addresses another limitation on participation, the constitutional prohibition of naturalized U.S. citizens becoming president.

Debate 22 about campaign finance reform also addresses participation. Those who argue that there should be strict limits on how much people and organizations can spend to support or oppose a candidate for office claim that the impact of money on politics makes a mockery of the idea that all citizens should have an equal say.

POLITICS SHOULD NOT ALWAYS AFFECT YOU

It is true that politics affects us all and that we should try to affect politics, but it is also a cornerstone of democracy that many aspects of our lives should be shielded from political control. This principle is the basis of, among other things, the Bill of Rights. Many of the debates in this volume address the line between where the government can make policy and where it is violating our political and civil rights. It is clear, for example, that the level of violence that children see on television has a negative impact on their development. What is unclear, as **Debate 7** struggles with, is whether the government should step in and, in what some claim is a violation of the First Amendment, regulate what is in the media.

A related matter of boundaries is taken up in **Debate 17** on how far the government can go to achieve racial integration in the country's schools. This debate focuses on the policy of the Seattle schools to try to achieve balance in the the racial composition of the district's schools by sometimes busing students.

PAY ATTENTION TO THE POLICY PROCESS

Process may seem less interesting than policy to many people, but you do not have to study politics very long to learn that *who* decides something very often determines *what* the policy will be. Process does not always determine which policy is adopted, but it plays a large role. Therefore, there are a number of debates in this volume whose outcome does not directly affect a specific policy, but which could have a profound impact on the policy process. For example, **Debate 2** on Federalism may seem abstract, but one of the cases on which the debate turns involved whether California could legalize the medical use of marijuana grown and distributed entirely within the state. Washington, D.C., opposed the California measure and claimed that it could regulate the drug under the interstate commerce clause, and the Supreme Court had to decide the issue in a case about the division of power between the Washington, D.C., and the state governments in the federal system. **Debate 20** also addresses federalism, and one advocate proposes to diminish the traditional power of the states to determine marriage law by amending the Constitution to bar marriages between homosexuals. There is little doubt that the president is the most powerful actor in the political process, and **Debate 12** examines one aspect of that authority: the president's ability to grant clemency to those who have committed criminal acts under federal law. **Debate 18** also addresses presidential power. The debate explores how power is allocated between the president and Congress in the process by which the government spends money. In the debate, one advocate suggests that the president be given more power by allowing him to cut specific items out of appropriations bills enacted by Congress. A second advocate argues giving this power to the president is an unwarranted transfer of power from one branch of government to another.

Policy is also a reflection, in part, of who serves, and Debates 9, 10, and 11 all focus on that issue. The Democrats have now lost two presidential elections in a row. **Debate 9** takes up whether the Democrats have the best chance of reversing their losing streak by making Senator Hillary Rodham Clinton (D-NY) their presidential nominee in 2008. Those who serve must, of course, come to office as the result of elections, but, for the president, whether that should be decided by a majority of the American voters or a majority of the Electoral College is featured in **Debate 10**. Both advocates in **Debate 11** argue that they want to give you more choice as to who will represent you in Congress. One advocate says the way to do that is to limit the term of federal legislators so that there will be regular turnover. The other advocate replies that doing so will limit your ability to be represented for many terms by an effective legislator whom you support.

The vast government bureaucracy is also part of the policy process. An ongoing issue concerns the degree to which career civil servants should be controlled in their statements and decisions by the president, as the elected head of the executive, or should be shielded from what some see as political interference. That matter is at the center of **Debate 13** over the White House's oversight of government scientists' recommendations on global warming.

It is also important to realize that the courts, especially the U.S. Supreme Court, are very much part of the policy process. That is evident in **Debate 14**, in which the advocates disagree on whether or not the recent appointment to the Supreme Court of Chief Justice John Roberts and Associate Justice Samuel Alito have swung the ideological composition of the court far to the right.

STATE AND LOCAL GOVERNMENTS ARE IMPORTANT, TOO

The federal government is just one of the more than 80,000 different governments in the United States. Each of the state and local governments has the power to pass laws, establish regulations, and tax and spend. For example, state and local governments now spend over $2 trillion a year. They also exercise a range of powers that, on a day-to-day basis, affect Americans more immediately than does federal law. One power exercised by state and local governments is the police power, sometimes with life-and-death consequences. That this is literally the case is clear in **Debate 15**. It considers the level of force that officers can use to stop a motorist who refuses to obey a police command to pull over to the side of the road and stop.

THERE ARE OFTEN MORE THAN TWO SIDES TO A QUESTION

Often public policy questions are put in terms of "pro and con," "favor or oppose," or some other such stark choice. This approach is sometimes called a Manichean approach, a reference to Manicheanism, a religion founded by the Persian prophet Mani (c. 216–276). It taught "dualism," the idea that the universe is divided into opposite, struggling, and equally powerful realities, light (good) and darkness (evil).

The view here is that many policy issues are more a matter of degree, and that the opinion of people is better represented as a place along a range of possibilities, rather than a black-or-white Manichean choice. Numerous debates herein are like that. For example, surveys of the American people on torturing suspected or proven terrorists, the subject of **Debate 23**, find that only about a third staunchly oppose torture under any circumstances, and even a smaller minority think it is regularly justified. That leaves about half of all Americans with a nuanced view, willing to support torture in some circumstances but not as a routine interrogation method. Opinion is similar about the death penalty, the focus of **Debate 16**. A large majority of Americans favor it, but surveys also show that people are troubled by a range of possible injustices, such as the relationship of wealth to the ability to mount a top-notch defense, the ability to execute people for crimes committed while a juvenile, and claims of racial injustice.

MANY ISSUES HAVE MULTIPLE ASPECTS

Often, political issues are like *matryoshkas*, the Russian nested dolls which come apart many times, each time revealing an ever-smaller doll inside. **Debate 1** is about "the right to bear arms." At its most specific, the issue is whether individuals have such a right. But deciding that involves the larger question of how to decide what those who wrote the Second Amendment meant. That matter, in turn, takes us to an even larger debate about whether we should follow the literal intent of those who wrote constitutional language, most of which is more than two centuries old, or apply the language of the Constitution within the context of the twenty-first century.

The discussion in **Debate 5** about how well recent immigrants are melding into the larger American culture also has multiple aspects, including both fact and values. At the objective level, the question is the degree of the immigrants' acculturation. How much of their old culture have immigrants and their families kept, and how "Americanized" have they become, especially after an extended time and into the second and third generations? Irrespective of the answer, there is also a question of values. How much should these newcomers and their families become homogenized? **Debate 19**, on poverty, also includes both objective and subjective aspects. How objectively do we determine who is poor? You will see that the formula for measuring poverty is very controversial. There is also the question of what and how much to do about poverty. To a degree, your views probably depend in part on whether you think an individual's success in life is the product of that person's abilities and effort or the product of society.

Everyone hates high gasoline prices, but there is little agreement on whether the government can or should try to do much about them. In **Debate 8**, one advocate argues that the oil industry has been profiteering, and that stricter regulations and taxes on the industry will help both keep prices down and generate revenues to support projects such as alternative fuel research. The other opponent claims that high gas prices have multiple causes, that these do not include gouging by the oil companies, and that government intervention would be unwarranted and counterproductive.

SOME CONCLUDING THOUGHTS

The points with which we began are important enough to reiterate. Whether you care about politics or not, it affects you every day in many ways. As the legendary heavyweight boxer Joe Louis put it after knocking out Billy Conn, a more agile but less powerful opponent, in their 1941 championship fight, "You can run, but you can't hide."

Simply paying attention is a good start, but action is even better. Everyone should be politically active, at least to the level of voting. Doing so is in your self-interest because decisions made by the federal, state, and local governments in the U.S. political system provide each of us with both tangible benefits (such as roads and schools) and intangible benefits (such as civil liberties and security). Also, for good or ill, the government takes things away from each of us (such as taxes) and restricts our actions (such as speed limits). It is also the case in politics, as the old saying goes, that squeaky wheels get the grease. Those who participate actively are more likely to be influential. Those who do not, and young adults are by far the age group least likely to even vote, are consigned to grumbling impotently on the sideline.

As an absolute last thought (really!), let me encourage you to contact me with questions or comments. My e-mail address is john.rourke@uconn.edu. Compliments are always great, but if you disagree with anything I have written or my choice of topics and readings, or if you have a suggestion for the next edition, let me know.

To the Faculty

Having plied the podium, so to speak, for three decades, I have some well-formed ideas of what a good reader should do. It is from that perspective that I have organized this reader to work for the students who read it and the faculty members who adopt it for use in their classes. Below is what I look for in a reader and how I have constructed this one to meet those standards.

PROVOKE CLASS DISCUSSION

The classes I have enjoyed the most over the years have been the ones that have been the liveliest, with students participating enthusiastically in a give-and-take among themselves and with me. Many of the debates herein have been selected to engender such participation in your classes by focusing on hot-button topics that provoke heated debate even among those who are not heavily involved in politics and who do not have a lot of background on the topic. The very first topic, gun laws, in Debate 1, is just such a subject. More than once I have had students get into spirited exchanges over the "right to bear arms," so I thought it would be a great debate to open the volume. Just a few of the other hot-button topics are medical marijuana use (Debate 2), use of the phrase "under God" in the Pledge of Allegiance (Debate 3), the death penalty (Debate 16), school busing (Debate 17), and gay marriage (Debate 20). I hope they rev up your classes as much as they have energized mine.

Another point about class discussion that I highlight in the preface section "To the students" is that, while the debate titles imply two sides, many policy topics are not a Manichean choice between yes and no. Instead, I have tried to include many issues on which opinion ranges along a scale. From that perspective, I often urge students to try to formulate a policy that can gain majority support, if not a consensus. You will also find that many of the issues herein are multifaceted, and I try to point that out to the students. For instance, the debate about gun control is about more than weapons, it is also about how we interpret and apply the Constitution.

BE CURRENT

An important factor in engaging the students is being current. Debating Franklin Roosevelt's court-packing scheme has importance, but it is not as likely to interest students as the acceptability of the Senate Democrats' current practice of sometimes filibustering President Bush's judicial nominees. Therefore, I vigorously update each edition. Even though *You Decide!* appears annually, more than half of the topics in *You Decide! 2008* are wholly new or are revised from *You Decide! 2007*. Additionally, some of the readings in the carry-over debates are new. Also for these debates, the "Continuing Debate" sections at the end are updated.

PROVIDE A GOOD RANGE OF TOPICS

I always look for a reader that "covers the waterfront" and have tried to put together this reader to do that. There are numerous debates on specific policy issues and others on process. All the major institutions are covered in one or more debates, and there are also debates touching on such "input" elements as parties, campaigns, interest groups, and the media. The primary focus of this book is on the national government, but federalism receives attention in Debate 2, and state and local government issues are taken up in Debate 15 on police powers. I have also included several debates that are at the intersection of domestic and foreign affairs, including Debate 23 (torturing terrorists) and Debate 24 (the U.S. presence in Iraq).

My sense of a good range of topics has meant balancing hot-button topics with others that, while they will draw less of an emotional response, are important to debate because they give insight about how the system works and how it might work differently. For example, Debate 20 relates to the hot-button topic of gay marriage, but as noted, its more basic point is federalism. I hope that the debate will get students to think of the federal system, which my experience tells me they mostly take as an unchanging given. Another example is the idea presented in Debate 11 of going from unlimited terms for members of Congress to limited terms.

GIVE THE STUDENTS SOME BACKGROUND FOR THE READING

Readers that work well provide students with some background material that is located just before the reading. This debate volume follows that scheme. There is a two-page introduction to each debate that establishes the context of the debate. As part of this setup, each introduction provides the students with several "points to ponder" as they read the debates.

Moreover, the introductions do more than just address the topic per se. Instead they try to connect it to the chapter for which it is designed. For example, the introduction to Debate 14 on the ideology of the U.S. Supreme Court begins with the power of the judiciary in the American system and how that makes judicial appointments such a high-stakes issue.

PROVIDE FOLLOW-UP POSSIBILITIES

One of the rewards of our profession is seeing students get excited about a field that intrigues us, and the reader provides a "continuing debate" section after each of the two readings. This section has three parts. "What Is New" provides an update of what has occurred since the date(s) of the two articles. "Where to Find More" points students to places to explore the topic further. I have particularly emphasized resources that can be accessed on the Internet on the theory that students are more likely to pursue a topic if they can do so via computer than by walking to the library. Needless to say, however, I think libraries are great and students should have to use them, so there are also numerous references to books and academic journals. Finally, the continuing debate section has a "What More to Do" part. This segment presents topics for discussion, suggests projects, and advises how to get active on a topic.

FIT WITH THE COURSE

I favor readers that fit the course I am teaching. I prefer a book with readings that supplement all or most of the major topics on my syllabus and that also allows me to spread the reading out so that it is evenly distributed throughout the semester. To that end, this book is organized to parallel the outline of the major introduction to American politics texts in use today. For those who favor the foundations-politics-institutions-policy approach, the table of contents of this volume should match almost exactly with their text and syllabus. For those who use a foundations-institutions-politics-policy scheme, a little, but not much, adjustment will synchronize the debates herein with your plans. Moreover to help with that, I have labeled each debate in the table of contents with the syllabus topic that fits with the debate. Additionally, for the 20 debates in the printed edition, I have indicated an alternative syllabus topic for each, and I have also made suggestions about how each of the six debates on the Web might fit with various text chapters and syllabus topics.

FLEXIBILITY

While there is a fair amount of similarity in the organization of the major introduction to American politics texts, I suspect that the syllabi of faculty members are a good deal more individualistic. With that in mind, I have provided flexibility in the reader. First, there are 18 debates in the printed edition, each of which is related to a topic, but each of which has suggestions in the table of contents for alternative assignments. Then there are six additional readings on the Longman Web site associated with *You Decide!* Each of these also has multiple uses and my suggestions about how to work each one into your syllabus. Thus, you can use all 24 debates or many fewer; you can substitute some on the Web for some in the printed edition; you can follow the order in the book fairly closely with most texts; or you can rearrange the order at will. As the Burger King slogan goes, "Have it Your Way!"

As a final note, let me solicit your feedback. Every text and reader that anticipates future editions should be a work in progress. *You Decide!* certainly is. Of course, I will be pleased to hear about the things you like, but I and the next edition of the text will surely benefit more from hearing how I could have done better and what topics (and/or readings) would be good in the next edition. Thanks!

1 | CONSTITUTION

GUNS, SAFETY, AND THE CONSTITUTION'S MEANING:
Individual Right *or* Subject to Regulation?

INDIVIDUAL RIGHT

ADVOCATE: Robert A. Levy, Senior Fellow in Constitutional Studies, Cato Institute

SOURCE: Testimony during hearings on "Oversight Hearing on the District of Columbia's Gun Control Laws," before the U.S. House of Representatives, Committee on Government Reform, June 28, 2005

SUBJECT TO REGULATION

ADVOCATE: The Brady Center to Prevent Gun Violence

SOURCE: Amicus Curiae brief to the U.S. Court of Appeals, District of Columbia Circuit in *Parker v. District of Columbia* (2006)

During World War II, British Prime Minister Winston S. Churchill famously described the Soviet Union as a "riddle wrapped in a mystery inside an enigma." Had he been commenting on the current debate in the United States over gun control, Churchill might have used the same description.

The riddle is the meaning of the words of the Second Amendment to the U.S. Constitution: "A well regulated Militia, being necessary to the security of a free State, the right of the people to keep and bear Arms, shall not be infringed." Does "people" mean individuals, or refer to the collective citizenry, as in "We the people"? The mystery is what, if anything, the framers of the U.S. Constitution and the Bill of Rights intended the amendment to accomplish. Scholars disagree about this issue. The enigma is whether 21st-century Americans should be bound by the literal meaning of words written more than 200 years ago, or should interpret them in the light of modern circumstances.

So far, the courts have not been crystal clear on these questions. Generally, they have upheld the authority of government to regulate the ownership of weapons, but the Supreme Court has never ruled directly on the essence of the Second Amendment. The most important case has been *United States v. Miller* (1939), in which the Supreme Court upheld a provision of the National Firearms Act (1934), requiring registration of sawed-off shotguns. The majority opinion held that "in the absence of any evidence...that possession [of a sawed-off] shotgun...has some reasonable relationship to...a well-regulated militia, we cannot say that the Second Amendment guarantees the right to keep and bear such an instrument." Notice that the opinion neither denies nor affirms a right to bear arms. It only rules that sawed-off shotguns are not protected, leaving it unclear if other weapons might be.

More recently, gun control opponents were buoyed by the decision of the Fifth U.S. Circuit Court of Appeals in *United States v. Emerson* (2001). The court construed the word "people" in the Second Amendment to mean individuals, and said that the clause "necessary to a well regulated militia," merely explained why individuals had the right to keep and bear arms. Still, it was a mixed case, because the judges also upheld the specific federal law that barred Timothy Emerson from owning a firearm based on his history of domestic violence. When the Supreme Court declined to hear Emerson's appeal, as it does in most cases, the major constitutional issues were left largely unresolved. The specific debate here relates to a District of Columbia law that virtually forbade the possession of handguns and required even tightly regulated possession of rifles and shotguns. Shelly Parker, a city resident who claimed she wanted to have a pistol in her home for self-protection, became the lead plaintiff along with five others in a suit, *Parker v. District of Columbia*, that challenged the law as violating the Second Amendment. The U.S. District Court dismissed the suit, arguing that "people" in the amendment meant militia, not individuals. In the following readings, Robert Cato in testimony before Congress supports Parker's position, which was then pending before the District of Columbia Circuit of the U.S. Courts of Appeals. In the second reading, the Brady Center to Prevent Gun Violence argues in an amicus curiae (friend of the court) brief to the appeals court that it should agree with the district court and reject Parker's appeal. The center is named after James Brady, a former White House press secretary who was shot in the head and disabled during the assassination attempt on President Ronald Reagan in 1981.

What would you decide? Considering weapons is one way to start thinking about the issues. Certainly, weapons have changed. Flintlock pistols and rifles were the personal firearms when the amendment was written in 1789. Today's weapons have much faster firing rates and higher muzzle velocities and, therefore, vastly greater killing power. There is no data on gun ownership in the 1790s, but it is widespread today. Almost 5 million firearms (including 1.7 million handguns) are manufactured or imported for the domestic U.S. market annually. About 40% of all homes contain a legal gun, and there are about 196 million such weapons, 30% of which are handguns, in the country. An uncertain but significant number of illegal weapons adds to these totals.

According to the most recent data, over 29,000 people in the United States are killed annually by gunshot and another 70,000 are wounded. Most (58%) of the dead are suicides. Another 37% are homicides, 3% accidents, 1.5% the result of police actions, and 0.5% instances of self-defense by individuals. Whether such statistics are relevant to a constitutional question and, if so, what they imply is your decision.

POINTS TO PONDER

➤ The most specific debate is about gun control policy and whether widespread gun ownership provides greater or less safety. Given your views on this issue, would you vote for a bill in Congress to ban the manufacture, importation, sale, and possession of all handguns?

➤ At a second level, the debate is about the specifics of the Second Amendment and the intent of those who drafted and ratified it. What do the two advocates claim that those who wrote the language of the Second Amendment intended it to mean?

➤ The third, most general, and most important dispute is over whether the Constitution is a fixed document whose meaning should be derived by "strict construction" of its words and the original intention of those who wrote it, or whether the Constitution is a "living document" that it should be interpreted in light of modern realities. What is your view? Should we be bound in the first decade of the 21st century by what people meant in the last decade of the 19th century when the Second Amendment was added to the Constitution?

Guns, Safety, and the Constitution's Meaning: Individual Right

ROBERT A. LEVY

This afternoon, I testify in support of the principles underlying H.R. 1288, The District of Columbia Personal Protection Act, which would repeal the District's ban on handguns and make other changes to the city's gun control laws. Although I support the underlying principles, I am nevertheless opposed to enactment of the legislation at this time. Essentially, I believe that advocates of gun owners' rights will be better served if *Parker v. District of Columbia*, a Second Amendment challenge to the D.C. handgun ban, is first resolved by the U.S. Court of Appeals for the District of Columbia Circuit, then presented to the U.S. Supreme Court for final review. Of course, *Parker* will be dismissed as moot if the challenged law is repealed.

My reasons for preferring the judicial route before proceeding with legislation are elaborated in Part IV below, "What Role Should Congress Play in Securing Second Amendment Rights?" First, however, some background in Part I, "Does the Second Amendment Secure an Individual or Collective Right?" That is followed by Part II, "Does the Second Amendment Apply to the District of Columbia?" Then Part III, "How Can District Residents Best Secure Their Second Amendment Rights?"

I. DOES THE SECOND AMENDMENT SECURE AN INDIVIDUAL OR COLLECTIVE RIGHT?

A question that has perplexed legal scholars for decades goes like this: Does the right to keep and bear arms belong to

us as individuals, or does it belong to us collectively as members of a militia? The answer has now been documented in an extended and scholarly staff memorandum opinion prepared for the Attorney General and released to the public last year. The memorandum opinion concluded that "The Second Amendment secures a right of individuals generally, not a right of States or a right restricted to persons serving in militias."

I concur. The main clause of the Second Amendment ("the right of the people to keep and bear Arms, shall not be infringed") secures the right. The subordinate clause ("A well regulated Militia, being necessary to the security of a free State") justifies the right. Properly understood, the militia clause helps explain why we have a right to bear arms. A well-regulated militia is a sufficient but not necessary condition to the exercise of that right. Imagine if the Second Amendment said, "A well-educated Electorate, being necessary to self-governance in a free state, the right of the people to keep and read Books shall not be infringed." Surely, no one would suggest that only registered voters (i.e., members of the electorate) would have a right to read. Yet that is precisely the effect if the Second Amendment is interpreted to apply only to members of a militia.

If the Second Amendment truly meant what the collective rights advocates propose, then the text would read, "A well regulated Militia being necessary to the security of a free State, the right of the states [or the state militias] to keep and bear arms shall not be infringed." But the

Second Amendment, like the First and Fourth Amendments, refers explicitly to "the right of the people." Consider the placement of the amendment within the Bill of Rights, the part of the Constitution that deals exclusively with the rights of individuals. There can be no doubt that First Amendment rights like speech and religion belong to us as individuals. Similarly, Fourth Amendment protections against unreasonable searches are individual rights. In the context of the Second Amendment, we secure "the right of the people" by guaranteeing the right of each person. Second Amendment protections were not intended for the state but for each individual against the state—a deterrent to government tyranny. Here's how Ninth Circuit judge Alex Kozinski put it [in his opinion in *Unites States v. Stewart* (2003)]:

> The institution of slavery required a class of people who lacked the means to resist.…All too many of the…great tragedies of history— Stalin's atrocities, the killing fields of Cambodia, the Holocaust—were perpetrated by armed troops against unarmed populations.

Maybe the threat of tyrannical government is less today than it was when our republic was experiencing its birth pangs. But incompetence by the state in defending its citizens is a greater threat. The demand for police to defend us increases in proportion to our inability to defend ourselves. That's why disarmed societies tend to become police states. Witness law abiding inner city residents, disarmed by gun control, begging for police protection against drug gangs—despite the terrible violations of civil liberties that such protection entails (e.g., curfews, anti-loitering laws, civil asset forfeiture, non-consensual searches of public housing, and even video surveillance of residents in high crime areas). An unarmed citizenry creates the conditions that lead to tyranny. The right to bear arms is thus preventive; it reduces the demand for a police state. When people are incapable of protecting themselves, they become either victims of the criminals or dependents of the state.

What do the courts have to say? In a 2001 Texas case, *United States v. Emerson*, the Fifth Circuit [of the U.S. Court of Appeals] held that the Constitution "protects the right of individuals, including those not then actually a member of any militia…to privately possess and bear their own firearms…suitable as personal individual weapons." That constitutional right is not absolute, said the court. For example, killers do not have a constitutional right to possess weapons of mass destruction. Some persons and some weapons may be restricted. Indeed, the Fifth Circuit held that Emerson's Second Amendment rights could be temporarily curtailed because there was reason to believe he posed a threat to his estranged wife. And the Tenth Circuit, in *United States v. Haney* [2004], ruled that machine guns were not the type of weapon protected by the Second Amendment. The Supreme Court declined to review either case.

The high Court has not decided a Second Amendment case since *United States v. Miller* in 1939. On that occasion, the challenged statute required registration of machine guns, sawed off rifles, sawed off shotguns, and silencers. First, said the Court, "militia" means all males physically capable of acting in concert for the common defense. That suggested a right belonging to all of us, as individuals. But the Court also held that the right extended only to weapons rationally related to a militia—not the sawed off shotgun questioned in *Miller*. That mixed ruling has puzzled legal scholars for more than six decades. If military use is the decisive test, then citizens can possess rocket launchers and missiles. Obviously, that is not what the Court had in mind. Indeed, anti-gun advocates, who regularly cite *Miller* with approval, would be apoplectic if the Court's military-use doctrine were logically extended.

Because *Miller* is so murky, it can only be interpreted narrowly, allowing restrictions on weapons, like machine guns and silencers, with slight value to law abiding citizens, and high value to criminals. In other words, *Miller* applies to the type of weapon, not to the question whether the Second Amendment protects individuals or members of a militia. That's the conclusion the Fifth Circuit reached in Emerson. It found that *Miller* upheld neither the individual rights model of the Second Amendment nor the collective rights model. *Miller* simply decided that the weapons at issue were not protected.

Enter former U.S. Attorney General John Ashcroft [2001–2005]. First, in a letter to the National Rifle Association, he reaffirmed a long-held opinion that all law-abiding citizens have an individual right to keep and bear arms. Ashcroft's letter was supported by 18 state attorneys general, including six Democrats, then followed by two Justice Department briefs, filed with the Supreme Court in the *Haney* and *Emerson* cases. For the first time, the federal government argued against the collective rights position in formal court papers.

Despite Ashcroft's view of the Second Amendment, the Justice Department declared that both *Emerson* and *Haney* were correctly decided. In *Emerson*, the restriction on persons subject to a domestic violence restraining order was a permissible exception to Second Amendment protection. And in *Haney*, the ban on machine guns applied to a type of weapon uniquely susceptible to criminal misuse.

Many legal scholars are now taking that same position. Harvard's Alan Dershowitz,

a former ACLU [American Civil Liberties Union] board member, says he "hates" guns and wants the Second Amendment repealed. But he condemns "foolish liberals who are trying to read the Second Amendment out of the Constitution by claiming it's not an individual right.... They're courting disaster by encouraging others to use the same means to eliminate portions of the Constitution they don't like." Harvard's Laurence Tribe, another respected liberal scholar, and Yale professor Akhil Amar acknowledge that there is an individual right to keep and bear arms, albeit limited by "reasonable regulation in the interest of public safety." In that respect, Tribe and Amar agree with the *Emerson* court and with Ashcroft on two fundamental issues: First, the Second Amendment confirms an individual rather than a collective right. Second, that right is not absolute; it is subject to regulation. To the extent there is disagreement, it hinges on what constitutes permissible regulation—i.e., where to draw the line.

To reinforce the views of Dershowitz, Tribe, Amar, and Ashcroft, let me comment briefly on a few of the underlying constitutional points.

- Three provisions limit the states' power over the militia. Article I, section 8, grants Congress the power to "organiz[e], arm[], and disciplin[e], the militia." Article I, section 10, says that "No state shall, without the consent of Congress,...keep troops in time of peace." Article II, section 2, declares the "President shall be Commander in Chief...of the Militia of the several States." Given those three provisions, how could the Second Amendment secure a state's right to arm the militia? No one argued then or argues now that the Second Amendment repealed all three earlier provisions.

• Consider the Supreme Court's pronouncement in *Miller*: "When called for service [in an organized militia] these men were expected to appear bearing arms supplied by themselves." If militia members were to arm themselves, the Second Amendment could not refer to states arming militias. Furthermore, if the *Miller* Court thought the Second Amendment merely enabled states to arm their militias, the Court would have dismissed the case on standing grounds. The plaintiff, *Miller*, was not a state and therefore had no standing to sue. The Court would never have reached the question whether a sawed off shotgun had military utility.

• Multiple provisions in the Bill of Rights refer to the right "of the people." In a 1990 case, *United States v. Verdugo-Urquidez*, the Court said, "'the people' protected by the Fourth Amendment, and by the First and Second Amendments, and to whom rights and powers are reserved in the Ninth and Tenth Amendments, refers to a class of persons who are part of a national community or have otherwise developed sufficient connection with this country to be considered part of that community." That statement contains no mention or even suggestion of a collective right

• What about the militia clause? That syntax was not unusual for the times. For example, the free press clause of the 1842 Rhode Island Constitution stated: "The liberty of the press being essential to the security of freedom in a state, any person may publish his sentiments of any subject." That provision surely does not mean that the right to publish protects only the press. It protects "any person"; and one reason among others that it protects any person is that a free press is essential to a free society.

• In the Militia Act of 1792, militia is defined as "every free able-bodied white male citizen…who is or shall be of the age of 18 years, and under the age of 45 years." That definition is expanded in the Modern Militia Act (1956–58) to read "all able-bodied males at least 17 years of age and…under 45 yrs of age [and] female citizens…who are members of the National Guard." The Act goes on to state that "the classes of the militia are (1) the organized militia, which consists of the National Guard and the Naval Militia; and (2) the unorganized militia, which consists of [all other members]." Ninth Circuit judge Andrew J. Kleinfeld wrote [in a dissenting opinion in *Silveira v. Lockyer* (2003) that the "militia is like the jury pool, consisting of 'the people,' limited, like the jury pool, to those capable of performing the service."

• Next, consider this historical context: Anti-federalists wanted three major changes prior to ratifying the Constitution: (1) include a Bill of Rights, (2) give states, not the federal government, power to arm the militia, and (3) eliminate federal power to maintain a standing army. Here was the federalist response, addressing those demands in reverse order: (1) Don't worry about the federal government maintaining a standing army; the federal militia power will obviate that need. (2) Don't worry about federal control over the militia; armed individuals will obviate those concerns. And (3) to ensure that individuals have a right to be armed, we will include such a provision in a Bill of Rights. So the federalist position depended on the people being armed. Clearly, the addition of the Second Amendment could not have been intended to eliminate that right. The Second Amendment's prefatory clause was the federalists' way of pacifying anti-federalists without limiting the power of the federal government to maintain a standing army or increasing the states' power over the militia.

• Here's a parallel view of that history, interpreting the term "well-regulated." In its 18th century context, well-regulated did not mean heavily regulated, but rather properly, not overly regulated. Looked at in that manner, the Second Amendment ensured that militias would not be improperly regulated—even weakened—by disarming the citizens who would be their members. The Framers feared and distrusted standing armies; so they provided for a militia (all able-bodied males above the age of 17) as a counterweight. But the framers also realized, in granting Congress near-plenary power over the militia, that a select, armed subset—like today's National Guard—could be equivalent to a standing army. So they wisely crafted the Second Amendment to forbid Congress from disarming other citizens, thereby ensuring a "well-regulated" militia.

For those of us eagerly awaiting a Supreme Court pronouncement on the Second Amendment, for the first time in 66 years, the Constitution is on our side....

That said, there is a legitimate and important reason for Congress to step aside until *Parker v. District of Columbia* is resolved. The *Parker* lawsuit was filed by upstanding D.C. residents who want to be able to defend themselves and their families in their own homes. *Parker* is now pending before the U.S. Court of Appeals for the D.C. Circuit. If H.R. 1288 is enacted, the lawsuit will be dismissed as moot. After all, plaintiffs cannot challenge a law that no longer exists.

Otherwise, *Parker* could well be headed to the Supreme Court; and that is where it belongs. The citizens of this country deserve a foursquare pronouncement from the nation's highest court about the real meaning of the Second Amendment for all Americans—not just the residents of D.C. Presently, because the Supreme Court has not resolved its view of the Second Amendment, the right to keep and bear arms under state law extends only as far as each state's constitution or statutes permit. That's unacceptable. A disputable Second Amendment right without a legally enforceable federal remedy is, in some states, no right at all.

Although the rights of D.C. residents can be secured by either legislation or litigation, a narrow bill aimed at the D.C. Code will do only part of the job. The bill could be repealed by the next anti-gun Congress. And more important, the bill will have no effect outside of the District. That means, of course, the bill will have negligible impact on gun owners' rights when contrasted with an unambiguous proclamation, applicable across the nation, from the U.S. Supreme Court.

If the Court should mistakenly hold that the Second Amendment provides a collective rather than an individual right, that would be the time for the legislative branch to ensure that D.C. residents have more protection than the judicial branch was willing to recognize. Until then, congressional action is premature.

Guns, Safety, and the Constitution's Meaning: Subject to Regulation

THE BRADY CENTER TO PREVENT GUN VIOLENCE

The Brady Center is a non-profit public interest organization dedicated to reducing gun violence through education, research, and legal advocacy. The Brady Center has a substantial interest in ensuring that the Second Amendment is not misinterpreted as a barrier to strong government action to prevent gun violence.

I. *UNITED STATES V. MILLER* ESTABLISHED THAT ANY SECOND AMENDMENT RIGHT MUST RELATE TO MILITIA SERVICE.

United States v. Miller (1939), the Supreme Court's last opinion construing the Second Amendment...is without question the seminal case interpreting [it]. Contrary to a long line of deliberate interpretation, [Shelly Parker and the other] plaintiffs contend *Miller* turned not on the substantive issue of *Miller's* right to bear arms, but on the nature of the weapon at issue (i.e., whether the weapon was suitable for militia service). But the plaintiffs' argument is wishful thinking, dependent upon a highly selective reading of *Miller*. As every federal appellate court save the Fifth Circuit recognizes, *Miller* firmly rejected the notion of a Second Amendment right unrelated to militia service. That decision is binding upon this [the U.S. Supreme] Court.

As Justice [James C.] McReynolds explained in *Miller*, it was the "obvious purpose" of the Amendment to "assure the continuation and render possible the effectiveness" of militia forces, and the Amendment "must be interpreted and applied with that end in view."

Historically, the Court noted, militia members were expected to supply their own arms....*Miller's* plain message was that the right to "keep and bear arms" in the Second Amendment refers only to arms borne in lawful militia service, not any rights of individuals to possess and use firearms for their own private ends. Because defendants [in the *Miller* case] failed to demonstrate that the "possession or use" of their firearm had "some reasonable relation to the preservation or efficiency of a well regulated militia," the Second Amendment gave them no defense.

Since *Miller*, the Supreme Court has twice affirmed the militia-based interpretation of the Second Amendment. In *Lewis v. United States* (1980), the Court addressed whether [a federal law] which criminalizes possession of a firearm by a convicted felon, could survive an equal protection challenge. The Court applied rational-basis review, rather than strict scrutiny, noting the statute at issue "[did not] trench upon any constitutionally protected liberties." Similarly, the Court dismissed the appeal of *Burton v. Sills* (1969), in which the [New Jersey supreme court] cited *Miller* in concluding that the Second Amendment did not confer a right to bear arms....This dismissal would have been inappropriate if the Court believed there was any doubt about whether *Miller* endorsed the militia-based view.

Thus, *Miller* firmly rejected the individual-rights view espoused by plaintiffs, and the Supreme Court has seen no need to revisit the issue since. With the exception of the Fifth Circuit in *United States v.*

Emerson (2001), this has been the accepted construction of *Miller* for more than six decades, including every published federal opinion since *Emerson*. This Court would be in error to overlook sixty-five years of unchanged Supreme Court precedent and the deluge of circuit case law [decisions by the various Federal Courts of Appeal] rejecting an individual right to bear arms not in conjunction with service in the militia.

II. TEXTUAL ANALYSIS CONFIRMS THAT THE SECOND AMENDMENT CONFERS NO INDIVIDUAL RIGHTS.

The unique textual structure of the Second Amendment sets it apart from all other provisions in the Bill of Rights. Courts and scholars agree that the meaning of the Second Amendment's right "to keep and bear arms" must be informed by the prefatory clause concerning a "well regulated militia." Even *Emerson* recognized that the prefatory clause must be given "its full and proper due." Under plaintiffs' reading, the first nine words of the Amendment serve no function whatsoever; the meaning of the Amendment would be the same if they were omitted entirely.

The Second Amendment's prefatory clause is much more than exhortatory preamble, as the plaintiffs suggest. Rather, the accepted reading—embraced by *Miller* and courts since—is that the prefatory clause helps shape and define the meaning of the substantive provision contained in the second clause, and thus of the amendment itself.

When the second clause is read in light of the first, so as to implement the policy set forth in the preamble,…the most plausible construction of the Second Amendment is that it seeks to ensure the existence of effective state militias in which the people may exercise their right to bear arms,

and forbids the federal government to interfere with such exercise.…

A. "Militia" Refers to an Organized Military Unit Under State Control.

The plaintiffs repeatedly insist that the "people" referenced in the Second Amendment are the same "people" mentioned elsewhere in the Bill of Rights. Their argument, however, assumes that the term "militia" can be reduced to the term "people"—that "the two are synonyms," and that "'militia' referred simply to members of the public," in their individual capacities, who were "capable of bearing arms in defense of the government." But as Pulitzer Prize-winning scholar Jack Rakove has explained, the plaintiffs' textual argument inappropriately requires one to presume that "people" should be "defined intratextually, by reference to its use in other amendments," but that "militia" should be interpreted as if it "leaps beyond the proverbial four corners of the document," and is not, in the Second Amendment, the same organized military unit well known to the framers [of the Constitution] and referenced repeatedly in the rest of the Constitution.

[Where] the word "militia" appears in the Constitution outside the Second Amendment, it can only be understood to refer to a military unit, and not to an undifferentiated mass of individuals. "Militia" first appears in Article I, which grants Congress the powers: "To provide for calling forth the militia to execute the Laws of the Union, suppress Insurrections and repel Invasions.…"; The "militia" of these provisions was no new creation, but an existing armed force in each state.…The Constitution, in a form of military federalism, preserved these state militias.…[In the second appearance,] Article II designates the president as the "Commander in Chief of the Army and

Navy of the United States, and of the militia of the several states, when called into the actual service of the United States," and [in the third appearance] the Fifth Amendment establishes a right to a grand jury "except in cases arising in the land or naval forces, or in the militia, when in actual service in time of War or public danger." In each of these provisions, the use of the term "militia"—paired with such other military bodies as "the Army and Navy" or "the land and naval forces"—denotes a legally organized military force, not a collection of private citizens independently exercising their individual rights.

The context of "militia" in the Second Amendment itself provides further evidence that it refers to a military unit. The Amendment begins: "A well regulated militia being necessary to the security of a free State...." This language makes clear that the Second Amendment does not envision the militia as [an unregulated body] of armed individuals, [as the plaintiffs claim]. Rather, only militias actively maintained and trained by the states can satisfy the 'well regulated militia' requirement of the Second Amendment. Additional support for this reading lies in the Amendment's concern for the "security of a free State," signaling that the Framers referred only to governmental militias that are actively maintained and used for the common defense. The absurdity of a "well regulated" people itself refutes the plaintiffs' assertion that the terms "militia" and "people" are "synonyms."

Finally, in *Miller*, the Supreme Court itself expressly drew the connection between the "well regulated militia" of the Second Amendment and the "militia" of Article I. The Court made express reference to the militia clauses of Article I, in finding that it was "[w]ith obvious purpose to assure the continuation and render possible the effectiveness of such forces the declaration and guarantee of the Second Amendment were made." The Court further defined the militia as "[a] body of citizens enrolled for military discipline." This definition of the militia is entirely inconsistent with the plaintiffs' argument that it was used in the Second Amendment as a synonym for "the people."

B. The Right to Keep and Bear Arms Is a Right of the People of Each State to Organize Themselves As a Military Force.

The Second Amendment's choice of words "to keep and bear arms"—rather than, for example, to possess or own arms—also pointedly connotes a militia-centered right. *Miller* itself cited a Tennessee Supreme Court case confirming that to "bear arms" means to take up arms "in a military sense," not for private, individual defense. The right to "bear arms" therefore served as a "right of the people" to a collective role in their government's military defense. Like jury duty, military service is not always so individually desirable as to be considered a "right." But as an institution, a right of the people, the state militias—like trial by jury—involved ordinary citizens in a crucial government function, allowing popular participation in the defense of a free State rather than relying on an untrustworthy and potentially rapacious professional army. The people of each free State were guaranteed, against federal interference, a right to bear arms in well-regulated state militia—a right that could not be exercised by private individuals for merely private ends.

Nor does the addition of the word "keep" alter the basic character of the right [as the plaintiffs argue]. It seems unlikely that the drafters intended the term "keep" to be broader in scope than the term "bear." Rather, the traditional interpretation of the amendment calls for the words "keep and bear" to be read together, much like "necessary and proper" [in Article I] or "cruel and unusual" [in the Eight Amendment]. Moreover, the inclusion of the word "keep" is most likely attributable to British troops' interference with the colonies' attempts to "keep" arms, and the word is used in this sense in the Articles of Confederation. In any event, the right to keep" arms in no way undercuts the strong implication that the right granted by the second clause relates to the performance of a military function, and not to the indiscriminate possession of weapons for personal use.

III. THE HISTORY OF THE SECOND AMENDMENT DEMONSTRATES THE FRAMERS DID NOT INTEND TO CREATE AN INDIVIDUAL RIGHT TO BEAR ARMS.

A. The Second Amendment's Purpose Was To Ensure The Militia Would Remain An Effective Fighting Force.

The Framers did not set out to secure an individual right to possess arms for private use. Rather, the Second Amendment arose largely in response to military concerns. The unamended [as written in 1787] Constitution contemplated a national and state defense system: authority would be divided between the national army and navy, exclusively controlled by the federal government, and the state militias, subject to congressional regulation and presidential command but officered and trained by the several states. The preservation of the state militias was crucially important to those ratifying the Constitution. As Madison pointed out in *Federalist No. 46*, these militias—not private citizens possessing arms—were viewed as the primary bulwark against abuses by a standing army: [I]t would not be going too far to

say, that the State Governments with the people on their side would be able to repel the danger [of a standing federal army]...opposed [to which would be] a militia amounting to near half a million of citizens with arms in their hands, officered by men chosen from among themselves, fighting for their common liberties, and united and conducted by governments possessing their affections and confidence.

The plaintiffs, who quote only the first half of Madison's sentence, claim that an individual right to gun possession was seen as necessary to maintaining a citizen militia. However, the historical materials reveal no concern that the federal government might confiscate guns from an armed citizenry. [According to one historian,] "There is not a single statement... [indicating] any congressman contemplated that [the Second Amendment] would establish an individual right to possess a weapon."

Instead, Americans worried that Congress might fail to provide the citizens with arms, allowing the militias to fall into disrepair, and thereby create an excuse to maintain a standing army. For example, George Mason [a Virginia delegate to the Constitutional Convention of 1787 who refused to sign it because it had no bill of rights] worried that Congress "may neglect to provide for arming and disciplining the militia, and the state Governments cannot do it, for Congress has an exclusive right to arm them....Should the national government wish to render the militia useless, they may neglect them, and let them perish, in order to have a pretense of establishing a standing army."

This fear of federal neglect, that Congress might not arm those who refused to arm themselves, would have been poorly addressed by an individual right to gun possession—especially given that private citizens would need not only weapons but also substantial training to be militarily effective. Rather, the Second Amendment was crafted to ensure that the states would have the ability to provide independently for the needs of the militia, so that the national government could not disarm the militia by failing to support it financially, while simultaneously divesting the states of authority to do so.

B. The Military Focus of the Amendment Is Apparent from Its Drafting History.

The drafting of the Second Amendment renders unambiguous the central role of the militia. Madison's initial proposal [for the language of the Second Amendment] provided: "The right of the people to keep and bear arms shall not be infringed; a well armed, and well regulated militia being the best security of a free country: but no person religiously scrupulous of bearing arms, shall be compelled to render military service in person." Though subsequently omitted, Madison's proposed exception for "religiously scrupulous" objectors supports two conclusions.

First, the clause clearly employs "bearing arms" in the military sense, rather than any individual activity such as hunting or self-defense. It follows that the same language, when used in the clause affirming the "right of the people to keep and bear arms," similarly pertains to military service.

Second, Madison's draft demonstrates that the overall thrust of the amendment was directed to the role of the militia. If the preceding two clauses were intended to affirm an individual right to bear arms, the proposed exemption for "religiously scrupulous" persons would have been unnecessary, and certainly would not have warranted a prefatory "but." The reason for the clause's removal is illuminating: Elbridge Gerry [a Massachusetts delegate] worried that Congress, in an "attempt to destroy the militia," might "declare who are those religiously scrupulous, and prevent them from bearing arms."

Other amendments to Madison's draft reaffirmed the centrality of the state militias. The House of Representatives altered the phrase "security of a free country" to "security of a free State," thereby showing that the Amendment was specifically designed to protect the several states rather than individual persons. It also added a clause (later removed by the Senate) providing that the militia would be "composed of the body of the people," which would have prevented Congress from defining the militia so as to exclude large classes of citizens from its ranks. The primary concern of the Amendment's drafters was not any individual right to bear arms, but the size, composition, and governance of the militia.

Finally, the existence of alternative contemporaneous proposals reveals that the Framers rejected the very individual rights model that the plaintiffs advance. Pennsylvania Anti-Federalists proposed fourteen amendments to the Constitution. While some were adopted virtually verbatim, the First Congress substantially modified the seventh proposal, which affirmed the right of the people to bear arms "for the defense of themselves and their own state" and prohibited the enactment of any law to disarm "the people or any of them unless for crimes committed, or real danger of public injury from individuals."

If Congress had incorporated these provisions into the Second Amendment, [one historian notes,] "the constitutional principle of private ownership of weapons would have been clear." Instead, "Madison and his colleagues in the First Congress emphatically rejected the goals and the language of the Pennsylvania Anti-federalists" relating to bearing arms, opting instead to create only a militia-based right.

C. The Framers Were Accustomed to and Accepted the Local Regulation of Firearms.

Although the plaintiffs present the individual-rights view as a product of the Anglo-American common-law heritage, or even of a natural right to self-defense, there is little historical support for such a view. [One historian writes,] "From the Revolution to the eve of the Civil War, there is precious little evidence that advocates of local control of the militia showed an equal or even a secondary concern for gun ownership as a personal right." Neither in England nor in the independent states were individual citizens granted a general right to possess weapons free of government regulation. Rather, regulation of firearms was commonplace.

1. Gun possession had been subject to strict regulation in England.

The laws and customs of England, the foundation of American law, traditionally restricted gun ownership. The Game Act of 1671 limited gun possession to the highest classes, a small fraction of the population. Following the 1688 ouster of [King] James II, who had begun arming English Catholics and disarming Protestants, the English Parliament negotiated limits on royal power—the Declaration of Rights—to which James's successor, William of Orange, acquiesced. Responding to James' attempt to act without Parliamentary authorization, and in order to protect the nation from the perceived Catholic menace, the Declaration provided that "the subjects which are Protestants may have arms for their defense suitable to their condition and as allowed by law." This provision not only restricted those who could possess arms

(Protestants of a suitable "Condition," i.e., class), but ensured that firearms possessions would be regulated by "law"—by Parliament, and not the Crown.

During the debates over the Declaration of Rights, no one complained that individuals lacked a general right to keep arms for personal use. Indeed, any such idea would have seemed strange, given Parliament's extensive regulation of personal ownership of arms both before and after the Declaration of Rights. The Declaration was primarily intended to reshape the relationship between Parliament and Crown, and within five years of approving the Declaration, while debating the Game Act of 1693, Parliament overwhelmingly rejected a provision that would have allowed ordinary Protestant subjects to keep arms in their homes.

2. Legal regulation of firearms continued after independence.

The regulation of gun ownership in America is not a modern invention; it was a practice accepted by the Framing generation. Firearms were commonly subject to police-power regulation in the states, and early Americans accepted the notion that groups of citizens could be disarmed without infringing state constitutions. For example, Pennsylvania, through the Test Acts of 1776, disarmed those who refused to take a loyalty oath. Similarly, early state governments monitored gun ownership and regulated weapons storage.

The Framers' broad understanding of the police power likewise supports a militia-based interpretation. Living in a time when various social and political upheavals seemed to threaten the survival of the new republic, the Framers would have been extraordinarily reluctant to eviscerate the capacity of the government to suppress domestic insurrections.

Yet the plaintiffs' theory of an individual right to bear arms assumes that the First Congress deprived itself of the power to regulate the flow of weaponry even in those places where it had plenary jurisdiction, such as the District of Columbia. Any such weakening of the government's ability to keep order would have been contrary to the overall thrust of the new Constitution. [According to one study,] "The goal was to prevent anarchy, violence, and rebellions. This prevention was accomplished by controlling the militias and the army and by retaining the right to limit weapons to those who formed 'A well regulated militia.'" If the Framers had intended to proscribe or restrict legislation limiting the ownership of dangerous weaponry one would expect at least some discussion of this controversial contraction of police power during the otherwise wide-ranging debates over the Bill of Rights.

Indeed, in more than two centuries of American jurisprudence, no decision of a federal court invalidating a gun-control law on the basis of the Second Amendment has been upheld. Even *Emerson* found that the gun-control law in question passed constitutional scrutiny because Second Amendment rights were not insulated from "limited, narrowly tailored specific exceptions or restrictions for particular cases that are reasonable." The federal courts' protracted and virtually unanimous acknowledgement of the right of states, municipalities, and the federal government to enact regulations limiting the private ownership and use of firearms is not just a jurisprudential curiosity; it is itself an important aspect of the Second Amendment's history. That history stands forthrightly opposed to the proposition that the Second Amendment creates a personal right to bear arms unrelated to militia service.

THE CONTINUING DEBATE:
Guns, Safety, and the Constitution's Meaning

What Is New

Shelly Parker and her co-plaintiffs prevailed in the appeals court. It decided by a 2 to 1 margin in March 2007 that the District of Columbia's law violated the Second Amendment by denying individuals to possess arms within their homes. D.C. Mayor Adrian Fenty vowed to appeal the case, arguing, "The handgun ban has saved many lives and will continue to do so if it remains in effect. Wherever I go, the response from the residents is, 'Mayor Fenty, you've got to fight this all the way to the Supreme Court.'" Whether the Supreme Court will agree the case remains uncertain. There have also been changes at the legislative level. For example, in 2004, Congress let lapse a 10-year-old ban that barred weapons from having muzzle-flash suppressors, large capacity ammunition magazines, and other characteristics commonly associated with military assault weapons. Anti–gun control forces won a further victory in 2005 when Congress enacted legislation barring most civil suits against most firearms makers for the use of their products in crimes and other instances where victims were killed or wounded.

Where to Find More

For data, laws, and related information on firearms go to the U.S. Bureau of Alcohol, Tobacco and Firearms Web site www.atf.treas.gov/pub/#Firearms. The most recent data on firearms deaths in the United States is available from the U.S. Public Health Service's Centers for Disease Control Web site at: www.cdc.gov/nchs/fastats/homicide.htm.

For policy advocacy, turn to the Web sites of two of the major opposing interest groups. The anti-gun control forces are represented by the National Rifle Association's Web site at www.nra.org. For the opposing view, the URL www.bradycampaign.org/ will take you to the Web site of the pro-gun control Brady Campaign to Gun Prevent Violence of the second reading. For a rebuke of both camps, read John Casteen, "Ditching the Rubric on Gun Control," *Virginia Quarterly Review* (Fall 2004).

For more on the politics of gun control, read Nicholas J. Johnson, "The Constitutional Politics of Gun Control," *Brooklyn Law Review* (2005). Several articles on various aspects of the issue are presented by the *Fordham Law Review* (2004) in a symposium issue on "The Second Amendment and the Future of Gun Regulation: Historical, Legal, Policy, and Cultural Perspectives."

What More to Do

One constant suggestion for this and every debate in this book is to get involved no matter which side you are on. The issue is important, and you can make a difference if you try. Also keep the larger constitutional questions in your mind as you read other debates in this book. Like this debate, some will involve questions about the meaning of words or phrases, such as "due process of law" in the Fourteenth Amendment. Other debates will also include the ongoing dispute over strict construction versus contemporary interpretation of the Constitution by the courts. Perhaps before any of this, though, think about and discuss with others the policy and constitutional issues presented in this debate. Then, as this book's title urges, You Decide!

2   FEDERALISM

FEDERAL REGULATION OF MEDICAL MARIJUANA:
Appropriate National Power *or* Usurpation of State Authority?

APPROPRIATE NATIONAL POWER

ADVOCATE: John Paul Stevens III, Associate Justice, U.S. Supreme Court

SOURCE: Opinion in *Gonzales v. Raich*, June 6, 2005

USURPATION OF STATE AUTHORITY

ADVOCATE: Sandra Day O'Connor, Associate Justice, U.S. Supreme Court

SOURCE: Opinion in *Gonzales v. Raich*, June 6, 2005

Students are commonly taught that one way the delegates to the Constitutional Convention of 1787 in Philadelphia sought to safeguard democracy was by creating a federal system that divides powers between the central government and the states. The true story is more complex than that, but James Madison, the "father of the Constitution," did argue in the *Federalist Papers* (No. 45), "The powers delegated by the proposed Constitution to the Federal Government, are few and defined. Those which are to remain in the State Governments are numerous and indefinite."

Whatever anyone thought or intended, the Constitution is very imprecise about the boundaries between the authority of Washington and that of the state capitals. As a result, the division of powers has been the subject of legal, political, and even physical struggle ever since. It has not, however, been an even contest. Since 1789 authority has generally flowed away from the states and toward the central government.

One reason for this shift is the congressional use and judicial view of the Constitution's interstate commerce clause. Located in Article I, section 8, it gives Congress the authority "to regulate commerce...among the several states." For many years, the Supreme Court usually rejected attempts by Congress to use the interstate commerce clause to assert national control over an area traditionally within the realm of the states. But beginning in the 1930s, the court became more willing to allow the expansion of federal power under the interstate commerce clause. During the 1960s and beyond, the Supreme Court also usually upheld federal civil rights laws' use of the commerce clause to attack discrimination. In *Heart of Atlanta Motel v. United States* (1964), the Supreme Court upheld federal action against the motel's restaurant, Ollie's Barbecue, which only served white people. The court ruled that even though Ollie's only served local people, it was subject to federal regulation because some of the food it served originated outside of Georgia. Scholar Richard S. Randall (*American Constitutional Development*, 2002) has termed such use of the interstate commerce clause a constitutional "revolution" that "transformed the commerce power into an almost unlimited federal grant" of authority.

Something of a counter-revolution occurred, however. The Supreme Court under Chief Justice William Rehnquist (1986–2005) made several decisions rejecting federal laws enacted under the logic of the commerce clause. This counter-trend brings us to the debate here. Throughout most of history, there was limited federal power to regulate drugs because many of them are produced, distributed, and used locally, and thus fell within the purview of the states.

This changed in 1970 when Congress issued a "finding" that drugs travel in and impacted interstate commerce and enacted the Controlled Substances Act (CSA). It regulated the production, distribution, and possession of five classes of "controlled substances." Of these all those listed in Schedule 1, including 42 opiates, 22 opium derivatives, and 17 hallucinogenic substances (including marijuana) were banned outright.

The specific debate here involves federal authority to regulate "medical marijuana." Many physicians believe that marijuana can be medically useful, especially in easing pain and other side effects of cancer. Based on this belief, a 1996 referendum in California approved the "Compassionate Use Act" permitting the use of marijuana on a doctor's recommendation. Patients could either grow their own or obtain the drug from a "caregiver" (grower) within the state. Ten other states enacted similar laws. In 2002, federal agents seized medical marijuana being used by several Californians, including Angel Raich, who was using marijuana to treat brain tumor symptoms. Raich sued the U.S. Attorney General. The District Court found against Raich, but the Ninth Circuit of the Court of Appeals ruled that locally grown and used marijuana was not involved in commerce and, therefore, federal regulation was unconstitutional. The Bush administration appealed to the Supreme Court, which brings us to the readings by Justices John Paul Stevens and Sandra Day O'Connor presenting their perspectives about whether or not regulation represented an abuse of federal authority by overextending the meaning of the interstate commerce clause.

POINTS TO PONDER

➤ Separate your views on the main point of this debate, federal authority, and the second point, medical marijuana. You can, for instance, believe that on the constitutional level, the growth of federal authority is positive and also believe that on the policy level, medical marijuana should be legal.

➤ As you read, think about how well Madison's portrayal of the federal government's powers as "few and defined" and those of the states as "numerous and indefinite" corresponds to federalism's current reality. Is the change or lack of change positive or regrettable?

➤ Not too far below the surface of some critics' position on federalism is the view that it is an outdated system. The argument is that the United States has become a single country economically and socially and, therefore, should also be a unified politically. The defenders of federalism argue that it still, as it did in 1789, protects freedom, promotes diversity, and permits policy experimentation. What do you think? Does federalism make sense any more?

Federal Regulation of Medical Marijuana: Appropriate National Power

JOHN PAUL STEVENS, III

California is one of at least nine states that authorize the use of marijuana for medicinal purposes. The question presented in this case is whether the power vested in Congress by Article I, §8, of the Constitution "[t]o make all Laws which shall be necessary and proper for carrying into Execution" its authority to "regulate Commerce with foreign Nations, and among the several States" includes the power to prohibit the local cultivation and use of marijuana in compliance with California law.

I

California has been a pioneer in the regulation of marijuana. In 1913, California was one of the first states to prohibit the sale and possession of marijuana, and at the end of the century, California became the first state to authorize limited use of the drug for medicinal purposes. In 1996, California voters passed Proposition 215, now codified as the Compassionate Use Act of 1996. The proposition was designed to ensure that "seriously ill" residents of the state have access to marijuana for medical purposes, and to encourage federal and state governments to take steps towards ensuring the safe and affordable distribution of the drug to patients in need. The act creates an exemption from criminal prosecution for physicians, as well as for patients and primary caregivers who possess or cultivate marijuana for medicinal purposes with the recommendation or approval of a physician. A "primary caregiver" is a person who has consistently assumed responsibility for the housing, health, or safety of the patient.

Respondents [those charged with violating the law] Angel Raich and Diane Monson are California residents who suffer from a variety of serious medical conditions and have sought to avail themselves of medical marijuana pursuant to the terms of the Compassionate Use Act. They are being treated by licensed, board-certified family practitioners, who have concluded, after prescribing a host of conventional medicines to treat respondents' conditions and to alleviate their associated symptoms, that marijuana is the only drug available that provides effective treatment. Both women have been using marijuana as a medication for several years pursuant to their doctors' recommendation, and both rely heavily on cannabis to function on a daily basis. Indeed, Raich's physician believes that forgoing cannabis treatments would certainly cause Raich excruciating pain and could very well prove fatal.

Respondent Monson cultivates her own marijuana, and ingests the drug in a variety of ways including smoking and using a vaporizer. Respondent Raich, by contrast, is unable to cultivate her own, and thus relies on two caregivers, litigating as "John Does," to provide her with locally grown marijuana at no charge. These caregivers also process the cannabis into hashish or keif, and Raich herself processes some of the marijuana into oils, balms, and foods for consumption.

On August 15, 2002, county deputy sheriffs and agents from the federal Drug Enforcement Administration (DEA) came to Monson's home. After a thorough investigation, the county officials concluded that her use of marijuana was entirely lawful as a matter of California law. Nevertheless, after a 3-hour standoff, the federal agents seized and destroyed all six of her cannabis plants.

Respondents thereafter brought this action against the Attorney General of the United States and the head of the DEA seeking injunctive and declaratory relief prohibiting the enforcement of the federal Controlled Substances Act (CSA) to the extent it prevents them from possessing, obtaining, or manufacturing cannabis for their personal medical use. In their complaint and supporting affidavits, Raich and Monson described the severity of their afflictions, their repeatedly futile attempts to obtain relief with conventional medications, and the opinions of their doctors concerning their need to use marijuana. Respondents claimed that enforcing the CSA against them would violate the Commerce Clause, the Due Process Clause of the Fifth Amendment, the Ninth and Tenth Amendments of the Constitution, and the doctrine of medical necessity.

The District Court denied respondents' motion for a preliminary injunction [in 2003]. Although the court found that the federal enforcement interests "wane[d]" when compared to the harm that California residents would suffer if denied access to medically necessary marijuana, it concluded that respondents could not demonstrate a likelihood of success on the merits of their legal claims.

A divided panel of the Court of Appeals for the Ninth Circuit [later in 2003] reversed and ordered the District Court to enter a preliminary injunction [to block federal action]. The [appellate] court found that respondents had "demonstrated a strong likelihood of success on their claim that, as applied to them, the CSA is an unconstitutional exercise of Congress' Commerce Clause authority." The Court of Appeals distinguished prior Circuit cases upholding the CSA in the face of Commerce Clause challenges by focusing on what it deemed to be the "*separate and distinct class of activities*" at issue in this case: "the intrastate, noncommercial cultivation and possession of cannabis for personal medical purposes as recommended by a patient's physician pursuant to valid California state law." The court found the latter class of activities "different in kind from drug trafficking" because interposing a physician's recommendation raises different health and safety concerns, and because "this limited use is clearly distinct from the broader illicit drug market—as well as any broader commercial market for medicinal marijuana—insofar as the medicinal marijuana at issue in this case is not intended for, nor does it enter, the stream of commerce."

...[This] case is made difficult by respondents' strong arguments that they will suffer irreparable harm because, despite a congressional finding to the contrary, marijuana does have valid therapeutic purposes. [A congressional finding is a statement within a law of what Congress believes is a fact related to the purpose of the law.] The question before us, however, is not whether it is wise to enforce the statute in these circumstances; rather, it is whether Congress' power to regulate interstate markets for medicinal substances encompasses the portions of those markets that are supplied with drugs produced and consumed locally. Well-settled law controls our answer. The CSA is a valid exercise of federal power, even as applied to the troubling facts of this case.

II

Shortly after taking office in 1969, President Nixon declared a national "war on drugs." As the first campaign of that war, Congress set out to enact legislation that would consolidate various drug laws on the books into a comprehensive statute, provide meaningful regulation over legitimate sources of drugs to prevent diversion into illegal channels, and strengthen law enforcement tools against the traffic in illicit drugs. That effort culminated in the passage of the Comprehensive Drug Abuse Prevention and Control Act of 1970.

This was not, however, Congress' first attempt to regulate the national market in drugs. Rather, as early as 1906 Congress enacted federal legislation imposing labeling regulations on medications and prohibiting the manufacture or shipment of any adulterated or misbranded drug traveling in interstate commerce. Aside from these labeling restrictions, most domestic drug regulations prior to 1970 generally came in the guise of revenue laws, with the Department of the Treasury serving as the federal government's primary enforcer. For example, the primary drug control law, before being repealed by the passage of the CSA, was the Harrison Narcotics Act of 1914. The Harrison Act sought to exert control over the possession and sale of narcotics, specifically cocaine and opiates, by requiring producers, distributors, and purchasers to register with the federal government, by assessing taxes against parties so registered, and by regulating the issuance of prescriptions.

Marijuana itself was not significantly regulated by the federal government until 1937 when accounts of marijuana's addictive qualities and physiological effects, paired with dissatisfaction with enforcement efforts at state and local levels, prompted Congress to pass the Marihuana Tax Act…(repealed 1970). Like the Harrison Act, the Marihuana Tax Act did not outlaw the possession or sale of marijuana outright. Rather, it imposed registration and reporting requirements for all individuals importing, producing, selling, or dealing in marijuana, and required the payment of annual taxes in addition to transfer taxes whenever the drug changed hands. Moreover, doctors wishing to prescribe marijuana for medical purposes were required to comply with rather burdensome administrative requirements. Noncompliance exposed traffickers to severe federal penalties, whereas compliance would often subject them to prosecution under state law. Thus, while the Marihuana Tax Act did not declare the drug illegal *per se*, the onerous administrative requirements, the prohibitively expensive taxes, and the risks attendant on compliance practically curtailed the marijuana trade.

Then in 1970, after declaration of the national "war on drugs," federal drug policy underwent a significant transformation. A number of noteworthy events precipitated this policy shift. First, in *Leary* v. *United States,* (1969), this Court held certain provisions of the Marihuana Tax Act and other narcotics legislation unconstitutional. Second, at the end of his term, President Johnson fundamentally reorganized the federal drug control agencies. The Bureau of Narcotics, then housed in the Department of Treasury, merged with the Bureau of Drug Abuse Control, then housed in the Department of Health, Education, and Welfare (HEW), to create the Bureau of Narcotics and Dangerous Drugs, currently housed in the Department of Justice. Finally, prompted by a perceived need to consolidate the growing number of piecemeal drug laws and to enhance federal drug enforcement powers, Congress enacted the Comprehensive Drug Abuse Prevention and Control Act.

Title II of that Act, the CSA, repealed most of the earlier antidrug laws in favor of a comprehensive regime to combat the international and interstate traffic in illicit drugs. The main objectives of the CSA were to conquer drug abuse and to control the legitimate and illegitimate traffic in controlled substances. Congress was particularly concerned with the need to prevent the diversion of drugs from legitimate to illicit channels.

To effectuate these goals, Congress devised a closed regulatory system making it unlawful to manufacture, distribute, dispense, or possess any controlled substance except in a manner authorized by the CSA. The CSA categorizes all controlled substances into five schedules. The drugs are grouped together based on their accepted medical uses, the potential for abuse, and their psychological and physical effects on the body. Each schedule is associated with a distinct set of controls regarding the manufacture, distribution, and use of the substances listed therein. The CSA and its implementing regulations set forth strict requirements regarding registration, labeling and packaging, production quotas, drug security, and recordkeeping.

In enacting the CSA, Congress classified marijuana as a Schedule I drug. This preliminary classification was based, in part, on the recommendation of the Assistant Secretary of HEW "that marihuana be retained within schedule I at least until the completion of certain studies now underway." Schedule I drugs are categorized [by the law] as such because of their high potential for abuse, lack of any accepted medical use, and absence of any accepted safety for use in medically supervised treatment. These three factors, in varying gradations, are also used to categorize drugs in the other four schedules. For example, Schedule II substances also have a high potential for abuse which may lead to severe psychological or physical dependence, but unlike Schedule I drugs, they have a currently accepted medical use. By classifying marijuana as a Schedule I drug, as opposed to listing it on a lesser schedule, the manufacture, distribution, or possession of marijuana became a criminal offense, with the sole exception being use of the drug as part of a Food and Drug Administration preapproved research study.

The CSA provides for the periodic updating of schedules and delegates authority to the Attorney General, after consultation with the Secretary of Health and Human Services, to add, remove, or transfer substances to, from, or between schedules. Despite considerable efforts to reschedule marijuana, it remains a Schedule I drug.

III

Respondents in this case do not dispute that passage of the CSA, as part of the Comprehensive Drug Abuse Prevention and Control Act, was well within Congress' commerce power. Nor do they contend that any provision or section of the CSA amounts to an unconstitutional exercise of congressional authority. Rather, respondents' challenge is actually quite limited; they argue that the CSA's categorical prohibition of the manufacture and possession of marijuana as applied to the intrastate manufacture and possession of marijuana for medical purposes pursuant to California law exceeds Congress' authority under the Commerce Clause.

In assessing the validity of congressional regulation, none of our Commerce Clause cases can be viewed in isolation....Our understanding of the reach of the Commerce Clause, as well as Congress' assertion of authority [under the cause] has evolved over time. The Commerce Clause emerged as the Framers' response to the central problem giving rise to the Constitution itself: the absence of any federal commerce power under the Articles of Confederation. For the first century of our history, the primary use of the Clause was to preclude the kind of discriminatory state legislation [against the products of other states] that had once been permissible. Then, in response to rapid industrial development and an increasingly interdependent national economy, Congress "ushered in a new era of federal regulation under the commerce power," beginning with the enactment of the Interstate Commerce Act in 1887.

Cases decided during that "new era," which now spans more than a century, have identified three general categories of regulation in which Congress is authorized to engage under its commerce power. First, Congress can regulate the channels of interstate commerce. Second, Congress has authority to regulate and protect the instrumentalities of interstate commerce, and persons or things in interstate commerce. Third, Congress has the power to regulate activities that substantially affect interstate commerce. Only the third category is implicated in the case at hand.

Our case law firmly establishes Congress' power to regulate purely local activities that are part of an economic "class of activities" that have a substantial effect on interstate commerce....We [the justices] have never required Congress to legislate with scientific exactitude. When Congress decides that the "'total incidence'" of a practice poses a threat to a national market, it may regulate the entire class. In this vein, we have reiterated [in an earlier case] that when "a general regulatory statute bears a substantial relation to commerce, the [importance or lack of importance of the] character of individual instances arising under that statute is of no consequence."

...Thus establishes that Congress can regulate purely intrastate activity that is not itself "commercial," in that it is not produced for sale, if it concludes that failure to regulate that class of activity would undercut the regulation of the interstate market in that commodity....

[In] this case...respondents are cultivating, for home consumption, a fungible commodity for which there is an established, albeit illegal, interstate market. ...[and] a primary purpose of the CSA is to control the supply and demand of controlled substances in both lawful and unlawful drug markets....[Therefore], Congress had a rational basis for concluding that leaving home-consumed marijuana outside federal control would similarly affect price and market conditions.

More concretely,...[a] concern making it appropriate to include marijuana grown for home consumption in the CSA is the likelihood that the high demand in the interstate market will draw such marijuana into that market....The diversion of home-grown marijuana tends to frustrate the federal interest in eliminating commercial transactions in the interstate market in their entirety. In both cases, the regulation is squarely within Congress' commerce power because production of the commodity meant for home consumption, [including] marijuana, has a substantial effect on supply and demand in the national market for that commodity....

Findings in the introductory sections of the CSA explain why Congress deemed it appropriate to encompass local activities within the scope of the CSA. The submissions of the parties and the numerous *amici* [supporting arguments submitted to the court by interested parties or "friends"] all seem to agree that...a national and international market for marijuana [exists]. ...Respondents nonetheless insist that the CSA cannot be constitutionally applied to their activities because Congress did not make a specific finding that the intrastate cultivation and possession of marijuana for medical purposes based on the recommendation of a physician would substantially affect the larger interstate marijuana market. Be that as it may, we have never required Congress to make particularized findings in order to legislate, absent a special concern such as the protection of free speech. While congressional findings are certainly helpful in reviewing the substance of a congressional statutory scheme, particularly when the connection to commerce is not self-evident, and while we will consider congressional findings in our analysis when they are available, the absence of particularized findings does not call into question Congress' authority to legislate.

In assessing the scope of Congress' authority under the Commerce Clause, we stress that the task before us is a modest one. We need not determine whether respondents' activities, taken in the aggregate, substantially affect interstate commerce in fact, but only whether a "rational basis" exists for so concluding. Given the enforcement difficulties that attend distinguishing between marijuana cultivated locally and marijuana grown elsewhere, and concerns about diversion into illicit channels, we have no difficulty concluding that Congress had a rational basis for believing that failure to regulate the intrastate manufacture and possession of marijuana would leave a gaping hole in the CSA. Thus…, Congress was acting well within its authority to "make all Laws which shall be necessary and proper" to "regulate Commerce…among the several States." That the regulation ensnares some purely intrastate activity is of no moment. As we have done many times before, we refuse to excise individual components of that larger scheme.

IV

…The activities regulated by the CSA are quintessentially economic. "Economics" [according to a dictionary] refers to "the production, distribution, and consumption of commodities." The CSA is a statute that regulates the production, distribution, and consumption of commodities for which there is an established, and lucrative, interstate market. Prohibiting the intrastate possession or manufacture of an article of commerce is a rational (and commonly utilized) means of regulating commerce in that

product. Such prohibitions include specific decisions requiring that a drug be withdrawn from the market as a result of the failure to comply with regulatory requirements as well as decisions excluding Schedule I drugs entirely from the market. Because the CSA is a statute that directly regulates economic, commercial activity, our opinion in *Morrison* casts no doubt on its constitutionality.

The Court of Appeals was able to conclude otherwise only by isolating a "separate and distinct" class of activities that it held to be beyond the reach of federal power, defined as "the intrastate, noncommercial cultivation, possession and use of marijuana for personal medical purposes on the advice of a physician and in accordance with state law." The court characterized this class as "different in kind from drug trafficking." The differences between the members of a class so defined and the principal traffickers in Schedule I substances might be sufficient to justify a policy decision exempting the narrower class from the coverage of the CSA. The question, however, is whether Congress' contrary policy judgment, *i.e.*, its decision to include this narrower "class of activities" within the larger regulatory scheme, was constitutionally deficient. We have no difficulty concluding that Congress acted rationally in determining that none of the characteristics making up the purported class, whether viewed individually or in the aggregate, compelled an exemption from the CSA; rather, the subdivided class of activities defined by the Court of Appeals was an essential part of the larger regulatory scheme.

First, the fact that marijuana is used "for personal medical purposes on the advice of a physician" cannot itself serve as a distinguishing factor. The CSA designates marijuana as contraband for *any* purpose; in fact, by characterizing marijuana as a Schedule I drug, Congress expressly found that the drug has no acceptable medical uses. Moreover, the CSA is a comprehensive regulatory regime specifically designed to regulate which controlled substances can be utilized for medicinal purposes, and in what manner. Indeed, most of the substances classified in the CSA "have a useful and legitimate medical purpose." Thus, even if respondents are correct that marijuana does have accepted medical uses and thus should be redesignated as a lesser schedule drug, the CSA would still impose controls beyond what is required by California law. The CSA requires manufacturers, physicians, pharmacies, and other handlers of controlled substances to comply with statutory and regulatory provisions mandating registration with the DEA, compliance with specific production quotas, security controls to guard against diversion, recordkeeping and reporting obligations, and prescription requirements. Furthermore, the dispensing of new drugs, even when doctors approve their use, must await federal approval. Accordingly, the mere fact that marijuana—like virtually every other controlled substance regulated by the CSA—is used for medicinal purposes cannot possibly serve to distinguish it from the core activities regulated by the CSA.

More fundamentally, if [it is true, as has been contended,] the personal cultivation, possession, and use of marijuana for medicinal purposes is beyond the "outer limits" of Congress' Commerce Clause authority, it must also be true that such personal use of marijuana (or any other homegrown drug) for recreational purposes is also beyond those "outer limits," whether or not a state elects to authorize or even regulate such use....One need not have a degree in economics to understand why a nationwide exemption for the vast quantity of marijuana (or other drugs) locally cultivated for personal use (which presumably would include use by friends, neighbors, and fam-

ily members) may have a substantial impact on the interstate market for this extraordinarily popular substance. The congressional judgment that an exemption for such a significant segment of the total market would undermine the orderly enforcement of the entire regulatory scheme is entitled to a strong presumption of validity. Indeed, that judgment is not only rational, but "visible to the naked eye" under any commonsense appraisal of the probable consequences of such an open-ended exemption.

Second, limiting the activity to marijuana possession and cultivation "in accordance with state law" cannot serve to place respondents' activities beyond congressional reach. The Supremacy Clause [in the U.S. Constitution] unambiguously provides that if there is any conflict between federal and state law, federal law shall prevail. It is beyond peradventure that federal power over commerce [prevails]...Just as state acquiescence to federal regulation cannot expand the bounds of the Commerce Clause, so too state action cannot circumscribe Congress' plenary commerce power.

Respondents acknowledge this proposition, but nonetheless contend that their activities were not "an essential part of a larger regulatory scheme" because they had been "isolated by the State of California, and [are] policed by the State of California," and thus remain "entirely separated from the market." The notion that California law has surgically excised a discrete activity that is hermetically sealed off from the larger interstate marijuana market is a dubious proposition, and, more importantly, one that Congress could have rationally rejected.

Indeed, that the California exemptions will have a significant impact on both the supply and demand sides of the market for marijuana is...is readily apparent. The exemption for physicians provides them with an economic incentive to grant their patients permission to use the drug. In contrast to most prescriptions for legal drugs, which limit the dosage and duration of the usage, under California law the doctor's permission to recommend marijuana use is open-ended. The authority to grant permission whenever the doctor determines that a patient is afflicted [according to the California law] with "any other illness for which marijuana provides relief" is broad enough to allow even the most scrupulous doctor to conclude that some recreational uses would be therapeutic. And our cases have taught us that there are some unscrupulous physicians who overprescribe when it is sufficiently profitable to do so.

The exemption for cultivation by patients and caregivers can only increase the supply of marijuana in the California market. The likelihood that all such production will promptly terminate when patients recover or will precisely match the patients' medical needs during their convalescence seems remote; whereas the danger that excesses will satisfy some of the admittedly enormous demand for recreational use seems obvious. Moreover, that the national and international narcotics trade has thrived in the face of vigorous criminal enforcement efforts suggests that no small number of unscrupulous people will make use of the California exemptions to serve their commercial ends whenever it is feasible to do so. Taking into account the fact that California is only one of at least nine states to have authorized the medical use of marijuana, Congress could have rationally concluded that the aggregate impact on the national market of all the transactions exempted from federal supervision is unquestionably substantial....

V

We...do note...the presence of...[an] avenue of relief....[The CSA] authorizes procedures for the reclassification of Schedule I drugs. But perhaps even more important than these legal avenues is the democratic process, in which the voices of voters allied with these respondents may one day be heard in the halls of Congress. Under the present state of the law, however, the judgment of the Court of Appeals must be vacated.

Federal Regulation of Medical Marijuana: Usurpation of State Authority

SANDRA DAY O'CONNOR

We enforce the "outer limits" of Congress' Commerce Clause authority not for their own sake, but to protect historic spheres of state sovereignty from excessive federal encroachment and thereby to maintain the distribution of power fundamental to our federalist system of government. One of federalism's chief virtues, of course, is that it promotes innovation by allowing for the possibility that [according to the often quoted words of Justice Louis D. Brandeis in 1932], "a single courageous State may, if its citizens choose, serve as a laboratory; and try novel social and economic experiments without risk to the rest of the country."

This case exemplifies the role of states as laboratories. The states' core police powers have always included authority to define criminal law and to protect the health, safety, and welfare of their citizens. Exercising those powers, California (by ballot initiative and then by legislative codification) has come to its own conclusion about the difficult and sensitive question of whether marijuana should be available to relieve severe pain and suffering. Today [in the decision written by Justice John Paul Stevens, III] the Court sanctions an application of the federal Controlled Substances Act that extinguishes that experiment, without any proof that the personal cultivation, possession, and use of marijuana for medicinal purposes, if economic activity in the first place, has a substantial effect on interstate commerce and is therefore an appropriate subject of federal regulation. In so doing, the Court announces a rule that gives Congress a perverse incentive to legislate broadly pursuant to the Commerce Clause—nestling questionable assertions of its authority into comprehensive regulatory schemes—rather than with precision....

I

What is the relevant conduct subject to Commerce Clause analysis in this case? The Court takes its cues from Congress, applying the above considerations to the activity regulated by the Controlled Substances Act (CSA) in general. The Court's decision rests on two facts about the CSA: (1) Congress chose to enact a single statute providing a comprehensive prohibition on the production, distribution, and possession of all controlled substances, and (2) Congress did not distinguish between various forms of intrastate non-commercial cultivation, possession, and use of marijuana. Today's decision suggests that the federal regulation of local activity is immune to Commerce Clause challenge because Congress chose to act with an ambitious, all-encompassing statute, rather than piecemeal. In my view, allowing Congress to set the terms of the constitutional debate in this way, *i.e.*, by packaging regulation of local activity in broader schemes, is tantamount to removing meaningful limits on the Commerce Clause.

The Court, [in the opinion written by Justice Stevens, argues that]...the CSA is "a lengthy and detailed statute creating a comprehensive framework for regulating the production, distribution, and possession of five classes of 'controlled substances.'" Thus, according to the Court,...the local activity that the CSA targets (in this case cultivation and possession of marijuana for personal medicinal use) cannot be separated from the general drug control scheme of which it is a part.

Today's decision allows Congress to regulate intrastate activity without check, so long as there is some implication by legislative design that regulating intrastate activity is essential (and the Court appears to equate "essential" with "necessary") to the interstate regulatory scheme.…The Court appears to reason that the placement of local activity in a comprehensive scheme confirms that it is essential to that scheme.…Furthermore, today's decision suggests we would readily sustain a congressional decision to attach the regulation of intrastate activity to a pre-existing comprehensive (or even not-so-comprehensive) scheme. If so, the Court invites increased federal regulation of local activity even if, as it suggests, Congress would not enact a *new* interstate scheme exclusively for the sake of reaching intrastate activity.

I cannot agree…[with the constitutionality of] such evasive or overbroad legislative strategies or that the constitutionality of federal regulation depends on superficial and formalistic distinctions. Likewise I did not understand our discussion of the role of courts in enforcing outer limits of the Commerce Clause for the sake of maintaining the federalist balance our Constitution requires as a signal to Congress to enact legislation that is more extensive and more intrusive into the domain of state power. If the Court always defers to Congress as it does today, little may be left to the notion of enumerated powers.

The hard work for courts, then, is to identify objective markers for confining the analysis in Commerce Clause cases. Here, respondents challenge the constitutionality of the CSA as applied to them and those similarly situated. I agree with the Court that we must look beyond respondents' own activities. Otherwise, individual litigants could always exempt themselves from Commerce Clause regulation merely by pointing to the obvious—that their personal activities do not have a substantial effect on interstate commerce. The task is to identify a mode of analysis that allows Congress to regulate more than nothing (by declining to reduce each case to its litigants) and less than everything (by declining to let Congress set the terms of analysis). The analysis may not be the same in every case, for it depends on the regulatory scheme at issue and the federalism concerns implicated.

A number of objective markers are available to confine the scope of constitutional review here. Both federal and state legislation—including the CSA itself, the California Compassionate Use Act, and other state medical marijuana legislation—recognize that medical and nonmedical (*i.e.*, recreational) uses of drugs are realistically distinct and can be segregated, and regulate them differently. Respondents challenge only the application of the CSA to medicinal use of marijuana. Moreover, because fundamental structural concerns about dual sovereignty [federal and state independent authority] animate our Commerce Clause cases, it is relevant that this case involves the interplay of federal and state regulation in areas of criminal law and social policy, where [according to earlier court decisions,] "States lay claim by right of history and expertise"…[Moreover, as found by the Court in another case,] "State autonomy is a relevant factor in assessing the means by which Congress exercises its powers" under the Commerce Clause. California, like other states, has drawn on its reserved powers to distinguish the regulation of medicinal marijuana. To ascertain whether Congress' encroachment is constitutionally justified in this case, then, I would focus here on the personal cultivation, possession, and use of marijuana for medicinal purposes.

Having thus defined the relevant conduct, we must determine whether, under our precedents, the conduct is economic and, in the aggregate, substantially affects interstate commerce. Even if intrastate cultivation and possession of marijuana for one's own medicinal use can properly be characterized as economic, and I question whether it can, it has not been shown that such activity substantially affects interstate commerce. Similarly, it is neither self-evident nor demonstrated that regulating such activity is necessary to the interstate drug control scheme.

The Court's definition of economic activity is breathtaking. It defines as economic any activity involving the production, distribution, and consumption of commodities. And it appears to reason that when an interstate market for a commodity exists, regulating the intrastate manufacture or possession of that commodity is constitutional either because that intrastate activity is itself economic, or because regulating it is a rational part of regulating its market. Putting to one side the problem endemic to the Court's opinion—the shift in focus from the activity at issue in this case to the entirety of what the CSA regulates. The Court's definition of economic activity for purposes of Commerce Clause jurisprudence threatens to sweep all of productive human activity into federal regulatory reach.

The Court uses a dictionary definition of economics to skirt the real problem of drawing a meaningful line between "what is national and what is local." It will not do to say that Congress may regulate noncommercial activity simply because it may have an effect on the demand for commercial goods, or because the noncommercial endeavor can, in some sense, substitute for commercial activity. Most commercial goods or services have some sort of privately producible analogue. Home care substitutes for daycare. Charades games substitute for movie tickets. Backyard or windowsill gardening substitutes for going to the supermarket. To draw the line wherever private activity affects the demand for market goods is to draw no line at all, and to declare everything economic. We have already rejected the result that would follow—a federal police power.

In [earlier cases], we suggested that economic activity usually relates directly to commercial activity. The homegrown cultivation and personal possession and use of marijuana for medicinal purposes has no apparent commercial character. Everyone agrees that the marijuana at issue in this case was never in the stream of commerce, and neither were the supplies for growing it. (Marijuana is highly unusual among the substances subject to the CSA in that it can be cultivated without any materials that have traveled in interstate commerce.) Possession is not itself commercial activity. And respondents have not come into possession by means of any commercial transaction; they have simply grown, in their own homes, marijuana for their own use, without acquiring, buying, selling, or bartering a thing of value....

Even assuming that economic activity is at issue in this case, the [federal] government has made no showing in fact that the possession and use of homegrown marijuana for medical purposes, in California or elsewhere, has a substantial effect on interstate commerce. Similarly, the [federal] government has not shown that regulating such activity is necessary to an interstate regulatory scheme. Whatever the specific theory of "substantial effects" at issue (*i.e.*, whether the activity substantially affects interstate commerce, whether its regulation is necessary to an interstate regulatory scheme, or both), a concern for dual sovereignty requires that Congress' excursion into the traditional domain of states be justified.

That is why characterizing this as a case about the Necessary and Proper Clause does not change the analysis significantly. Congress must exercise its authority under the Necessary and Proper Clause in a manner consistent with basic constitutional principles. Congress cannot use its authority under the Clause to contravene the principle of state sovereignty embodied in the Tenth Amendment. Likewise, that authority must be used in a manner consistent with the notion of enumerated powers—a structural principle that is as much part of the Constitution as the Tenth Amendment's explicit textual command. Accordingly, something more than mere assertion is required when Congress purports to have power over local activity whose connection to an intrastate market is not self-evident. Otherwise, the Necessary and Proper Clause will always be a back door for unconstitutional federal regulation.

There is simply no evidence that homegrown medicinal marijuana users constitute, in the aggregate, a sizable enough class to have a discernible, let alone substantial, impact on the national illicit drug market—or otherwise to threaten the CSA regime. Explicit evidence is helpful when substantial effect is not "visible to the naked eye." And here, in part because common sense suggests that medical marijuana users may be limited in number and that California's Compassionate Use Act and similar state legislation may well isolate activities relating to medicinal marijuana from the illicit market, the effect of those activities on interstate drug traffic is not self-evidently substantial....

The Court [in Justice Steven's opinion] refers to a series of declarations in the introduction to the CSA saying that (1) local distribution and possession of controlled substances causes "swelling" in interstate traffic; (2) local production and distribution cannot be distinguished from interstate

production and distribution; (3) federal control over intrastate incidents "is essential to effective control" over interstate drug trafficking....[These clauses] amount to nothing more than a legislative insistence that the regulation of controlled substances must be absolute. They are asserted without any supporting evidence—descriptive, statistical, or otherwise....

In particular, the CSA's introductory declarations are too vague and unspecific to demonstrate that the federal statutory scheme will be undermined if Congress cannot exert power over individuals like respondents. The declarations are not even specific to marijuana. (Facts about substantial effects may be developed in litigation to compensate for the inadequacy of Congress' findings; in part because this case comes to us from the grant of a preliminary injunction, there has been no such development.) Because here California, like other states, has carved out a limited class of activity for distinct regulation, the inadequacy of the CSA's findings is especially glaring. The California Compassionate Use Act exempts from other state drug laws patients and their caregivers "who posses[s] or cultivat[e] marijuana for the *personal* medical purposes of the patient upon the written or oral recommendation of a physician" to treat a list of serious medical conditions. The Act specifies that it should not be construed to supersede legislation prohibiting persons from engaging in acts dangerous to others, or to condone the diversion of marijuana for nonmedical purposes. To promote the Act's operation and to facilitate law enforcement, California recently enacted an identification card system for qualified patients. We generally assume states enforce their laws and have no reason to think otherwise here.

The [federal] government has not overcome empirical doubt that the number of Californians engaged in personal cultivation, possession, and use of medical marijuana, or the amount of marijuana they produce, is enough to threaten the federal regime. Nor has it shown that Compassionate Use Act marijuana users have been or are realistically likely to be responsible for the drug's seeping into the market in a significant way. The [federal] government does cite one estimate that there were over 100,000 Compassionate Use Act users in California in 2004, but does not explain, in terms of proportions, what their presence means for the national illicit drug market. [A study by the U.S.] General Accounting Office, Marijuana: Early Experience with Four States' Laws That Allow Use for Medical Purposes" (2002) [found that] in four California counties before the identification card system was enacted, voluntarily registered medical marijuana patients were less than 0.5 percent of the population; in Alaska, Hawaii, and Oregon, statewide medical marijuana registrants represented less than 0.05 percent of the states' populations. It also provides anecdotal evidence about the CSA's enforcement. The Court also offers some arguments about the effect of the Compassionate Use Act on the national market. It says that the California statute might be vulnerable to exploitation by unscrupulous physicians, that Compassionate Use Act patients may overproduce, and that the history of the narcotics trade shows the difficulty of cordoning off any drug use from the rest of the market. These arguments are plausible; if borne out in fact they could justify prosecuting Compassionate Use Act patients under the federal CSA. But, without substantiation, they add little to the CSA's conclusory statements about diversion, essentiality, and market effect. Piling assertion upon assertion does not, in my view, satisfy the substantiality test.

III

We would do well to recall how [in *Federalist* No. 45] James Madison, the father of the Constitution, described our system of joint sovereignty to the people of New York: "The powers delegated by the proposed constitution to the federal government are few and defined. Those which are to remain in the state governments are numerous and indefinite....The powers reserved to the several states will extend to all the objects which, in the ordinary course of affairs, concern the lives, liberties, and properties of the people, and the internal order, improvement, and prosperity of the state."

Relying on Congress' abstract assertions, the Court has endorsed making it a federal crime to grow small amounts of marijuana in one's own home for one's own medicinal use. This overreaching stifles an express choice by some states, concerned for the lives and liberties of their people, to regulate medical marijuana differently. If I were a California citizen, I would not have voted for the medical marijuana ballot initiative; if I were a California legislator I would not have supported the Compassionate Use Act. But whatever the wisdom of California's experiment with medical marijuana, the federalism principles that have driven our Commerce Clause cases require that room for experiment be protected in this case. For these reasons I dissent.

THE CONTINUING DEBATE:
Federal Regulation of Medical Marijuana

What Is New

One June 6, 2005, the Supreme Court handed down its decision in *Gonzales v. Raich*. By a 6 to 3 vote, the court reversed the ruling of the Court of Appeals and held that the federal government could regulate marijuana under the interstate commerce clause. The decision applies to California and, by extension, to all other states permitting the use of medical marijuana. In one of the last cases over which he presided before his death in September, Chief Justice Rehnquist, who had often sided with the states, did so again and dissented along with Justice O'Connor and Justice Clarence Thomas. On the day of the decision, John P. Walters, President George Bush's director of national drug control policy, proclaimed, "Today's decision marks the end of medical marijuana as a political issue." Walters was almost certainly wrong. Seven months after the *Raich* decision, Rhode Island became the eleventh state to legalize medical marijuana, New Mexico became the twelfth to do so in 2007, and proposals to legalize the drug are pending in several other states. Moreover, 72% of Americans support the use of medical marijuana, and the effort to get Congress to change federal law or to get the Justice Department to reconsider its stance are ongoing.

Where to Find More

For an entertaining view of the history of non-medical drug control, read "The History of the Non-Medical Use of Drugs in the United States" a speech to the California Judges Association 1995 annual conference at www.druglibrary.org/schaffer/History/whiteb1.htm. An authoritative review, "Workshop of the Medical Utility of Marijuana," sponsored by the National Institute for Health is available at www.nih.gov/news/medmarijuana/MedicalMarijuana.htm. Also worthwhile is Lawrence O. Gostin, "Medical Marijuana, American Federalism, and the Supreme Court," *JAMA: Journal of the American Medical Association* (2005). For the views of a group favoring the use of medical marijuana, go to the Web site of the Drug Policy Alliance at www.drugpolicy.org/marijuana/medical/. The view of an anti-use organization, the U.S. Drug Enforcement Administration, in its report, "Exposing the Myth of Smoked Medical Marijuana: The Facts" is at www.usdoj.gov/dea/ongoing/marijuana.html.

What More to Do

Analyze the positions of those in your class on this subject by dividing them into four groups according to each person's view of whether or not the expansive view of the commerce clause is acceptable or not and whether or not medical marijuana should be legalized. How many people have a constitutional position and a policy position that, in this case, are at odds with one another? Another project is to pick a different policy area that you think should not be subject to federal law under your concept of how federalism should work. Spend a little time finding out if there are federal laws governing that policy area. A group or an entire class can do this project together, with each person taking a different policy area.

CIVIL LIBERTIES

THE PHRASE "UNDER GOD" IN THE PLEDGE OF ALLEGIANCE:
Violation of the First Amendment *or* Acceptable Traditional Expression?

VIOLATION OF THE FIRST AMENDMENT

ADVOCATE: Douglas Laycock, Professor, School of Law, University of Texas; and Counsel of Record for 32 Christian and Jewish clergy filing an Amicus Curiae brief with the Supreme Court in *Elk Grove School District v. Newdow*

SOURCE: A discussion of the topic "Under God? Pledge of Allegiance Constitutionality," sponsored by the Pew Forum on Religion and Public Life and held before the National Press Club, Washington, D.C., March 19, 2004

ACCEPTABLE TRADITIONAL EXPRESSION

ADVOCATE: Jay Alan Sekulow, Chief Counsel, American Center for Law and Justice; and Counsel of Record for 76 members of Congress and the Committee to Protect the Pledge filing an Amicus Curiae brief with the Supreme Court in *Elk Grove School District v. Newdow*

SOURCE: A discussion of the topic "Under God? Pledge of Allegiance Constitutionality," sponsored by the Pew Forum on Religion and Public Life and held before the National Press Club, Washington, D.C., March 19, 2004

This debate focuses on the establishment clause of the Constitution's First Amendment, which requires that "Congress shall make no law respecting an establishment of religion." It is clear that the authors of the First Amendment were reacting against the British practice of establishing and supporting an "official" church, in that case the Church of England. Also certain is that Congress meant the amendment to prohibit any attempt to bar any religion or religious belief. There the certainties end. For example, freedom of religion does not mean that the government cannot proscribe certain religious practices. Polygamy, animal sacrifice, and taking illegal drugs are just a few of the practices exercised in the name religion that have been legally with subsequent court approval.

Nevertheless, religion has always had a presence in government in the Untied States. The Great Seal of the United States, adopted in 1782 (and found on the back left of one dollar bills) contains an "all seeing eye of Providence," which probably means God, especially given that it is framed in a triangle, thought to represent the Christian trinity. The Great Seal also contains the Latin phrase "annuit coeptis," which translates as "It/He (Providence/God) has favored our undertakings." Also, first adopted in 1964 and currently on all U.S. paper currency is the motto "In God We Trust." That phrase is also found in the fourth stanza of the Star Spangled Banner (written 1813; officially adopted 1931), which concludes, "And this be our motto: "In God is our trust." Finally, in 1957 Congress added "under God" after one nation" to the Pledge of Allegiance. This last reference to God is the specific issue in this debate.

Government also has and continues to support religion and to choose among religions in other ways. For example, the military employs chaplains for all the major religious faiths, but does not employ atheist counselors. There is also a level of choosing among religions in having chaplains for the major religions, but not for the minor ones. Each year the president lights an immense Christmas tree, although these days in a bow to restrictions on religious displays on public property the giant fir is call the "national tree" and is lighted as part of the "Pageant of Peace," which, of course, corresponds with the Christmas season. Historically, it has been common to find the Ten Commandments carved in the walls of public buildings or otherwise displayed in them.

Traditionally, displays of the Ten Commandments or similar religious symbols on public property, prayers in public schools, references to God on the country's currency, or affirmations of patriotism were not high profile issues. This began to change because of the increasing stress on civil rights and liberties and because in *Everson v. Board of Education* (1947) the Supreme Court ruled that the due process cause of the Fourteenth Amendment made the establishment clause of the First Amendment applicable to the states, as well as federal government. During the ensuring years, a significant number of cases involving practices at the state and local levels were brought before the Supreme Court. With regard to the establishment clause, the Court struck down prayers and religious invocations in public schools, most religious displays on public property, and other explicit and implicit supports of religion by public officials. However, the Supreme Court has also allowed religious groups to meet in public buildings as long as there is no discrimination, has supported prayers opening legislative sessions, and having student groups fees go to student religious groups.

In this setting, Michael Newdow filed suit arguing that a California rule requiring students to recite the Pledge of Allegiance with its affirmative reference to God violated the establishment clause of the First Amendment. A U.S. District Court ruled for the school district, but the "Ninth Circuit of the U.S. Court of Appeals found for Newdow, and the Elk Grove school district appealed to the U.S. Supreme Court. Shortly before the High Court heard oral arguments, two opposing attorneys who had filed amicus curiae ("friend of the court") briefs with the Court debated the issue and responded to questions from the audience in the readings that follow.

POINTS TO PONDER

➤ Expressing an absolutist position when writing the majority opinion in the *Everson* case, Justice Hugo Black argued that the wall between church and state "must be kept high and impregnable. We [should] not approve any breach." What would be the implications of adopting that no-compromise standard?

➤ Compare the argument of Douglas Laycock that the Pledge, as government sanctioned religious expression, is "coercive" and Jay Sekulow's contention that the phrase "under God" is merely a "historical statement" reflecting the belief in God by most Americans throughout history.

➤ Does it make any difference that students are not required to say the pledge, only that schools must lead its recitation?

The Phrase "Under God" in the Pledge of Allegiance: Violation of the First Amendment

Douglas Laycock

Jay [Sekulow, the author of the second article in this debate] and I were on the same side in a case [*Locke v. Davey*, 2004] that the [Supreme] Court decided earlier this year, involving the student from Washington [State] who wanted to take his state scholarship to go to seminary with it. With this case, we're on opposite sides. How does that happen? What's up with me? Explaining that is relevant to what I think about the Pledge of Allegiance.

I come to these cases with a fairly simple theory, which is that people of every religion, including the majority and the minority, and people of no religion at all, are entitled to believe their own beliefs, speak their own beliefs, and act on their own beliefs as long as they're not hurting anybody else, and to be left alone by government and have government not take sides. And a corollary of that is that none of these groups can use the government to try to force the other side to join in or participate in their own religious observances. So when government tries to stop a student prayer club from meeting on its own after school, I think government is wrong. And when that student prayer club—or the supporters of that student prayer club—moves into the classroom and tries to induce everyone else who didn't want to come to participate anyway, I think they're wrong. And I think the Pledge of Allegiance falls on that side of the line.

The country has been fighting about this issue in various forms since the 1820s, when Catholics objected to Protestant religious observances in public schools. We've gotten better about it. In the 1840s and '50s, we had mobs in the street; we had

people dead. We don't do that to each other any more, and that's progress. And "one nation under God" may seem like a pretty minimal violation of whatever principle is at stake here. The Supreme Court for 40 years has said consistently, without an exception, that government may not sponsor religious observances in the public schools, and they've said it with respect to things that were pretty short. The first school prayer case, *Engel v. Vitale* in 1962, was a pretty generic, monotheistic prayer composed not by clergymen but by the New York Board of Regents, and it was 22 words long, and the Court said you can't ask children to recite that prayer.

Now we're down to only two words, and it's not a prayer, and it's mixed up in the Pledge of Allegiance, and the question is, Does that change the answer? And the Supreme Court has repeatedly suggested, never in a holding, but over and over in what lawyers call dictums—side comments explaining what this opinion doesn't decide—there is some kind of threshold. It's got to be big enough to matter before it's an Establishment Clause violation [of the First Amendment to the Constitution]. There are little, ceremonial, rote, repetition things that the Court is not going to get involved in striking down. "In God We Trust" on the coins is a classic example; various state mottos around the country; certainly religious references in historical documents and in politicians' speeches, the Supreme Court is not going to strike down. And they have said—without a holding—two or three times that the Pledge of Allegiance is like "In God We Trust" on the coins. It's very short, and it's repeated by rote, and nobody really thinks about it much. Well, most people don't really think about it much.

The Court may say the Pledge of Allegiance—the religious part of the Pledge of Allegiance—is just too short to worry about. It's what lawyers call *de minimis*. That may happen.

I think the Pledge of Allegiance is different from all these other examples of things that might be de minimis. It's different from "In God We Trust" on the coins. It's different from politicians making speeches and so forth. The reason it's different is really unique in the culture. Government doesn't do this to adults; it doesn't do this to children in any other context. In the Pledge of Allegiance, we ask every child in the public schools in America every morning for a personal profession of faith. You don't have to take out your coin and read and meditate on "In God We Trust." You don't have to pay any attention when the politician is talking, and lots of us don't.

But this asks for a personal affirmation: I pledge allegiance to one nation under God. Now if God does not exist, or if I believe that God does not exist, then that isn't one nation under God. We can't have a nation under God unless there is a God. It doesn't say one nation under our god, or some gods, or one of the gods. It pretty clearly implies there is only one God, and if there is only one God, then the God of the Pledge is the one true God, and other alleged gods around the world are false gods.

It says one other thing about this God—it doesn't say much, can't say much in two words—but the nation is "under God." God is of such a nature that God exercises some sort of broad superintending authority so that it is possible for a whole nation to be under Him. Now that doesn't exclude many folks, but it excludes some,

right? This is not God as First Cause who set the universe in motion and doesn't intervene any more; this is not God as a metaphor for all the goodness imminent in the universe or imminent in the population. This is God exercising some kind of authority over at least this nation; maybe over all nations.

It's a pretty generic concept of God, and it's comfortable for a lot of people. But we may overestimate how many people. The largest private opinion polls have about 15 percent of the population not subscribing to any monotheistic conception of God. Who is in that 15 percent? Buddhist and other non-theists, Hindus and other polytheists, those with no religion, atheist, agnostic, humanist, ethical culturalists. That's 15 percent of the population, with 7.2 million children in public schools who are being asked to personally affirm every morning a religious belief that is different from the religious belief that is taught or held in their home and by their parents. And it is the personal affirmation request in the Pledge, it seems to me, that makes the Pledge unique. It is different from all the other kinds of ceremonial deism that go on in the country.

In the attempt to defend the Pledge, government and the various friends of the Court supporting the Pledge have said a remarkable variety of things, but probably the most common thing they've said is variations on what appears in the brief of the United States. It is not religious. We don't mean for them to take it literally. We ask the children to say the nation is under God, but we don't expect them to really believe that the nation is under God. Here is a quote from the government's brief: "What it really means is, I pledge allegiance to one nation, founded by individuals whose belief in God gave rise to the governmental institutions and political order they adopted, indivisible, with liberty and justice for all."

Now if that were what it means, if anybody thought that was what it meant, we would not have had the great political outcry in response to the Ninth Circuit's decision. If people want to get mad about this because it had some recital about what the founders believed, or because of the other point the government makes—that it's in reference to historical and demographic facts that most Americans over time have believed in God—that would be one thing. But people don't get angry at a recital of historical and demographic facts. People get angry because they know what it means; it's plain English. They believe what it means, they want people to say what it means, they want their kids to say what it means. And I'll tell you a dirty little secret: They want to coerce other kids to say what it means and what they believe to be true. They know that "under God" means under God.

And if it doesn't mean under God, if we were to take the government seriously for asking children every morning to say the nation is under God but not to mean the nation is under God, well, Christians and Jews have a teaching about that, too. "Thou shalt not take the name of the Lord Thy God in vain." If we don't mean it, if it's a vain form of words that doesn't mean what it says, then it is indeed a taking of the name of the Lord in vain. That is why the [amicus curiae] brief that I filed [with the Supreme Court in the case of *Elk Grove School District v. Newdow*] is on behalf of 32 Christian and Jewish clergy who do care, not only about not coercing other people to practice their religion, but also care that if we are going to practice religion, we mean it seriously. We don't want a watered down religion that we don't really believe.

Jay Sekulow's version [in an opposing amicus curiae brief] is a little different. He says there's a category—and there's some of this in the government's brief as well—of patriotic observances with religious references. You can't do religion in the school, but you can do patriotism with a religious reference. The consequence of that would be, I suppose, that we could undo all the school prayer cases as long as we wrapped them in a coat of patriotism.

Mingling the patriotic and the religious seems to me to make it worse, not better. Think about what the Pledge does to a child who cannot in good faith affirm that the nation is under God and who actually thinks about it. And let me tell you, kids think about it. You don't think about it if you're comfortable with it, if it doesn't challenge anything you believe, you blur right over it. You can say it pretty fast, and most of us don't stop to reflect on the Pledge anymore. But for kids who don't believe it, and maybe most especially for kids who once went to a church and now don't believe it, whether or not to say "under God" becomes a big issue. I don't claim it becomes a big issue for all 7.2 million whose parents show up in opinion polls, but for a substantial minority of kids, to say "under God" or not becomes an issue.

Some kids drop it out. One of the saving graces here is that it's only two words, so you can get away with dropping it out, and your friends may not notice. But there are people who refuse to say those two words because they don't believe them, and there are a few who refuse to say those two words because it's religious in a governmental context, and it shouldn't be there. It belongs somewhere else.

And for the child who cannot say it, here's what we do by putting the religious reference in the middle of the Pledge of Allegiance to the nation: If you are doubtful about the existence of God, you are of doubtful loyalty to the nation. What kind of a citizen can you be? You can't even say the Pledge of Allegiance in the prescribed form that Congress has written. You can't pledge your loyalty to the nation without pledging your belief in the existence of God.

Now over and over and over the Supreme Court has said the reason it will not allow the government itself to take a position on a religious question, will not allow the government to endorse a religious viewpoint or an anti-religious viewpoint is because government should not make any citizen's political standing in the community depend upon his religious beliefs, not even implicitly, not even by implication. The Court says repeatedly that if the government says this is a Christian nation or this is a religious nation, then non-Christians and non-religious folks will think the government really views them as a second-class citizens. That's pretty indirect and implicit. This is very direct and explicit. Now, children, it is time to pledge your allegiance to the United States of America, and to do that, you have to pledge that the nation is under God. We have linked religion and politics, religion and patriotism, religious faith and patriotic standing inseparably right in the middle of one sentence. And the only way to avoid the religious part is literally to drop out mid-sentence and then come back in.

What would follow from a Supreme Court either striking down or upholding the Pledge? I think because of the fact that the Pledge is unique in asking for a personal affirmation, not much follows about other cases from a decision striking it down. Political volcano is going to follow, but not much is going to follow legally. "In God We Trust" doesn't come off the coins, the other religious references in the school curriculum don't come out. Of course the government can teach historical documents that have religious references in them because that is part of the history curriculum. I think they can teach music with religious references in it because that's music. It's important in the culture. I think schools should be more sensitive than they are about the problems faced by nonbelieving children when they're asked to sing

that music. I think we can deal with those problems, but I don't think the Constitution requires that all—indeed, I think it forbids—certainly, it's sound educational policy—forbids stripping all religious references out of history. Religion is part of history.

None of those things ask the child to personally affirm his belief that the nation is under God, so in this sense, the Pledge case is unique. A decision taking "under God" out of the Pledge would not really portend much change on anything else.

A decision upholding the Pledge, well, you've got to see how they write it. If the Court wants to say the Pledge is special, we're going to let this go by, but it doesn't mean we're unraveling all the school prayer cases, it doesn't mean anything else much changes. They can write this very narrowly. There is a whole list of objective factors that are special about the Pledge that cut the other way. They could say it is only two words; it is recited by rote; it is not a prayer; it has been around in exactly the same form for 50 years before we got a hold of it; kids don't have to say it—we settled that in 1943 [in West Virginia v. Barnette]; they don't have to say it. For those reasons, in combination with all those reasons, we're going to uphold this. Nothing else will satisfy all those reasons. Nothing else is only two words, for starters, and that would be an opinion that doesn't change much.

If they write an opinion that's like the government's brief—we're going to declare that this really isn't religious—the problem with that is that it's completely standardless and therefore it's completely boundless. It's a fiat. The plain language is religious, but five of us on the Supreme Court—hey, with five votes, you can do anything—we're going to tell the country this is not religious. The Fifth Circuit recently held the Ten Commandments are not religious. A big monument across the top, giant letters, "I am the Lord, thy God. Thou shalt have no other gods before me." Not religious, the Fifth Circuit [of the U.S. Court of Appeals] says.

If the Supreme Court adopts that kind of approach—we'll just decree things not to be religious—then everything's up for grabs. If you're going to arbitrarily decree religious things to be secular, you can do it in any case, and district judges will be asked to do it in any case. So that would be a much scarier opinion, a much more potentially wide-ranging opinion, and then other possibilities sort of range in between. Any religion is okay if you're wrap it in patriotism. I think that's pretty wide open, too, because political officers can be pretty clever about wrapping things in patriotism.

So we may get an opinion either way—we may get a very narrow opinion either way or a very broad opinion, particularly if they uphold it. Watch not only for the result; watch for how they write it.

Question: Please comment on the "notion…of ceremonial deism," the idea that "references to God become meaningless if recited often enough in public places."

Mr. Laycock: I think you're right. I think the principal religious division in the country used to be Protestant-Catholic. It's not that anymore. It is a continuum from intense anti-religion to intensely religious. Intensely devout Protestants, Catholics, Muslims, Jews find themselves on the same side of a lot of issues, given that divide, and ceremonial deism is very comfortable for the vast range in the middle. The religious center in America is low-intensity theist.

I think these ceremonial references are very problematic for the anti-religious and for the seriously religious, and many of the seriously religious, in good faith, defend that kind of watered-down ceremonial deism in court on the theory that it's better than nothing; that's all they'll let us have, that's all we can get in a government-sponsored forum,

and it's not for me to tell them they're making a mistake. But it seems to me it is a mistake, and a lot of folks who are intensely religious aren't comfortable with it, and to some extent, it is a position only for the Court. So the Justice Department, representing the United States, says, This is not religious at all. But the form letter from the White House that goes out to people who write in about this issue says it is profoundly religious. They're telling the Court one thing and the public something completely different. The ceremonial deism is a placeholder.

Question: Just to follow up,…comment on whether there is a path that we go down that essentially declares that the public realm—whatever is supported by government—must necessarily be godless, or is there an alternative to this? Does this case take you there or does it not necessarily take you there?

Mr. Laycock: There's no path that leads to the public sphere being godless. There is a path that leads to any activity sponsored by government being godless. The simple absolutist rule is that if the government's sponsoring it, there's no mention of God. In the public schools, the Court has never found a case where a government could mention God, but they've never said this is an absolutist rule with no exceptions either.

This case does not take us there. It does not present the question whether there can ever be any exceptions because this case has the unique feature of requesting a personal affirmation. So a decision in this case wouldn't say anything about whether the rule about what the teacher can do is absolute or the rule about what the president or the governor or the mayor at a public ceremony can do. That's never going to be absolute.

Question: I was wondering what implications this case would have for currency in the message "In God We Trust" on the U.S. dollar notes and coins?

Mr. Laycock: I'm sure there are people who fear it portends that any governmental reference to God goes, and so the currency all has to be changed. I don't think that follows at all because no one has to agree with the currency or pledge allegiance to the currency or even pay any attention to what it says on the currency, beyond the number.

Question: [You argue] "that the Pledge requires an affirmation of personal faith and consequently has got to go." Mr. Sekulow argues, "no, it doesn't—it's not an affirmation of personal faith, so it's okay. One point of view that's not represented here…is that yes, it requires an affirmation of personal faith and that's fine. And the Court should say that's fine. Is that a possible outcome? Can you play around with that a little bit?

Mr. Laycock: I think that's quite unlikely. It's not impossible, but let me just give you 30 seconds of the background. What the Court has said over the years on political issues the government can try to lead public opinion—which it does all the time, it tries to rally public support for its own agenda—but it cannot coerce people to agree with the government or to say that they agree with the government. And that's why in 1943, when the Pledge was entirely secular, it didn't have "under God" in it, and the Pledge case got to the Supreme Court, they said, You can't make students say it. Any student can opt out, but the teacher can lead it. On religious questions in the school prayer cases, they've said opt out isn't enough, because it's really outside the government's jurisdiction, the government isn't responsible for leading public opinion on religion, so the government can't do it at all. It can't ask the kids, even with an opt-out right, to say anything religious, and that's why I agree with Jay [Selulow].

It would be quite unlikely for them to say this really is religious, it really is an affir-

mation of faith and the government can ask you to say it as long as it gives you the right to opt out. That would be a striking departure from the structure of doctrine they've set up over the past 60 years.

Question: Much has been made of the fact that there are only two words here, but one of those words is a preposition, which, to at least some ears, implies a particular type of God, one that we are under, one that is transcendent. And I wonder if consideration of that aspect would move this particular phrase beyond ceremonial deism? I guess my concern is that if you reject the historical document argument, it does seem to imply that we're asking people to affirm a particular type of God, which in 2004, many, many people do not affirm.

Mr. Laycock: I think that if you want to talk about history, let's talk about history. "One nation under God" does not talk about history. It talks about theology and the relation of this nation today to God today and it does say we're under, that is a particular kind of God. I don't think that's going to trouble the Court much because it doesn't eliminate many conceptions of God, but it does eliminate some, as I said. But it's hard to talk about God without talking about some conception of God. It's impossible to be truly neutral in God-talk because humans have evolved too many radically diverse understandings of God.

Question: If our nation was not under Christianity at the birth of our Constitution, which I think scholars generally acknowledge Thomas Jefferson, whether he was a deist or a heretical Christian or a Unitarian, whatever he was, he was a religious man, obviously. But whether he was a Christian or not isn't relevant as far as the Constitution goes. But why did our Constitution refer to a Christian Sabbath, not a Jewish or a Muslim or an atheist Sabbath? And why was the document dated in the year of our Lord? Would anyone dare to say that Lord is anyone other than Jesus Christ?

Mr. Laycock: I agree with most of what Jay just said. Let me elaborate a little bit further and add a piece that I think is very important here. The founding generation fought hard about religious liberty, but they fought about the issues that were controversial in their time. And the religious liberty issue that was controversial in their time was how do you fund the church? And it was controversial because Protestants disagreed about it, because Episcopalians and Congregationalists had had tax support and nobody else did, and fixing that, not surprisingly, produced a huge fight.

They did not fight about these sort of religious references in public documents and public events because there was broad diversity of opinion, but the country was overwhelmingly Protestant and there wasn't any disagreement there big enough to get a fight going. The disagreement became big enough to get a fight going in the 1820s, when they started creating public schools and conservative Protestants said you Unitarians—Horace Mann was a Unitarian, and he was the founder of the public school movement—you Unitarians are putting watered down Christianity. It's not much more than Unitarianism in the public schools. We want real religion in the public schools. And then the huge Catholic immigration began and you got much bigger fights between Protestants and Catholics about what to do with the schools. And really, today's battles over prayer in the public schools and funding for private religious schools both of those battles date to those early 19th century disputes and the Protestant-Catholic conflicts that comes all the way down.

Now if the Religion Clauses of First Amendment are a guarantee of principle that government will leave each of us alone, give us as much religious liberty as we can, that principle encountered a whole new set of applications when religious diversity became greater and when the public schools got going. And so to say that in the Declaration of Independence, which is our founding political theory but it's also a political document to rally opinion, that they invoked both the secular rationale, natural law, and the religious rationale, nature's God and our Creator, they did both, that's true. And that was shrewd, but I don't think that tells us anything about how the government should handle religion when it has other people's children in its custody.

The Phrase "Under God" in the Pledge of Allegiance: Acceptable Traditional Expression

JAY ALAN SEKULOW

First, let me say that I probably agree with Doug [Laycock] on more cases than I disagree. In fact, the very first case I argued at the Supreme Court of the United States [*Airport Commissioners v. Jews for Jesus*]—which seems like a long time ago, because it was—Justice [Sandra Day] O'Connor wrote for the Court, and she relied primarily on an article that was written by Professor Laycock. So I've always appreciated that unanimous opinions are rare and getting rarer every day, especially in the Religion Clause cases.

Let me give you five reasons why the Pledge of Allegiance is constitutional and should be affirmed by the Court as not violating the Establishment Clause [of the First Amendment].

1. The Pledge of Allegiance is not in a form of prayer.

2. The Pledge of Allegiance does not refer to Christianity or any other particular religion.

3. The religious portion of the Pledge of Allegiance is only two words.

4. The Pledge of Allegiance was recited unchanged for 50 years before the Court considered the question.

5. And no one can be required to recite the Pledge of Allegiance.

That's the closing portion of the [amicus curiae] brief Professor Laycock filed [in *Elk Grove School District v. Newdow*], where he argued that if the Court was going to rule in favor the Pledge of Allegiance, here's five ways to do it. And it may well be what the Supreme Court does, because it does give a very specific approach, and I think a fairly persuasive one.

Doug [Laycock] talked about the 40 or 50 years of history when the Supreme Court has dealt with the school prayer issue and not allowing for school prayer in that context. There's another history that's over 200 years now, and it goes something like this: "God save the United States and this Honorable Court"—that's how this Supreme Court oral argument's going to start when Dr. [Michael] Newdow presents his arguments before the Supreme Court [in *Elk Grove School District v. Newdow*] next Wednesday.

So the fact of the matter is that the Supreme Court itself has had this cry as part of its opening ceremony described as an invocation. Students attend oral arguments frequently, including kids in high school and even elementary school. And when those justices stand up or walk in, the students stand up. And while they don't have to repeat it, students also don't have to repeat the Pledge of Allegiance, and correctly so, since the Supreme Court's decision in [West Virginia State Board of Education v. Barnette [(1943)]], which is now dating back almost 60 years, said you can't be compelled to violate your conscience [by being required to recite the Pledge of Allegiance], and in that way, if you are objecting to the form of the Pledge of Allegiance.

I think that the words "God save the United States and this Honorable Court," like the words of the Pledge of Allegiance, echo what our founding fathers thought, and that was that our freedoms, rights and liberties are derived not from government but rather from God granting them to mankind. And in a sense, it's a very Lockean [English political philosopher John Locke, 1632–1704] concept. Thomas Jefferson talks about it. And even, of course, in the Declaration of Independence itself, how often have we learned or were required to learn and recite in school the words, the famous portion of the Declaration of Independence where it's written, "We hold these truths to be self-evident, that all men are created equal, endowed by their Creator with certain unalienable rights. Amongst them are life, liberty and the pursuit of happiness."

If the Pledge of Allegiance were to say something like that, I would suspect that there would be the same objection. Why? Because of its reliance on a Creator, and it is a concept where the Creator endows us with our rights. But in the context of the history of our country, that makes a lot of sense. Our country was founded on the concepts that the rights of man don't derive from a king and they can't be taken away from us by a king. The rights of mankind, the basic rights of mankind—liberty, freedom, the things that we cherish in this country—derive from a Creator. That's what our founding fathers mean.

It's often talked about, Thomas Jefferson's famous letter [in 1801] to the Danbury Baptist Connecticut Association, where he talked about what he called the "high and mighty duty in this wall of separation between church and state." There's something else that Jefferson wrote several years before he wrote that famous letter to the Danbury Baptists, and that was during the debates on the First Amendment and also in discussions with friends about the concept of liberty. He wrote, "Can the liberties of a nation be thought secure when we have removed their only firm basis, a conviction in the minds of the people that

the liberties are a gift of God and that they are not violated but with His wrath?"

Now, Thomas Jefferson, in the classic understanding of his religious belief, would not fall within what most people would consider an orthodox Christian position. In my view of history anyway, I would not consider him to be—and I'm not speaking as a theologian—He had various views on religion and faith. I don't think faith was insignificant in his life, I don't mean to suggest that at all, but it wouldn't be what we would typically talk about today as a Protestant form of Christianity or Catholic form of Christianity. He kind of had his view of faith, Christianity, and the deity of Jesus, and that's a whole different topic.

But he recognized something very fundamental in that our rights don't come from a king; they are endowed to us. So if the requirement of the school district in *Elk Grove* was that we begin each school day by reminding ourselves, as students, that we should remember the history of this great nation, that we are endowed by our Creator with these rights, they're inalienable, and that the Creator bestowed them upon us—life, liberty and the pursuit of happiness—I submit that many people, Dr. Newdow included, would object, saying again it's this compelled reliance.

Now, nobody can be compelled, nor should they be, as I said, to recite the Pledge. Let's talk about the more recent history, and that is, what happened in 1954? Now, of course, the issue upon which certiorari is granted—and I am frequently reminded of that both when I'm watching arguments and when I argue them myself—is not the congressional action here, which is interesting. The United States asked for review of the 1954 congressional act amending the Pledge of Allegiance. The Supreme Court denied review there. They granted the school district's policy for review, which is a policy that said the school day will start with a patriotic expression. The Pledge of Allegiance would meet that patriotic expression.

In 1954, though, when the Pledge was modified to include the phrase "under God," what was motivating Congress? There were a lot of things motivating Congress. We were in the midst of the Cold War. There was this desire to treat and to establish the difference between how we viewed our rights and liberties, and how communism viewed these things, which is any rights that you have, whatever they might be, are derived from the state; the state is supreme. Congress, reflecting, again, on what the founding fathers thought, said, No, it doesn't work that way. We believe the foundation of our country is different, and this shows the difference. We believe that our rights come from God to mankind.

And I don't know if this is a true fact or not, but it's in one of the briefs, that Dr. Newdow is actually an ordained minister with the Universal Life Church, and I'm not sure if that's correct. What the Universal Life Church has as one of their—and I know they have a pretty broad view of what constitutes God—mission statements, it says that—and they use the phrase "gods" in terms of recognizing that individuals, us, are given what he calls "God-given rights"—freedoms, liberties. Again, this is part of the American experience.

Now, no one's required to believe that, and I don't think that that's the intent of saying the Pledge. Students who don't want to participate don't have to participate, and I think acknowledging the historical significance of how our rights are derived in the foundation of America is correct. The idea that you would be able to tell a student, You cannot be compelled to memorize the Declaration of Independence—which many of us remember having to do—and recite it because of its reference to a Creator, I would think would be wrong. Now, could you argue that there should be a religious

exemption? Probably you could argue that under the Free Exercise Clause. These days, though, I don't know if any of us would be too persuasive on how that would go. But I will tell you this much: that is the historical fact. Our founding fathers did recognize—This was part of the Lockean concept of the rights of mankind, and you don't have to be a historian to check this out....

But I don't think it's correct contextually, with due respect, and that is "one nation"—the Pledge of Allegiance, "I pledge allegiance..." one nation under God," and of course ellipses in between. But that's not what the Pledge of Allegiance says. It doesn't say "one nation under God," and context matters in Establishment Clause cases. And I think the context of the Pledge and the history of how this country came into existence is going to point to what I would expect to be a Supreme Court decision affirming the constitutionality of the Pledge.

Let me close with this, and then I know there's going to be some questions. I think it would be revisionist history if we're going to start saying that students cannot say the Pledge of Allegiance, and revisionist in this context: the history, granted, of the Pledge itself is only 50 years old—it's not that old. But I'll tell you something: the religious heritage of the country goes back to its founding, and whether you take the very strict view of church-state separation or a more accommodationist view, or somewhere in between, denying the history is denying the fact. And I think that mandating a change in the Pledge or finding that those statements, those two words, as Professor Laycock pointed out so well in his brief, those two words create a constitutional crisis, I would hope the Court does not go there.

Question: [Pease comment on the] notion...of ceremonial deism...the idea that "references to God become meaningless if recited often enough in public places."

Mr. Sekulow: I'll go quickly, because I addressed the issue and covered it, but I'll give you two quick thoughts.

I don't for those who are anti-religious—and I know there are people who are anti-religious—I mean, the fact of the matter is you could be anti-something or pro-something; it's a free country, and neither the anti-religious nor the majority religion have a veto right over everybody else. And I think that's one thing.

Number two, a lot of people on my side of these issues normally, Doug [Laycock], get nervous about the phrase ceremonial deism. I've never had a problem with it. I think what Justice O'Connor said is right. It's one of these phrases that does tend to solemnize an occasion. It expresses hope for the future and reflects our past, but again, you're not compelling anybody to say this. You're not compelling anybody to believe this, but I suspect there'll be a lot of questions—I mean, I'm guessing again—on the issue of ceremonial deism. I've had that happen on a couple of the cases that I argued on those issues where prayer came up, and even in some of the earlier cases, in the early '90s. That's an issue that's going to come up. The ceremonial deism question is going to, I think, play in this probably significantly.

Question: Just to follow up,…comment on whether there is a path that we go down that essentially declares that the public realm—whatever is supported by government—must necessarily be godless, or is there an alternative to this? Does this case take you there or does it not necessarily take you there?

Mr. Sekulow: I think this case says you don't have to be godless. You can accurately reflect the historical precedent of the country's founding. That's how I would pitch this case. If I were arguing this case to the Court, I would be talking about the historic fact of patriotic expression. Sure, it's

got religious overtones, but so does the "Star Spangled Banner" and a host of other religious music and songs and documents of our country. It's part of who we are.

So, yes, I think it can reflect—If you don't want to be in a situation where the next thing—and maybe some do—that we're fighting over is whether you really can have those students memorize the Declaration of Independence and be required to recite it as my teacher required me to recite it flawlessly, and if you didn't do it flawlessly you did it again, and it could go on, for many of us, for weeks.

Question: "I was wondering what implications this case would have for currency in the message "In God We Trust" on the U.S. dollar notes and coins?

Mr. Sekulow: I do think the lawsuit will follow, though. If the Pledge of Allegiance is declared unconstitutional—There have already been a series of cases on the national motto. Most recently, I handled one in Kansas. The district court ruled in our favor, and there was no appeal taken in that case. But I would expect that whether it applies or not, you will see those kind of lawsuits being filed if they declare the Pledge unconstitutional.

Whether they'll succeed or not, that's going to depend on how this opinion's written and what the Court says. But to say that it's not going to have far reaching consequences if the Pledge is struck down as unconstitutional—even if it is a four-four decision, which, as Professor Laycock said, is just an affirmance of the judgment—I will tell you that there will be school districts all over the United States that are going to say, Well, look, we're going to not read the tea leaves here. We don't want to get sued and lose again, so we're just going to stop saying the Pledge. I think that will be a ripple effect of this, too.

Question: Mr. Laycock argues "that the Pledge requires an affirmation of personal faith and consequently has got to go." Mr. Sekulow argues, "no, it doesn't—it's not an affirmation of personal faith, so it's okay." One point of view that's not represented here…is that yes, it requires an affirmation of personal faith and that's fine. And the Court should say that's fine. Is that a possible outcome? Can you play around with that a little bit?

Mr. Sekulow: I can't imagine the Court saying that—if they hold the Pledge constitutional, I think—actually, if they hold the Pledge constitutional, I think, it's going to be for the five reasons that Professor Laycock laid out in his brief. I think that is a pretty straightforward way for the Court to go if they decide it's constitutional. I can't imagine them saying the Pledge is constitutional, and you must believe it when you say it.

Question: "Much has been made of the fact that there are only two words here, but one of those words is a preposition, which, to at least some ears, implies a particular type of God, one that we are under, one that is transcendent. And I wonder if consideration of that aspect would move this particular phrase beyond ceremonial deism? I guess my concern is that if you reject the historical document argument, it does seem to imply that we're asking people to affirm a particular type of God, which in 2004, many, many people do not affirm.

Mr. Sekulow: But it's an historical fact that the phrase under God—Most people think it originated in the Gettysburg Address, when President Lincoln said "This nation under God shall have a new birth of freedom." But actually it predates that by almost a hundred years, because General Washington—I think he was Colonel Washington then actually—in his order to the Continental Army said, "Millions of lives are in jeopardy, both born and unborn"—talking about posterity—"and this army under God"—now, does that mean that this army's under God? That's

how they viewed the interplay of Divine Providence. That's what they meant by that.

And, again, the Pledge is an historic statement. You can't change the history; you can debate what the history means, but the words they used are—Fortunately for all of us, we have them, and that's what they meant and that's what they said.…

Let's say you don't agree with the historical document, say the Declaration of Independence. Again, Mrs. Sopher requiring us to memorize it when I was in junior high. There's no dispute that that's what the document says. It says we're endowed by our Creator with these rights. It was a Lockean concept that rights derived not from the King of England, because then the king could take them away, but derived from God to mankind. That's what they thought, whether they were deists or whatever their views were theologically, that is what their overall and overarching propositions were, and that's their thought process. So you could say you don't agree with the historical documents or you don't assume they're historic, you could argue anything, but I think they're pretty clear.

Question: If our nation was not under Christianity at the birth of our Constitution, which I think scholars generally acknowledge Thomas Jefferson, whether he was a deist or a heretical Christian or a Unitarian, whatever he was, he was a religious man, obviously. But whether he was a Christian or not isn't relevant as far as the Constitution goes. But why did our Constitution refer to a Christian Sabbath, not a Jewish or a Muslim or an atheist Sabbath? And why was the document dated in the year of our Lord? Would anyone dare to say that that Lord is anyone other than Jesus Christ?

Mr. Sekulow: I've just completed a dissertation on a lot of the historical backgrounds, mostly focusing on the Supreme Court justices, not on the founding fathers.

But what becomes very clear is that a lot of terminology was used by the founding fathers and by Supreme Court justices that we take in one context and, culturally, at the time, meant something very different. It's not to say that they were not people of faith, but there is no doubt about it, I mean, if you study history in America, it was a pretty broad—even within the founding fathers, a pretty broad swath of faith.

And statements like "In the year of our Lord" were the customary ways in which these documents were signed. It does not mean that they were anti-religious. Obviously they included them in there. The Declaration of Independence, I think, as a foundational document established how

Americans viewed the relationship between rights, liberty, mankind and God, and I think they did it in one document and actually in one portion of that document.

A lot of the justices, for instance, had said this is a Christian nation, in 1892, 1864. We're Unitarians. Now, I'm not saying that they weren't Unitarians, weren't Christians, it's just that it wasn't what you would typically think of as Protestantism as we know it. So you've got to look at the cultural context to understand.

Now, having said all of that, to remove that history, I think, would be very dangerous. The fact that there was this general belief in the way rights derived to mankind, to remove that, I think, would be wrong....

THE CONTINUING DEBATE:
The Phrase "Under God" in the Pledge of Allegiance

What Is New

The Supreme Court in essence ducked when it ruled in *Elk Grove Unified School District v. Newdow*. Instead of deciding the question, the Court dismissed the case on the grounds that since Michael Newdow's ex-wife had custody of their daughter, he did not have "standing" (enough legal interest) to sue on the girl's behalf. That almost certainly served only put off the day when the Court will have to rule. New law suits have been filed, and in 2005 a U.S. District Court judge found the Pledge unconstitutional. Taking an opposite view, North Carolina and other states have added a requirement that teachers in some school levels lead the pledge, and the U.S. House of Representatives passed a bill denying to the federal courts the authority to rule against the Pledge. How the Supreme Court might rule is unclear because it continues to demonstrate a careful, some might say inconsistent, view about the establishment clause. In *Van Orden v. Perry* (2005), the Court allowed a monument to the Ten Commandments to remain on the grounds of Texas' capitol building. The Court found the monument to be a historical reflection of the country's traditional recognition of the importance of the Ten Commandments and argued, "Simply having religious content or promoting a message consistent with a religious doctrine does not run afoul of the establishment clause." On the very same day, however, the Court also ruled in *McCreary County v. ACLU* (2005) that displays of the Ten Commandments in Kentucky state court houses, violated the establishment clause because, "When the government acts with the ostensible and predominant purpose of advancing religion, it violates…[the] central establishment clause."

Where to Find More

One site of a group that believes in a wall between church and state is the "nontheist" Freedom From Religion Foundation at www.ffrf.org/. Taking the opposite view is the Rutherford Institute at www.rutherford.org/issues/religiousfreedom.asp. A comprehensive view of the Supreme Courts role in the church-state issue is James Hitchcock, *The Supreme Court and Religion in American Life, Vol. 1: The Odyssey of the Religion Clauses* (Princeton University Press, 2004). Looking at the current strains over what the establishment clause means is Noah Feldman, *Divided by God: America's Church-State Problem—and What We Should Do About It* (Farrar, Straus and Giroux, 2005). The history of and controversies about the Pledge itself can be found in Richard J. Ellis, *To the Flag: The Unlikely History of the Pledge of Allegiance* (University of Kansas Press, 2005).

What to More to Do

One way to try to approach this debate and the difference between what is not permissible and what merely reflects tradition and is permissible is to ponder the seemingly contradictory decisions of the Supreme Court in *Van Orden v. Perry* (2005) and *McCreary County v. ACLU*. You can read opinions of the justices in these cases and also find supporting material at the site of the First Amendment Center at www.firstamendmentcenter.org/. Enter the name of the case in the search window. Once your views are clear, try jotting down some notes for a hypothetical essay, "How High Should the Wall Between Church and State Be?"

CIVIL RIGHTS

BARRING STUDENTS FROM ADVOCATING ILLEGAL DRUG USE:
Abridging Free Speech *or* Permissible Restriction?

ABRIDGING FREE SPEECH

ADVOCATE: Center for Individual Rights

SOURCE: Amicus Curiae brief to the U.S. Supreme Court in *Morse v. Frederick* (2007)

PERMISSIBLE RESTRICTION

ADVOCATE: Paul D. Clement, U.S. Solicitor General

SOURCE: Amicus Curiae brief to the U.S. Supreme Court in *Morse v. Frederick* (2007)

No "freedom" under the Bill of Rights is absolute. For example, it is well established that there are limits to the freedom of speech under the First Amendment. One standard was enunciated in *Schenck v. United States* (1919) by the Supreme Court when it held that the government could limit free expression when it created "a clear and present danger" to the public welfare, such as "shouting fire in a crowded theater." However, the courts have also applied the "strict scrutiny" standard. This places the burden of proof on the government when it moves to suppress free speech. Generally even advocating illegal activity is protected, unless there is a clear and present danger that someone might immediately be incited and cause substantial harm.

Another facet of freedom of speech doctrine relates to who is expressing themselves. One issue is whether grade school and high school students, who are minors, have the same freedom as adults. In one important case, officials at a Des Moines high school sent student John Tinker home when he refused to removed an anti-Vietnam War an antiwar black armband he was wearing. Eventually the Supreme Court ruled In *Tinker v. Des Moines* (1969) that the school had violated his rights, reasoning that, students do not "shed their constitutional rights to freedom of speech or expression at the schoolhouse gate." But the court also suggested that limits could be applied if the prohibited act would "materially and substantially interfere with the requirements of appropriate discipline in the operation of the school."

One important case where the Supreme Court upheld a restriction was *Bethel School District v. Fraser* (1986). The case began when school officials suspended student Matthew Fraser for making a speech during a high school assembly that was full of obvious sexual innuendos. In *Fraser*, the majority decision held that "the constitutional rights of students in public school are not automatically coextensive with the rights of adults in other settings" and that the rights of students had to be "applied in light of the special characteristics of the school environment."

The *Tinker* and *Fraser* decisions set the stage for the case, *Morse v. Frederick* (2007), at the center of this debate. The controversy began when students at Alaska's Juneau High School were allowed to exit the school to watch a runner carrying the Olympic torch go by. As the runner passed, student Joseph Frederick, who was standing across the street from the school, unfurled a 14-foot banner that read, "BONG HiTS 4 JESUS." Principal Deborah Morse believed that the banner advocated the use of illegal drugs, was directed toward other students, and violated school policy. She asked Frederick to take it down. He refused, she then suspended him for 10 days, and the city's school board upheld the suspension.

Frederick then filed suit in U.S. District Court claiming that Morse and the school board had violated his First Amendment rights because he was not on school grounds, at a school-sponsored event, or advocating the illegal use of drugs. He claimed that "the words [on the banner] were just nonsense meant to attract television cameras" and, later, that the banner was meant to "show that—to reassure myself that this is America. I have a Bill of Rights....The Constitution doesn't just protect deep speech." The district court found for the school district, but the U.S. Court of Appeals for the Ninth Circuit, which includes Alaska, disagreed with the lower court and sided with Frederick. The Supreme Court was the next and final stop, and in this debate the two positions are advocated in amicus curiae (friend of the court) briefs, with the Center for Individual Rights supporting Frederick and the U.S. Solicitor General taking the view of Principal Morse and the school board.

POINTS TO PONDER

➤ Whose interpretation of what "BONG HITS 4 JESUS" should prevail, Frederick's or Morse's?

➤ Should it make any difference whether watching the event was or was not a "school event" or whether Frederick was on the same side of the street as the school or across from it in determining whether Morse had a right to regulate Frederick's freedom of expression?

➤ Think about this debate in terms of free speech rather than marijuana use as such.

Barring Students from Advocating Illegal Drug Use: Abridging Free Speech

CENTER FOR INDIVIDUAL RIGHTS

The Center for Individual Rights ("CIR") is a public interest law firm. It has participated in the litigation of numerous cases concerning issues related to the First Amendment, especially those involving students in college and high school. The CIR believes that the standard set forth by petitioners Principal Deborah Morse and the Juneau School Board on the underlying First Amendment question, that is, speech that interferes with a school's basic educational mission is unprotected by the First Amendment, is far too expansive and vague. It submits this amicus brief to point out the dangers of adopting such a standard.

INTRODUCTION

Joseph Frederick, eighteen and idealistic, was engaging in an age-old form of expression—political satire—when, on a January morning in 2002, he and his friends stood on a public sidewalk holding a banner that read "Bong Hits 4 Jesus" as the Olympic Torch Relay traveled through the streets of Juneau, Alaska....The free speech message that Mr. **Frederick** sought to convey referenced a robust and highly public debate concerning the legal status of marijuana—a debate that has gripped Alaskans for more than a quarter century, has led to the repeated intercession of all three branches of state government, and has reverberated on the national political scene loud enough to prompt White House intervention.

This brief begins by providing this Court with a fuller understanding of the historical, political and cultural contexts in which Mr. Frederick's speech took place and from which it cannot be divorced when assessing its First Amendment implications. To be sure, Mr. Frederick's use of pop-culture slang juxtaposed with a jarring religious reference was disturbing to some, humorous to others, and nonsensical to most. Indeed, it is difficult, if not impossible, to divine from his banner a single, discernible meaning. [The school authorities'] actions and argument boil down to the dubious claim that speech that references drug is synonymous with drug use. This Court should reject this premise as unfounded. First, the facts of this case require that [school's] actions be judged under the strict scrutiny standard. When Mr. Frederick held up his banner he was eighteen years of age, permissibly absent from school, standing on a public thoroughfare, observing a city-wide event of national and international significance. Moreover, although some students at the high school chose to view the event as it passed in front of their school, the Olympic Torch Relay was not properly considered a school-sponsored event: attendance was not mandated, nor did school officials undertake special measures to organize the student body. For these reasons, the "student speech" doctrine, with its lesser First Amendment protections, does not apply here. Second, if the Court disagrees with the application of strict scrutiny, then this case should be analyzed under the standard set forth in *Tinker v. Des Moines* (1969). Although Mr. Frederick's speech can perhaps be characterized as opaque and ill-conceived, it could not be "reasonably forecasted substantially disrupt, or materially interfere with, school activities."

ARGUMENT

Morse and the school board] are compelled to invest [respondent Joseph] Frederick's flippant speech with great import in order to justify their obvious overreaction to it. It was, they say, speech designed to, or with the effect of, promoting illegal drug use, which is contrary to the School's basic educational mission of preventing such use. Even granting them the questionable premise of interpreting Frederick's speech in this way, their argument that the School can punish any speech inconsistent with its "basic educational mission" during any "school-sponsored activity" is not supported by this Court's cases.

1. Morse and the school board rely heavily on *Bethel School District v. Fraser* (1986) in arguing that a school may punish speech inconsistent with its "basic educational mission." But *Fraser* hardly stands for the proposition that a school can define its mission in any way it chooses. Rather, Fraser focuses on the means that the student there chose to communicate his point, rather than the substance of it:

> [T]he penalties imposed in this case were unrelated to any political viewpoint. The First Amendment does not prevent the school officials from determining that to permit a vulgar and lewd speech such as respondent's would undermine the schools' basic educational mission. A high school assembly or classroom is no place for a sexually explicit monologue directed towards an unsuspecting audience of teenage students.

[In *Fraser*] this Court analogized rules for appropriate means of communication to the rules for the conduct of debates promulgated in each house in Congress. This Court never held that there were certain topics that would be off-limits—or worse, that student expression on certain topics is permissible only if one agrees with the school's own viewpoint.

That is a rather large and significant step. It moves the school's pedagogic interest from punishing anti-social behavior (speech must comply with rules of decorum in a civilized society) to conformity of opinion (speech must not disagree with the school's own belief system). Perhaps such a step might be justified where the school's message is an actual pedagogic topic. If a student refuses to learn evolution in his high school biology class and answers all questions on an exam related to that topic with the theory of evolution is contrary to the Bible, a school can give him a failing grade without violating the First Amendment. But the School's pedagogic interest here is far more remote than that. It is concerned that students will take messages like [Joseph] Frederick's [the respondent] seriously, smoke marijuana, and thus be less able to learn.

If a school can define its "basic educational mission"—or, as Morse and the school board put it, "work of the school"—as broadly as it wishes and punish speech inconsistent with that "mission" or "work," it is hard to envision what a school cannot regulate. Surely, any speech that might encourage an activity harmful to health can be regulated under this theory. Obesity, for example, is an increasing problem for students of all ages, and it apparently has significant deleterious effects on related health problems and resulting absenteeism. Under the expansive notion of "basic educational mission" proffered by Morse and the school board a school can define its basic educational mission to include inculcating healthful eating habits in its students. An invitation to a birthday party at which sweets and birthday cake will be consumed can be speech inimical to that mission, and punished.

In an effort to confine such a dangerously expansive notion of school authority over student speech, Morse and the school board also argue that Frederick's speech promoted an illegal activity. But this gambit costs the theory whatever coherence it might have had. Why should a school's mission be defined only by external goals set in society at large? One might think that failing to devote time to homework is even more detrimental to a high school student's ability to succeed than driving five miles per hour over the speed limit, even though the broader society has rules against the latter but not the former. Why should speech discouraging homework be protected while "Go Speed Racer" t-shirts, which might encourage student-drivers to exceed the speed limit, are not?

In any event, the drop in coherence does not even buy much of a reduction in the theory's expansiveness. For example, sexual intercourse and other kinds of sexual acts between high school students are illegal, and often felonious, in many states. Moreover, it obviously can lead to conditions, such as teen-age pregnancy or sexually transmitted diseases, inimical to students' education. Even under the narrower version of the "basic educational mission" theory, every statement in the locker room or hallway deemed to "promote" such crimes can be prohibited.

None of this speech restriction is at all necessary. Schools have the ability to speak themselves to send a message to their students. Both the schools and society itself have the means to combat actual illegal activity. If there is speech that school officials reasonably believe will directly disrupt the educational process, by causing illegal or other activity undermining the educational process in a way both temporally near and reasonably likely to occur, it

can be punished under *Tinker v. Des Moines* (1969). By seeking an expansion of *Fraser* to cover this situation, Morse and the school board ask here for bludgeon to kill a flea.

2. Morse and the school board tie the expansive notion of "basic educational mission" with an equally broad concept of "school-sponsored activity" at which the school's full speech-suppressing authority is available. "Even [though] the Olympic torch relay was an event occurring partly off-campus and with minimal school supervision, and Frederick's banner was displayed outside the classroom [and] across the street from the school, Morse and the school board [still] insist that the school's full speech-suppressing authority should be available at anything that can be called a "school event." Moreover, while advocating a bright line between "school-sponsored events" and other activity, Morse and the school board do little to define where it is drawn—except to insist that the students' observation of the Olympic Torch Relay falls on their side of it.

Is a football game or other sporting event held after hours a "school event" for this purpose? Would it matter if the school's pep band attended as a group? Or if the event did not take place at the school's facilities, but at some third-party site? If students are told to visit a museum over the next week and report on something they see there, is each student's separate trip a "school event"? Morse and the school board cannot answer these questions because they do not identify where the bright line between "school-sponsored events" and other events is drawn.

Not everything involving a student during school hours constitutes a "school-sponsored event," regardless of its attenuated connection to school authorities or its degree of school supervision. If it did, every student given permission to study in the town's public library during school hours—as shown in Part II of this Argument, there is evidence to show less than that here—would be participating in a "school event," and their speech subject to the full panoply of school regulation, just as if they were speaking in the middle of calculus class. Morse and the school board complain about courts "overseeing a typology of school-related activities," but some lines must be drawn if students' entire lives are not to be given over to schools' speech-suppressing agenda—and Morse and the school board just refuse to do so.

[Clearly, the event in question was not schools sponsored. Student] Micaela F. Croteau testified [in the lower court hearing] as follows:

> On the day on which the Olympic Torch Relay was to be run through Juneau, the school allowed students to go out to the street to watch it…We were not required to stay together as a class, and I think only the gym class stayed together. We were just told to come back to our next class at a particular time.

Similarly, [student] Sara Croteau testified:

> [W]hen the torch relay was being run near our school, the teacher announced that we could go watch it. Some students did, others did not, and the teacher made no effort to keep those of us who did go out together. We stood in the snow for a long time waiting for the torch to come by. Many people got bored and left. The school administrators weren't stopping any of the people who left…I could have done whatever I wanted.

If the only thing that teachers told students at Juneau Douglas High School was

that they had to be back to their next class at a particular time, and school administrators did nothing to stop even one of the many students who chose to leave the torch relay route, then it is reasonable to infer that the students had a free period to do what they wanted. While this surely was done to accommodate those who wanted to watch the Olympic Torch Relay, students had no obligation to watch it or to stay anywhere near the high school. Under these circumstances, the school had no reasonable basis for believing that this was a "school event" at all at which it could regulate the speech of its students. A school cannot offer its students an opportunity to go out to the public square unsupervised, and then punish them for doing what any other citizen in the public square could do. This Court may affirm the judgment of the Ninth Circuit on the ground that there was an issue of fact relating to whether this was a "school event" at all.

In addition to claiming that Frederick's speech was at a school-sponsored activity, Morse and the school board also try to characterize Frederick's speech as school-sponsored speech, i.e., speech with the school's imprimatur Specifically, the school argues that it would have given its imprimatur (or would have been perceived to have done so) had it not punished Frederick. In short, Morse and the school board argues that all speech at a school-sponsored activity is school-sponsored speech. Since classes and walking in the halls between classes are "school-sponsored activities," there is little expression that could not be characterized as "sponsored" by the school.

The School claims that it punished Frederick because his speech violated its policy 5520 in that it "advocated the use of substances that are illegal to minors." Frederick presented evidence [in district court] that this was a pretext. Specifically, Frederick testified that the school tolerates all kinds of t-shirts with messages promoting drug or alcohol use. If so, a reasonable [person] could conclude that his speech was punished not for its content, and not because it interfered with the school's interest in deterring the use of illegal substances, but because Morse was embarrassed that the message could be seen by non-students. But the school has no legitimate interest in restricting student speech to outsiders when it permits the same speech to be made to other students.

[One last] argument deserves brief mention. Morse and the school board assert that local school board control is important and that this Court should not attempt to micromanage the thousands of local school districts in this nation. The short answer is that this Court does not "micromanage" anything except its own area of expertise: the individual rights of citizens of the United States.

Barring Students from Advocating Illegal Drug Use: Permissible Restriction

PAUL D. CLEMENT

This case concerns the authority of public schools to prohibit student speech that promotes illegal drug use, and the qualified immunity of school officials who punish students for engaging in such speech. The United States [government] has a substantial interest in those questions. The federal government has provided billions of dollars to support state and local drug-prevention programs. The United States administers numerous other programs that seek to deter illegal drug use, particularly among children. The federal government also operates hundreds of primary and secondary schools on military installations and Indian reservations. Finally, the same principles of qualified immunity that apply in suits against state and local officials apply in similar actions against federal officials.

THE FIRST AMENDMENT DOES NOT PROTECT STUDENT SPEECH CONTRARY TO A SCHOOL'S BASIC EDUCATIONAL MISSION, INCLUDING SPEECH THAT ADVOCATES ILLEGAL DRUG USE

While students do not "shed their constitutional rights to freedom of speech or expression at the school house gate," [as the Supreme Court said in *Tinker v. Des Moines*, (1969)], [it is also true, as the court said in *Bethel School District v. Fraser* (1986) that] "the constitutional rights of students in public school are not automatically coextensive with the rights of adults in other settings." Instead, the First Amendment—like other constitutional rights—must be "applied in light of the special characteristics of the school environment" [as the Court also said in *Tinker*].

Because the task of educating the Nation's children vests public schools with responsibility to teach impressionable young students, a school may prohibit student speech [according to *Fraser*] that "would undermine the school's basic educational mission" and "need not tolerate student speech that is inconsistent with its basic educational mission, even though the government could not censor similar speech outside the school. Indeed, even outside of the school context, this Court has repeatedly recognized the governmental interest in protecting children from harmful materials, and has therefore upheld restrictions on expression [such as the sale of pornography to children] that would be unconstitutional if applied to adults.

Student advocacy of illegal drug use at a school event is manifestly inconsistent with a public school's basic educational mission, and therefore outside of the First Amendment's protection.

First, there are few greater threats to the nation's school children and public education system than illegal drugs. School authorities act *in loco parentis* [in place of parents], with responsibility for the health and safety of students entrusted to their custody. In discharging that responsibility, the Juneau public schools, like public schools across the country, have adopted a health and safety curriculum that, among other things, educates students about the dangers of illegal drug use and discourages them from engaging in such activity. The health and safety mission of our public schools is especially pronounced in the context of this case. School children are not only more vulnerable to drug use than adults, but such abuse is more likely to devastate their lives. Certainly, a school can conceive of its mission as involving not only the graduation of well-educated students, but students who have emerged from their K-12 years free from the scourge of illegal drugs.

Second, not only does student advocacy of illegal drug use undermine a school's anti-drug curriculum, it also places the school curriculum as a whole in jeopardy, for the use of illegal drugs harms the educational process itself. Students who use illegal drugs are more likely to suffer from impaired cognitive capabilities, more likely to struggle in the classroom, and more likely to leave school prematurely. Moreover, [one study finds that] the effects of illegal drug use by students "are visited not just upon the users, but upon the entire student body and faculty, as the educational process is disrupted."

Finally, advocating any illegal behavior—including use of illegal drugs—is antithetical to the educational mission. As this Court emphasized in *Fraser*, schools must "inculcate fundamental values necessary to the maintenance of a democratic political system." Respect for the law is a fundamental democratic value, be cause our society depends on the willingness of its members to work to change objectionable laws, rather than simply violating them. Advocacy of unlawful conduct therefore strikes at the heart of a school's basic educational mission to teach fundamental democratic values.

Given the extent to which students conform their actions to the behavior and values of their peers, speech advocating the use of illegal drugs is particularly damaging when it comes from students. Peer pressure is a major factor in children's decision to use drugs. As a result, an effective anti-drug program must not only teach the dangers of drugs; it must also protect impressionable young people from the countervailing effects of peer pressure. At a minimum, such a program entails prohibiting student advocacy of illegal drug use in school or at school events, where students are entrusted to the schools' care.

In the Safe and Drug-Free Schools and Communities Act of 1994, Congress recognized the importance of sending a "clear and consistent message" to impressionable school-age children that illegal drug use is unacceptable. Congress authorized federal grants under that statute to support, among other things, "local programs of school drug prevention." Significantly, applications by local educational agencies must contain "assurance[s] that drug prevention programs supported [by the grant] convey a clear and consistent message that the illegal use of drugs [is] wrong and harmful." By prohibiting student advocacy of illegal drugs, the schools are not only acting on the basis of their own educational judgments; they are acting consistent with federal policy.

The anti-drug curriculum in schools is especially important in light of the drug problem in our nation's schools. In 2005, approximately one-half of all students in the twelfth grade had used an illicit drug, and more than one-half of those students had used an illicit drug other than marijuana. Indeed, approximately one-fourth of twelfth graders had used an illicit drug in the past 30 days. In light of the gravity of the problem, this Court has recognized that the governmental interest in deterring drug use by school.

WHILE STUDENT SPEECH MAY NOT BE BANNED MERELY TO AVOID CONTROVERSY, IT MAY BE BANNED IF IT IS INCONSISTENT WITH A SCHOOL'S BASIC EDUCATIONAL MISSION

The court of appeals [in this case] erred in concluding that *Tinker* prevents schools from prohibiting student advocacy of illegal drug use at school events. This case is governed not by *Tinker*, which applies when a school merely seeks to avoid controversy and prevent disturbances, but instead by *Fraser*, which confirms that a school can prohibit speech inconsistent with its basic educational mission.

The court of appeals believed that under *Tinker*, "students retain First Amendment expression rights at school, which may be suppressed only if authorities reasonably forecast substantial disruption of or material interference with school activities." The "only" in that sentence is where the Ninth Circuit went wrong.

In *Tinker*, a school prohibited students from wearing armbands to school to protest the Vietnam war. After explaining that the school prohibited the armbands "to avoid the controversy which might result from the expression" (out of a belief that "the schools are no place for demonstrations"), this Court held that "to justify prohibition of a particular expression of opinion, [a school] must be able to show that its action was caused by something more than a mere desire to avoid the discomfort and unpleasantness that always accompany an unpopular viewpoint." It was only in that context—where the asserted governmental interest was preventing controversy—that the Court stated that a student "may express his opinions, even on controversial subjects like the conflict in Vietnam, if he does so without materially and substantially interfering with the requirements of appropri-

ate discipline in the operation of the school and without colliding with the rights of others."

Significantly, the *Tinker* Court made clear that schools can restrict student speech for reasons other than avoiding controversy. The Court stressed, for example, that "this case does not concern speech or action that intrudes upon the work of the schools," because "there is here no evidence whatever of petitioners' interference, actual or nascent, with the schools' work."

Hence, the circumstances in Tinker were quite different in several respects. The asserted governmental interest here is not preventing controversy, but preventing illegal drug use—a matter that, as discussed, directly threatens the basic educational mission of schools. While the students in *Tinker* opposed the Vietnam war, they did not advocate lawless action, such as illegal resistance to the draft or vandalism of recruiting stations.

Moreover, while the court of appeals viewed this case as presenting the general question whether a school can prohibit "a social message contrary to the one favored by the school," this case does not involve just any "social message"—it involves advocacy of dangerous drug use, which, unlike the speech in *Tinker*, interferes with the work of the school. The educational mission and in loco parentis responsibilities of schools do not require them to take a stand on the advisability of a foreign war waged by the federal government. But they most certainly do require schools to protect students' health, safety, and ability to learn.

Any remaining doubt should be resolved in favor of the school district's educational judgment, set forth in its written policies. The school board's decision to oppose illegal drug use as part of its basic educational mission, and to disassociate itself from pro-drug speech by banning it at school events, represents an unassailable, common-sense educational judgment entitled to deference from the federal courts. The appeals court's test, by contrast, would put federal courts in a difficult position of second-guessing local school boards and the reasonableness with which local officials forecast disruption of school activities. As this case amply demonstrates, that is not an appropriate role for a federal court.

In any event, even if *Tinker's* "interference with school activities" standard applied in this context, it would be satisfied. Tinker did not consider only whether classroom activities were disrupted. Instead, it looked broadly to whether there was interference—"actual or nascent"—with "the work of the schools or any class." If schools permitted advocacy of illegal drugs, such speech could counteract, if not drown out, the schools' anti-drug message, especially because of peer pressure. Permitting students to make light of the school's anti-drug message or launch a prodrug use campaign would undermine both that message and the school's disciplinary authority generally. There is no reason a school should have to wait and see whether speech promoting illegal drug use actually has that effect before taking action, especially where, as here, the question concerns the educational message conveyed to students, not the avoidance of controversy.

Here, moreover, the school had gathered its students to view the relay of the Olympic torch. The juxtaposition between an event honoring amateur athletic competition and the use of marijuana made the speech particularly disruptive. By unveiling his bong-hits banner just as the torch passed, respondent [Joseph Frederick] both exploited the event to maximize the impact of his message and interfered with the work of the schools by distracting others' attention from the very

event the school wanted them to observe. And the potential reach of the message was magnified still further by the fact that respondent unfurled the banner right as a television camera crew walked by, which had the potential of increasing the publicity surrounding the banner.

Any doubt regarding the validity of petitioners' response is removed by *Fraser.* [in which] the Ninth Circuit [court of appeals] held that *Tinker* barred a school from punishing a student for making a sexually suggestive speech at a school assembly. This Court reversed [the appeals court and] held, "The First Amendment does not prevent the school officials from determining that to permit a vulgar and lewd speech would undermine the school's basic educational mission."

The court of appeals attempted to limit *Fraser* to its facts by stating that this case, unlike *Fraser,* does not involve sexually offensive speech. As discussed above, however, the reason this Court held that sexually offensive speech could be prohibited is that it is "inconsistent with the 'fundamental values' of public education." Nothing in *Fraser* supports the novel proposition that only sexual speech can be inconsistent with a school's basic educational mission. While sexual innuendo may be damaging to students, there is no comparison with the toll that illegal drug use may have on the lives of school children and the threat posed by illegal drugs in the nation's schools.

RESPONDENT WAS PARTICIPATING IN A SCHOOL EVENT

The court of appeals acknowledged that petitioners might be able to prohibit respondent's message during some school events, but held that they could not do so here because the Olympic torch relay was not an "official school activity," but instead "took place out of school while students were released." [To the contrary, Joseph Frederick] was a student, school was in session, the school released students from their classrooms for the specific purpose of watching the Olympic torch relay in front of the school, and the students were subject to at least some measure of supervision.

That the relay occurred on a public street and not in a classroom is of no moment. The process of educating our youth for citizenship in public schools is not confined to books, the curriculum, and the civics class. Field trips, for example, are an integral part of the learning experience, and the fact that they take place off campus does not deprive them of their educational character or diminish the authority of school officials to regulate student conduct and expression to ensure that the school's educational mission is not undermined. A fortiori, the fact that students cross the street to participate in a school event does not deprive the event of its educational character.

The court of appeals acknowledged that "one can hypothesize off-campus events for which the students might be released that would be educational and curricular in nature," but decided that "a Coca Cola promotion as the Olympic torch passed by on a public street was not such an event." The court gave no basis for that distinction, and there is none. Coca Cola may have sponsored the relay, but the school sponsored its students' attendance at that event, just as a school sponsors its students' attendance at a museum, theatrical production, or other cultural event that may enjoy corporate sponsorship. Here, because school was in session, the school's decision to authorize students to view the event was the only reason respondent was not required to be in a classroom.

Nor is there is any basis in the First Amendment for applying different levels of scrutiny to student conduct or expression at different off-campus school events. Regardless of the type of event, the school's educational mission, custodial responsibilities, and interest in regulating student conduct and expression remain, no matter how much the Ninth Circuit might question the pedagogical significance of this or any other event. Indeed, schools have an additional interest in establishing standards of appropriate behavior when students attend school events away from school premises, in order to prepare students for life in the broader world and instill values of respect and civility when they interact with others outside the immediate school environment. Applying different standards at different off-campus events would send mixed signals to students, and would make it very difficult for courts, let alone school administrators and teachers with little or no legal training, to do their jobs.

This is a particularly unlikely case for heightened scrutiny because the Olympic torch relay passed directly in front of respondent's school, and students watched from both sides of the street. Which side of the street respondent chose to stand on during a school event is simply not a constitutionally [important] fact. Moreover, respondent unfurled his banner in view of students who were watching the relay from school grounds. Especially when a student displays a message to other students who are on school grounds during normal school hours, normal student-speech principles apply.

PETITIONERS REASONABLY UNDERSTOOD RESPONDENT'S BANNER TO ADVOCATE ILLEGAL DRUG USE

School administrators' day-to-day experiences with students committed to their custody and care give them by far the best understanding of the meaning of students' language, how that language is understood by other students, and the risks the speech poses in the school environment. Similarly, disciplinary decisions are ordinarily committed to school administrators' discretion, in part because [this Court has said,] "Events calling for discipline are frequent occurrences," requiring that discipline be both "swift and informal" to be effective. And school administrators may impose corporal punishment based on their reasonable belief that it is necessary for a child's education. It would be anomalous at best to employ a more stringent standard of review for a school official's factual assessments underlying a student's suspension than for assessments underlying a student's corporal punishment.

Morse and the Juneau School Board reasonably understood Joseph Frederick's banner to advocate illegal drug use. Following an administrative process during which respondent was represented by counsel, the superintendent found that respondent was disciplined "because his speech appeared to advocate the use of illegal drugs." The phrase "bong hit" is a slang reference to a particular way of smoking marijuana. Frederick himself admitted [in the District Court case] that the terms he used, including 'bong' and 'hit,' could be understood to refer to drugs," and that "many people have taken that to be the meaning," While the additional phrase "4 Jesus" is presumably unusual in this context, the fact remains that the banner advocated "bong hits," i.e., illegal marijuana use, and that petitioners were in the best position to evaluate how the banner would be perceived by other students. Neither of the lower courts took issue with that conclusion. The district court held that the school "administrator's interpretation [of respondent's message] is reasonable," and the court of appeals likewise "proceed[ed] on the basis that the banner expressed a positive sentiment about marijuana use, however vague and nonsensical." There is no reason for this Court to reach a different conclusion.

The court of appeals expressed the view that "it is not so easy to distinguish speech about marijuana from political speech" in Alaska, in part because "referenda regarding marijuana legalization repeatedly occur" there. Respondent expressly advocated bong hits, however, not the legalization of bong hits.

In any event, even if respondent's banner were some how understood to advocate legalization of marijuana, that would not immunize it from school discipline. Under *Fraser* and *Tinker*, the ultimate question is not whether student speech could be considered "political," but whether it is inconsistent with the schools' basic educational mission. "Legalize" is not a magic word that clothes speech advocating drug use from school discipline. And students do not have a First Amendment right to display "legalize marijuana" banners at school assemblies—or at school—supervised events like the one at issue here. As a practical matter, whether student speech is protected will depend on context, and courts should defer to the reasonable judgments of school administrators on such contextual evaluations.

THE CONTINUING DEBATE:
Barring Students from Advocating Illegal Drug Use

What Is New

By a 5 to 4 vote in *Morse v. Fredrick*, the Supreme Court found for the school author-ities. Writing for the majority, Chief Justice John G. Roberts rejected Frederick's con-tention that no school event was involved and also agreed with Principal Deborah Morse that the banner advocated illegal drug use and violated school policy. Therefore, the chief justice concluded, "Because schools may take steps to safeguard those entrusted to their care from speech that can be reasonably regarded as encour-aging illegal drug use, the school officials in this case did not violate the First Amendment." Dissenting Associate Justice John Paul Stevens wrote, "It is one thing to restrict speech that advocates drug use. It is another thing entirely to prohibit an obscure message with a drug theme that a third party subjectively—and not very rea-sonably—thinks is tantamount to express advocacy." Note that even the dissenting justices would not have supported school action against a clear advocacy of illegal activity by a student.

Where to Find More

More on the background to the case, the majority opinion, and other concurring and dissenting opinions by the justices is available at www.supremecourtus.gov/ opinions/06pdf/06-278.pdf. To read the transcript of the oral arguments by oppos-ing counsel before the Supreme Court, the questions that the justices ask, and how the attorney's respond. For this case, the transcript can be found at www.supremecourtus.gov/oral_arguments/argument_transcripts/06-278.pdf. The Web site of the Center for Individual Rights, which wrote the amicus brief used here supporting Frederick is at www.cir-usa.org/. An overview of freedom of speech issues in the United States and elsewhere is in Eric Baredt, *Freedom of Speech* (Oxford University Press, 2007).

What More to Do

In addition to discussing whether you agree with the decision in *Morse v. Frederick*, follow and debate some even more recent disputes regarding students' freedom of expression in school setting. Information can be found on the Web site of the Student Press Law Center at www.splc.org/ under "News Flash." For example, do you agree with the July 2007 decision of federal district court in Missouri upholding a school ban against clothes displaying a Confederate flag? What is your view of another July 2007 decision, this time by the Sixth Circuit U.S. Court of Appeals that upheld the dismissal of four football players from their team after they petitioned their Tennessee school to replace their coach? Also consider college actions, such as the lawsuit filed in August 2007 against the University of Delaware after it suspended student Maciej Murakowski for posting material including satirical essays that the school claims were offensive to some students on his blog hosted on a university server.

5 | AMERICAN PEOPLE/ POLITICAL CULTURE

THE CULTURAL ASSIMILATION OF IMMIGRANTS:
The Melting Pot Is Broken *or* Blending Satisfactorily?

THE MELTING POT IS BROKEN

ADVOCATE: John Fonte, Director, Center for American Common Culture, Hudson Institute

SOURCE: Testimony during hearings on "Comprehensive Immigration Reform: Becoming Americans—U.S. Immigrant Integration" before the U.S. House of Representatives, Committee on the Judiciary, Subcommittee on Immigration Citizenship, Refugees, Border Security, and International Law, May 16, 2007

BLENDING SATISFACTORILY

ADVOCATE: Gary Gerstle, James Stahlman Professor, Department of History, Vanderbilt University

SOURCE: Testimony during hearings on "Comprehensive Immigration Reform: Becoming Americans—U.S. Immigrant Integration" before the U.S. House of Representatives, Committee on the Judiciary, Subcommittee on Immigration Citizenship, Refugees, Border Security, and International Law, May 16, 2007

The face of America is changing. A nation that was once overwhelmingly composed of European heritage whites is becoming more diverse ethnically and racially. In 1960 the U.S. population was approximately 82% white, 11% black, and 6% Hispanic, 0.5% Asian American, and 0.5% Native American. By 2000 the U.S. population had become 69% white, 12% African American, 13% Latino, 4% Asian American, and 1% Native American. This diversification is expected to continue, with the U.S. Census Bureau estimating that in 2050, the U.S. population will be 52% white, 24% Latino, 15% African American, 9% Asian American, and 1% Native American. One reason for the change is varying fertility rates, which is the average number of children a woman in her child-bearing years will have. In 2000 the fertility rate was 2.0 for whites, 2.1 for African Americans, 2.3 for Asian Americans, 2.5 for Native Americans, and 2.9 for Hispanics.

Immigration changes are a second factor accounting for growing diversity. As late as the 1950s, more than 70% of immigrants were coming from Europe or from Canada and other European-heritage countries. Then Congress amended the immigration laws in 1965 to eliminate the quota system that favored immigration from Europe. Now, only about 16% of newcomers are from Europe, compared to 48% from Latin America and the Caribbean, 32% from Asia, and 4% from Africa. Adding to this influx are those who come to the United States without going through established immigration procedures. There are an estimate 10 million such immigrants in the United States, and between 400,000 and 500,00 new ones were arriving each year. About 80% of these illegal immigrants are from Central America, especially Mexico.

Not only the racial and ethnic composition of those coming to the United States changed dramatically since the 1960s. There has also been a dramatic increase in the number of immigrants. Legal immigration has nearly tripled from an annual average of 330,000 in the 1960s to annual averages of 978,000 in the 1990s and 1,016,000 between 2000 and 2006. These numbers seems huge, but relative to the U.S. population they are not as high as earlier periods in history. For example, the immigrants who arrived during the decade 1900–1909 equaled 10.4% of the population. Those arriving legally in the ten years between 1997 and 2006 came to 2.9% of the population, with the net inflow of about 4 million illegal immigrants during those years increasing that figure to about 4.3%

The classic image Americans have of what has occurred with immigrants is in the melting pot analogy, with new immigrants being "Americanized," that is learning English and adopting existing American values and customs. In reality, of course, new immigrants also changed the nature of the American "stew" in the pot by introducing new words, ideas, foods, and other things that exiting Americans adopted. Be that as it may, the increased rate of immigration and its increasingly non-European complexion have raised concerns in some quarters that the melting pot is not working adequately and even that some immigrants have no wish to blend in. This view came into particular focus with the book, *Who We Are: The Challenges to America's National Identity* (Simon & Schuster, 2004) written by Harvard University political scientist Samuel P. Huntington. As the *Washington Post* noted, Huntington posed "some of the most critical questions facing our nation" including, "How can a people already preoccupied with ethnic identity absorb and acculturate the millions of immigrants being driven to our shores by global economics?" and "How in the long run will America cohere if everyone feels they belong to a minority?" Huntington was concerned about the melting pot, and his view is furthered in the first reading by John Fonte of the conservative think tank, the Hudson Institute. That is followed by a much more optimistic view of the assimilation process given by historian Gary Gerstle of Vanderbilt University.

POINTS TO PONDER

➤ The traditional goal has been a cultural melting pot in which immigrants merged into existing American culture. Some people now advocate multiculturalism, the coexistence of more than one culture. What are the benefits and drawbacks of the melting pot and multicultural images?

➤ There are people who argue that at least some of those who raise concerns about assimilation are closet racists who are concerned about the "de-Europanization" of the United States, both in culture and the color of its citizen's skins. What is your view?

➤ Think about what changes to immigration policy and naturalization (becoming a U.S. citizen) policy you might make.

The Cultural Assimilation of Immigrants:
The Melting Pot Is Broken

JOHN FONTE

WHAT DO WE MEAN BY INTEGRATION?

Let us start by using the more serious and vigorous term "assimilation." There are different types of assimilation: linguistic, economic, cultural, civic, and patriotic. Linguistic assimilation means the immigrant learns English. Economic assimilation means the immigrant does well materially and, perhaps, joins the middle class. Cultural assimilation means that the immigrant acculturates to the nation's popular cultural norms (for both good and ill). Civic assimilation or civic integration means that the immigrant is integrated into our political system, votes, pays taxes, obeys the law, and participates in public life in some fashion.

These forms of assimilation are necessary, but not sufficient. We were reminded again last week, in the Fort Dix conspiracy that there are naturalized citizens, legal permanent residents, and illegal immigrants living in our country who speak English, are gainfully employed (even entrepreneurs) who would like to kill as many Americans as possible [Fort Dix conspiracy: Six foreign-born Muslim men were arrested in May 2007 and charged with plotting to detonate a terrorist bomb at the U.S. Army installation. Three of the men were illegal immigrants, one was a naturalized citizen, one was a legal immigrant, and the status of the six man was unknown]. The type of assimilation that ultimately matters most of all is patriotic assimilation: political loyalty and emotional attachment to the United States. What do we mean by patriotic assimilation? First

of all, patriotic assimilation does not mean giving up all ethnic traditions, customs, cuisine, and birth languages. It has nothing to do with the food one eats, the religion one practices, the affection that one feels for the land of one's birth, and the second languages that one speaks. Multiethnicity and ethnic subcultures have enriched America and have always been part of our past since colonial days.

Historically, the immigration saga has involved some "give and take" between immigrants and the native-born. That is to say, immigrants have helped shape America even as this nation has Americanized them. On the other hand, this "two way street" is 2 not a fifty-fifty arrangement. Thus, on the issue of "who accommodates to whom"; obviously, most of the accommodating should come from the newcomers, not from the hosts.

So what is patriotic assimilation? (or as well shall soon discuss "Americanization"). Well, one could say that patriotic assimilation occurs when a newcomer essentially adopts American civic values, the American heritage, and the story of America (what academics call the "narrative") as his or her own. It occurs, for example, when newcomers and their children begin to think of American history as "our" history not "their" history. To give a hypothetical example, imagine an eighth-grade Korean-American female student studying the Constitutional Convention of 1787.

Does she think of those events in terms of "they" or "we"? Does she envision the creation of the Constitution in Philadelphia as something that "they" (white males of European descent) were involved in 200 years before her ancestors came to America, or does she imagine the Constitutional Convention as something that "we" Americans did as part of "our" history? Does she think in terms of "we" or "they"? "We" implies patriotic assimilation. If she thinks in terms of "we" she has done what millions of immigrants and immigrant children have done in the past. She has adopted America's story as her story, and she has adopted America's Founders—[James] Madison, [Alexander] Hamilton, [Benjamin] Franklin, [George] Washington—as her ancestors. (This does not mean that she, like other Americans, will not continue to argue about our history and our heritage, nor ignore the times that America has acted ignobly).

OUR HISTORIC SUCCESS WITH AMERICANIZATION

Historically America has done assimilation well. As *Washington Post* columnist Charles Krauthammer put it, "America's genius has always been assimilation, taking immigrants and turning them into Americans."

This was done in the days of Ellis Island because America's leaders including Democrat [President] Woodrow Wilson and Republican [President] Theodore Roosevelt believed that immigrants should be "Americanized."

They were self-confident leaders. They were not embarrassed by the need to assimilate immigrants into our way of life and by explicitly telling newcomers that "this is what we expect you to do to become Americanized." Indeed, they didn't use weasel words like "integration," that suggests a lack of self-confidence. They believed in "Americanization." For example, on July 4, 1915 President Woodrow Wilson declared National Americanization Day. The President and

his cabinet addressed naturalization ceremonies around the nation on the subject of Americanization. The most powerful speech was delivered by future Supreme Court Justice, Louis Brandeis at Faneuil Hall in Boston in which Brandeis declared that Americanization meant that the newcomer will "possess the national consciousness of an American."

In a sense the views of Theodore Roosevelt, Woodrow Wilson and Louis Brandeis on the need to foster assimilation go back to the Founders of our nation. Indeed, President George Washington explicitly stated the need to assimilate immigrants in a letter to Vice President John Adams. [Washington wrote:]

> The policy or advantage of [immigration] taking place in a body (I mean the settling of them in a body) may be much questioned; for, by so doing, they retain the language, habits, and principles (good or bad) which they bring with them. Whereas by an intermixture with our people, they, or 4 their descendants, get assimilated to our customs, measures, laws: in a word soon become one people.

The Present Day: Americanization and Anti-Americanization

During the 1990s, one of the great members of the House of Representatives, the late Congresswoman Barbara Jordan (D-TX) called for a revival of the concept of Americanization and for a New Americanization movement. Jordan wrote an article in the *New York Times* on September 11, 1995 entitled the "The Americanization Ideal," in which she explicitly called for the Americanization of immigrants. We should heed her words today. Unfortunately, for decades we have implemented what could truly be called anti-Americanization, anti-assimilation, and anti-integration policies—Multilingual ballots, bi-lingual education, [presidential] executive order 13166 that insists on official multilingualism, immigrant dual allegiance including voting and running for office in foreign countries, and the promotion of multiculturalism over American unity in our public schools. [Executive Order 13166, Improving Access to Services for Persons With Limited English Proficiency, issued August 11, 2000.] The anti-assimilation policies listed above did not place in a vacuum. They are all connected and related to the larger picture. All of these policies and attitudes have hurt assimilation.

Let us examine how assimilation has become more problematic in recent years.

Traditionally the greatest indicator of assimilation is intermarriage among ethnic groups and between immigrants and native-born. Unfortunately a new major study published in the *American Sociological Review* by Ohio State Professor Zhenchao Qian found a big decline in inter-ethnic marriage. Professor Qian declared, "These declines…are significant a departure from past trends" and "reflect the growth in the immigrant population" with Latinos marrying Latinos and Asians marrying Asians.

The survey found that even as recently as the 1970s and 1980s there was an increase in intermarriage between immigrants and native born citizens. In the 1990s however, this situation was reversed with intermarriage between immigrants and native-born declining. Mass low-skilled immigration was an implicit factor cited in the *Ohio State University Research Bulletin*. The researchers pointed out the immigrants with higher education levels were more likely to marry outside their immediate ethnic group and the reverse

was true for immigrants with less education. In recent years our immigration policy favors the less education and lower skilled.

My fellow witness, Professor Rumbaut has done some excellent work examining assimilation among the children of immigrants. With Professor Alejandro Portes he produced the "The Children of Immigrants Longitudinal Study," of over 5,000 students from 49 schools in the Miami, Florida and San Diego, California areas. Portes carried out the research in Miami. Their joint findings were published by the University of California Press in 2001 as *Legacies: The Story of the Immigrant Second Generation*. The parents of the students came from 77 different countries, although in the Miami area they were 5 primarily from Cuba, Haiti, Nicaragua, and Columbia. In San Diego there were large numbers from Mexico, the Philippines, and Viet Nam.

Portes and Rumbaut pointed out that it is significant that although the youths' knowledge of English increased during their three or four years of school between the longitudinal interviews, their American identity decreased:

> Moreover, the direction of the shift is noteworthy. If the rapid shift to English…was to have been accompanied by a similar acculturative shift in ethnic identity, then we should have seen an increase over time in the proportion of youths identifying themselves as American, with or without a hyphen, and a decrease in the proportion retaining an attachment to a foreign national identity. But…results of the 1995 survey point in exactly the opposite direction.

In other words, linguistic assimilation has increased, but patriotic assimilation has decreased. After four years of American high school the children of immigrants are less likely to consider themselves Americans. Moreover, the heightened salience (or importance) of the foreign identity was very strong. Portes and Rumbaut declare that:

Once again, foreign national identities command the strongest level of allegiance and attachment: over 71% of the youths so identifying considered that identity to be very important to them, followed by 57.2% hyphenates [as in, for example, Irish-American], 52.8% of the pan-ethnics [such as Latino, a regional, rather than specific country reference], and only 42% of those identifying as plain American. The later [plain American] emerges as the 'thinnest' identity. Significantly, in the 1995 survey, almost all immigrants groups posted losses in plain American identities....Even private-school Cubans, over a third of whom had identified as American in 1992, abandoned that identity almost entirely by 1995–1996.

In 2002 the Pew Hispanic Survey revealed that around seven months after 9/11 only 34% of American citizens of Hispanic origin consider their primary identification American. On the other hand, 42% identified first with their parent's country of origin (Mexico, El Salvador, etc.) and 24% put ethnic (Latino, Hispanic) identity first.

An empirical survey of Muslims in Los Angeles was conducted in the 1990s by religious scholar Kambiz Ghanea Bassiri (a professor at Reed College). The study found that only one of ten Muslim immigrants surveyed felt more allegiance to the United States than to a foreign Muslim nation. Specifically, 45% of the Muslims surveyed had more loyalty to an Islamic nation-state than the United States; 32% said their loyalties "were about the same" between the U.S. and a Muslim nation-

state; 13% were "not sure" which loyalty was stronger; and 10% were more loyal to the United States than any Muslim nation. All of this data suggests problems with assimilation.

In a Chicago *Tribune* article on April 7, the head of the Office of New Americans in Illinois, the person in charge of assimilation in the state, made the following statement. "The nation-state concept is changing. You don't have to say, 'I am Mexican,' or, 'I am American.' You can be a good Mexican citizen and a good American citizen and not have that be a conflict of interest. Sovereignty is flexible."

He is a dual citizen who is actively involved in Mexican politics. He votes in both the U.S. and Mexico and is active in political campaigns in both nations. His political allegiance is clearly divided. He will not choose one nation over the other. One hundred years ago the President of the United States in 1907, Theodore Roosevelt, expressed a different point of view:

If the immigrant who comes here in good faith becomes an American and assimilates himself to us, he shall be treated on an exact equality with everyone else, for it is an outrage to discriminate against any such man because of creed, or birthplace, or origin. But this is predicated upon the man's becoming in very fact an American, and nothing but an American...There can be no divided allegiance here. we have room for but one sole loyalty and that is a loyalty to the American people.

Those are two very different views of the meaning of the oath of allegiance in which the new citizens promises to "absolutely and entirely" renounce all allegiance to any foreign state.

What is to be done?

What do we do then, in a practical sense? For one thing, it makes no sense to enact so-called comprehensive immigration reform, which means both a slow motion amnesty and a massive increase in low skilled immigration further exacerbating our assimilation problems. What we do need is comprehensive assimilation reform for those immigrants who are here legally.

First, we have to dismantle the anti-assimilation regime of foreign language ballots, dual allegiance voting by American citizens in foreign countries, bilingual education, and executive order 13166.

Second, we should follow Barbara Jordan's lead and explicitly call for the Americanization of immigrants, not integration.

Third, we should enforce the oath of allegiance. The Oath should mean what it says:

> I hereby declare, on oath, that I absolutely and entirely renounce and abjure all allegiance and fidelity to any foreign prince, potentate, state, or 7 sovereignty, of whom or which I have heretofore been a subject or a citizen; that I will support and defend the Constitution and laws of the United States of America against all enemies foreign and domestic; that I will bear true faith and allegiance to the same; that I will bear arms on behalf of the United States when required by law; that I will perform noncombatant service in the Armed Forces of the United States when required by law; that I will perform work of national importance under civilian direction when required by law; and that I take this obligation freely, without any mental reservation or purpose of evasion; so help me God.

Clearly, if we are a serous people, naturalized citizens should not be voting and running for office in their birth nations.

Fourth, Senator Lamar Alexander of Tennessee has introduced bi-partisan legislation "to promote the patriotic integration of prospective citizens into the American way of life by providing civics, history and English as a second language courses." There is a "specific emphasis" on "attachment to the principles of the Constitution" and to the "heroes of American history (including military heroes)." This initiative will be administered by the Office of Citizenship in the United States Citizenship and Immigration Services (USCIS). Also, this legislation incorporates "a knowledge and understanding of the Oath of Allegiance into the history and government test given to applicants for citizenship." This amendment passed the Senate last year by 91–1. Its enactment should be implemented with or without any "comprehensive" measure.

Fifth the mandate of the Office of Citizenship should be to assist our new fellow citizens in understanding the serious moral commitment that they are making in taking the Oath, and "bearing true faith and allegiance" to American liberal democracy.

Because we are a multiethnic, multiracial, multireligious country, our nationhood is not based on ethnicity, race, or religion, but, instead, on a shared loyalty to our constitutional republic and its liberal democratic principles. If immigration to America is going to continue to be the great success story that it has been in the past, it is essential that newcomers have an understanding of and attachment to our democratic republic, our heritage, and our civic principles.

To this end, the Office of Citizenship should strengthen the current educational materials used by applicants for American citizenship. Since the Oath of Allegiance is the culmination of the naturalization process, an examination of the Oath and what it means, "to bear true faith and allegiance" to the United States Constitution should be part of those educational materials, and should be included on any citizenship test. Further, the Office could (1) examine ways to make citizenship training and the swearing-in ceremony more meaningful; (2) cooperate with other government agencies that work with immigrants such as the U.S. Department of Education's English Literacy-Civics 8 program; and (3) continue to reexamine the citizenship test to see how it can be improved (as it is currently doing, so kudos to the Office of Citizenship on this point). Sixth English Literacy Civics (formerly English as a Second Language-Civics or ESLCivics) is a federal program that provides grants to teach English with a civics education emphasis to non-native speakers. The program is administered by the U.S. Department of Education through the states. The money goes to adult education schools, community colleges, and non-governmental organizations to integrate civic instruction into English language learning.

Logically, EL-Civics is a program that should promote the Americanization of immigrants. As noted, in becoming American citizens, immigrants pledge, "True faith and allegiance" to American liberal democracy. This requires some knowledge of our history and our values. If the money expended annually on EL-Civics assisted our future fellow citizens in understanding America's heritage and civic values, the money would be well spent. This appears to have been the intent of Congress in creating the program in the first place.

Unfortunately, there are problems with EL-Civics programs. In many federally funded EL-Civics classes "civics" is defined narrowly as pertaining almost exclusively to mundane day to day tasks such as how to take public transportation or make a doctor's appointment. Obviously, these "life-coping skills" (as they are called in the jargon) could be part of EL-Civics classes, but the classes should focus primarily on American values, or what veteran civic educator Robert Pickus calls "Idea Civics."

The problem is that many state guidelines for EL-Civics are rigid and inflexible. These state guidelines have been influenced heavily by language professionals; who define "civics" in a very narrow way, and resist the idea of teaching American values through English language training.

It is time to put American civic principles at the head of the taxpayer supported English Literacy Civics program. Federal guidelines to the states should be revised, insisting on the use of solid content materials that emphasize our American heritage, and our civic and patriotic values. In our post-9-11 world, "Idea Civics," that will assist newcomers in understanding the meaning of "bearing true faith and allegiance" to our democratic republic must be emphasized.

In sum, it is time to promote the patriotic assimilation of immigrants into the mainstream of American life. Today as in the past, patriotic assimilation is a necessary component of any successful immigration policy. This does not mean that we should blindly replicate all the past Americanization policies of Theodore Roosevelt and Woodrow Wilson. But it does mean that we have much to learn from our great historical success. In the final analysis it means that we should draw on a usable past, exercise common sense, and develop an Americanization policy that will be consist with our principles and effective in today's world.

What about "Comprehensive Immigration Reform"?

The irony is that so-called "comprehensive" immigration reform is not "comprehensive." There are no serious assimilation components to the legislation. Moreover the eventual promised amnesty and the massive increase in low-skilled immigration promoted formula would weaken assimilation. Assimilation policy cannot be separated from immigration policy. We need comprehensive assimilation reform (for legal immigrants), before we need comprehensive immigration.

Unfortunately, comprehensive immigration reform is primarily about the special needs of particular businesses, not the interests of the American people as a whole, ignores assimilation and puts the market over the nation, but Americans must always remember that we are a nation of citizens before we are a market of consumers.

The Cultural Assimilation of Immigrants: Blending Satisfactorily

Gary Gerstle

Since its founding, the United States has arguably integrated more immigrants, both in absolute and relative terms, than any other nation. In the years between the 1820s and 1920s, an estimated 35 million immigrants came to the United States. Approximately 40 to 50 million more came between the 1920s and 2010s, with most of those coming after 1965. The successful integration of immigrants and their descendants has been one of the defining features of American society, and, in my view, one of this country's greatest accomplishments. Can we find descendants of the immigrants who came in such large numbers one hundred years ago who today do not regard themselves as Americans? We can probably identify a few, but not many. Even those groups once known for their resistance to Americanization—Italians, for example—today count themselves and are considered by others as being among the America's most ardent patriots. Throughout the nation's history, moreover, newer Americans and their descendants have contributed a dynamic quality to our society through their Americanization. As President Woodrow Wilson proudly told a group of immigrants in 1915, America was "the only country in the world that experiences a constant and repeated rebirth," and the credit went entirely to the "great bodies of strong men and forward-looking women out of other lands" who decided to cast their lot with America.

In my testimony today, I have four aims: first, to acquaint you with the so-called "new immigrants" who came by the millions to the United States one hundred years ago and who were widely regarded as lacking the desire and ability to integrate themselves into American society; second, to discuss with you how these immigrants and their children confounded their critics by becoming deeply and proudly American; third, to lay out for you what I think a successful process of immigrant integration requires; and fourth, to suggest to you ways this earlier experience of successful integration can guide an exploration of the prospects of integrating immigrants who are living in America today.

My most important point is twofold. First, that the United States has been enormously successful in making Americans out of immigrants, even among immigrant populations who were thought to have cultures and values radically different from America's own. Second, immigrant integration does not happen overnight. Typically it takes two generations and requires both engagement on the part of immigrants with American democracy and an opportunity for them to achieve economic security for themselves and their families. If we approach questions of immigration today with a realistic and robust sense for what a successful process of immigrant incorporation requires, we have reason to be optimistic that America will once again demonstrate its remarkable ability to absorb and integrate foreign-born millions.

THE "NEW IMMIGRANTS" OF ONE HUNDRED YEARS AGO

An estimated 24 million immigrants came to the United States between the 1880s and the 1920s. They entered a society that numbered only 76 million people in 1900. A large majority of these new immigrants came from Europe, and they came mostly from impoverished and rural areas of eastern and southern Europe: from Italy, Russia, Poland, Lithuania, Hungary, Slovakia, Serbia, Greece, and other proximate nations or parts of the Austro-Hungarian Empire. Few of these immigrants were Protestant, then the dominant religion of the United States; most were Catholic, Christian Orthodox, or Jewish. The integration process of these turn-of-the century immigrants, however, was not quick and it was not easy. Indeed, the label applied to these immigrants— "the new immigrants"—was meant to compare them unfavorably to the "old immigrants" who had come prior to 1880 from the British Isles, Germany, and Scandinavia and who were then thought to have been the model immigrants: industrious, freedom-loving, English-speaking, and ardently patriotic. If I could parachute you, the members of this Subcommittee into American society in a year when the "new immigration" was at its height—in 1910, for example, or 1920—you would encounter a pessimism about the possibilities of integrating these immigrants more intense than what exists in American society today. That the outcome was so positive and so at variance with the pessimistic expectations of 1910 or 1920 should caution us against giving ourselves over to pessimism today.

In the early years of the twentieth century, a majority of Americans were Protestants who cared deeply about the Protestant character of their society. Protestantism, in their eyes, had given America its mission, its democracy, its high regard for individual rights, and its moral character. These Americans worried that the largely Catholic, Orthodox, and Jewish immigrants who dominated the ranks of the "new immigrants" would subvert cherished American ideals, and that the great American republic would decline or even come to an end.

America, at the time, was also a deeply racist society. Black-white segregation was at its height. Chinese immigrants had been largely barred from coming to the United States in 1882 and Japanese immigrants were largely barred in 1907. A naturalization law stipulated that only those immigrants who were free and white were eligible for citizenship, a law that effectively prohibited almost all East and South Asians immigrants from becoming citizens between 1870 and 1952. For a twenty year period in the early twentieth century, the U.S. government attempted to rule that several peoples from the Middle East and West Asia, including Arabs and Armenians, were nonwhite and thus also ineligible for U.S. citizenship. In 1924, Congress stopped most eastern and southern Europeans from coming to the United States because these peoples were also now thought to be racially inferior and thus incapable of assimilating American civilization and democracy. This is how a member of Congress (Fred S. Purnell of Indiana, R) described eastern and southern European immigrants in 1924, [saying,] "There is little or no similarity between the clear-thinking, self-governing stocks that sired the American people and this stream of irresponsible and broken wreckage that is pouring into the lifeblood of America the social and political diseases of the Old World."

Purnell quoted approvingly the words of a Dr. Ward, who claimed that Americans had deceived themselves into believing that "we could change inferior beings into superior ones." Americans could not escape the laws of heredity, Ward argued. "We cannot make a heavy horse into a trotter by keeping him in racing stable. We can not make a well bred dog out of mongrel by teaching him tricks." The acts that Ward dismissed as "tricks" including the learning by immigrants of the Gettysburg Address and the Declaration of Independence.

Given these attitudes, it is not surprising that many immigrants felt unwelcome in the United States. Nevertheless, America was then what it is today: a society for the enterprising, for those who wanted to raise themselves up in the world. Many immigrants perceived America as a land in which they could improve their economic circumstances. They worked endless hours to make that happen. But would America become for them more than a place to work? Would it become their home, a place where they would feel comfortable, where they would raise their families, where they could come to consider themselves—and be considered by others as—Americans? Many immigrants doubted that this would ever be the case. Many intended to make some money in the United States and return home. In the early years of the 20th century, it is estimated that the repatriation rates (those who chose to return home) among Italian immigrants ran as high as 40 to 50 percent. Among immigrants from the Balkans in the years prior to the First World War, it is estimated that as many 80 percent returned home. Those who did not or could not return to their original lands often sent remittances to their families in Europe. For many of these immigrants, becoming U.S. citizens and learning English were goals that were secondary to the primary challenge of earning a living and raising the standard of one's family, either in the United States or one's home country. Yet these immigrants and their children did become integrated into America and deeply committed to

America. How and when did this integration happen?

INTEGRATING THE "NEW IMMIGRANTS"

Three factors are particularly important for understanding the integration of the "new immigrants": learning to practice American democracy; the transition in immigrant communities from the first to second generation; and the achievement of economic security.

Practicing American Democracy: As anti-immigrant sentiment grew in America across the early decades of the 20th century, immigrants who had been reluctant to enter American politics now believed that they had no alternative but to become so involved, if only to protect their most basic interests. In the 1920s, they began to naturalize and then to vote in large numbers. Immigrants wanted to elect representatives who supported their freedom to enter the United States, to pursue a trade or occupation of their choice, to school their children and raise their families in ways that corresponded to their cultural traditions and religious beliefs. They also wanted the government to end discrimination against immigrants in employment, housing, and education. Immigrants lost some major elections, as in 1928, when Herbert Hoover (R) defeated the pro-immigrant candidate, Al Smith (D) [for the presidency], but they also scored some major victories, as when Franklin D. Roosevelt (D) won a landslide re-election in 1936 with the help of millions of new voters, many of them immigrant, casting their ballots for the first time. These immigrant voters believed that FDR was opening up American politics to immigrant participation in ways that few previous presidents had done. In response to this opening, these new immigrants and their children became an important part of the Democratic Party voting majority that would keep Democrats in the White House and in control of Congress for a majority of years between the mid-1930s and late 1960s.

Political parties were important in brokering the entrance of immigrants into American politics. The Democratic Party in particular played a pivotal role not just in registering immigrants to vote but in teaching them the practical arts of American politics—running for office, building constituencies, raising money for campaigns, getting out the vote, writing legislation and building coalitions. The "political boss" and "political machines" were central institutions in many American cities of the time, and both played important roles in bringing immigrants into politics. Although the national Republican Party was not as important as the Democratic Party in assisting immigrants, particular state and local Republican parties often were important players in this brokerage process.

The ability of immigrants to participate in politics and to feel as though their votes made a difference was crucial to their engagement with and integration into America. In the 1920s and 1930s, immigrants began to assert their Americanness and their right to participate in debates about America's best interests. In the short term, this generated more political conflict than political consensus, as immigrant Americans often disagreed sharply with the native-born about what course to chart for America's future, and whether (and how) to open up American workplaces, occupations, universities, and neighborhoods to the full participation of immigrants. But there can be no doubt that immigrant engagement in American politics, with all the conflict it entailed, worked to bind the native-born and foreign born together, and

make both groups feel part of one American nation. And that engagement worked, too, to change America in ways that allowed Catholics and Jews to assert their claims on America and to assert that they had as much right to live in America, to speak on its behalf, and to access its opportunities as did long-settled populations of American Protestants.

Generational Transition: Equally important to the integration of the new immigrants was a shift in the balance of power within immigrant families from the first to second generation. This shift occurred sometime between the 1920s and the 1940s, as the immigrant generation aged and the second generation came into maturity. The children of immigrants (or those who had come to America as very small children) were comfortable with their Americanness in ways that their parents frequently had not been. Some of this second-generation Americanization occurred invisibly, through the daily experiences of these children with American society—walking down the streets of their cities, scouring the ads in newspapers and magazines for alluring consumer goods, listening to the radio, going to the movies, playing sports, and discovering the latest innovation in American popular music. Popular culture in America has always been a great assimilator. Some of the second generation's Americanization occurred more formally, through institutions, most notably high schools (which significantly expanded their enrollments in the 1930s and 1940s) and the World War II military, which took more than sixteen million young Americans out of their homes and neighborhoods between 1941 and 1945, mixed them up with other young Americans from every region of the country, and then asked every one of them to give their life for their country.

Even prior to their entry into these powerful institutions, mother-tongue monolingualism had fallen dramatically among these young men and women. For the second generation, bilingualism or English monolingualism became the norm; the third generation, meanwhile, was almost entirely English monolingual. Most members of the third generation could not speak and not even understand the language of their grandparents. By this time, too, many private institutions in "new immigrant" ethnic communities—churches, synagogues, fraternal and charitable organizations, ethnic newspapers—had begun to see themselves as agents of Americanization, in part to keep the younger generation engaged with issues of concern to the ethnic community.

Economic Security: We should not underestimate the importance of economic security in persuading immigrants to cast their lot with America. The welfare of one's family was almost always a key consideration for the "new immigrants" of the early 20th century. While some immigrants found opportunities in America and prospered, many were stuck in low paying, unskilled jobs in American manufacturing and construction, with little promise of advancement and no security that they would be able to keep even these jobs. Many had to make do with wages that were chronically insufficient. Many lived with the fear that they would fail as breadwinners, that the American dream would never be theirs, and that their employers would toss them aside for yet younger and cheaper workers. When the Great Depression plunged the

U.S. economy into crisis for twelve long years, this fear spread to the second generation who were trying to find their first jobs at a time when neither the private nor public sector was able to bring the

nation's unemployment rate below 15 percent. In these dire circumstances, many immigrants and their children began to turn to collective institutions of economic self help, the most important of which was the labor movement. Labor unions were Americanizing institutions during these years, convincing ethnic workers both that they had rights as American workers and that their ability to improve their circumstances would contribute to the overall well-being of American society. Labor movement advocates argued that wages must be raised to a decent level, that hours of work should not exceed human endurance, that the government must make some provision for those who lost their jobs through no fault of their own, and that those who had spent a life time at work should be rewarded by the government with an old age pension. The labor movement provided critical support for two of the most important government policies of the 1930s and 1940s, the Social Security Act and the GI Bill of Rights, both of which meant a great deal to the new immigrants and their children. One can make the case that the labor movement played a major role in helping to lift immigrant workers and their children out of poverty and thereby in giving them a stake in the American dream.

To identify the labor movement as an important institution of immigrant incorporation is to venture onto controversial political terrain. But whatever one thinks of the proper role of labor unions, it remains the case that questions of economic security and opportunity must be part of our discussion of immigrant integration. An immigrant population that finds itself unable to move out of poverty or to gain the confidence that it can provide a decent life for its children is far more likely to descend into alienation than to embrace America.

By 1950s, the integration of the "new immigrants" and their children had been successfully accomplished. Most of the children and grandchildren of these immigrants were enthusiastic Americans. But the success of the process had taken forty to fifty years and had required immersion in the practice of American democracy, a transition in generational power from the first o the second generation, and the achievement of economic security.

TODAY'S IMMIGRANTS: QUESTIONS AND ANSWERS

Today's immigrants are sometimes depicted by their critics as are far more different from "us" than were past waves of immigrants and as far less interested in integrating themselves into American society. The charge is also leveled that there are simply too many of immigrants residing in America today for this country to absorb and integrate. Below I examine each of these beliefs in light of the background I have provided on the "new immigrants" who came between the 1880s and 1920s.

1. *Are today's immigrants too different from "us?"* Immigrants today are different from earlier waves of immigrants in the diversity of their origins, in the diversity of their economic backgrounds, and in the fact that a majority are nonwhite. At earlier periods of U.S. history, most immigrants came from Europe. Today they come from every continent, with South America (and Latin America more generally), Asia, and Africa being the largest sources. Today's immigrants are also more diverse in economic backgrounds than any previous wave of immigrants. In earlier waves, the immigrants were overwhelmingly poor and generally lacking in education. Such individuals are amply represented in the ranks of immigrants today, but so too are those who are highly trained professionals, managers, and small retailers who have decided that their skills will be more fully used and rewarded in the United States than at home, and that the opportunities for their children will be greater here as well. Thus the proportions of professionals and managers in the immigrant streams coming from the Philippines, India, Taiwan, and Korea regularly reach or exceed fifty percent. These immigrants are generally thought not to be "problem immigrants" and so they don't form a significant part of our discussion about immigration today. But these kinds of immigrants are well represented in today's immigrant population, especially among those groups who have come from East and South Asia. They are generally thought to be important contributors to America, and so they should be included in any overall assessment of current immigration.

Discussion of today's immigrants generally focuses on those who are at the poor end of the immigrant spectrum. Poverty alone, of course, is hardly a distinguishing feature of today's immigrants, since past groups of immigrants were overwhelmingly poor. What does distinguish today's immigrant poor is that they are non-European. Coming from nonEuropean cultures, they are sometimes thought by their critics to lack the cultural attributes—what we commonly refer to as the values of "western civilization"—that allowed earlier waves of poor immigrants to climb out of their poverty, to embrace America's creed of freedom and individualism as their own, and to become active contributors to American enterprise and American democracy.

The irony of this critique is that the "Europeans" held up as model immigrants of yesteryear were, at the time of their immigration, depicted much as poor nonwhite immigrants are today: as so racially and culturally different from Americans, as so different from the earlier waves of immigrants who had come from western and northern Europe, that they could never close the gap between who they were and what "we," America, wanted them to be. Because they were allegedly unassimilable, the United States made a fateful decision in the 1920s to all but close its immigrant gates to eastern and southern Europeans. America was successful in barring them from entry, but it was wrong to believe that they lacked the ability to integrate themselves into American society. As I have argued in earlier sections of this testimony, the millions of eastern and southern Europeans already here did Americanize, and today we celebrate them as exemplary Americans. Why repeat that earlier mistake today and designate large sections of the world's population as inappropriate material for inclusion in America? To do so is not only to discriminate on the grounds of race but also to confess our own lack of faith in the promise and transformative power of American freedom.

2. Are today's immigrants too little interested in integrating themselves into American society? It is true that many immigrants today retain strong ties to their homeland and that many return home or aspire to do so. Technological innovations have made travel back and forth relatively easy, and the communications revolution has made it possible to stay in constant and instantaneous touch with one's family and friends back home. Many immigrants are not eager to relinquish the cultures they brought with them. Among adult immigrants who work in unskilled occupations where literacy is not important (construction, agriculture, landscaping, and personal services), some are slow to learn English. But these patterns are hardly novel. To the contrary, they are similar to patterns evident among the European immigrants who came at the

beginning of the twentieth century. They are patterns that tend to be characteristic of immigrant groups in which recent arrivals form a large part of the immigrant population.

If we want to develop an accurate picture of the progress of integration (or lack thereof), we should not be content to take snapshots of a group at a particular point in time. We should want to supplement those snapshots with an examination of immigrants across time and across generations. Studies done by social scientists are beginning to supply us with this kind of data, and they are revealing patterns of integration that are similar to those associated with European immigrants a hundred years ago. For example, among the children of Latino immigrants, the rates of Spanish monolingualism (those who speak only Spanish) are very low and the rates of English-Spanish bilingualism are very high. Moreover, English monolingualism has made surprising inroads among the children of Latino immigrants, so much that some Latino parents worry that their children are losing touch with their cultural roots. These patterns become even more pronounced among third generation immigrants. The patterns of language loss and acquisition among today's immigrant generations, in other words, seem to be similar to those that shaped the lives of the European immigrants who came one hundred years ago.

Successful integration depends not simply on language and generational transition but on immigrant engagement with American democracy and on the experience of economic opportunity, advancement, and security. Some social scientists have argued that institutions that were once so important in involving past generations of immigrants in American politics (political parties) and for helping them to achieve economic security (the labor movement) have either so changed in nature or have become so weak that they can no longer perform a similar function with today's immigrants. There is some truth to this argument, although the events of the past two years have demonstrated both that political parties still retain the capacity to mobilize immigrants and that labor unions, in cities such as Los Angeles where they remain strong, can still play an important role in promoting immigrant economic interests. Nevertheless, it seems clear that the successful integration of today's immigrants requires either that these older institutions find ways to broaden their involvement with immigrants or that other institutions step forward to engage immigrants in the practice of American democracy and to assist the poor among them with the pursuit of economic opportunity and security. Among Latino immigrants, the Catholic Church has demonstrated that it can become an important mechanism for immigrant integration. Ideally, institutions that assist immigrants in the pursuit of economic opportunity will bring them into alliance rather than conflict with the native-born poor.

3. *Has the number of immigrants coming to America reached such a numerical level that integration has become impossible?* In absolute terms, the number of immigrants is at all time high: approximately 35 million. A few years ago, the number arriving in a single year passed one million and topped the previous one year record that had been recorded in the early years of the twentieth century. In proportional terms, however, we have not yet reached the immigrant density that prevailed in America in the early twentieth century. The million who were arriving annually in those years were entering a society that possessed between one-fourth and one-third the population of America today. To reach that earlier level of immigrant density, America would have to admit three to four million immigrants a year and sustain that rate for a decade or more.

It is possible, of course, for a society to reach levels of saturation whereby the numbers coming overwhelm mechanisms of integration. Saturation can be a national phenomenon or one that affects a particular region or city. Current immigrant density in the United States, however, is not at an all time high. Moreover, it is wrong to assume that demography is destiny, and that, for the sake of integration, we must close the immigrant gates once a pre-selected immigration density index is reached. If we can put in place mechanisms or institutions that broaden immigrant immersion in the practice of American democracy and broaden the access of poor immigrants to economic opportunity and security, then we can have every reason to believe that the integration of this wave of immigrants will be as successful as the last one was. The process will take time and we should expect it to be complex and contentious. But it can yield success, proving yet again the remarkable ability of America to take in people from very different parts of the world, to make them into Americans, and to allow them an important role in defining what it means to be an American.

THE CONTINUING DEBATE:
The Cultural Assimilation of Immigrants

What Is New

Immigration has been a hotly debated subject during the last few years. So far, though, the focus of that debate has been illegal immigration. Most Americans agree that illegal immigration is a major problem, but there are such wide disagreements about what to do that Congress could not pass legislation on the issue in 2007 despite the concerted efforts of the president and the leadership in both houses to move a bill forward. As for general immigration, polls in 2007 showed that Americans are of mixed mind. Most (57%) said recent immigrants on average contribute to the country, with only 28% answering "cause problems," and 15% saying both or unsure. Nevertheless, a plurality (45%) want to decreased the level of immigration, while 35% would maintain the current level, 16% would increase it, and 4% were unsure. There is also disquiet about the acculturation of immigrants. Those who agreed that "immigration has gone too far and many of today's immigrants are not learning the language or assimilating into American culture" outnumbering those who disagreed by a 5 to 4 margin. Language is a major focus, with 91% of Americans thinking immigrants should be required to learn English to become citizens and 77% thinking they should learn it to even stay in the country.

Where to Find More

A review of immigration policy is the Congressional Budget Office's *Immigration Policy of the United States* (February 2006) at the agency's Web site, www.cbo.gov/. A group favoring tough immigration laws is NumbersUSA at www.numbersusa.com/. An opposing viewpoint is held by the National Immigration Forum at www.immigrationforum.org/. An important source of information about matters such as the attitudes and language capabilities of Latinos, the largest group of immigrants, is the Pew Hispanic Center at www.pewhispanic.org/. Valuable to explore the view of Asian Americans is the *San Jose Mercury News*/Kaiser Family Foundation Survey of Asians in the Bay Area at www.kff.org/newsmedia/pomr121204pkg.cfm. A book that takes a negative view of immigration is Patrick J. Buchanan, *State of Emergency: The Third World Invasion and Conquest of America* (Thomas Dunne Books, 2006). A much more positive view is presented in Michael Barone, *The New Americans: How the Melting Pot Can Work Again* (Regency Publishing, 2006).

What More to Do

One thing to do is to be careful of the history of immigration. It is common to think that things once went smoothly and now have somehow gone off the tracks. Is that true. Talk to people who are, say, third and fourth generation Americans and see what they can recall about how fast their parents, grandparents, and great grandparents "melted in the pot." Then talk to first or second generation Americans, especially from the newer immigrant groups, such as Latinos. Also explore the data on the acculturation of immigrants from these groups and the generations that follow them at the Pew and Kaiser sites noted above and others that are available. Has acculturation really slowed?

6   PARITICIPATION

QUALIFIED TO BE PRESIDENT:
"Born in the U.S.A." Only *or* All Citizens?

"BORN IN THE U.S.A." ONLY

ADVOCATE: Matthew Spalding, Director, Center of American Studies, The Heritage Foundation

SOURCE: Testimony during hearings on "Maximizing Voter Choice: Opening the Presidency to Naturalized Americans," before the U.S. Senate, Committee on the Judiciary, October 5, 2004

ALL CITIZENS

ADVOCATE: Prepared Statement by John Yinger, Professor of Economics and Public Administration, The Maxwell School, Syracuse University

SOURCE: Testimony during hearings on "Constitutional Amendment to Allow Foreign-Born Citizens to be President," before the U.S. House of Representatives Committee on the Judiciary, Subcommittee on the Constitution, July 24, 2000

It is a constant theme in the mythology of American democracy: Any boy or girl can grow up to be president. American children learn about such humble beginnings as Abraham Lincoln being born in a log cabin. And politicians trumpet them. For example, the first line of Richard Nixon's autobiography, *RN*, is, "I was born in the house my father built." Similarly, President Jimmy Carter's wife Rosalyn has recalled that in the elementary school both she and the president attended, their teacher Julia Coleman would tell her students, "We had to be prepared for the outside world. She reminded us that in a country as great as ours, 'any...one of [us], might grow up to be President of the United States'."

As it turns out, though, it is not true that any American boy or girl can theoretically grow up to be president. Young Henry Kissinger could not, even though he would one day become Secretary of State. Neither could Madeleine Albright, the girl who grew up to be the first female Secretary of State. More currently, the youths who grew up to be Governor Jennifer Granholm of Michigan and California's Governor Arnold Schwarzenegger are also ineligible. Indeed, well over a hundred million boys and girls growing up in the United States throughout its history have been unable to aspire to lead their country.

What stands between Governor Granholm, Governor Schwarzenegger, and millions of other Americans from being inaugurated as president is Article II, section 1 of the Constitution, which reads, "No person except a natural-born citizen, or citizen of the United States at the time of the adoption of this Constitution, shall be eligible to the office of president." With all Americans who were foreign-born in 1789 long gone, this means that anyone who is not a citizen of the United States by birth cannot become president. According to the 2000 census, this includes 28.4 million resident of the United States, or about 10% of the population, who are foreign-born, legal immigrants. Of these, 10.6 million have already become citizens, and another 17.6 million are eligible for U.S. citizenship when they have completed the naturalization process under U.S. laws. Oddly, although the process of becoming a citizen is officially called *naturalization*, that does not imply that those granted citizen are natural-born citizens.

It should be noted that this does not mean that being born in a foreign country as such creates the barrier. The rules are complex, but generally children born of American parents anywhere are American citizens, and they would almost certainly be considered natural born. Among other things, the First Congress enacted legislation in 1790 specifying, "The children of citizens of the United States that may be born beyond sea, or outside the limits of the United States, shall be considered as natural-born citizens of the United States." Beyond this, there are some cases where who are natural-born citizens and who are statutory citizens (naturalized, have become citizens according to provisions of statutory law) is not totally clear because the courts have never dealt with this issue. For example, there is disagreement about whether Puerto Ricans born in Puerto Rico can become president because they were made citizens by statute in 1917, and because Puerto Rico is a commonwealth of the United States, not fully part of it.

Why were foreign-born citizens constitutionally barred from becoming president? The answer is not entirely clear because the direct historical record from the documents of the Constitutional Convention and the *Federalist Papers* is nearly nonexistent, as the advocates in the two accompanying articles explain. But they also discuss the general feeling among historians about the origins of the clause based on indirect evidence.

The issue of the ineligibility of naturalized citizens for the presidency has regularly arisen in Congress, with legislators as diverse as Senator Orrin Hatch (R-UT) and Representative Barney Frank (D-MA) introducing amendments to the Constitution that would allow foreign-born citizens to become president. Such proposals engendered the hearings from which the two articles below are drawn.

To return briefly to the idea that every boy and girl can become president, that bit of Americana does not mean that parents or their children necessarily want that to happen on a personal level. In one survey, 53% of adults thought their children could grow up to be president, but only 30% wanted them to do so. Teenagers were more optimistic about their chances, with 62% thinking they could someday be president. But they were even more turned off than their parents by the prospect, with only 17% wanting to one day occupy the Oval Office.

POINTS TO PONDER

➤ Advocates Matthew Spalding and John Yinger both extensively detail the views of the framers of the Constitution on the subject of eligibility for the presidency. More than two centuries later, how relevant are such views?

➤ Do you think there is a relationship between people's views on this topic and their views on some other debates, especially Debate 5 on immigration?

➤ If John Yinger is correct that allowing naturalized citizens to become president is a matter of equal rights, should the age restriction also be abolished to make adult citizens ages 18 through 34 eligible to be president?

Qualified to Be President:
Natural-Born Citizens Only

MATTHEW SPALDING

More than any other nation in history, this country and its system of equal justice and economic freedom beckons not only the downtrodden and the persecuted—indeed, all those "yearning to breathe free"—but also those who seek opportunity and a better future for themselves and their posterity.

By the very nature of the principles upon which it is established, the United States encourages immigration and promotes the transformation of those immigrants into Americans—welcoming newcomers while insisting on their learning and embracing America's civic culture and political institutions, thereby forming one nation from many peoples.

"The bosom of America is open to receive not only the opulent and respectable stranger," George Washington wrote, " but the oppressed and persecuted of all Nations and Religions; whom we shall welcome to a participation of all our rights and privileges if, by decency and propriety of conduct, they appear to merit the enjoyment."

Yet there is one legal limitation on the potential rights of immigrant citizens: only those who are native born can become president of the United States. Why the exception to this otherwise universal principle? The immediate answer seems to be clear: Poland, where in 1772, as the historian Forrest McDonald explains, "the secret services of Austria, Prussia and Russia had connived to engineer the election of their own choice for king, whereupon the entirety of Poland was partitioned and divided among those three powers." Indeed, South Carolina delegate Charles Pinckney worried that "in not many years

the fate of Poland may be that of the United States."

Perhaps with this in mind, John Jay, then Superintendent of Foreign Affairs wrote to Washington, as president of the Convention, urging that it would be "wise & seasonable to provide a strong check to the admission of Foreigners into the administration of our national Government; and to declare expressly that the Command in chief of the American army shall not be given to, nor devolve on, any but a natural born Citizen." Thus the phrase, as Justice Joseph Story later explained in his *Commentaries on the Constitution*, "cuts off all chances for ambitious foreigners, who might otherwise be intriguing for the office."

But there is something more going on here as well, that points back to the Founders' general views about immigration. The purpose of immigration policy, as Hamilton put it succinctly, was for immigrants "to get rid of foreign and acquire American attachments; to learn the principles and imbibe the spirit of our government." The immediate fear was a foreign takeover, but the larger concern was foreign influence.

At the Constitutional Convention there was a lively and illuminating debate about the eligibility of foreign immigrants for federal office. Elbridge Gerry wanted to restrict membership to those born in the United States, while Gouverneur Morris and Charles Pinckney advocated a qualifying period of at least 14 years before eligibility. George Mason was all for "opening a wide door for emigrants; but did not choose to let foreigners and adventurers make law for and govern us." Indeed, were it not for the many immigrants who had acquired great merit in the Revolution, he, too, would be "for restraining the eligibility into the Senate to natives."

Other, more numerous delegates vigorously criticized this position. Scottish-born James Wilson knew from experience "the discouragement and mortification [immigrants] must feel from the degrading discrimination now proposed." Benjamin Franklin opposed such illiberality and argued that when a foreigner gives a preference to America "it is a proof of attachment which ought to excite our confidence and affection." James Madison wanted to maintain the "character of liberality" of the state governments and "to invite foreigners of merit and republican principles among us," while West Indies-born Alexander Hamilton spoke of attracting respectable immigrants who would "be on a level with the First Citizens."

These views prevailed and the Constitution required relatively modest residency periods for immigrant citizens who aspired to the federal legislature: seven years for the House and nine years for the Senate. This was long enough, Madison later wrote in The Federalist, to assure that legislators are "thoroughly weaned from the prepossessions and habits incident to foreign birth and education."

But again, why the natural born citizenship requirement for the presidency? In the House of Representatives and the Senate, members check each other and diffuse the influence of any one individual. Not so in the case of the president. With a single executive, at the end of the day, there are no checks, no multiplicity of interests that would override the possibility of foreign intrigue or influence, or mitigate any lingering favoritism—or hatred —for another homeland.

The attachment of the president must be absolute, and absolute attachment comes most often from being born and raised in— and educated and formed by—this country, unalloyed by other native allegiances. "The safety of a republic," as Hamilton observed, "depends essentially on the energy of a common national sentiment; on a uniformity of principles and habits; on the exemption of the citizens from foreign bias, and prejudice; and on that love of country which will almost invariably be found to be closely connected with birth, education, and family." The natural born citizen requirement for the presidency seeks to guarantee, as much as possible, this outcome where it matters most.

And while the practical circumstances have changed—there is no threat of a foreign royal taking the reins of power—the underlying concerns about foreign attachments and favoritism, and the need for absolute allegiance and loyalty in the executive, still make sense....

Let me add [two other brief points]:

1. Opening the presidency to naturalized citizens, who in theory but often not in practice have renounced their past allegiances, compels us to consider the question of Dual Citizenship. This is a significant issue and...could be a particularly thorny problem. If the natural born citizen requirement violates the idea that anyone can become an American, so the reality of multiple citizenships violates the idea that becoming an American is meaningful.

2. I am concerned about the politicization of this question....It should not be resolved based on immediate calculations to advance or hinder the political aspirations of any particular individual or party....

Qualified to Be President:
All Citizens

JOHN YINGER

1. INTRODUCTION

One of the cornerstones of American democracy is the "self-evident truth" in the Declaration of Independence that "all men are created equal." This truth leads directly to the principle that all citizens should have equal rights. The U.S. Constitution made historic contributions, of course, to the establishment of this principle, by, among other things, setting up the popular election of members of the House of Representatives and by allowing even naturalized citizens, after a waiting period of a few years, to run for the Senate or the House of Representatives.

It is equally true, of course, that the Founding Fathers did not fully implement the equal-rights principle, and throughout its history, this nation has moved toward completing this task. The Constitution's most important limitations on this score obviously were that it allowed the states to disenfranchise people on the basis of sex and race. The Fourteenth, Fifteenth, and Nineteenth Amendments to the Constitution, along with extensive civil rights legislation, have been passed to remove these limitations. The vast majority of American citizens now embrace the principle that all citizens should have equal rights, and our equal-rights legislation has made us a beacon of hope for people around the world striving for freedom and justice.

[We should follow]…the path toward equal rights, namely, ensuring that naturalized American citizens have exactly the same rights as natural-born American citizens. The only difference in rights between these two groups is that naturalized citizens cannot run for president or vice president. This difference comes from the clause in the Constitution that limits the presidency to natural-born citizens, along with the Twelfth Amendment to the Constitution, which implicitly extends this limitation to the office of Vice president. Thus, the quintessential dream of our democracy, the dream of being able to grow up to be president, is withheld, for no good reason, from millions of naturalized American citizens.…

The provision in the Constitution that limits presidential eligibility to natural-born citizens grew out of the Founders' fear of foreign influence. As I will show in this statement, however, the Founders expressed serious doubts about this provision, and, as the Founders' own arguments make clear, this provision is both unwise and unnecessary. We should not let a misplaced fear of foreigners prevent us from removing this anachronistic provision from the Constitution and thereby reaffirming the principle of equal rights for all American citizens.

2. THE FOUNDERS' DOUBTS ABOUT THE NATURAL-BORN CITIZEN REQUIREMENT

The issue of presidential eligibility was first raised at the Constitutional Convention fairly early in the deliberations. On July 26, 1787, George Mason of Virginia moved that a committee "be instructed to receive a clause requiring certain qualifications of landed property and citizenship of the United States in members of the legislature." Two other delegates, Charles Pinckney and Charles Cotesworth Pinckney of South Carolina, then "moved to insert by way of amendment the words Judiciary & Executive so as to extend the qualifications to those departments." This motion carried unanimously. Hence, the Founders' first instinct was to allow all citizens, naturalized and natural-born, to run for president. Moreover, the first draft of the presidential eligibility clause, which appeared on August 22, includes only a time-of-citizenship requirement.

The version of the presidential eligibility clause that excludes naturalized citizens did not appear until the final grand compromise on September 4, less than two weeks before the Constitution was signed by most of the delegates. This version was accepted unanimously with no record of any debate. In fact, however, the Founders provided considerable evidence concerning their feelings about restricting the rights of naturalized citizens, and most of these feelings were negative. In this section, I discuss three examples of this evidence: the grandfather clause concerning presidential eligibility, the Founders' recognition that second-class citizenship for naturalized citizens violates the equal-rights principle, and the Founders' demonstrated trust in naturalized citizens.

The Grandfather Clause

The first source of evidence about the Founders' views concerning the treatment of naturalized citizens comes from the presidential eligibility clause itself, which reveals that the Founders did really not want to prevent all naturalized citizens from running for president. To be specific, this clause grants presidential eligibility to any "Citizen of the United States at the time of the Adoption of this Constitution."

This "grandfather" clause gave presidential eligibility to tens of thousands of naturalized citizens, included seven of the people who signed the Constitution. If the Founders thought that, among people meeting the fourteen-year residency requirement, naturalized citizens were inherently unqualified to be president or that naturalized citizens were inherently more likely than natural-born citizens to be subject to foreign influence, then they would not have included this provision.

According to this clause, presidential eligibility was granted to all naturalized citizens at the time the Constitution was adopted in 1789. Based on information available from the U.S. Census, I estimate that roughly 60,000 foreign-born American citizens were eligible to run for president in the elections of 1796 and 1800. Moreover, about 1,500 of these people were born in France and about 10,000 were born in Great Britain, countries that were at odds with the United States in those years.

Thus, the grandfather clause granted presidential eligibility to about 60,000 foreign-born citizens, including citizens from countries in conflict with the United States. The Founders' ambivalence about limiting presidential eligibility to natural-born citizens is evident in the presidential eligibility clause itself for anyone to see.

Statements That Second-Class Citizenship for Naturalized Citizens Violates the Equal-Rights Principle

Although the records of the Constitutional Convention contain no mention of a debate about the presidential eligibility clause itself, they contain evidence about the Founders' views concerning second-class citizenship for naturalized citizens.

This evidence comes from the debates concerning the time-of-citizenship requirements for the Senate and the House of Representatives....The key issue in these debates was whether to set long or short time-of-citizenship requirements. The delegates all agreed that long requirements placed an extra burden on naturalized citizens, but some delegates thought this extra burden was appropriate and others did not.

A few of the delegates raised the issue of restricting eligibility to natural-born citizens, but no delegate moved to include such a restriction in the Constitution, and only one delegate, Elbridge Gerry of Massachusetts, made a statement in support of such a restriction.

In contrast, numerous delegates spoke out against long time-of-citizenship requirements and, implicitly, against stronger restrictions on naturalized citizens, such as making them ineligible altogether. The most eloquent statements on this matter come from James Madison, who is often called the father of the Constitution. Madison declared that a severe restriction on the rights of naturalized citizens would be "Improper: because it will give a tincture of illiberality to the Constitution." He was seconded by Benjamin Franklin "who was not against a reasonable time [that is, a reasonable time-of-citizenship requirement], but should be very sorry to see any thing like illiberality inserted in the Constitution."

Another important argument about naturalized citizens was then made by Edmond Randolph of Virginia, who "could never agree to the motion for disabling them for 14 years to participate in the public honors. He reminded the Convention of the language held by our patriots during the Revolution, and the principles laid down in all our American Constitutions." Randolph is referring to the state constitutions passed shortly after the Declaration of Independence, none of which placed limits on the rights of naturalized citizens....

At the time of independence, eleven of the thirteen original colonies adopted new state constitutions. Not one of these constitutions restricted the rights of naturalized citizens. Two cases are particularly instructive. In Virginia, a draft constitution was written by Thomas Jefferson in June, 1776. This document has special historical signif-icance because it contains a preliminary version of the grievances that would appear in the Declaration of Independence the next month. In addition, this draft includes the following naturalization clause:

> All persons who by their own oath or affirmation, or by other testimony shall give satisfactory proof to any court of record in this colony that they propose to reside in the same 7 years at the least and who shall subscribe the fundamental laws, shall be considered as residents and entitled to all the rights of persons natural born.

The draft goes on to say that "every person so qualified to elect shall be capable of being elected" and thereby explicitly makes naturalized citizens eligible for all statewide offices. Although this specific wording was edited out of the final version of the Virginia Constitution, its spirit remained, and this constitution does not place any restrictions on the rights of naturalized citizens.

In the case of New York, the constitution of 1776, which was drafted by John Jay, gives the right of suffrage to "every male inhabitant of full age, who shall have personally resided within one of the counties of this State for six months" and who is a "freeholder," that is, a person who owns property. This constitution also says that the "freeholders" must elect the governor, with no explicit statement about the governor's qualification. Among other powers, the governor was declared to "be general and commander-in-chief of all the militia, and admiral of the navy of this State." Finally, this constitution gives the state legislature the power to naturalize foreigners and to make them "subjects of this state," with no qualifications concerning their rights.

John Jay's role in drafting this constitution is intriguing because many historians believe that Jay is responsible for the natural-born citizen requirement in the U.S.

Constitution thanks to a letter he wrote George Washington, who presided over the Constitutional Convention. Jay, who was well known but not a delegate to the Convention, suggested that foreign influence could be minimized by limiting the "command in chief of the American army" to "a natural born citizen." Thus, John Jay's own position appears to be contradictory: he saw no need for a natural-born citizen requirement for New York's governor and commander in chief, but then, a decade later, called for such a requirement for the nation as a whole.

In short, speaking though the state constitutions and the debate at the Constitutional Convention, many of our Founding Fathers considered restrictions on the rights of naturalized citizens to be violations of the fundamental principle of equal rights for all citizens. As Madison put it many years later, "Equal laws, protecting equal rights, are found, as they ought to be presumed, the best guarantee of loyalty and love of country."

Demonstrated Trust in Naturalized Citizens

Presidents George Washington, John Adams, and James Madison revealed their lack of concern about nativity by, among other things, offering high-level federal positions to some of the foreign-born delegates to the Constitutional Convention. Washington appointed William Paterson and James Wilson to the U.S. Supreme Court; he made James McHenry Secretary of the Army; he offered to make Robert Morris Secretary of the Treasury and then gave the job to Alexander Hamilton when Morris turned him down. Adams kept McHenry and Hamilton in his cabinet, later appointed Hamilton as Inspector-General of the Army, and made William Davie first a brigadier general and then Peace Commissioner to France. Finally,

Madison offered Davie an appointment as a major-general, but this offer was declined.

An even more dramatic declaration of the Founders' ambivalence, if not outright hostility, toward the natural-born-citizen requirement came out of the U.S. Senate in 1798. In this year, the Senate was full of men who had participated in the founding of the United States. Two senators (John Langdon of New Hampshire and Charles Pinckney of South Carolina) had been delegates to the Constitutional Convention. All but three of the remaining senators had served in at least one of the following: the American Army during the Revolutionary War, the Continental Congress, a state convention to ratify the U.S. Constitution, and the House of Representatives. In December, these men elected a naturalized citizen, John Laurance of New York, to be President Pro Tempore of the Senate.

This action is particularly significant for two reasons. First, the grandfather clause applied to Laurance. He was born in England in 1750, sailed to America in 1767, and was admitted to the bar in 1772—all well before the adoption date of 1789. Second, the Presidential Succession Act of 1792 placed the President Pro Tempore second in the line of succession to the presidency. For a brief period in 1798, therefore, a naturalized citizen, John Laurance, stood behind only Vice President Thomas Jefferson in the sequence of succession.

During this year, the notorious XYZ affair stirred up American patriotism, and tensions between the United States and both Great Britain and France were very high. In the summer of 1798, the Senate responded by passing the infamous Alien and Sedition Acts, which authorized the president to deport "dangerous" aliens and also imposed penalties for "malicious writing." Moreover, the year before, William Blount, a natural-born citizen who had been a delegate to the Constitutional

Convention, was expelled from the Senate for the "high misdemeanor" of conspiring with the British.

Despite the turbulence of the times, however, the Senate clearly believed that a man with a distinguished record of service to the United States, namely Laurance, should not be disqualified for the presidency simply because he was born in another country, even a country at odds with the United States.

3. THE CASE FOR REMOVING THE NATURAL-BORN CITIZEN REQUIREMENT

Thanks to 9/11, this country once again finds itself in a time characterized by concern about the influence of foreigners in the United States. Why is this a good time to eliminate the natural-born citizen requirement? In this section, I evaluate key argument for and against such a change.

Arguments for Removing the Natural-Born Citizen Requirement

The natural-born citizen requirement (including its implicit extension to the vice president in the Twelfth Amendment) is the only provision in the Constitution, or in our laws, for that matter, that explicitly denies rights to an American citizen based on one of that citizen's indelible characteristics. The equal-rights principle is fundamental to our democracy, and throughout our history we have struggled to extend it. By sanctioning one exception to this principle, we leave open the door to other exceptions. We will strengthen out democracy by closing this door.

The Fourteenth Amendment, which is one of the crowning achievements in this nation's struggle to promote equal rights, says, in part, all persons born or naturalized in the United States, and subject to the jurisdiction thereof, are citizens of the United States and of the state wherein they

reside. No state shall make or enforce any law which shall abridge the privileges or immunities of citizens of the United States; nor shall any state deprive any person of life, liberty, or property, without due process of law; nor deny to any person within its jurisdiction the equal protection of the laws.

This amendment prohibits the states from treating naturalized citizens any differently from natural-born citizens. The same prohibition should apply to the federal government. As the U.S. Supreme Court said in another context, "it would be unthinkable that the same Constitution would impose a lesser duty on the federal government." In the case of the natural-born citizen requirement, however, the Constitution does impose a lesser duty on the federal government than the duty imposed on the states by the Fourteenth Amendment. This "unthinkable" contradiction should be removed.

Eliminating the natural-born citizen requirement from the Constitution would also send a powerful message to people around the world about this nation's commitment to equal rights. We will judge all or our citizens on their merits, this change would say, not on their place of birth. In these troubled times, a statement of this type can only serve to enhance our reputation as the world's standard bearer for democratic values.

Arguments against Removing the Natural-Born Citizen Requirement

Some people have argued recently that we need to keep the natural-born citizen requirement because it makes this country safer. This argument is simply not true.

The delegates to the Constitutional Convention obviously wanted to protect the United States from foreign influence. This concern played an important role in many of their decisions, including the creation of a strong central government, the design of the Electoral College, and the system of checks and balances.

The relationship between foreign influence and the provisions in the Constitution is discussed at length in the Federalist Papers, which are, of course, key documents in interpreting the Founders intentions. Essays 2 through 5, which were written by John Jay, were titled "Concerning Dangers from Foreign Force and Influence." Although the main focus of these essays is on the need for a strong central government to protect a nation from foreign military action, they also suggest that a strong central government can help protect a nation from "foreign influence." Concern about foreign influence also appears in essay 20, written by Hamilton and Madison; essay 43 by Madison; and essays 66, 68, and 75 by Hamilton.

The role of the presidential selection mechanism, and in particular of the Electoral College, in limiting foreign influence is explicitly discussed by Hamilton in essay 68. Neither this essay, however, nor any of the others, refers to the natural-born citizen requirement. To these three influential Founders, this requirement is not important enough to mention. Even John Jay, whose letter may have inspired the requirement, does not bring it up.

Despite all the protections built into the governmental system created by the Constitution, some people still insist that we gain additional protection from the natural-born citizen requirement. If naturalized citizens were allowed to run for president, these people argue, foreign powers might scheme to have their citizens elected here. In fact, however, this Manchurian Candidate imagery has two major flaws. The first flaw was articulated by…Representative Charles T. Canady (R-FL)…during hearings…on this issue in 2000. According to Canady, eliminating the natural-born citizen require-

ment would not give naturalized citizens "a right to be president"—only a right to run for president.

Moreover, any naturalized citizen running for president would face an extremely high burden convincing a majority of the American people that he or she is the best candidate for president. This point was made by Madison [in 1787]. "For the same reason that they [men with foreign predilections] would be attached to their native country, our own people would prefer natives of this Country to them. Experience proved this to be the case. Instances were rare of a foreigner being elected by the people within any short space after his coming among us."

The second flaw in the Manchurian Candidate image is that any foreign power wishing to undermine our government is more likely to use a natural-born citizen than a naturalized one, precisely because of the suspicion falling on naturalized citizens. This argument was forcefully made by Madison at the Constitutional Convention. He said that "He was not apprehensive …that foreign powers would make use of strangers as instruments for their purposes. Their bribes would be expended on men whose circumstances would rather stifle than excite jealousy and watchfulness in the public."

Restricting the rights of all naturalized citizens out of the fear than one of them might try to undermine our government by running for president is an extreme form of profiling with no basis in logic or history. Does it make sense to discriminate against 12.8 million naturalized citizens, including over 250,000 foreign-born adoptees, because one of them might both harbor negative attitudes toward this country and decide to run for president? Of course not: It makes no sense at all. The natural-born citizen requirement may make some people feel better, but it adds nothing of substance to the extensive protection provided by our constitutional election procedures, by our checks and balances, and by the judgment of the American people.

Another argument against changing the natural-born citizen requirement is that it is a poor subject for a constitutional amendment, either because it is tied to the political fortunes of a particular person or because it is just not important enough to justify altering the Constitution.

A constitutional amendment to eliminate the natural-born citizen requirement might, depending on its time-of-citizenship requirement, enable two current governors, Arnold Schwarzenegger of California and Jennifer Granholm of Michigan to run for president. Both of these governors are naturalized citizens. Some people have argued for or against an amendment because of their feelings about one of these governors. In my view, however, this amendment is about principle, not politics.

We do not disqualify other potential presidential candidates on the basis of their experience or their stands on substantive issues, and we should not disqualify Governors Schwarzenegger or Granholm, either. The principle of equal rights for all American citizens should not have an exception based on nativity—or on any other indelible characteristic—and these two governors should be allowed to run for president if they choose to do so.

This principle does not imply, of course, that voters would have to ignore a candidate's nativity, and, as Madison said long ago, it might be more difficult for Governors Schwarzenegger and Granholm than for a natural-born candidate to convince voters that they would act in our country's best interests. Instead, the principle of equal rights simply requires than neither of these governors nor any other citizen be automatically disqualified from the presidency because of their place of birth.

The argument that presidential eligibility is not substantive enough for a constitutional amendment also does not hold up under scrutiny. The distinguished, non-partisan organization called the Constitution Project has developed a series of guidelines for constitutional amendments. According to these guidelines, a constitutional amendment "should address matters…that are likely to be recognized as of abiding importance by subsequent generations," "should be utilized only when there are significant practical or legal obstacles to the achievement of the same objectives by other means;" "should not be adopted when they would damage the cohesiveness of constitutional doctrine as a whole;" and "should embody enforceable, and not purely aspirational, guidelines."

An amendment to eliminate the natural-born citizen requirement clearly meets all of these tests. The equal-rights principal is a matter of "abiding importance." Because the natural-born citizen requirement is in the Constitution, there are significant legal obstacles to obtaining equal rights through other means. As pointed out earlier, this requirement contradicts the Fourteenth Amendment, so eliminating it would actually enhance constitutional doctrine as a whole. And an amendment to eliminate this requirement would obviously be easy to enforce.…

4. A SIMPLE MATTER OF EQUAL RIGHTS

The principles on which our democracy is founded need to be protected, extended, and reaffirmed.…[by amending the Constitution and thus supporting one of our most fundamental principles, namely, the principle that all American citizens should have equal rights.

In practical terms, the right to run for president is not the most important right a citizen can have. After all, the vast majority of American citizens will never attempt to run for president. In symbolic terms, however, the right to run for president is vitally important.

Commentators, politicians, and teachers are fond of saying that the United States is a country where anyone can grow up to be president, because this expression conveys the essence of our democracy. This expression clearly sends the signal that political offices in this country are not inherited or restricted to a select few, but instead are open to anyone who can convince the voters of his or her merit.

THE CONTINUING DEBATE:
Qualified to Be President

What Is New

Although proposals to make foreign-born citizens eligible to become president continue to be introduced in Congress, none has moved passed the committee stage to the floor of either house for general debate. One reason this idea has never gotten very far is public opinion about it. One national poll found that 64% of respondents opposed making naturalized citizens eligible to be president, with 29% in favor and 7% unsure. Another possibility is that changing the Constitution would most immediately favor Governor Arnold Schwarzenegger, and neither Democrats nor many conservative Republicans are disposed to clear the way for a presidential run by California's charismatic governor.

Whatever one many think of Schwarzenegger, changing demographics have brought new prominence to the issue and are apt to contribute to ongoing pressure to amend the Constitution. Changed immigration laws have increased the percentage of foreign-born citizens, and that figure continues to grow. Moreover, politics is becoming more diverse, with an increased number of naturalized citizens in prominent positions. Ironically, two members of President George W. Bush's cabinet in 2007 whose office put them in the line of succession to the presidency are constitutionally excluded. These two Cabinet members are Secretary of Labor Elaine Chao, who was born in Taiwan, and Secretary of Agriculture Carlos Gutierrez, a native of Cuba.

Where to Find More

You can find out more on the attempt in the House and Senate during the 110th Congress (2007–2009) or any previous Congress to amend the constitution on this issue by going to Thomas, the Web site of Congress, at thomas.loc.gov/. For the proposals made in 2005, search for House Joint Resolutions 2, 15, and 42.

There is surprisingly little written on this subject. However, further information is available from Jill A. Pryor, "The Natural-Born Citizen Clause and Presidential Eligibility: An Approach for Resolving Two Hundred Years of Uncertainty," *Yale Law Journal* (1988); Robert Post, "What Is the Constitution's Worst Provision?" *Constitutional Commentary* (1995); and Sarah P. Herlihy, "Amending the Natural Born Citizen Requirement: Globalization as the Impetus and the Obstacle," *Chicago Kent Law Review* (2006).

What More to Do

There are two suggestions here about what more to do, and they parallel similar suggestion in many of the other debates herein. First, stimulate your intellect by finding out more about what is going on and the arguments pro and con, then debating or discussing the issue with your friends and classmates. At least as important, perhaps more so, is to get involved in the national debate by letting your members of Congress know what you think, by writing an op-ed piece for a newspaper or other publication, by joining a group that is active on the issue, or by taking any one of the myriad other steps available to ensure you have a voice. It is, after all, your country; it is a democracy, albeit an indirect one; and the mantra for each citizen in a democracy with this and every other issue in this volume should be, You Decide!

MEDIA

CHILDREN'S ACCESS TO VIOLENCE ON TELEVISION:
Regulate or Leave to Parental Oversight?

REGULATE

ADVOCATE: Dale Kunkel, Professor, Department of Communication, University of Arizona

SOURCE: Testimony during hearings on "The Effects of Television Violence on Children" before the U.S. Senate, Committee on Commerce, Science, and Transportation, June 26, 2007

LEAVE TO PARENTAL OVERSIGHT

ADVOCATE: Laurence H. Tribe, Carl M. Loeb University Professor, Harvard University and Professor of Constitutional Law, Harvard Law School

SOURCE: Testimony during hearings on "The Effects of Television Violence on Children" before the U.S. Senate, Committee on Commerce, Science, and Transportation, June 26, 2007

There is proverbial bad news and good news about today's entertainment offerings. The bad new, at least in the view of many, is that except perhaps for those who have lived in war zones or in other horrific circumstances, we all—including children—are surrounded by more violence than people have been at any time in history. Films, television programs, computer games, and other forms of "entertainment" feature frequent and graphic violence. This is a major shift from the past. In the 1950s, for example, "good guys" used subdued "bad guys" with one punch or by shooting the gun out of their hand. If some actually did get shot or otherwise, it was almost always very antiseptic, with little blood the norm, and gaping slashed throats, smashed skulls, and other gruesome wounds taboo.

Moreover, there are many more points of access to violence. Parents worrying about what their children were taking in the 1950s had to deal with a few movie houses, no more than a couple of broadcast television stations, and comic books. They all generally subscribed to the strict limits on the portrayal of violence, but even if they had not, parents could oversee the access of their children too them relatively easily. Now of course, there are many more broadcast stations; cable television, which is largely not subject to the regulations that apply to broadcast stations, have added scores, even hundreds of more points of programming, and entirely new technologies such as video games and the Internet have added a multitude of channels through which violence can be brought into almost any child's living room or bedroom.

According to a study Kaiser Family Foundation, the average youngster between the ages of 8 and 18 spends 44.5 hours a week watching television, playing video games or on the Internet. This is more time than spent on any activity, including school, except for sleeping. A lot of what these youth's experience is violent. At study done in the 1990s found that even then the average person would see 200,000 acts of violence, including 40,000 murders, on television by age 18.

Most experts consider exposure to such repeated images of graphic violence to be corrosive to the development of children. A joint statement issued in 2000 by the American Academy of Pediatrics, American Academy of Child & Adolescent Psychiatry, American Psychological Association, American Medical Association, American Academy of Family Physicians, and American Psychiatric Association concluded that studies "point overwhelmingly to a causal connection between media violence and aggressive behavior in some children. The conclusion of the public health community…is that viewing entertainment violence can lead to increases in aggressive attitudes, values and behavior, particularly in children."

Adding to the problem, changes in society have put more parents in the workplace and left fewer at home during some hours when children are also at home. In 1950, 56% of all families had one parent working and a second parent at home. Currently, less than 25% of all families fit that image. Of the vast majority of families where there is no "at home" parent, two-thirds have both parents working, and one-third are single parent families. As a result, 31% of elementary and high school children, some 11.5 million kids, take care of themselves in the afternoons.

The good news is that no one has to watch anything they do not want to. Moreover, there are methods parents can use to monitor and if they wish restrict their children's entertainment consumption. It is possible to block a fair amount of programming and material on the Internet, and people do not have to subscribe to cable or even to an Internet ISP if they do not wish to. Yet it is also true, that cable television and the Internet are becoming essential part of living in a modern world, and not subscribing is no more reasonable than deciding not to have a telephone.

The immediate debate here between Professors Dale Kunkel of the University of Arizona and Laurence Tribe of Harvard University was sparked in April 2007 when the Federal Communications Commission issued a report recommending that Congress enact legislation regulating violence on television, and Congress moved to do just that. The FCC concluded that steps such as program rating systems and V-chips were not sufficient to protect children from the ill effects of what it portrayed as excessive, gratuitous, and graphic violence on television. "Clearly, steps should be taken to protect children from excessively violent programming," FCC head Kevin J. Martin urged. Others hastened to disagree. Caroline Fredrickson, an American Civil Liberties Union official, called the FCC recommendations "political pandering," and warned, "The government should not replace parents as decision makers in America's living rooms. There are some things that the government does well. But deciding what is aired and when on television is not one of them." Similarly, a spokesman for the National Cable and Telecommunications Association suggested that parents "are the best judge of which content is appropriate for their household."

POINTS TO PONDER

➤ Note the clash here between to fairly clear and opposing factors: that exposure to violence is bad for children and that the Constitution gives little room to regulate the media.

➤ Pay attention to the specific recommendations of the FCC. Ignoring for the moment the constitutional issue, do the FCC's proposals seem overly burdensome?

➤ How would you craft a standard about what is acceptable and unacceptable of violence?

Children's Access to Violence on Television: Regulate

Dale Kunkel

I have studied children and media issues for over 20 years, and am one of several researchers who led the National Television Violence Study (NTVS) in the 1990s, a project widely recognized as the largest scientific study of media violence. In my remarks here today, I will briefly report some key findings from the NTVS project, as well as summarize the state of knowledge in the scientific community about the effects of media violence on children.

THE EFFECTS OF TELEVISION VIOLENCE

Concern on the part of the public and Congress about the harmful influence of media violence on children dates back to the 1950s and 1960s, and remains strong today. The legitimacy of that concern is corroborated by extensive scientific research that has accumulated over the past 40 years. Indeed, in reviewing the totality of empirical evidence regarding the impact of media violence, the conclusion that exposure to violent portrayals poses a risk of harmful effects on children has been reached by the U.S. Surgeon General, the National Institutes of Mental Health, the National Academy of Sciences, the American Medical Association, the American Psychological Association, the American Academy of Pediatrics, and a host of other scientific and public health agencies and organizations.

These harmful effects are grouped into three primary categories:

(1) children's learning of aggressive attitudes and behaviors;

(2) desensitization, or an increased callousness towards victims of violence; and

(3) increased or exaggerated fear of being victimized by violence.

While all of these effects reflect adverse outcomes, it is the first—an increased propensity for violent behavior—that is at the core of public health concern about televised violence. The statistical relationship between children's exposure to violent portrayals and their subsequent aggressive behavior has been shown to be stronger than the relationship between asbestos exposure and the risk of laryngeal cancer; the relationship between condom use and the risk of contracting HIV; and exposure to second-hand smoke in the workplace and the risk of lung cancer. There is no controversy in the medical, public health, and social science communities about the risk of harmful effects from children's exposure to media violence. Rather, there is strong consensus that exposure to media violence is a significant public health concern.

KEY CONCLUSIONS ABOUT THE PORTRAYAL OF VIOLENCE ON TELEVISION

Drawing upon evidence from the National Television Violence Study, as well as other related research, there are several evidence-based conclusions that can be drawn regarding the presentation of violence on television.

1. Violence is widespread across the television landscape.

Turn on a television set and pick a channel at random; the odds are better than 50–50 that the program you encounter will contain violent material. To be more precise, 60% of approximately 10,000 programs sampled for the National Television Violence Study contained violent material. That study identified an average of 6,000 violent interactions in a single week of programming across the 23 channels that were examined, including both broadcast and cable networks. More than half of the violent shows (53%) contained lethal acts, and one in four of the programs with violence (25%) depicted the use of a gun.

2. Most violence on television is presented in a manner that increases its risk of harmful effects on child-viewers.

More specifically, most violence on television follows a highly formulaic pattern that is both sanitized and glamorized.

By sanitized, I mean that portrayals fail to show realistic harm to victims, both from a short and long-term perspective. Immediate pain and suffering by victims of violence is included in less than half of all scenes of violence. More than a third of violent interactions depict unrealistically mild harm to victims, grossly understating the severity of injury that would occur from such actions in the real world. In sum, most depictions sanitize violence by making it appear to be much less painful and less harmful than it really is.

By glamorized, I mean that violence is performed by attractive role models who are often justified for acting aggressively and who suffer no remorse, criticism, or penalty for their violent behavior. More than a third of all violence is committed by attractive characters, and more than two-thirds of the violence they commit occurs without any signs of punishment.

Violence that is presented as sanitized or glamorized poses a much greater risk of adverse effects on children than violence that is presented with negative outcomes such as pain and suffering for its victims or negative consequences for its perpetrators.

3. The overall presentation of violence on television has remained remarkably stable over time.

The National Television Violence Study examined programming for three years in the 1990s and found a tremendous degree of consistency in the pattern of violent portrayals throughout the television landscape. Across the entire study of roughly 10,000 programs, the content measures which examined the nature and extent of violence varied no more than a percent or two from year to year. Similar studies that have been conducted since that time have produced quite comparable results.

This consistency clearly implies that the portrayal of violence on television is highly stable and formulaic—and unfortunately, this formula of presenting violence as glamorized and sanitized is one that enhances its risk of harmful effects for the child audience.

In sum, the evidence clearly establishes that the level of violence on television poses substantial cause for concern. It demonstrates that violence is a central aspect of television programming that enjoys remarkable consistency and stability over time.

IMPLICATIONS FOR PUBLIC POLICY

It is well established by a compelling body of scientific evidence that television violence poses a risk of harmful effects for child-viewers. While exposure to media violence is not necessarily the most potent factor contributing to real world violence and aggression in the United States today, it is certainly the most pervasive. Millions of children spend an average of 20 or more hours per week watching television, and this cumulative exposure to violent images can shape young minds in unhealthy ways.

Given the free-speech guarantees of the First Amendment, the courts have ruled that there must be evidence of a "compelling governmental interest" in order for Congress to take action that would regulate television content in any way, such as the indecency regulations enforced by the FCC. In my view, the empirical evidence documenting the risk of harmful effects from children's exposure to televised violence clearly meets this threshold, and I should note that former Attorney General Janet Reno offered an identical opinion to this Committee when she testified before it on this same issue in the 1990s.

There has been a lot of talk in recent weeks about the U.S. Court of Appeals (2nd Circuit) ruling regarding "fleeting expletives" that were cited as indecent by the FCC [Federal Communications Commission] (*Fox et al. v. FCC*, June 4, 2007). Some have suggested this ruling threatens the future of any content-based television regulation. While I am not a legal expert, let me draw several important distinctions between this indecency case and the situation policy-makers face with the issue of television violence. First, there is no clear foundation of empirical evidence to document the effects of children's exposure to indecent material in any quantity, much less modest and fleeting examples of it. In contrast, there is an elaborate, solid foundation of evidence regarding the cumulative effects of televised violence on children. While "fleeting expletives" occur occasionally on television, they are generally quite rare. In con-

trast, violent portrayals are not only common, they are pervasive across the television landscape, and are found in a majority of programs.

Indeed, it is the cumulative nature of children's exposure to thousands and thousands of violent images over time that constitutes the risk of harmful effects. Just as medical researchers cannot quantify the effect of smoking one cigarette, media violence researchers cannot specify the effect of watching just a single violent program. But as exposure accrues over time, year in and year out, a child who is a heavy viewer of media violence is significantly more likely to behave aggressively. This relationship is the same as that faced by the smoker who lights up hour after hour, day after day, over a number of years, increasing their risk of cancer with every puff.

The scientific evidence about the effects of televised violence on children cannot clarify which path is the best for policy-makers to pursue to address the problems that research in this area has identified. That decision rests more in value judgments, based upon the relative importance that each of you place on protecting children's health as contrasted with the other competing interests involved, such as freedom of speech concerns. But when you make that judgment—as each Member of this committee will eventually be called upon to do—it is critical that you understand that television violence harms large numbers of children in this country, and significantly increases violence in our society.

To conclude, the research evidence in this area establishes clearly that the level of violence on television poses substantial cause for concern. Content analysis studies demonstrate that violence is a central aspect of television programming that enjoys remarkable consistency and stability over time. And effects research, including correlational, experimental, and longitudinal designs, converge to document the risk of harmful psychological effects on child-viewers. Collectively, these findings from the scientific community make clear that television violence is a troubling problem for our society. I applaud this Committee for considering the topic, and exploring potential policy options that may reduce or otherwise ameliorate the harmful effects of children's exposure to television violence.

Children's Access to Violence on Television: Leave to Parental Oversight

Laurence H. Tribe

Thank you for inviting me to testify about the constitutionality of the legislative proposals made by the Federal Communications Commission (FCC) in its recent report on television violence. That report concludes that there is evidence—which the report concedes to be mixed and uncertain—that certain depictions of violence on television correlate with harmful effects on children, including short-term aggressive behavior and feelings of distress, and that the existing V-chip regime, based on the industry's voluntary ratings system, has been insufficiently effective at keeping violent content from children. On that basis, the report recommends three legislative responses: time channeling, which would ban some content during certain hours; a mandatory, government-run ratings program to replace the current voluntary system; and mandatory unbundling, or à la carte cable/satellite programming, to require cable and satellite providers to give consumers a choice of opting in or out of channels or bundles of channels.

The fundamental error of the FCC Report lies in its belief that the most appropriate response to concerns about television programs containing violent scenes or elements is more intrusive governmental control over the free flow of speech, rather than more narrowly tailored and far less restrictive alternatives to facilitate greater parental control. Such use of centralized government regulation is antithetical to the letter and spirit of the Constitution.

I. THE FIRST AMENDMENT PROTECTS DEPICTIONS OF VIOLENCE ON SUCH MEDIA AS TELEVISION.

The FCC Report concedes that the First Amendment protects depictions of violence, but the scope and rationale of this protection nevertheless deserve emphasis here. In *Winters v. New York* (1948), the Supreme Court considered the constitutionality of a state law criminalizing the sale of magazines that displayed "stories of bloodshed, lust or crime." The Court rejected [the law] holding, Though we can see nothing of any possible value to society in these magazines, they are as much entitled to the protection of free speech as the best of literature."

[In the same way,] violent television content—whether it educates or merely entertains—is protected by the First Amendment. This conclusion properly recognizes that depictions of violence have always been an integral part of expressive speech. From Greek mythology to the stories in the Bible, from Grimm's Fairy Tales to innumerable great plays, novels, and movies, depictions of violence have long played a role in the stories, fables, and narratives that illustrate and inform our notions of crime and punishment, evil and justice, right and wrong. The use of violence in television programming is no different. Depictions of violence and its effects and consequences can contribute powerfully to a show's portrayal of our often violent world or its equally violent history, and the use of violence—however disquieting—adds emphasis that is nearly impossible to achieve otherwise. For example, news programs reporting on a war could not be as truthful, nor achieve the same impact, if they shied away from violence, and a Holocaust documentary that unflinchingly portrays the atrocities of that era is both more honest and more effective than a documentary on the same subject that avoids any such video or pictorial depictions. These are contexts in which excising elements of violence would lie by omission.

The important role of depictions of violence holds for fictional programming as well. Many of our most popular and critically acclaimed television shows are indelibly associated with depictions of violence. *Law and Order*, *CSI*—these and scores of other police and detective series would be severely weakened, artistically and dramatically, if they could not depict with some degree of verisimilitude the commission and consequences of violent crimes and the physical conduct sometimes necessary on the part of law enforcement to bring wrongdoers to justice. Similarly, shows about espionage, science fiction the supernatural, and doctors would be greatly diminished in their power and their story-telling if they could not contain some scenes of violence or its effects, as well as scenes showing surgical and other medical procedures.

My point here is not that violence is necessary for television programs to express any "message," or that it is impossible for these shows or others to continue in some form without portraying violence. Rather, my point is that all of these programs and many others would be drastically different—and considerably less valuable as speech—if they were forbidden to portray physical violence and its consequences in the way that they do. Whether

fictional or nonfictional, journalistic or artistic, depictions of violence in television programming are entitled to the powerful protection of the First Amendment.

II. THE FCC'S PROPOSALS RELY UPON A CONSTITUTIONALLY UNACCEPTABLE CONCEPTION OF "IMPERMISSIBLE" DEPICTIONS OF VIOLENCE.

The FCC Report does not, of course, recommend that all violence on television be regulated. Rather, it recommends regulating only those depictions of violence that the FCC views as somehow crossing the line from "permissibly violent" to "impermissibly violent."

Although the distinction between permissible and impermissible views of violence thus lies at the heart of all of the FCC's proposals, the Report provides little meaningful guidance on the content of this distinction or on how to translate it into operative language. The FCC's silence is telling. It is not difficult to see why any attempt to distinguish between permissible and impermissible displays of violence—using words and concepts like "excessive," "gratuitous," and so on—could not pass muster under First Amendment scrutiny [a Supreme Court doctrine that requires the government to show that when it regulates speech, it (1) has "compelling governmental interest" to do so, (2) that the restricting is as "narrowly applied" as possible, and (3) that the restriction is the "least restrictive means" for achieving the objective.]

A. Any definition that prohibits a significant amount of the violent content that the FCC is concerned about will be unacceptably vague because it will be impossible at the end of the day to tell what the definition regulates and what it does not.

The prohibition on vagueness becomes no less stringent simply because "a particular regulation of expression...was adopted for the salutary purpose of protecting children," as the Supreme Court held in *Interstate Circuit, Inc. v. City of Dallas* (1968). There, the Court invalidated a statute that permitted a movie review board to censor films that the board deemed "unsuitable" for consumption by children if, among other things, they described or portrayed "brutality, criminal violence or depravity in such a manner as to be, in the judgment of the Board, likely to incite or encourage crime or delinquency." The Court found the phrase "likely to incite" insufficiently determinate, in effect granting the board a "roving commission" to censor any films of which it disapproved.

The impenetrable darkness into which such definitions would plunge writers, producers, broadcasters, cable/satellite operators, and other creators and distributors of content is easily illustrated by reference to a recent report on television violence by a group that strongly backs government regulation of television violence. Among the examples of television programming that the group deems objectionable, and which it presumably would want to subject to government regulation and fines:

- A little girl pulls another girl's hair on an episode of *America's Funniest Home Videos*";
- A "dead and bloodied body" is shown on an autopsy table in an episode of *Medical Investigation*;
- A witness describes an alleged rape (never shown) on *Law and Order*;

In any of these cases, how is a government regulator to decide whether the violence is "gratuitous," "excessive," and/or "patently offensive," as the group listing these examples evidently believes? Any such inquiry would be unavoidably, and almost entirely, subjective, leaving a creator or distributor of content no choice but to steer far clear of anything that might be deemed objectionable by the most sensitive viewer.

The phrases suggested by the FCC to delimit a class of impermissibly violent content—"outrageously offensive," "rough," "intense," and the like—are no more definite than other statutory phrases deemed unconstitutionally vague by the Supreme Court, [such as] "patently offensive." Because these phrases have no historically or legally established meaning, they provide little guidance for those subject to punitive measures for failing to comply with the statute's imprecise commands.

B. Any plausible definition of impermissible television violence will [also] unconstitutionally discriminate based on the viewpoint expressed.

Much of the drive to regulate televised violence responds less to violence as such than to what a particular depiction appears to say about the use of violence—whether it appears to glamorize or condemn such use, whether it seems to approve or disapprove of some form or degree of violent behavior in a given context, and what attitude about or perspective on violence viewers might be expected to take away from the experience. But any law, regulation, or enforcement practice that explicitly or implicitly restricted "excessively violent" programming in this way, or in any way that considered the purpose or message behind the use of violence, would necessarily be subject to—and would almost certainly fail—the strictest First Amendment scrutiny.

C. Any plausible definition of impermissible television violence will be unconstitutionally overbroad.

An intrinsic problem with defining impermissible violence is that any such definition that manages to sweep in enough violent content to accomplish Congress's goals will at the same time sweep in far more speech than may permissibly be suppressed. Whatever interests Congress may assert to regulate televised violence, they do not justify prohibiting adults (or, for that matter, older children) from seeing the violent but protected depictions that the FCC hopes to prevent young children from seeing. Even a statute enacted with the best of intentions, and even one undoubtedly effective in achieving its objectives, is "unconstitutional on its face if it prohibits a substantial amount of protected expression," according to *Ashcroft v. Free Speech Coalition* (2002).

It has long been settled that the First Amendment prohibits limiting permissible expression to speech that would be suitable for the very young. In the landmark case of *Butler v. Michigan* (1957), the Supreme Court considered the constitutionality of a Michigan statute that criminalized distribution of books that contained language "tending to the corruption of the morals of youth." Court emphatically rejected this argument, famously observing [that if upheld, the law would] "Surely, this is to burn the house to roast the pig....The incidence of this enactment is to the adult population of Michigan to reading only what is fit for children."

D. Any plausible regulation of supposedly unacceptable television violence will contain too many internal inconsistencies to meet First Amendment standards.

The FCC has identified several interests that are arguably served by centrally regulating televised violence, including:

- enabling parents to protect their children from material that the parents believe will make their children too insensitive to the evils of hurting others,

- enabling parents to protect their children from material that the parents believe will make their children too fearful of being violently injured or killed, and

- protecting children from material their parents would not want them to see but are unable to keep from their children despite that wish.

However legitimate or even compelling these interests might be, they are at war with one another to such a degree that they will ironically render any statute that was closely tailored to serve any one of those interests self-defeating with respect to others, leaving it unconstitutionally ill-fitting under the First Amendment.

The ostensible interest in protecting children from frightening material, for example, would suggest that any depiction of violence should be cartoonish and sanitized, as in the madcap violence of the Roadrunner cartoons or the Three Stooges or the stylized heroics of the old Batman series; but this would undercut the asserted interests in making children understand the real-life consequences of violence and in avoiding material that proponents of regulation fear children might imitate. Further, if some obviously protected categories of violent depictions, such as those in news or sports, were exempted in order to save regulation of television violence from unimaginable overbreadth, the result would be to prevent Congress's goals from being meaningfully served: children who would imitate the physical brawling on a detective drama would be no less likely to imitate the hard-hitting tackles on televised football games, assuming the risk of imitative behavior to be as the proponents suggest it is. And if the fictional bloodletting on *The Shield* scares young children, then surely the very real violence that children might see while watching news about the war in Iraq would be no less frightening. The First Amendment forbids speech regulation that selectively targets some speech while exempting other speech that is likely to have similar effects.

E. Many less restrictive alternatives exist to respond to violent television programming.

The FCC Report surveys only a small fraction of the options available, limiting its discussion of current technologies to the V-Chip and cable operator-provided parental controls, coupled with voluntary ratings systems. But the FCC substantially underreports the extent to which existing technologies can give effect to the government's goal of limiting the exposure of children to television programming that their parents deem unacceptably violent. Parents have access to a wide range of tools—shortchanged or ignored by the FCC report—with which they can limit their children's exposure to such programming should they wish to do so. As Commissioner McDowell notes in his separate statement, "Never have parents been more empowered to choose what their children should and should not watch." First, all televisions sets manufactured in the United States or shipped in interstate commerce with a screen larger than 13 inches must be equipped with a "V-Chip" that can be programmed to block programming that parents do not want their children to view. Even if it is correct that only half of televisions in use are equipped with V-chips, that is irrelevant in light of the fact that 100% of new televisions available for purchase are equipped with V-chips. And while it is up to individual parents to decide whether to use it, information on using the V-chip is readily available. The FCC itself has posted a website that gives detailed instruction to parents on how to use the V-Chip, and industry and private groups have provided similar information via websites and tutorials.

Second, V-chip-like devices are also available on nearly all cable and satellite services, allowing parents to block either entire channels or just those shows that the parents believe include unacceptably violent (or otherwise objectionable) content. Furthermore, on-screen guides are standard features of most cable and satellite services, and almost all cable and satellite providers allow viewers to establish special menus tailored to their own preferences so as to block channels they do not want their children to watch. These parental controls are readily available to the 87.7 percent of American households that currently subscribe to cable or satellite services.

Third, parents can choose to subscribe to family-friendly cable and satellite options, such as Comcast's Children and Family channels, Dish Network's Family Pak, and DirecTV's Family Choice Plan, which enable individual households to limit their children to child-friendly content.

Fourth, parents can use time-shifting technologies (such as VCRs and DVRs) to record certain programs they deem appropriate for their children, and allow their children to watch only pre-recorded programming.

Fifth, parents can employ a number of after-market solutions to limit the channels their children watch and the time of day their children are allowed to watch television, such as the TV Channel Blocker or various timers that allow televisions to work only at certain times.

Sixth, parents can watch television with their children and/or establish and enforce rules about what children can watch and when they can watch it. Many resources, such as the Pause, Parent, and Play Project, provide resources enabling parents to involve themselves directly in the programming that their children see.

There are also a number of ratings systems that parents can access to guide their choices in using all of the above tools. In addition to the industry's voluntary ratings program, many independent groups provide ratings guides that use their own criteria to tell parents what may or may not be appropriate for their children to watch.

All of these alternatives, and the voluntary ratings systems that accompany them, serve the government's interests in protecting children and increasing parental control while being far less restrictive in their effect on First Amendment rights. Two features of these alternatives are crucial: they allow more fine-grained blocking of violent programming, so that blocking can be done by subject matter, time, channel, program, show, and so on; and they accomplish this blocking by empowering parents rather than empowering government. As a result, these voluntary technologies impose a significantly smaller burden on First Amendment speech rights. These alternatives foreswear imposing burdens of any sort at the source of speech and instead strengthen the ability of each individual household to govern the content that reaches children. They do not restrict access to programming across the board, denying such access even to the vast majority of American households that contain no young children. Moreover, rather than depriving parents of their right to provide their children with violent programming that they think is appropriate or even necessary (such as war movies), parents will retain freedom to decide for themselves what is appropriate for their younger children.

F. The FCC's criticisms of these alternatives do not save its proposals under the First Amendment.

The FCC criticizes a number of less restrictive alternatives, focusing primarily on the V-chip, cable blocking technologies, and the voluntary ratings system. These criticisms fail on both factual and legal grounds and do not excuse the government from its obligation to use the less restrictive means outlined above.

Inexplicably, the FCC simply ignores almost all of the alternative technologies discussed above. As a result, the FCC report never tackles the legal significance of the ever-improving voluntary blocking technologies now available to parents, even though the First Amendment mandates a careful appraisal of such alternatives. Moreover, the FCC engages in a broad-brushed criticism of the V-chip and the voluntary ratings system without acknowledging a core analytic confusion that renders its criticisms incomplete and even incoherent. Blocking technology that fails to shield children from things the government might prefer they not see but that their parents would like them to see (or are at least indifferent about their seeing) cannot on that account be deemed constitutionally ineffective. Yet much of the evidence cited by the FCC for the ostensible failings of existing alternatives focuses on statistics about parental inaction that give no indication that determined parents are unable to control what their children end up watching. For instance, the FCC reports that "only 15 percent of all parents have used the V-chip," and "20 percent of parents know they have a V-chip, but have not used it." But these numbers, even if accurate, say nothing about whether parents are dissatisfied with the V-chip, whether they instead use one of the many other methods of controlling what their children watch, or whether [they are unconcerned about what their children watch]. In other words, that the children of such parents may be seeing content that the government would rather they not see certainly does not establish that they are seeing content that their parents would rather they not see. Given the First Amendment's preference for parent- and individual-focused voluntary blocking over more restrictive forms of speech regulation, many of the FCC's criticisms are misdirected.

In fact, the study cited by the FCC for its figures itself calls into question the FCC's conclusion that the V-chip is ineffective. The study reports, for instance, that "the vast majority of parents who have used the V-Chip say they found it useful, including 61% who say it was 'very' useful and 28% who say 'somewhat' useful," and it notes that "among parents who are aware that they have a V-Chip but have chosen not to use it, 60% say the main reason is that an adult is usually nearby when their kids watch TV, and 20% say it's because they trust their children to make their own decisions."

THE CONTINUING DEBATE:
Children's Access to Violence on Television

What Is New

Members of Congress introduced numerous pieces of legislation, such as the Child Safe Viewing Act of 2007 (S. 602), related to children and violence on television and in other media. None had moved beyond the committee stage by late summer 2007. If it were up to the American people, limits would soon be enacted. Two-thirds said in a 2006 poll that they favored "new regulations to limit the amount of sex and violence in TV shows during the early evening hours, when children are most likely to be watching." Yet people are also resistant to any proposal to restrict their freedom. One of the difficulties with regulation violence—or indecency—on television is that the primary vehicle for doing so has been the ability of Congress to regulate the "public airwaves," those that carry broadcast, "over-the-air" television. Cable television is much more insulated from regulation because it is carried by wire and because it cannot be received unless someone subscribed to it. When a recent survey asked people if they favored an extension of government authority to regulate "programs available by subscription to cable or satellite television systems" much the same as broadcast television, only 35% said yes, with 60% saying no, and 5% unsure.

Where to Find More

Violent Television Programming and its Impact on Children, the recent FCC report that sparked this debate can be found at fjallfoss.fcc.gov/edocs_public/ openAttachment.do?link=FCC-07-50A1.pdf. Two groups that favor increased regulation are Teachers Resisting Unhealthy Children's Entertainment (TRUCE) at www.truceteachers.org/ and the Parents Television Council at www.parentstv.org/. Both site contain considerable information of the impact of media violence on children. There are no groups specifically dedicated to opposed regulation, but most of the media associations do. Opposition also come from groups opposed to censorship and other violations of the First Amendment. An example is Robert Corn-Revere, FCC television-violence report: a conclusion in search of an analysis, April 27, 1907, on the Web site of the First Amendment Center at www.firstamendmentcenter.org/commentary.aspx?id=18493. For the rare view that media violence is a positive influence, see Gerard Jones, "Violent Media is Good for Kids," June 28, 2000 on the *Mother Jones* Web site, www.motherjones.com/ commentary/columns/2000/06/violent_media.html.

What More to Do

Because an argument can be made that the government has a compelling interest in protecting the country's children, Laurence Tribe's constitutional argument against regulation rests heavily on his argument that it is impossible to work out an acceptable definition of what is to be regulated. Work in the class to try to come up with standards that are both clear and specific.

8 INTEREST GROUPS

THE OIL INDUSTRY AND ENERGY PRICES:
Profiteering *or* Responding to Market Forces?

PROFITEERING

ADVOCATE: Tyson Slocum, Director, Public Citizen's Energy Program

SOURCE: Testimony during hearings on "Prices at the Pump: Market Failure and the Oil Industry" before the U.S House of Representatives, Committee on the Judiciary, Antitrust Task Force, May 16, 2007

RESPONDING TO MARKET FORCES

ADVOCATE: John Felmy, Chief Economist, American Petroleum Institute

SOURCE: Testimony during hearings on "Prices at the Pump: Market Failure and the Oil Industry" before the U.S House of Representatives, Committee on the Judiciary, Antitrust Task Force, May 16, 2007

It is indisputable that the price of gasoline at the pump—the price consumers pay—has increased dramatically in recent years. In June 2002, the average cost of gasoline including taxes was $1.42. Since then the average price in June has been $1.53 (2003), $2.02 (2004), $2.20 (2005), $2.93 (2006), and $3.12 (June 2007). Thus gasoline prices more than doubled (+120%) between mid 2002 and mid 2007. Whether the increase is due in major part to oil company greed or to due to market forces is the issue in this debate.

In addition to the price of gasoline, other statistics also inform this debate. One is the rising price of crude petroleum. During the same June 2002–June 2007 period, the price of a barrel of crude petroleum rose from $22.97 to $66.65. That is 190%, a steeper increase than the price of gasoline. As of November 2006, according to the U.S. Energy Information Administration (EIA), the price of gasoline could be broken down into 55% for the cost of the crude, 20% for state and local taxes, 15% for refining costs and profits, and 8% for distribution costs and marketing. Note that barrel of crude contains 42 gallons, but equating that directly to the price of gasoline if difficult because a barrel of crude yields no more than 20 gallons of gasoline and often less depending on its quality. Moreover, what is left after gasoline has been extracted has value in that it is used to make many petroleum-based products. There have been many reasons for the increased price of crude but two stand out. One has been the instability in many oil-producing areas such as the Middle East and Nigeria. The second reason is that increasing demand for oil by developing countries, especially China, is putting an increasing squeeze on the supply part of the supply-and-demand equation.

Whatever the reasons, the increased costs are important. For the individual consumer, increasing gasoline prices do more than add to personal transportation costs. They also have an important "downstream" impact on prices, increasing the cost of the making or growing and transporting almost everything a society consumes.

Indeed, rising fuel prices have been the most important component of inflation in the U.S. economy for several years.

Rising fuel price also put a heavy strain on the U.S. economy. Americans consume about 25% of the world's annual petroleum production even though they make up less than 5% of the world population and produce only 8% of the world oil. Because American use three times more petroleum than they produce, the rest must be imported. During 2006 the United States imported about $325 billion in oil. This and similar annual imports are a major component of the massive and troublesome U.S. annual trade deficit. Indeed, the 2006 oil imports equaled roughly half that year's trade deficit.

While the price of crude oil and the accompanying price of gasoline has risen steeply in recent years, a longer-term perspective presents a different picture. Gasoline cost an average of 27 cents a gallon in 1950 measured in "current dollars," the price at the time. Over the next forty years gasoline prices actually decreased measured "real dollars," the value of the dollar controlled for inflation. Using 2005 as a base year for the dollar's value, the price of gasoline dropped from a real dollar value of $2.00 in 1950 to $1.50 in 2002, before beginning a steep rise that took it to an average 2006 real price of $3.00. Thus the real price of gasoline increased only a very modest 50% between 1950 and 2006. Had that occurred evenly, it would have not raised notice. But because real prices declined through 2002 by 25%, then doubled over the next four years, the price increases shocked the public. From the longest perspective, when the world's first oil well was drilled in 1859 in Titusville, Pennsylvania, oil sold initially for $25 a barrel. In 2007, that would come to about $625 a barrel in real dollars.

A last final few statistics to inform this debate between Tyson Slocum of the Public Citizen's Energy Program and John Felmy of the American Petroleum Institute over whether the oil industry is price gouging American consumers have to do with the supply of oil and gasoline. As noted, Americans import about two-thirds of the petroleum products they use. Of these imports, about 75% is crude oil and 9% is refined gasoline, with the balance a wide range of petroleum products such as kerosene. Over the years, U.S. imports have risen sharply, and the burgeoning demand for gasoline and other petroleum products has increasingly outstripped U.S. production. While no new refineries have been built in many years, the supply of gasoline has risen through expanding the capacity of current refineries and importing more already refined gasoline. As a result, the daily supply of gasoline to the U.S. market rose from 315 million gallons in 1991, to 365 million gallons in 2001, to 400 million gallons in August 2007. The stock of gasoline at the daily use rate at the time has declined from 28 days in 1991, to 24 days in 2001, to 22 days in August 2007.

POINTS TO PONDER

➢ The potential to make profits is the driving force in the U.S. capitalist economy, but is there a limit to how much profit should be allowed?

➢ If it is fair to tax "windfall profits?" Should taxpayers subsidize oil companies in years when their profit margins are low or they suffer losses?

➢ Do American consumers bear any of the blame for increased prices?

The Oil Industry and Energy Prices: Profiteering

Tyson Slocum

My name is Tyson Slocum and I am Director of Public Citizen's Energy Program. Public Citizen is a 36-year-old public interest organization with over 100,000 members nationwide. We represent consumer interests through research, public education and grassroots organizing.

Gasoline prices have nearly tripled in the last five years, creating financial hardship for millions of families, as the average annual expenditure on gasoline increased $1,000 for the typical family over that time. While some households have been able to reduce their consumption in response to these high prices by either investing in a more fuel-efficient or alternative-fuel car, taking mass transit or weatherizing their home to cut down on home heating oil costs, most lack the financial resources to make such investments or lack access to alternatives to driving in their car. That explains why, even in the face of skyrocketing gasoline prices, consumption has not moderated.

While American families pay record high prices, oil companies are enjoying the strongest profits in the economy. Since 2001, the largest six oil companies operating in the United States—ExxonMobil, ChevronTexaco, ConocoPhillips, BP, Shell and Valero—recorded $477 billion in profits. Recent entries to oil markets like investment banks, hedge funds and private equity firms have also been posting record earnings. While some of their profit clearly stems from certain aspects of global supply and demand, investigations show that a portion of these record earnings are fueled by market manipulation and other

anti-competitive practices, made possible by the wave of recent mergers and weak regulatory oversight, thereby denying Americans access to competitive markets. To add insult to injury, oil companies enjoy billions of dollars worth of subsidies courtesy of the U.S. taxpayer at a time when the industry records record profits. Investing in America's communities—not Big Oil—is needed to provide families with access to alternatives. Public Citizen research shows that oil companies aren't adequately investing these record earnings into projects that will help consumers, as the largest capital expenditure in 2006 was to buy back stock and pay dividends to shareholders. America's addiction to oil is a major source of greenhouse gas emissions that cause global warming. Forty-four percent of America's world-leading carbon dioxide emissions are from the burning of petroleum products. Until the oil industry takes the lead on prioritizing investments to curb America's addiction, Congress should take steps to revoke oil company subsidies or impose a windfall profits tax to finance sustainable energy solutions.

In addition, energy trading markets, where futures prices of oil and gasoline are set, were recently deregulated, providing new opportunities for oil companies and financial firms to manipulate prices. Investigations show that energy trading firms have not only exploited recently weakened regulatory oversight, but a new trend of energy traders controlling energy infrastructure assets like pipelines and storage facilities provide additional abilities to use "insider" information to help manipulate markets.

Public Citizen has a five point plan for reform:

- Repeal all existing oil company tax breaks, close loopholes allowing oil companies to escape paying adequate royalties and/or implement a windfall profits tax, dedicating the new revenues to financing clean energy, energy efficiency and mass transit.

- Strengthen antitrust laws by empowering the Federal Trade Commission to crack down on unilateral withholding and other anti-competitive actions by oil companies. Re-evaluate recently approved mergers.

- Establish a Strategic Refining Reserve to be financed by a windfall profits tax on oil companies that would complement America's Strategic Petroleum Reserve.

- Re-regulate energy trading exchanges to restore transparency and impose firewalls to stop energy traders from speculating on information gleaned from the companies' affiliates.

- Improve fuel economy standards to reduce gasoline demand.

RECENT MERGERS, WEAK ANTI-TRUST LAW THREATEN CONSUMERS

According to the U.S. Government Accountability Office, over 2,600 mergers have been approved in the U.S. petroleum industry since the 1990s. In just the last few years, mergers between giant oil companies—such as Exxon and Mobil, Chevron and Texaco, Conoco and Phillips—have resulted in just a few companies controlling a significant amount of America's gasoline, squelching competition. And the mergers continue unabated as the big just keep getting bigger. In 2005 [for example],

ChevronTexaco acquired Unocal. Exxon-Mobil, ChevronTexaco, ConocoPhillips, BP and Shell produce 10 million barrels of oil a day—more than the combined exports of Saudi Arabia and Qatar.

Consumers are paying more at the pump than they would if they had access to competitive markets, and five oil companies are reaping the largest profits in history. Since 2001, the six largest oil companies operating in America have recorded $477 billion in profits. While of course America's tremendous appetite for gasoline plays a role, uncompetitive practices by oil corporations are a cause—more so than OPEC [Organization of Petroleum Exporting Countries] or environmental laws—of high gasoline prices around the country.

High prices are having a detrimental impact on the economy and national security. Imported oil represents one-third of America's trade deficit, slows economic growth, adds to inflationary pressures and creates financial hardship for families and businesses.

Motorists are not getting any bang for their buck. While drivers are stuck paying record high prices, oil companies are spending more money buying back their own stock then they are on investing in their ageing infrastructure. The industry leader, ExxonMobil, spent $25.4 billion buying back its stock and paying dividends to its shareholders in 2006, while spending only $17.7 billion worldwide on its oil exploration and refining capital investment.

In just the last few years, mergers between giant oil companies—such as Exxon and Mobil, Chevron and Texaco, Conoco and Phillips—have resulted in just a few companies controlling a significant amount of America's gasoline, squelching competition. Public Citizen research shows that in 1993, the largest five oil refiners controlled one-third of the

American market, while the largest 10 had 55.6 percent. By 2005, as a result of all the mergers, the largest five now control 55 percent of the market, and the largest 10 dominate 81.4 percent. This concentration has led to skyrocketing profit margins. As a result of all of these recent mergers, the largest five oil refiners today control as much capacity as the largest 10 did a decade ago.

The consolidation of downstream assets—particularly refineries—plays a big role in determining the price of a gallon of gas. Recent mergers have resulted in dangerously concentrated levels of ownership over U.S. oil refining. A recent government study revealed that the "source of potential market power in the wholesale gasoline market is at the refining level because the refinery market is imperfectly competitive and refiners essentially control gasoline sales at the wholesale level" and concluded that "mergers and increased market concentration generally led to higher wholesale gasoline prices in the United States."

The industry has plenty of incentive to intentionally keep refining markets tight. ExxonMobil's new CEO told *The Wall Street Journal* that even though American fuel consumption will continue growing for the next decade, his company has no plans to build new refineries [because of] the "shift toward fuel efficiency that Exxon thinks will cause fuel consumption by North American cars and light trucks to peak around 2020—and then start to fall."

ExxonMobil and other major oil companies are not building new refineries because it is in their financial self interest to keep refining margins as tight as possible, as that translates into bigger profits. Margins for U.S. oil refiners have been at record highs. In 1999, U.S. oil refiners enjoyed a 18.9 cent margin for every gallon refined from crude oil. By 2005, they

posted a 48.8 cent margin for every gallon of gasoline refined, a 158 percent jump. Indeed, BP's most recent financial report shows that refining profit margins at their US operations are more than double the margins in other countries. In 2006, BP earned $9.14 for every barrel they refined in the Midwest, $12/barrel in the Gulf Coast and $14.84/barrel on the West Coast. Compare these returns with those at BP's English operations ($3.92/barrel) and Singapore ($4.22/barrel).

Concentration of refinery markets has been compounded by consolidation in gasoline marketing. Refiners get gasoline to the market by distributing their product through terminals, where jobbers then deliver to retail gas stations. The number of terminals available to jobbers in the U.S. was cut in half from 1982 to 1997, leaving retailers with fewer options if one terminal raises prices.

As a result of this strategy of keeping refining capacity tight, energy traders in New York are pushing the price of gasoline higher, and then trading the price of crude oil up to follow gasoline.

Since gasoline futures are a more localized market than crude oil, it is easier for oil companies, hedge funds and investment banks to manipulate gasoline markets. Now that crude oil trading often follows the gasoline markets, the ability of these traders to exploit America's underregulated futures markets raises concerns that consumers are being price-gouged.

High domestic inventories are not suppressing prices. In April 2006, U.S. commercial inventories of crude oil surpassed 347 million barrels—the highest level since May 1998. Current amounts remain at historically high levels, demonstrating that while we have plenty of surplus crude, problems lie with accessing refined products. Consumers are paying a premium not because of problems in crude oil markets, but rather the problems in the refining markets. And the biggest problem in the refining market is the industry lacks financial incentive to expand capacity to create a surplus.

The U.S. Federal Trade Commission found evidence of anti-competitive practices in its March 2001 Midwest Gasoline Price Investigation:

> An executive of [one] company made clear that he would rather sell less gasoline and earn a higher margin on each gallon sold than sell more gasoline and earn a lower margin. Another employee of this firm raised concerns about oversupplying the market and thereby reducing the high market prices. A decision to limit supply does not violate the antitrust laws, absent some agreement among firms. Firms that withheld or delayed shipping additional supply in the face of a price spike did not violate the antitrust laws. In each instance, the firms chose strategies they thought would maximize their profits.

Although federal investigators found ample evidence of oil companies intentionally withholding supplies from the market in the summer of 2000, the government has not taken any action to prevent recurrence. A congressional investigation uncovered internal memos written by major oil companies operating in the U.S. discussing their successful strategies to maximize profits by forcing independent refineries out of business, resulting in tighter refinery capacity. From 1995–2005, 97 percent of the nearly 929,000 barrels of oil per day of capacity that has been shut down were owned by smaller, independent refiners. Were this capacity to be in operation today, refiners could use it to better meet today's reformulated gasoline blend needs.

TAXING OIL COMPANY PROFITS

Apologists for record oil company profits argue that the companies need and deserve record windfalls to provide the necessary market incentive to invest more money into increased energy production.

Public Citizen's analysis of oil company profits and their investments show that they are spending unprecedented sums on benefits for their shareholders in the form of stock buybacks and dividend payments and not adequately investing in sustainable energy that is necessary to end America's addiction to oil. Since January 2005, the top five oil companies have spent $172 billion buying back stock and paying out dividends. In addition, they held $56 billion in cash. This not only represents a huge transfer of wealth from consumers to oil company investors, but shows that oil companies are squandering opportunities to use their record profits to make investments that will end America's addiction to oil.

With nearly $1 trillion of combined assets tied up in extracting, refining and marketing petroleum and natural gas, the big five oil companies' entire business model is designed to squeeze every last cent of profit out of their monopoly control over fossil fuels. They simply will not make significant investments in anything else until their monopoly control over oil is spent.

And this monopoly control translates into unprecedented profits. When communicating to the general public and lawmakers, oil companies downplay these record earnings by calculating profits differently than they do when they speak to Wall Street and shareholders. Conversing with lawmakers and the general public, the oil industry highlights the small profit margins (typically around 8 to 10 percent) that measuring net income as a share of total revenues produces.

But that's not the calculation ExxonMobil and other energy companies use when talking to investors and Wall Street. For example, [ExxonMobil's] 2005 annual report [to its investors argued] return on average capital employed (ROCE) is the [best measure of financial performance. [By that measure,] ExxonMobil's 2006 earning report shows that that the company's global operations enjoyed a 32 percent rate of return on average capital employed.

It isn't just oil producing nations like Saudi Arabia that get rich when the price of a barrel of oil exceeds $60—major oil producing corporations get rich, too. On average, it costs an oil company like ExxonMobil about $20 to extract a barrel of oil from the ground, while they sell that barrel to American consumers at the market price of $60/barrel.

With oil companies failing to take action to protect America's middle- and low-income families from the high energy prices that fuel their profits, oil industry subsidies should be repealed with the proceeds invested in renewables, alternative fuels, energy efficiency and mass transit.

Naysayers argue that increasing taxes on oil companies or enacting a Windfall Profits Tax didn't work the last time it was tried. The Windfall Profits Tax of 1980–88 was ineffective not because of the tax itself, but because oil prices fell shortly after enactment of the tax due to global events unrelated to U.S. tax policy. But that was then. *The Wall Street Journal* recently concluded that "a crash [in oil prices] looks unlikely now, both because supplies remain tight and because of the large volumes of money that investors are pouring into oil markets."

In addition to a Windfall Profits Tax, Congress needs to reform the royalty system imposed on companies drilling for oil and natural gas on public land. One-third of the oil and natural gas produced in the United States comes from land owned by the taxpayers, but royalty payments by oil companies have not been keeping up with the explosion in energy prices and profits enjoyed by the industry. A recent Inspector General audit of the U.S. Department of the Interior's Minerals Management Service concludes that oil companies are pumping oil from federal land without paying adequate royalties to taxpayers for the privilege. Taxpayers must be fairly compensated for allowing oil companies the privilege of extracting resources from federally-owned land.

Public Citizen also recommends repealing all federal subsidies currently enjoyed by the oil industry and transferring those expenditures to renewable energy, energy efficiency and mass transit. Public Citizen estimates that the oil industry receives 65 percent of all federal government energy tax breaks and government spending programs, estimated at as much as $8 billion annually.

Other countries often feature higher gas prices than the U.S., but that is because they impose higher taxes on gasoline than we do. For example, the average federal, state and local gas taxes in the United States are 39 cents/gallon, compared to $2.06/gallon in Japan, $3.77/gallon in France; $4.12/gallon in Germany; and $4.33/gallon in the United Kingdom. These high taxes are not only a disincentive to drive, but generate the revenue the countries need to help subsidize mass transit and other sustainable energy investments to actively provide citizens with alternatives to driving.

FTC NOT ADEQUATELY PROTECTING CONSUMERS

The Federal Trade Commission has contributed to the problem by allowing too many mergers and taking a stance too permissive to anti-competitive practices, as evidenced by the conclusions in its most recent investigation, for example, finding evidence of price-gouging by oil companies but explaining it away as profit maximization strategies and opposing federal price-gouging statutes. This stands in stark contrast to the May 2004 conclusions reached by a U.S. Government Accountability Office report which found that recent mergers in the oil industry have directly led to higher prices.

The FTC consistently allows refining capacity to be controlled by fewer hands, allowing companies to keep most of their refining assets when they merge, as a recent overview of FTC-approved mergers demonstrates. [For example,] the major condition demanded by the FTC for approval of the August 2002 Conoco-Phillips merger was that the company had to sell two of its refineries—representing less than four percent of its capacity. Phillips was required only to sell a Utah refinery, and Conoco had to sell a Colorado refinery. But even with this forced sale, ConocoPhillips remains the largest domestic refiner, controlling refineries with capacity of more than 2.2 million barrels of oil per day, or 13 percent of America's entire capacity. And the FTC allowed ConocoPhillips to purchase Premcor's 300,000 barrels/day Illinois refinery in 2004.

CONCLUSION

This era of high energy prices and record oil company profits isn't a simple case of supply and demand, as the evidence indicates that consolidation of energy infrastructure assets, combined with weak or non-existent regulatory oversight of energy trading markets, provides opportunity for energy companies and financial institutions to price-gouge Americans. Forcing consumers suffering from inelastic demand to continue to pay high prices—in part fueled by uncompetitive actions—not only hurts consumers economically, but environmentally as well, as the oil companies and energy traders enjoying record profits are not investing those earnings into sustainable energy or alternatives to our addiction to oil. As a result, our consumption of fossil fuels continues to grow, and the impacts of global warming take their toll on our environment. Reforms to strengthen regulatory oversight over America's energy trading markets and bolster anti-trust enforcement are needed to restore true competition to America's oil and gas markets.

The Oil Industry and Energy Prices: Responding to Market Forces

JOHN FELMY

I am John Felmy, chief economist of [the American Petroleum Institute] API, the national trade association of the U.S. oil and natural gas industry. API represents nearly 400 companies involved in all aspects of the oil and natural gas industry, including exploration and production, refining, marketing and transportation, as well as the service companies that support our industry. The oil and natural gas industry understands America's frustrations about gasoline prices. Higher prices are a burden to households and potentially threaten the economy. However, the evidence overwhelmingly demonstrates that higher prices reflect an imbalance between supply and demand, worsened at least in part by policy failures, which the current price-control proposals will make still worse. The contention that higher prices are driven by market failure or market manipulation, including the holding back of supplies, is not credible. The prices are a symptom of larger energy challenges facing the nation and must be addressed in other ways.

U.S. oil companies are working extremely hard to provide Americans with the fuels they need and demand. U.S. refineries have been making record amounts of gasoline, about 8.85 million barrels per day to date this year [about 4% more than last year]. However, less imported gasoline has been available. Typically, imports make up about 12 percent of gasoline supply. Less foreign gasoline has been available in part because of spring refinery maintenance in Europe and an 18-day French port-workers' strike

in March, which led some European refiners to reduce production. As a result, total U.S. gasoline supplies have struggled to keep up with demand, which has been extremely strong. During the first quarter of 2007, total U.S. gasoline demand set a record, increasing almost 2 percent over the same period in 2006.

The most important factor in higher gasoline prices has been higher crude oil prices. More than half the cost of gasoline is attributable to the cost of crude oil. Crude oil prices have fluctuated significantly, driven by lingering geopolitical tensions, OPEC's continuing production controls, and worldwide demand growth. Oil companies do not set the price of crude. It is bought and sold in international markets, with the price for a barrel of crude reflecting the market conditions at the time of purchase. It is well recognized that the market for crude oil has tightened. World oil demand reached unprecedented levels in 2006 and continues to grow due to strong economic growth, particularly in China and the United States. World oil spare production capacity—crude that can be brought online quickly during a supply emergency or during surges in demand— is near its lowest level in 30 years. In addition, the annual switchover to "summer blend" gasoline required by EPA [the U.S. Environmental Protection Agency] has occurred, and this warm-weather gasoline is more expensive to produce. The switchover lowers yields per barrel of oil and requires a large supply drawdown to meet regulations, which reduces inventories.

Finally, despite record U.S. gasoline production, regularly scheduled refinery maintenance and unexpected problems relating to extreme weather, external power outages and other incidents have prevented refiners from making even more gasoline. Maintenance is a normal procedure, though it has been delayed, in some cases, by damage suffered from the catastrophic hurricanes in 2005. While maintenance curtails refining operations temporarily, it helps ensure the long-term viability of the refinery and protects the health and safety of workers.

In short, the recent price increases reflect the forces of supply and demand. And the same is true for past price increases that have been thoroughly investigated by government agencies who would not have hesitated to take the industry to task if illegal or improper activity had been discovered. Invariably, these agencies have explained price spikes by supply/demand conditions. The evidence is overwhelming that refiners are not withholding supplies or otherwise manipulating the market.

Here, for example, is what the U.S. Federal Trade Commission said in May 2006 as a result of an investigation:

> The best evidence available through our investigation indicated that companies operated their refineries at full sustainable utilization rates. Companies scheduled maintenance downtime in periods when demand was lowest in order to minimize the costs they incur in lost production. Internal company documents suggested that refinery downtime is costly, particularly when demand and prices are high. Companies track these costs, and their documents reflected efforts to minimize unplanned downtime resulting from weather or other unforeseen calamities. Our investi-

gation uncovered no evidence indicating that refiners make product output decisions to affect the market price of gasoline. Instead, the evidence indicated that refiners responded to market prices by trying to produce as much higher-valued products as possible, taking into account crude oil costs and other physical characteristics. The evidence collected in this investigation indicated that firms behave competitively.

Those who persist in suspecting, despite the massive evidence to the contrary, that the industry is holding back supplies often cite the lack of new refinery construction. While it is true that no new refinery has been built since the 1970s, companies have steadily increased the capacity of existing refineries and continue to do so. Over the past ten years, existing refineries have expanded capacity equivalent to building 10 new refineries and, based on public announcements of refinery expansions, are projected to add capacity equivalent to an additional eight new refineries by 2011.

Another explanation advanced to explain higher prices is industry mergers. As with all industries, mergers have occurred only after careful FTC scrutiny to ensure the competitiveness of markets. There is no shortage of competitors today, and market power is not heavily concentrated. The eight biggest refiners account for 66 percent of the market, a level of concentration that compares favorably to other consumer product industries. There are close to 60 refining companies, about 142 refineries, and about 165,000 retail outlets, all but a small percentage of these outlets owned by small businessmen and women. A 2004 report by the FTC [U.S. Federal Trade Commission] said that the share of U.S. refining capacity owned by independent refiners with no production operations rose from 8 percent in 1990 to over 25 percent in 2006.

A 2003 GAO [U.S. General Accountability Office] report says that mergers affected prices by less than one half of one cent per gallon at the wholesale level, but the FTC dismissed the report as "fundamentally flawed" and full of "major methodological mistakes." It says the report's conclusion "lack any quantitative foundation." Beyond this suspect GAO report, we are unaware of anything in the professional literature tying higher prices to mergers. Indeed, in part as a result of the mergers, the industry has become more efficient, which has reduced costs to consumers, though this benefit has been masked by sharp increases in crude oil prices.

Proponents of "price-gouging" proposals say they are partly justified by the oil and natural gas industry's large earnings. There is considerable misunderstanding about this. Companies' earnings are typically in line with other industries and often lower. For 2006, the industry's annual earnings averaged 9.5 cents on each dollar of sales. The average for all manufacturing industries was 8.2 cents or about a penny lower. From 2002 to 2006, average earnings for the industry stood at approximately 7.4 cents on each dollar of sales—a penny above the five-year average for all U.S. manufacturing industries.

It should not be forgotten that the energy Americans consume today is brought to us by investments made years or even decades ago. Today's oil and natural gas industry earnings are invested in new technology, new production, and environmental and product quality improvements to meet tomorrow's energy needs. Between 1992 and 2005, the industry invested more than $1 trillion—on six continents—in a range of long-term

energy initiatives: from new exploration and expanding production and refining capacity to applying industry leading technology. In fact, over this period, our cumulative capital and exploration expenditures exceeded our cumulative earnings.

Furthermore, the industry's future investments are not focused solely on oil and natural gas projects. For example, one oil company is among the world's largest producers of photovoltaic solar cells; another oil company is the world's largest developer of geothermal energy; and the oil and gas industry is the largest producer and user of hydrogen. Over the last five years in North America alone, we have invested $12 billion in renewable, alternative and advanced non-hydrocarbon technologies. In fact, when you add up all of the various types of emerging energy technologies, our industry, over the five years, has invested almost $100 billion—more than two and half times as much as the federal government and all other U.S. companies combined.

It also requires billions more dollars to maintain the delivery system necessary to ensure a reliable supply of energy and to make sure it gets where it needs to go: to industry customers. According to the EIA [U.S. Energy Information Administration], Americans will need 28 percent more oil and 19 percent more natural gas in 2030 than in 2005. The industry is committed to making the reinvestments that are critical to ensuring our nation has a stable and reliable supply of energy today and tomorrow.

It is also important to understand that those benefiting from healthy oil and natural gas industry earnings include numerous private and government pension plans, including 401K plans, as well as many millions of individual American investors. While shares are owned by individual investors; firms, and mutual funds, pension plans own 41 percent of oil and natural gas company stock. To protect the interest of their shareholders and help meet future energy demand, companies are investing heavily in finding and producing new supplies.

None of the arguments advanced to justify the price-control proposals has a strong factual and analytical basis, yet even if all did, price-control legislation would be a supremely bad idea. The proposals could interfere with the operation of the law of supply and demand, hamstringing efforts to secure and deliver ample supplies of fuel to consumers.

Today's proposals are cousins of the disastrous price and allocation controls of the 1970s. Those policies established price ceilings on domestically produced crude oil and refined products, keeping them artificially low compared to world prices. This resulted in decreased domestic crude oil production while domestic demand for crude oil and refined products increased, leading to a worsening of shortages and increased oil imports. It was the era of gasoline lines, odd or even days, and millions of angry motorists, victims of the misguided policies of their own government, which should have known better.

If price controls are enacted, the 12 percent of our daily gasoline consumption met by imports could be jeopardized. Overseas suppliers would not have an incentive to ship to U.S. markets if the price were kept artificially low. Also, they might prefer to ship to other markets rather than risk jail time or exorbitant fines in the U.S.

In addition, today's proposals contain vague pricing requirements that make it virtually impossible for marketers to know in advance if their actions will be found to be in or out of compliance and, therefore, will be extremely difficult to enforce fairly. For example, under these bills, how is a gas station operator to know whether a price increase of five, ten or fifteen cents a gallon will be considered "unconscionable?" This legal uncertainty, especially when coupled with the serious risk of jail time or exorbitant fines, could discourage a supplier from doing business in areas affected by a natural disaster when supplies have been substantially reduced, thus delaying a return to normal conditions.

Price-control laws will not solve today's problems. The U.S. oil and natural gas industry is doing everything it can to produce the fuel supply needed to meet consumer energy needs. Congress needs to allow the oil and gas industry to invest today's earnings in meeting tomorrow's energy needs and continue to operate within a market system, which has done far more for consumers than price controls could ever hope to. However, the industry cannot meet U.S. energy challenges alone. Our nation's energy policy needs to focus on increasing supplies; encouraging energy efficiency and conservation in all sectors of the economy, including transportation; and promoting responsible development of alternative and non-conventional sources of energy.

At a minimum, we must do no harm. Price control laws threaten consumers and the nation's energy security. We can do much, much better.

THE CONTINUING DEBATE:
The Oil Industry and Energy Prices

What Is New

To ease the long-term price pressures on gasoline, President George W. Bush in his 2007 State of the Union called for a 20% reduction in gasoline consumption by 2017. To accomplish that, Bush asked Congress to enact legislation that would, among other things, lead to the production of at least 35 billion gallons of renewable and alternative vehicle fuels, such as ethanol, and an increase in the Corporate Average Fuel Economy (CAFE) standards for private passenger vehicles including pickup trucks. Bush also called for increasing domestic oil production to lessen U.S. imports. Each of these is controversial. Critics of ethanol claim, for example, that it takes as much energy to produce it as the product yields. There are also some indications that the diversion of a good part of the country's corn production is increasing the cost of livestock feed and thus the country's food supply. Achieving higher CAFE standards could cost the already staggering U.S. auto industry billions and arguably would also force some Americans to abandon the SUV, pickup, and other large vehicles they favor. Increasing the supply of domestic oil would require drilling in environmentally sensitive off-shore and inland places. Various other, more dramatic proposals have been made such as price controls, significantly increasing gasoline taxes, and adding substantial "gas-guzzler tax" that increased for every mile less than say 20 mpg a vehicle gets. Some legislators have also called for financing alternative fuel research by enacting a windfall tax of an estimated $21 billion dollars on the oil companies. What, if anything, Congress will do remains to be seen.

Where to Find More

Data on the production, use, and cost of gasoline, as well as other energy sources, is available through the U.S. Energy Information Administration at www.eia.doe.gov/. An even broader perspective on energy is available from the U.S. Department of Energy at www.energy.gov/. The president's most recent energy plan is outlined at www.whitehouse.gov/stateoftheunion/2007/initiatives/energy.html. To check gasoline prices in other countries, go to www.nationmaster.com/graph/ene_gas_pri-energy-gasoline-prices. The last significant attempt to regulate the oil industry came in the late 1970s, and its impact is explored in J. P. Kati, *Economics and Politics of Oil-price Regulation: Federal Policy in the Post-embargo Era* (MIT Press, 1981). For a contemporary look at the U.S. energy picture within the global framework see Toyin Falola and Ann Genova *The Politics of the Global Oil Industry* (Praeger, 2005) and Anthony H. Cordesman, *The Global Oil Market: Risks And Uncertainties* (Center for Strategic & International Studies (March 20, 2006). An exploration of the oil companies themselves is available in Valerie Marcel with John V. Mitchell, *Oil Titans* (Brookings Institution, 2006).

What More to Do

Go to Thomas, the congressional Web site at thomas.loc.gov, and find out what Congress is doing. Bring specific proposals that it is considering to class and debate them in order to see why passing comprehensive energy reform is so difficult.

9   POLITICAL PARTIES

HILLARY CLINTON AND THE 2008 PRESIDENTIAL ELECTION:
The Democrats' Best Bet *or* a Problematic Candidate?

THE DEMOCRATS' BEST BET

ADVOCATE: Carl Cannon, White House correspondent for the *National Journal*

SOURCE: "She Can Win the White House," *Washington Monthly,* July/August 2005

A PROBLEMATIC CANDIDATE

ADVOCATE: Amy Sullivan, editor, *Washington Monthly*

SOURCE: "Not So Fast," *Washington Monthly*, July/August 2005

K̲ermit the Frog has often sung a plaintiff tune that begins, "It's not easy being green." Members of the currently out-of-power political party in the United States can identity with Kermit's struggle because for them, "It's not easy being a Democrat." Once that was easier. Indeed the Democrats had a great run beginning with Franklin D. Roosevelt's entry into the White House in 1933. From then until 1969, a Democrat sat in the Oval Office for all but eight years (1953–1961, Dwight D. Eisenhower). Making life even happier for the Democrats, they also controlled both houses of Congress except for four years (1947–1949 and 1953–1955).

Then the political fortune of the Democrats began to decline. Republican Richard M. Nixon became president in 1969, and since then a Republican has been president two-thirds of the time (exceptions: Jimmy Carter, 1977–1981; Bill Clinton, 1993–2001). The power of the Democrats also declined in Congress, although they held on longer there. The Republicans took control of the Senate in 1981 and held it for six years. They then lost the majority to the Democrats for eights years but regained control in 1997 and have held it to 2007. Democrats ceded power in the House even more slowly, but they lost it in 1997 and remain the minority party. Republicans also dominate marginally at the state level. In 2005, Republican state governors outnumber their Democratic counterparts 28 to 22. Of the various state legislative chambers, Republicans control 50, the Democrats 47; one is tied.

This tale of nearly 40 disappointing years for the Democrats brings us to the 2008 presidential election and the potential of New York Senator Hillary R. Clinton as the Democratic nominee. Prior to that, of course, there is the 2006 congressional elections. With public discontent over the war in Iraq and other matters hurting the popularity of President Bush and, by extension, other Republicans, the Democrats have the best chance in a decade to regain a majority in one or both houses of Congress. However, the Republicans have enough of a majority in both houses and the chances of defeating incumbents are so slim, that Democratic control of the Senate would be a major upset and there is only a fifty-fifty chance the Democrats will control the House. Thus 2008 is a key year for the Democrats. With President

Bush ineligible to run again, the Democratic incumbent will not have to run against an incumbent president. Moreover of the 33 Senate seats up for election in 2008, Republicans are vulnerable because they hold 19 of them. Additionally, a winning Democratic presidential "coat tails," even if limited, could provide the margin of victory to gain a majority in the House.

Is Senator Clinton the candidate most likely to lead Democrats to control of the White House and both houses of Congress in 2009? That is the issue which divides Carl Cannon, who believes she is, and Amy Sullivan, who contends that she is not.

Clinton was born on October 26, 1947, as Hillary Diane Rodham and grew up in Park Ridge, Illinois. She began her active political career while at Wellesley College, where she served as president of the Wellesley College Chapter of the College Republicans. During her junior year, however, Rodham became a Democrat. She first gained a glimmer of national note when her valedictory graduation speech at Wellesley was considered so outstanding that she was featured in a *Life* magazine article. After that, she attended Yale Law School, where she met future husband Bill Clinton, and from where she graduated in 1972. After marrying Clinton in 1975, she moved to Arkansas, where she practiced law.

Hillary Clinton became first lady in 1993, and was soon appointed by her husband to head the Task Force on National Health Care Reform. Its eventual recommendations were much too far reaching to be accepted by Congress and were soon abandoned. This ended any overt political role for Ms. Clinton until the very end of her husband's tenure in the White House. It was not, however, the last of her trouble during those years. There were charges of unethical, even illegal activities in the huge gain she had made in 1979, turning an investment of $1,000 into $100,000, trading cattle futures on the Chicago Mercantile Exchange. Later, in the so-called Whitewater scandal, Ms. Clinton was summoned to testify before a grand jury regarding any part she might have played in a real estate fraud involving a venture in which she and her husband were among the partners. Several of the partners went to jail, but the Clintons were not charged. Ms. Clinton's time in the White House was also troubled by her spouse's alleged and acknowledged extra-marital affairs, most notably with White House intern Monica Lewinsky. With her husband's years as president ending, Ms. Clinton sought and won the Democratic nomination for the U.S. Senate in New York, then handily beat her Republican opponent with 55% of the vote. It was widely thought that she would use the New York Senate seat as a base to seek the presidency, and that proved correct. After winning a second Senate term in November 2006 with 67% of the vote, she launched her presidential campaign in January 2007 with the declaration, "I'm in. And I'm in to win."

POINTS TO PONDER

➤ For this early in a campaign, Senator Clinton has an unusually high percentage of "positive" and "negatives," people who like and dislike her. The authors disagree about what this means. Who is right?

➤ What, if anything, would it mean to have former president Bill Clinton in the White House as the "first gentleman"?

➤ To what degree if any is gender a reasonable standard to any voter to make a decision for or against supporting Clinton?

Hillary Clinton and the 2008 Presidential Election: The Democrats' Best Bet

CARL CANNON

In 1978, while covering California politics, I found myself on election night at the Century Plaza Hotel in Los Angeles, which was serving as a kind of election central. Waiting for the returns to come in, I was sitting in the lobby having a drink with my father—who, then as now, was the leading expert on Ronald Reagan. As iron cue, the former actor and ex-California governor came striding into the hotel. Even then Reagan looked the part: wide-shouldered, flanked by a security detail, sporting his trademark blue serge suit, every black hair in place.

The only thing missing, I thought, was the Marine Corps Band.

No one back east took Reagan nearly as seriously as he seemed to be taking himself. Despite a devoted following among what were then known as Goldwater Republicans, the Washington cognoscenti casually dismissed Reagan as too conservative, too old, a B-movie actor who once played second fiddle to a chimpanzee— "Who does he think he is?" I asked my dad. "The president of the United States?"

"No," came the reply. "He thinks he's the next president of the United States." After a pause, he added, "And he might be."

I remember that vignette every time a political sage says authoritatively that [Senator] Hillary Rodham Clinton (D-NY) will "never" be president.

This is a particularly entrenched bit of conventional wisdom, which seems to have metastasized into a kind of secret handshake. If you "know" Clinton can't be president, you're a member of the Washington in-crowd. If you don't, you're an outsider,

some boob from the sticks of, I don't know, Sacramento or somewhere. Suburban Chicago, maybe. You know the rap: She's too liberal, too polarizing, a feminist too threatening to male voters. Too much baggage. Too...*Clinton*.

And these are Democrats talking. Bizarrely, the party's insiders are going out of their way to tear down the credentials and prospects of one of their rare superstars. Conservative columnist Robert Novak ran into this phenomenon recently while speaking to eight local Democratic politicians in Los Angeles. Novak told them matter-of-factly that Hillary was the odds-on favorite to be their party's 2008 nominee—and that no one was in second place. Novak was surprised by their reaction: Not one was for Mrs. Clinton. Why? "They think she is a loser," said one of the Democrats.

With some exceptions, the journalistic pack seems nearly as negative about Hillary Clinton's chances. I'm a charter member of an informal lunch group of writers who runs the gamut from conservative to liberal, and each month when we meet, Hillary's name arises. Around the table it goes: She can't be elected in a general election; men aren't willing to vote for a woman like Hillary; women don't think much of her marriage—or her, for staying in it; which red state could she possibly carry? What swing voter would she convince? Each month, I marshaled my arguments in favor of Hillary's candidacy until finally I began sparing my friends the whole rap by just noting—for the minutes of the meeting, as it were—that I disagree with them.

Perhaps my lunch mates, those worried activist Democrats, and the majority of Washington pundits are correct. But I don't think so.

They certainly weren't right about Reagan.

Conservatives (and liberals) would consider it heresy to compare Ronald Reagan and Hillary Clinton. And Reagan is certainly a hard act to follow. He combined Main Street sensibilities and a soothing Middle America persona with an uplifting vision of America's place in the world that earned him a stunningly decisive victory in 1980—and 60 percent of the vote when he ran for reelection four years later. Senator Clinton is a more polarizing figure, in more polarized times. Yet Clinton, like Reagan, can lay claim to the passions of diehard grassroots members of her party. With the exception of incumbents and vice presidents, no candidate since Reagan has had a hammerlock on his or her party's nomination this long before the election. And like Reagan, the charisma gap between her and any would-be challengers in her own party is palpable.

Of course, the question is not whether she can win in the primary. Most Democrats concede the primary is probably hers for the taking. "I don't know how you beat her for the Democratic nomination," former Senator Bob Kerrey (D-NE) told *New York* magazine. She's a rock star. But that, as the cognoscenti see it, is the problem. She can't lose the primary, and she can't win the general election. And so they look vainly for an alternative—Warner? Biden? Bayh? Oh my!—always circling back to the same despairing fear of another four years in the political wilderness. Democrats have raised this kind of defeatism to a high art. But it's time for Democrats to snap out of it and take a fresh look at the hand they've been dealt. Hillary Rodham Clinton can win the general elec-

tion no matter who the Republicans throw at her. The Democrats just might be holding aces.

POLL POSITIONED

The available data do not suggest she is unelectable—they suggest just the opposite. A Gallup poll done a week before Memorial Day showed Senator Clinton with a favorable rate of 55 percent. True, her unfavorable number is 39 percent, which is high enough for concern—but one that is nearly identical to Bush's on the eve of his reelection. And the unfavorable rating registered by Republican contender [Senator] Bill Frist (R-TN) was nearly as high as his favorable numbers, with 32 percent saying they'd never heard of him.

Then there was this eye-opening question:

If Hillary Rodham Clinton were to run for president in 2008, how likely would you be to vote for her—very likely, somewhat likely, not very likely, or not at all likely?

Very likely	29%
Somewhat likely	24
Not very likely	7
Not at all likely	40
No opinion	1

At the risk of laboring the point, 29 percent plus 24 percent adds up to a majority. I can hear my pals answering this as they read these numbers: "Yes, but that's before the conservative attack machine gets a hold of her…"

Well, no, it isn't. They've been going at her with verbal tire irons, machetes, and sawed-off shotguns for 12 years now. Senator Clinton's negatives are already figured into her ratings. What could she be accused of that she hasn't already confronted since she entered the public eye 14 years ago? Clinton today is in a position similar to Bush's at the beginning of 2004. Democrats hoped that more information about the president's youth would "knock him down." But voters had already taken the president's past into account when they voted for him in 2000. More information just wasn't going to make a dent. In fact, as the spring of 2005 turned to summer there were yet another book and a matched spate of tabloid broadsides. In the face of it all, Hillary appears, if anything, to be getting stronger. Indeed, the more the right throws at her, the easier it is for her to lump any criticism in with the darkest visions of the professional Clinton bashers.

Let's also look deeper into that Gallup survey because the closer you look at it, the more formidable Senator Clinton seems. Thirty percent of the poll's respondents consider Hillary a "moderate," while 9 percent described her a "conservative." Now, I'm not sure which newspapers that 9 percent have been reading (the *Daily Worker?*), but the fact that nearly 40 percent of the electorate does not identify her as liberal mitigates the perception that she's considered too far to the left to be a viable national candidate.

Such perceptions are hardly set in stone, however, and senators' voting records can come back to haunt them in the heat of a campaign as [Senator] John Kerry (D-MA) learned in 2004 and countless others have learned before him. It's no accident that the last sitting U.S. senator elected president was John F. Kennedy. Thus, Clinton's Senate voting record, and where it puts her on the ideological scale, is worth some additional scrutiny.

The most comprehensive annual analysis of voting records is undertaken by my magazine, *National Journal*, which for 2004 used 24 votes on economic issues, 19 votes on social issues, and 17 foreign policy-related roll calls to rate all 100 U.S. senators. Its resulting ranking of John Kerry as the Senate's most liberal member (at least during 2003) was a gift from on high for the Bush campaign, and the Massachusetts senator spent the better part of his campaign trying to explain away this vote or that. But Senator Clinton is harder to pigeon-hole. For 2004, Clinton's composite liberal score was 71 percent—putting her roughly in the middle of the Democratic caucus. While adhering to her party's liberal dogma on issues such as race, gun control, and judicial appointees, Hillary lists slightly toward the center on economic issues, and even more so on national security and foreign-policy issues. There's no telling at this point how the war in Iraq will play in 2008, but one thing is certain: Senator Clinton won't struggle the way Kerry did to reconcile a vote authorizing the war with one not authorizing the $87 billion to pay for it. For better or worse, she voted "aye" both times.

Yet another piece of received Washington wisdom holds that the party could never nominate someone in 2008 who has supported the Iraq war. Perhaps. But history suggests that if Bush's mission in Iraq flounders, a politician as nimble as Clinton will have plenty of time to get out in front of any anti-war movement. If it succeeds, Hillary would have demonstrated the kind of steadfastness demanded by the soccer moms turned security moms with whom Bush did so well in 2004.

On domestic issues, Senator Clinton has also shown a willingness to step out of the safety zone. She is bolstering her bipartisan credentials by teaming up with Republicans from the other side of the aisle, such as [Senator] Lindsey Graham (R-SC) and Frist himself, making her more difficult to portray as some kind of radical. And while her liberal voting record on social issues remains intact, she has taken rhetorical steps toward the middle. The most notable example occurred during a January speech in Albany, in which she advised abortion-rights activists to seek "common ground …with people on the other side." While pledging to defend *Roe v. Wade*, Mrs. Clinton relented to abortion as a "sad, even tragic, act" and called on Democrats to embrace a moral language for discussing the issue. Some conservatives even seemed receptive. In some quarters, Hillary's centrist posture was portrayed as new; but it actually isn't: She butted heads with the Arkansas teachers' union in the mid-1980s over a proposal she led to improve teacher quality.

The abortion speech was reminiscent of her husband's 1992 campaign-trail criticism of Sister Souljah for advocating violence against white people. Her remarks simultaneously showed she was willing to talk common sense to a key Democratic interest group while putting herself in sync with the ambivalent sensibilities most Americans have toward abortion. And because of the high standing she enjoys among Democratic women, she was able to do it without any fear of liberal backlash. Let's face it: When a feminist with Hillary's credentials discusses abortion in the way she has, it causes people to sit up and take notice.

Which brings us to the ultimate question: Hillary's gender. Will Americans vote for a woman?

They certainly say they will: 74 percent told Gallup that they'd be either "somewhat" or "very" likely to vote for a woman in 2008. This number is actually on the low side compared to polls from the pre-Hillary era, for the obvious reason that Clinton casts a shadow over 2008, and many of the respondents are Republicans who plan to vote against her. Again, I can hear some of my friends murmuring that these voters aren't telling the truth. But that's precisely the kind of snobbish thinking that never gets Democrats anywhere, that is usually wrong, and that infuriates swing voters. My advice to my Democratic friends is to ignore your inner elitist, and trust the

American people to tell the truth, and, moreover, to do the right thing.

In fact, there is no reason to doubt them, as they've been proving their willingness to pull the lever for female candidates for a long time. In 1999, when Hillary first entered the national scene, 56 women sat in the House of Representatives, and nine in the Senate. Only three women were governors, but many women were in the pipeline in state government: Nearly 28 percent of statewide elective offices in the country were occupied by women. In one state, Arizona, women held the top five statewide offices. And that pipeline produced. Six years later, there are 14 women in the Senate, and 66 in the House (along with another three non-voting delegates). There are eight, not three, women governors. "The day will come when men will recognize woman as his peer, not only at the fireside, but in councils of the nation," [Women's suffrage leader] Susan B. Anthony [1820–1906] once predicted. That day is fast approaching whether or not conservatives are ready for it, and whether or not liberals are willing to acknowledge it.

Nonetheless, anyone who maintains that the American electorate is ready for a female president (and this particular female candidate) must at some point confront the Electoral College map. This, my skeptical friends claim, is where Hillary's hopes run aground. Putting it plainly, they challenge anyone to come up with a red state that Hillary can carry—someplace, anyplace, where Senator Clinton could run stronger than the Kerry/Edwards ticket.

It is, of course, absurd to look at electoral politics at such an atomic level this far out. In due time, pollsters and the press will christen 2008's must-have swing voters and must-win swing states. But calibrating a candidacy to the last election is a fool's errand. The near-frozen electoral map of the last five years has been an historical anomaly, not the rule. So there's no reason to believe that a 2004 electoral map would be terribly useful three years hence.

But if we must, let's play along. What red state could Clinton snatch away from the GOP column? How about Florida? The Gold Coast considers itself part of New York anyway, and Clinton's moderate overtures might draw swing voters from upstate. Cuban Americans are no longer the sole Latino voting bloc in Florida—and even Cubans are no longer monolithic. If not Florida, how about Iowa and New Mexico? They are centrist, bellwether states—and states Hillary's husband carried both times he ran. Meanwhile, the Republican Party hardly has a lock on Ohio, which went for Clinton twice, and which was close in 2000 and 2004.

The fact is, there are a thousand movable parts in a presidential campaign, but the two most indispensable are (1) a candidate with charisma, money, and a broad following in his or her party; and (2) a ticket that espouses values and policies that Middle Americans agree with. A candidate, the polls now suggest, like Hillary Clinton. Or [Senator] John McCain (R-AZ).

THE BUBBA FACTOR

After dissecting an upcoming race, any good horse player will look at the *Racing Form* again and figure out if he (or she) missed anything: Who could beat the obvious horse? For the 2008 presidential run, there is an answer that jumps off the page: If the Republican faithful are smart enough to nominate him, John Sydney McCain III would probably be their most formidable candidate—if he gets the GOP nomination, a big "if."

It's fanciful to suggest that anyone is unbeatable this far out, even McCain. While he makes the media swoon, the Arizona senator would have to thread a pretty tight needle to get to the White House. A Quinnipiac Poll taken in March showed a McCain-Clinton election virtually tied, 43–41. These are good numbers, but they're hardly in the Colin Powell range. The Republican conservative base remains leery of him. That this antipathy is self-defeating (or even inexplicable) makes it no less real. In addition, the easiest circumstances to envision that would benefit McCain would be if there were widespread disillusion with Bush. But the issue most likely to bring that about—a dire result to the occupation in Iraq—probably doesn't help McCain anyway: If anything, he's been more hawkish on foreign policy than the president. Even if other factors—a rotten economy or a scandal—led to a McCain general election candidacy, a GOP meltdown might carry McCain to the nomination, but it wouldn't help him against Hillary Clinton. First, if conservatives could muster only halfhearted passion for the man (not unlike the less-than-enthusiastic support John Kerry received from many Democrats), well, we've seen that movie. No candidate is without vulnerabilities, and certainly Hillary has hers. (I'll leave their enumeration to my counterpart, Amy Sullivan.) The difference between a winning and losing campaign, though, is whether you have the strategy to weather the inevitable rough waters.

On the USS *George W. Bush*, Karl Rove is considered the indispensable navigator. But when one looks on the Democratic side, who is a match for the man Bush called "The Architect" of his triumph? What recent Democrat has shown such an ability to see the political chessboard 20 moves ahead and plot a winning game plan? Only one, and to find him, Senator *Clinton* need only look to the other side of the breakfast table.

President Clinton doesn't come without strings attached. While it is an article of faith among the Clintonistas that Al Gore hurt his own campaign in 2000 by not using Bill Clinton more on the stump, there was plenty of polling to back up Gore's gambit. While Clinton could stir up the party faithful, his presence wasn't always a net plus. Hillary faces a similar dilemma when it comes to her husband—and a lot closer to home. But in addition to being able to draw upon Clinton's strategic gifts, Senator Clinton would almost certainly not make the more serious mistake Gore made: not being able to successfully make use of the Clinton administration's record of 22 million new jobs; steady income growth for workers of every level; precipitous declines in the welfare rolls; and an expanded NATO [North Atlantic Treaty Organization] alliance that ushered in the post–Cold War geopolitical map.

Will Americans remember the optimism and idealism espoused in 1992 by The Man From Hope [a reference to Hope, Arkansas, the childhood home of Bill Clinton], and the way Clinton would parry policy questions with long, coherent, informative answers? Or will they remember their disgust at the revelations about the infamous blue dress, and how Clinton often shaded the truth?

No repentance, however sincere, could spare Bill Clinton from his eternity as fodder for the tabloids and late-night monologues. But he seems to be growing increasingly sure-footed and confident in his role as elder statesman. He has formed a friendship with the man he defeated for the office, and a productive working relationship with the current president. If he is to help his wife, all Clinton needs to do is remind us of his better angels, as he did during his tour of tsunami-devastated South Asia.

This brings us back to Hillary herself. Even if Bill Clinton rises to the occasion, voters are going to remember the yin and the yang of our 42nd president, and they are going to chew on the fact that the woman who wants to be our 44th is married to him. She will be asked about the marriage. How she answers will go a long way toward determining the viability of her candidacy. In his astute book [*The Survivor*: Random House, 1992] on the Clinton presidency, John F. Harris recounts how aides broached the subject of her marriage as Hillary prepared to run for the Senate. How would she answer this basic question: Why had she stayed with him?

"Yes, I've been wondering that myself," Hillary says playfully.

Then Bill interjects: "Because you're a sticker! That's what people need to know—you're a sticker. You stick at the things you care about."

Clintonites love this story, but there are a couple of things wrong with it. First, Bill Clinton is providing the answer, but it's not his answer to give. Second, it's a talking point. The Clintons are good at slogans, but this is a question women will have for Hillary Clinton, women looking to identify with her. A sound bite answer just might confirm voters' fears that her marriage is a sham, and that she's an opportunist. On the other hand, if the answer emerges that she loves Bill Clinton, despite his flaws, and that she's in an imperfect marriage—well, most marriages are imperfect. Moreover, if she suggests that the deciding factor was her concern for their daughter, well, that's the kind of pro-family cred that really matters. Cute answers won't cut it. Authenticity will. And there's every reason to believe both Clintons could summon it when talking about the daughter to whom they are so obviously devoted.

Finally, there is one perceived pitfall—and that's Hillary's penchant for the jugular. Party activists admire her for this, but successful general election candidates learn to temper the instincts that result in outbursts like the "vast, right-wing conspiracy."

In upstate New York, Senator Clinton has charmed independent Yankee farmers and small-town Republican businessmen from Buffalo with an inclusive, upbeat style of campaigning and governing. This is the dress rehearsal for running nationwide, yet when she gets going on the red meat circuit Senator Clinton retains a fondness for ad hominem attacks and paranoid world views.

"There has never been an administration, I don't believe in our history, more intent upon consolidating and abusing power to further their own agenda," Clinton said at a recent Democratic fundraiser. "Why can't the Democrats do more to stop them? I can tell you this: It's very hard to stop people who have no shame about what they're doing....It is very hard to stop people who have never been acquainted with the truth." The crowd loved it, but this rant manages to ignore Nixon, while simultaneously sounding Nixonian. Hillary can definitely have a tin ear.

Hillary Clinton, whether she realizes it or not, is relieved of the obligation to pander in this way. She has paid her dues to the Democratic Party, and she doesn't have to prove her bona tides to anyone. From now on, she only need emulate Reagan, a fellow Illinois native, who campaigned with positive rhetoric and a smile on his face, trusting that the work he'd done cultivating his base would pay off, and that he needed mainly to reassure independent-minded voters. When we in the press corps tried to bait Reagan into going negative by asking why he'd abandoned the party of his youth, he invariably smiled, cocked his head, and gave the same line. "I didn't leave the Democratic Party," Reagan would say. "The Democratic Party left me."

As a girl, Hillary Rodham was a Goldwater Republican. She could use the same line in reverse. It might remind swing voters why they are looking, once again, at casting their lot with a candidate named Clinton. She can do this because Democrats are poised to back her already, and because much of the rest of America is watching, open-minded, half-hoping that she gives them a reason to support her, too.

Hillary Clinton and the 2008 Presidential Election: A Problematic Candidate

AMY SULLIVAN

For a first-time candidate and controversial first lady, Hillary Clinton's bid for the open New York Senate seat in 2000 was going surprisingly well. From the beginning, she had staked out a seemingly impossible strategy; given who she was: ignore the press, go straight to the voters, and focus exclusively on issues, never on herself. "You make a mistake if you let any campaign become about you," she told Michael Tomasky, one of the reporters who followed her that year. Given that even campaigns not involving Hillary Clinton sometimes manage to become about Hillary Clinton, it was difficult to imagine how she could pull off this feat. Still, she stuck doggedly to policy talk, boring the press corps but impressing New York voters. Two weeks before Election Day, she enjoyed a comfortable lead, polling eight points ahead of opponent [Republican candidate, Representative] Rick Lazio.

And that's when Lazio decided to take matters into his hands and make the race about Clinton whether she liked it or not. His campaign put together a commercial intended to target her biggest vulnerability: white suburban women. All throughout the campaign, this demographic had been the most skeptical; in focus groups, even women who liked Clinton said she reminded them of an unpleasant woman in their lives—a mother-in-law or a stern Catholic nun or a judgmental neighbor. The ad sought to remind them that, deep down, they didn't really like Hillary Clinton, that they thought she was too ambitious. On the screen, a woman making dinner in a kitchen talked on a phone, her tone angry:

"We started out at the bottom and worked our tushes off to get somewhere. No, but Hillary, she wants to start at the top, you know, the senator from New York?"

The ad was the most personal of the race, and it worked. Within days, Clinton's lead had shrunk to three points, within the margin of error. Although she recovered to win the Senate seat with 55 percent of the vote, Clinton's advantage among women was only half that of Al Gore's, who won New York's female vote by a margin of 65 to 31.

Five years later, Senator Clinton is a major player on the political scene. Her name is first on the lips of anyone who talks about the 2008 race for the White House. Potential rival John McCain says she would make a fine president. Conservatives such as [former Speaker of the U.S. House of Representatives] Newt Gingrich and Bill Kristol [editor of *The Weekly Standard*] are talking up Clinton, warning their partisan colleagues that she would be a formidable opponent. That's not surprising—after all, Republicans have long fantasized about the prospect of taking on Hillary Clinton again at a national level. But now, talk of her candidacy has gone from conservative wishful thinking to serious discussions within her own party, which is anxious to end its losing streak and is considering the advantages of closing ranks behind an early frontrunner. One glance at polls showing that 53 percent of Americans are willing to consider putting Clinton in the White House makes visions of sugar plums and oval offices dance in the heads of Democratic Party leaders. The high name recognition, impressive early poll numbers, and desperate party all carry the Senate whiff of inevitability that accompanied George W. Bush's campaign for the 2000 election.

In the face of this momentum, someone has to say it, so here goes: Please don't run, Senator.

Don't get me wrong. I'm a longtime Hillary Clinton fan. As in a back-when-she-was-still-wearing-headbands fan. I have found her warm and utterly charming in person; more than that, she understands the challenges facing Democrats in a way that few others in the party do, and her ability to absorb policy nuances rivals her husband's. This country is long past due for a female president, and I would love to see Hillary Clinton in that trailblazing role (and not just because it would make Ann Coulter break out in giant hives). But—at the risk of getting myself permanently blackballed by her loyal and protective staff while Clinton can win nearly any debate that is about issues, she cannot avoid becoming the issue in a national campaign. And when that happens, she will very likely lose.

NO SUCH THING AS UNDECIDED

It's not exactly news that Hillary Clinton is a polarizing figure. Ever since Newt Gingrich's mother whispered to Connie Chung on national television that she thought Mrs. Clinton was, well, a bitch, Americans have understood that the ex-first lady provokes intense emotions on all sides. Still, it's not hard to see why Hillary boosters are tempted to think that voters might be willing to take a new look at her and why politically astute people are turning cartwheels over the idea of her candidacy.

Over the last five years, Clinton has developed into perhaps the most interesting politician in America. She has a reputation for bipartisanship in the Senate, forming partnerships with some of her most conservative Republican colleagues, including Bill Frist (R-TN), Rick Santorum (R-PA), and Sam Brownback (R-KS). She has quietly, but firmly, assumed a leadership role in her own caucus. And she has shown vision and backbone in a party that is accused of having none.

Years before most Washington Democrats started worrying about the party's reputation on "moral values," Clinton was bringing Jim Wallis and other progressive religious leaders to talk with her colleagues about reclaiming the concepts of faith and values. She voted for the Iraq war when that wasn't a popular position for a Democrat to take, and has been willing to speak uncomfortable truths in difficult venues. In January, she told a crowd of over 1,000 assembled pro-choice activists that the way they have been talking about abortion is wrong, that many Americans won't even listen to them until they admit that it would be better if most women didn't have to face the "sad, even tragic choice" of having one. More recently, she cosponsored the "Workplace Religious Freedom Act" after intense lobbying from women's groups that oppose the legislation.

There's no one tougher. No one understands better that Middle America cares about both economic issues and cultural concerns. At the same time, no one is better at firing up the liberal base. Add to all of that approval ratings in the high 50s, and it sounds like you have the makings of a sure-fire winner for the Democrats.

And if it were any other candidate, that might be true. But with Hillary Clinton, everything's more complicated.

Let's look at those poll numbers that have Democrats pasting "Hillary '08" bumper stickers onto their Subaru Outbacks and Republicans pulling their Whitewater files out of the basement. Right now, Clinton is leaving her fellow Democratic contenders—including Sens. John Kerry (D-MA), John Edwards (D-

NC), and Joseph Biden (D-DE)—in the dust. In polls that ask voters to identify which potential Democratic nominee they would back in 2008, she regularly clocks in at around 40 percent while her closest competitor rarely breaks the 20 percent mark.

It's important to remember, however, that polls taken this early in the process tend simply to reflect how well known a candidate is. (Kerry is surely as well-known as Clinton, but may be suffering in the polls from Democratic loser fatigue.) In 1997, for instance, George W. Bush led most polls of Republican prospects, in large part because many respondents thought they were being asked about his father. Hillary Clinton occupies the spot held by Al Gore at this point in the 2004 election cycle. She may well be the candidate most Democrats want to see as their nominee; or she could just be the one they know best. Right now, it's too early to know for certain.

In addition, while her "favorables" are good—57 percent of Americans have a positive impression of her—her negatives are disturbingly high as well. This long before an election, most voters have yet to make up their mind about a candidate. Even as close to the primaries as December 2003, 66 percent of voters didn't know what they thought of John Kerry. That's not the case with Clinton. While at this point in George W. Bush's first presidential campaign, Bush also had favorable ratings around the mid-50s, an additional 30 percent of voters said they either hadn't made up their minds about him or they didn't know who he was. Compare that to Hillary: Only 7 percent of respondents aren't sure what they think of her, and—not surprisingly—no one says they haven't heard of her.

Never in American political history has a candidate faced such a decided electorate at this early a point in a presidential race. That's a disadvantage when you consider that one of the lessons of 2004 was that once voters develop a perception about a candidate, it's as immovable as superglue. No one who thought George W. Bush was a likable, friendly guy could be convinced that he was corrupt or misleading. And once John Kerry became identified in voters' minds as a "flip-flopper," no amount of arguing could change that image. It's a problem for any candidate. For Senator Clinton, it could be fatal. Americans know exactly what they think of her. And nearly 40 percent say they would never consider voting for her.

SHAKING HANDS, CHANGING MINDS

Of course, there is one proven way that Hillary Clinton has damaged voters' perceptions. In her first Senate race, the strategy was simple: Meet as many voters as possible, and ignore the scandal-focused press. It paid off—when Clinton hunched her campaign, only 41 percent of New Yorkers were prepared to vote for her; she won in November 2000 with 55 percent of the vote after having visited each of the state's 62 counties, many of them repeatedly.

Operation Smother the Voters worked in large part because the real Hillary Clinton is a far cry from the caricature of a manipulative, power-hungry, shrewish woman that has been propagated by the right. One of the unexpected benefits of being demonized and attacked by conservatives for more than a decade turns out to be that voters are surprised and relieved when she doesn't fly into town on a broomstick. Tomasky relates the response of voters when they actually met the woman they'd heard so much about for eight years in *Hillary's Turn*, his excellent book about Clinton's 2000 campaign. "People had expected Hillary to instruct and talk, and, let's face it, to come across as pushy and judgmental," he wrote. "So when she paid genuine attention to the things people were saying, she really threw them." Indeed, the first time I met the Clintons, the president distractedly shook some hands after a speech and then left fairly quickly while the first lady was the one who displayed the vaunted Clinton political skills—chatting easily about policy details, focusing intently on what my colleague and I had to say, and then throwing her arms around our shoulders for a photo that looks more like three college friends than two awed congressional staffers and a first lady.

The strategy also succeeded because many voters—weaned on a diet of conservative talking points during the 1990s—expected Clinton to be a liberal of the bluest sort, to the left of Ted Kennedy and unable to understand their concerns. What they found was that her positions on welfare, crime, and foreign policy, among other issues, were far more centrist than liberal. In addition, while most professional political observers dismissed her "Listening Tour" as a stunt, Clinton actually used it to query New Yorkers about their problems and obsessively study up on local issues.

All of this is impressive. But if the ability to work a rope line or a town hall meeting was the key ingredient to winning a national race, our political history would be quite different. In *What It Takes*, his chronicle of the 1988 presidential race, the journalist Richard Ben Cramer describes watching Dick Gephardt entrance voters with his earnest, determined approach and piercing blue eyes. "Sweet Jesus, he is terrific," Cramer writes. "There aren't ten voters in the country who would work against him, once he's had them face-to-face." Similarly, last winter, many political reporters chalked up John Kerry's surprising comeback in Iowa to the fact that he'd spent countless evenings in individual homes, talking to voters until he had convinced each person to support him. No candidate, however,

meets every voter face-to-face en route to the White House.

Anyone running for office would prefer to meet as many voters as possible in person. The stakes are higher for Hillary Clinton: She has to meet personally with voters in order to have a chance of changing their minds about her. If she runs for the White House, the vast majority of Americans will learn what they know about her campaign through the media. And that's where the second half of Senator Clinton's New York strategy falls apart.

"NURSE RATCHED"

When a candidate's name recognition is at 100 percent in a statewide campaign, she can afford to turn a few campaign saws about the media upside-down. For the 2000 Clinton campaign, no press was good press; "the smaller the circus, the better," one of her staffers told Tomasky. They considered it a victory when the traveling press corps—bored by the lack of news made by Clinton's "Listening Tour" and its endless focus on the minutiae of dairy compacts and traffic conditions on the Canadian border—winnowed from 250 reporters to 70 to about a dozen permanent scribes. Although the *New York Post*, and columnist Dick Morris in particular, nipped at Clinton's heels for the length of the campaign, she was able to conduct her image transformation largely in a vacuum.

It's safe to say that wouldn't be the case in 2008. The only way to reach voters in a nationwide campaign is through the media, both through purchased airtime and what is referred to as "free" media—coverage of campaign events and interviews with print and television reporters. It's a two-sided coin for candidates. They need journalists in order to get their messages across to the majority of Americans who won't get a chance to hear them in person, but they have no control over what gets reported or how it's framed in the press. Any Democrat running in the general election would face that challenge, although they might not yet know precisely how the press would cover their candidacy. Senator Clinton, however, knows all too well what to expect. Her instincts were correct in 2000: When you're Hillary Clinton, "free" media always comes with a cost.

Journalists are often no different from voters in general—when they form an impression of a politician, many reporters filter coverage through what they think they know about the candidate. Reporters "knew" Al Gore was a serial exaggerator, that Kerry was an out-of-touch, aristocratic elitist, and that Bush was an amiable goof. They may not let ideological leanings color their coverage, but personal biases can affect what they choose to report and the narratives they choose to tell.

Jill Lawrence, one of *USA Today*'s campaign correspondents in 2004, has observed that very few political reporters wrote about the way Kerry used religious language—even though, she noted, it occurred every week on the campaign wail—because they assumed that Democratic candidates weren't deeply religious. "The stereotype of the Democratic Party is so deep that it never broke through," she said. That's already happening with Clinton, whose religious references and comments on abortion generated headlines early in 2005. Most news outlets characterized her remarks as a distinct break from the past—implying that she was transforming herself for a White House run—even though she is a former Sunday School teacher who has spoken publicly about religion for decades and her comments on abortion were consistent with her husband's mantra that abortion should be "safe, legal, and rare?"

Chemistry is also important for the press corps. Reporters are attracted to straight-talkers like [Senator] John McCain [R-AZ],

Rudy Giuliani [former Republican mayor of New York City], and—in 2003, at least—Howard Dean [former Democratic governor of Vermont]. Inaccessibility is definitely a turn-off; in the early years of the Clinton administration, the First Lady famously fought with the *Washington Post* over the release of documents about Whitewater. Her chilly relationship with the press has warmed considerably during her first term in the Senate, but Hillary Clinton still has far more skeptics than fans have the press corps.

Sometimes they go far beyond reportorial cynicism. The *Washington Post*'s reporter assigned to cover Clinton's first Senate race, [*Washington Post* reporter] Michael Grunwald, provides one illustration of how the press corps already feels about her. Describing the first lady as "bor[ing] New York into submission, droning on endlessly about focus-grouped Democratic issues," Grunwald accused her of "baldly deceptive and intentionally vacuous behavior" and "an intellectually and emotionally dishonest scheme to get a job without a résumé" and charged that "her only consistent ideology was a faith in political popularity." Ouch. More recently, on the Feb. 20, 2005, installment of "The Chris Matthews Show," a panel discussed Hillary's candidacy while calling her "Nurse Ratched" [an unflattering reference to a domineering, repressed character in the 1975 film *One Flew Over the Cuckoo's Nest*] and a "castrating female persona" things really got going when journalist Gloria Borger mimicked Clinton's laugh and mannerisms while her colleagues sniggered.

And that's coming from members of the mainstream media. The conservative press—never shy when it comes to Hillary Clinton—has spent the spring teeing up for another game of Hillaryball. The trial of David Rosen, the fundraiser for Clinton's 2000 campaign, who was accused of hiding about $800,000 of costs for a campaign event held in Los Angeles, came first. In the three months leading up to the verdict (Rosen was acquitted), the FOX News Channel ran more than a dozen segments on Rosen, including a "Hannity & Colmes" segment titled "Are Hillary's Presidential Chances Over?" Rosen's eventual acquittal merited barely a hiccup on FOX, which simply replaced Rosen coverage with segments on the next Clinton scandal story—yet another bestselling book taking on the Senator.

THE HILLARY EFFECT

Edward Klein's *The Truth About Hillary: What She Knew, and How Far She'll Go to Become President* [Sentinel, 2005] is, even by the low standards of the genre, vile. In seeking to portray Hillary Clinton as a cold, manipulative woman who will do anything for power, Klein relies on wholly unsubstantiated accusations of corruption, lesbianism, and marital rape. Most conservatives who gleefully anticipated the book's release are now distancing themselves from it. And liberals have derived some joy from scenes such as right-wing talk show host Scan Hannity sharply questioning Klein over his use of sources.

Klein apparently didn't get the memo about anti-Hillary strategy. Frontal assaults and reckless accusations are sooo 1990s, definitely déclassé. More to the point, they make conservatives sound scary and are counterproductive. But while Democrats are surely hoping that these attacks will spur a backlash and sympathy for Clinton, the more likely outcome is a draw. Americans may have lost their appetite for books like *Madame Hillary: The Dark Road to the White House* [by R. Emmett Tyrrell, Jr., and Mark W. Davis, 2004] and *Hillary's Scheme: Inside the Next Clinton's Ruthless Agenda to Take the White House* [by Carl Limbacher, 2004], but many of them share the under-

lying concern about Clinton's motives and character. Likewise, while a Republican nominee would benefit from anti-Hillary donations—in the last few months of the 2000 race, Lazio averaged $1 million each week in hard money contributions from Hillary-haters outside of New York—Senator Clinton's prodigious fundraising has the potential to neutralize that effort.

Conservatives won't trot out supposed lesbian lovers in 2008; they'll go after her more subtly. They know that 40 percent of the country can't stand Senator Clinton, another 40 percent adores her, and the remaining 20 percent (which, according to those recent polls, seem to feel generally positive about her) is made up of fairly soft support. The best way to turn that support into opposition is to voice those age-old questions about the Clintons: She's inappropriately power-hungry and ambitious—remember that Tammy Wynette crack? He lacks moral character—do you really want him roaming the White House again? And don't forget health care—who elected her to that post anyway?

Another golden oldie—the charge that the Clintons will say anything to get ahead—is already being revived elliptically by conservatives. The day after Senator Clinton's news-making abortion speech this past January, conservatives were all over the media, charging that she was undergoing a "makeover" of her political image. "I think what we're seeing is, at least rhetorically, the attempt of the ultimate makeover," Gary Bauer told the *Washington Times. Investors Business Daily* editorialized: "When husband Bill did it, it was called triangulation....Now another Clinton running for president is telling different audiences what they want to hear." In the six months since, the "makeover" charge has been repeated more than 100 times in the press. Give them another six, and "makeover" will be the new "flip-flop."

The target audience for these whispers and insinuations—and, let's not be naive, occasional television commercials—is a familiar demographic: suburban women. Democrats lost ground in the 2004 elections among white, married, working women, and it's generally accepted that to win back the White House, the party needs a nominee who can appeal to these women. There's no reason to think that Republicans wouldn't revive the same kind of personal attacks that Lazio brought out in the last week of the 2000 campaign. In that race, the Hillary effect that resulted in the loss of suburban women was masked by gains among upstate men. She'll have a much harder time winning their counterparts in those essential swing states, which makes it even more important that she be able to count on the women's vote. If the Republican strategy in 2008 results in the same outcome as 2000—if, in other words, Clinton's advantage among women was half that of Gore's—the margin of victory in states like Iowa, Minnesota, New Mexico, and Wisconsin will disappear. Game, set, match.

No, Democrats, it's not fair. Hillary Clinton is smart, she's paving a promising new path for her party, she's a much better campaigner than anyone ever expected, and she's already survived more personal assaults than anyone should have to endure. But wishing the country would grow up and get over the 1990s already, that she could wage a campaign of issues and be evaluated on her political merit, won't make it so. What's more, those daydreams—pleasant as they are to contemplate on a sunny afternoon—cast a shadow over the Democratic field that makes it difficult for a potentially viable candidate to emerge.

It's too early for anyone to say with certainty that Hillary Clinton can't win the White House. But it's far too early—and dangerous—to conclude that she's the best chance that Democrats have.

THE CONTINUING DEBATE:
Hillary Clinton and the 2008 Presidential Election

What Is New

When Hillary Clinton announced her candidacy for president in January 2007, she became the instant front-runner for the Democratic nomination. Some thought she would not even be strongly challenged, but that changed a month later when Senator Barak Obama of Illinois announced his candidacy. Among other Democratic announced hopefuls, the party's 2004 vice presidential candidate, former Senator John Edwards of North Carolina also presented a credible challenge, with some wondering whether former Vice President Al Gore might emerge, especially if the nomination was in doubt when the Democratic convention convened in 2008.

Several factors will influence Clinton's prospects in 2008. First of course, she must win the nomination. As of August 2007, Clinton was favored by 40% of Democrats for the nomination, with Obama at 21%, Edwards at 12%, with the rest split among other announced and potential candidates. Clinton could stumble, though, if she does not do well in states with early tests of strength. For those, very early polls showed Clinton in a near dead with Edwards in Iowa, substantially ahead of the pack in New Hampshire, and leading Obama by only 4% in South Carolina.

As for her possible Republican opponents if she is nominated, the polls in August 2007 put her even with former New York City Mayor Rudolph Giuliani and ahead of all the other major Republican contenders by from 4% to 10%. In addition to the normal political consideration, Clinton is an unusual candidate because she is a woman and because of her high profile as a former first lady. As for the impact of gender on the campaign, only 9% of Americans say they would not vote for a woman for president. But another poll that gave respondents a bit more leeway, found 19% saying they were "somewhat" or "entirely uncomfortable" with the thought of a woman president. Yet another poll recorded 34% saying that most people they knew would not vote for a woman. Such polls are somewhat offset, however, by others that show, for instance, that 13% of Americans are "somewhat" or "much more likely" to vote for a presidential candidate because she is a woman.

Because of Clinton's high visibility, opinions on her tend to be strong. Not boding well for her, her "unfavorable" rating (49%) in August 2007 was a bit higher than her "favorable" rating (47%). Only 3% had not formed an opinion, a very low percentage that early in the race. Additionally, the electorate is moderate, and the Republicans will portray her as a liberal. In mid 2007, 53% of Americans already saw her that way. Furthermore, the liberal tag is supported by Clinton's voting record, which the liberal group Americans for Democratic Action has given a "liberal quotient" of 95%, for her first term in the Senate.

Where to Find More

Autobiographies are worth reading if not fully believing, and Hillary Clinton's is *Living History* (Simon & Schuster, 2003). In somewhat the same genre, visit her presidential campaign site at www.hillaryclinton.com/ and her Senate office site at clinton.senate.gov/. An unofficial Hillary Clinton for president organization is Votehillary at www.votehillary.org/. Directly rebutting Clinton's autobiography is *Rewriting History* (Regan Books, 2004) by Dick Morris, a former top political adviser to President Clinton. A group that takes a dim view of the senator is Against Hillary at www.againsthillary.com/.

What More to Do

Whether you support or oppose Senator Clinton, you should take a role in her campaign or in an effort to defeat her campaign to win the Democratic presidential nomination and then the White House. If you are not sure, gather information about Clinton, form an opinion, then get active.

10 VOTING/CAMPAIGNS/ELECTIONS

THE ELECTORAL COLLEGE:
Abolish *or* Preserve?

ABOLISH

ADVOCATE: Becky Cain, President, League of Women Voters

SOURCE: Testimony during hearings on "Proposals for Electoral College Reform: H.J. Res. 28 and H.J. Res. 43" before the U.S. House of Representatives Committee on the Judiciary, Subcommittee on the Constitution, September 4, 1997

PRESERVE

ADVOCATE: Judith A. Best, Professor of Political Science, State University of New York at Cortland

SOURCE: Testimony during hearings on "Proposals for Electoral College Reform: H.J. Res. 28 and H.J. Res. 43" before the U.S. House of Representatives Committee on the Judiciary, Subcommittee on the Constitution, September 4, 1997

Sometimes figuring out your course grade in college can get pretty complicated. Your raw score on tests may not exactly equate to your final "curved" grade. Determining the final score in the Electoral College can be a little like this. The raw score (the popular vote) and the final score (the vote of the electors) never match up. In 1980, for example, Ronald Reagan received 90.1% of the electors' votes, while getting only 51.6% of the popular vote. It is even possible in the Electoral College to have a higher raw score than anyone else, yet lose. Al Gore received 51,003,238 popular votes to only 50,459,624 votes for George Bush in the 2000 presidential election. Yet Bush received 50.4% of the electoral vote compared to 49.4% for Gore.

Then, like in some college grading, the Electoral College has other variables. For example, electors selected by the voters in many states can legally vote for someone other than the candidate to whom they are pledged. Such unexpected votes are not common, but they have occurred in 11 elections. Most recently, an elector from Minnesota voted for John Edwards for president even though he was the vice presidential nominee on the Democratic ticket with John Kerry. Thus the official electoral vote for 2004 was George Bush 286, John Kerry 251, John Edwards 1.

These oddities and other quirks bring up three questions. What is the Electoral College? Where did it come from? Should we keep it? The first two questions are easier. The Electoral College is an indirect process for selecting the U.S. president. Each state selects a number of electors equal to its representation in Congress, and the District of Columbia gets three electors, for a total of 538 electors. The exact process for choosing electors varies by state, but as a general rule each party or candidate selects a slate of electors. It is for one of these slates that the people vote in November. In all states except Maine and Nebraska, there is a "winner-take-all" system in which the slate that receives the most votes wins. Then the individual electors cast their separate ballots for president and vice president in December. The ballots are sent to Congress, where they are counted in early January. It takes a majority of all electoral votes (270) to win. If no individual receives a majority, then the House selects a president from among the candidates with the three highest electoral votes. Each state casts one vote in the House, and it requires a majority of the states (26) to win. The Senate, with each member voting individually, chooses a vice president from among the top two electoral vote recipients. It is not possible to detail here all the possible permutations, but the choice has gone to the House twice (1800 and 1824), and on three occasions (1876, 1888, and 2000) the candidate with the most popular votes has lost the electoral vote.

The Electoral College was established for two reasons. One is that it stressed the role of the states. They can choose electors as they wish and are not even obligated to have popular elections. The second motive for the Electoral College was to insulate the selection of president from the people. As Alexander Hamilton explained in *Federalist* #68 (1788), he and others worried that the "general mass" would not "possess the information and discernment requisite to such complicated investigations," raising the possibility of "tumult and disorder."

The question is whether to abolish or preserve the Electoral College. Throughout its history, the process has been controversial, and it has provoked over 700 proposals in Congress to reform or eliminate it. Yet it survives. The following articles lay out their respective attack on and defense of the Electoral College, but beyond those substantive arguments, the process continues for two additional reasons. One is that changing it would require a constitutional amendment, most probably through a two-thirds vote by each house of Congress and ratification by three-fourths of the state. Obtaining such supermajorities is very difficult. The second procedural reason the Elector College survives is that, for contradictory reasons, it appeals to many states. States with big populations, such as California with its 55 electoral votes (more than 20% of those needed to win), believe they gain political advantage through their hefty share of the electoral votes. States with small populations also see political advantage. Wyoming may have only 0.55% of the electoral vote, but that is more than three times the state's 0.17% of the U.S. population. States in a middle position come out mathematically about right. For example, New Jersey with 8.1 million people and 15 electoral votes has 2.86% of the population and 2.78% of the electoral votes. Thus the Electoral College can seem either politically favorable or neutral to almost every state, making an amendment even more difficult to pass and ratify.

POINTS TO PONDER

➤ Becky Cain, testifying in 1997, predicts a fiasco if, once again, a candidate were to lose the electoral vote while winning the popular vote. Three years later that occurred, yet there were no widespread protest demonstrations. Why not?

➤ Judith Best contends that abolishing the Electoral College would diminish the influence of minority groups. Why might this occur?

➤ Which is more important, the aspect of federalism that is part of the Electoral College vote calculation or the principle of "one person—one vote"?

The Electoral College:
Abolish

BECKY CAIN

Mr. Chairman, members of the subcommittee, I am Becky Cain, president of the League of Women Voters.

I am pleased to be here today to express the support of the League [League of Women Voters of the United States] for a constitutional amendment to abolish the Electoral College and establish the direct election of the President and Vice President of the United States by popular vote of the American people.

The League of Women Voters of the United States is a non-partisan citizen organization with 150,000 members and supporters in all fifty states, the District of Columbia and the Virgin Islands. For over 75 years, Leagues across the country have worked to educate the electorate, register voters and make government at all levels more accessible and responsive to the average citizen.

Since 1970, the League has supported an amendment to the Constitution that would abolish the Electoral College and establish a direct, popular vote for the President and Vice President of the United States. The League arrived at this position through its time-honored study and consensus process. Leagues in over 1,000 communities across the country participated in the study and came to the same conclusion: our method of electing a President must be changed to ensure a more representative government.

Political developments since the 1970s have only underscored the need for the elimination of the Electoral College system. The downward trend in voter participation, coupled with increased cynicism and skepticism amongst the public about the ability of elected leaders to provide meaningful representation are the warning signs of a potential electoral fiasco.

Picture if you will a future national election in which a presidential candidate receives a majority of the popular vote, but is denied the 270 votes necessary for election by the Electoral College. This has already happened once in our nation's history, when, in 1888, Grover Cleveland outpolled Benjamin Harrison in the popular vote but lost the Electoral College vote by 233 to 168. It caused a public furor then, when political office was often gained through back-room deals and closed-door maneuvering. Imagine the public outcry today, after a long primary campaign and a grueling race for the Presidency. Imagine the public's rage at being denied their candidate of choice.

Now go one step further. Consider a close three-way race for President in which no candidate earns the necessary Electoral College votes to win. This has happened twice before in our nation's history, in 1801 and 1825, when the House of Representatives chose Thomas Jefferson and John Quincy Adams, respectively. While the League believes both of these men were great presidents, we are troubled about the potential for a future presidential candidate with the highest number of popular votes to lose the election in a House of Representatives dominated by one or another political party.

In the twentieth century, we have only narrowly avoided a series of constitutional crises in which the Electoral College could have over-ruled the popular vote.

- In the 1916 presidential election, a shift of only 2,000 votes in California would have given Charles Evans Hughes the necessary electoral votes to defeat Woodrow Wilson, despite Wilson's half-million vote nationwide plurality.

- In 1948, a shift of only 30,000 votes in three states would have delivered the White House to Governor [Thomas] Dewey, in spite of the fact that he trailed President Truman by some 2.1 million popular votes.

- In 1960, a shift of only 13,000 votes in five states (5,000 in Illinois, 5,000 in Missouri, 1,200 in New Mexico, 1,300 in Nevada and 200 in Hawaii) would have made Richard Nixon president.

- In 1968, a shift of 42,000 votes in three states (Alaska, Missouri and New Jersey) would have denied Nixon an Electoral College victory and thrown the election into the House of Representatives.

- In 1976, a shift of only 9,300 votes (5,600 from Ohio and 3,700 from Hawaii) would have elected Gerald Ford, even though he trailed Jimmy Carter in the popular vote by 1.6 million ballots.

Apart from the public outcry that would be caused by a circumvention of the popular will, there are a number of other serious flaws in the Electoral College system.

The Electoral College system is fundamentally unfair to voters. In a nation where voting rights are grounded in the one person, one vote principle, the Electoral College is a hopeless anachronism.

The current system is unfair for two reasons.

First, a citizen's individual vote has more weight if he or she lives in a state with a small population than if that citizen lives in a state with a large population. For example, each electoral vote in Alaska is equivalent to approximately 112,000 people. Each electoral vote in New York is equivalent to approximately 404,000 eligible people (based on 1990 census data). And that's if everyone votes!

The system is also unfair because a citizen's individual vote has more weight if the percentage of voter participation in the state is low. For example, if only half of all people in Alaska vote, then each electoral vote is equivalent to roughly 56,000 people.

Moreover, the electoral vote does not reflect the volume of voter participation within a state. If only a few voters go to the polls, all the electoral votes of the state are still cast.

Finally, the Electoral College system is flawed because the constitution does not bind presidential electors to vote for the candidates to whom they have been pledged. For example, in 1948, 1960 and 1976, individual electors pledged to the top two vote-getters cast their votes for third place finishers and also-rans. Defecting electors in a close race could cause a crisis of confidence in our electoral system.

For all these reasons, the League believes that the presidential election method should incorporate the one-person, one-vote principle. The President should be directly elected by the people he or she will represent, just as the other federally elected officials are in this country. Direct election is the most representative system. It is the only system that guarantees the President will have received the most popular votes. It also encourages voter participation by giving voters a direct and equal role in the election of the President.

Of course, a direct popular vote does not preclude the possibility of a close three-way race in which no candidate receives a majority, or even a plurality, of the votes. The League believes that if no candidate receives more than 40 percent of the popular vote, then a national run-off election should be held.

Until there is a constitutional amendment to abolish the Electoral College, the League supports the early establishment of clear rules and procedures for the House and Senate to handle their responsibilities in electing the President and Vice President if there is no majority vote in the Electoral College.

Procedures should be established to avoid the last-minute partisan wrangling that would inevitably take place. In addition, we believe any congressional vote for President must take place in full public view, with individual representative's votes entered into the Congressional Record.

When the constitution was first written, our nation was a vastly different kind of democracy than it is today. Only white, male property owners could vote. The 15th Amendment gave black men the right to vote. The 17th Amendment provided for direct popular election of the Senate. The 19th Amendment gave women the vote. The 26th Amendment established the right of citizens 18 years of age and older to vote.

The time has come to take the next step to ensure a broad-based, representative democracy. Fairness argues for it. Retaining the fragile faith of American voters in our representative system demands it. We urge the House and the Senate to pass a constitutional amendment abolishing the Electoral College system and establishing the direct popular election of our President and Vice President.

The Electoral College:
Preserve

JUDITH A. BEST

Critics of the electoral vote system believe that the principle of democratic legitimacy is numbers alone, and therefore they think the system is indefensible. On the contrary, the electoral vote system is a paradigm—the very model—of the American democracy, and thus is quite easy to defend. For all practical purposes it is a direct popular federal election. (The Electors are mere ciphers, and the office of elector, but not the electoral votes, can be abolished.) The critics' principle of democratic legitimacy is inadequate because it is apolitical and antifederal. Logically it boils down to: the majority must win and the minority must lose no matter what they lose. It is a formula for majority tyranny. But majority rule is not the principle of our Constitution. Rather it is majority rule with minority consent. The critics, however, think that because the system does not follow an arithmetical model it may produce the "wrong" winner. In fact, I contend, because it is federal it produces the right winner.

The following passage from my recent book, *The Choice of the People? Debating the Electoral College* explains my point:

> Politics and mathematics are two very different disciplines. Mathematics seeks accuracy, politics seeks harmony. In mathematics an incorrect count loses all value once it is shown to be wrong. In politics even though some people are out-voted they still have value and must be respected in defeat. Efforts must be made to be considerate and even generous to those who lost the vote, to make then feel they are part of the community, for if they feel alienated they may riot in the streets. Further, mathematical questions, like those in all the sciences, deal with truth and falsehood. But politics is an art, not a science. Political questions do not deal primarily with truth and falsehood, but with good and bad. We do not ask whether a political decision on war or taxation or welfare or agricultural subsidies is true. We ask, is the policy good for the country? And, will it actually achieve its purpose?

> Those who confuse politics and mathematics, the head counters, operate on an unstated assumption that the will of the people is out there like some unsurveyed land, and all we need do is send out the surveyors with accurately calibrated instruments to record what is there. They also assume that our democratic republic is a ship without a specific destination. Whatever most of the people want, most of the people must get, and the minority be damned. Mathematical accuracy being their sole criterion for legitimacy, they make a great fuss about politically imposed devices, intermediary institutions like the electoral vote system with its federal principle and its winner-take-all rule. From their perspective, such majority building and structuring devices complicate their self-assigned task, distort the accuracy of their count and possibly produce the "wrong" result.

> If their assumptions were correct they would have a point. But their assumptions are false. Ours is a ship

of state bound for a port called Liberty. On such a ship majority rule doesn't suffice without the consent of the minority. Their assumption about the will of the people is particularly false in this vast and varied country, in a continental republic populated by a people who do not share a common religion, race, or ethnic heritage, in a commercial republic populated by people with diverse and competing economic interests. In such a country the will of the people and the will of the majority can be two very different things. Therefore, the will of the people—that one thing which all can share, which is the goal of liberty for all—must be constructed and periodically reconstructed. This requires a political, not a mathematical process.

In this country, it requires a federal political process. The federal principle is one of the two fundamental structural principles of our Constitution (the other being the separation of powers). The proposals to abolish the Electoral College are proposals to abolish the federal principle in presidential elections. All of our national elective offices are based on the federal principle—they are state based elections for we are a nation of states. Thus our national motto: *E Pluribus Unum*.

The federal principle in presidential elections forces presidential candidates to build broad cross-national political coalitions. Thereby it produces presidents who can govern because of their broad cross-national support. In politics as well as in physics there is such a thing as a critical mass. In presidential elections numbers of votes are necessary but not sufficient. To create the critical mass necessary for a president to govern, his votes must be properly distributed. This means he must win states and win states in more than one region of the country.

Under the federal presidential election system, a successful candidate can't simply promise everything to one section of the country and neglect the others. Analogy: Why are professional football teams required to win games in order to get into the playoffs and win the Super Bowl? Why not simply select the teams that scored the most points during the regular season? Any football fan can tell you why. Such a process wouldn't produce the right winner. Teams would run up the score against their weakest opponents, and the best teams in the most competitive divisions would have the least chance to get into the playoffs. Such a system isn't the proper test of the team talent and ability. A nonfederal election is not a proper test of support for the president.

If we abandon the federal principle in presidential elections, we will be abandoning a national consensus building device by allowing candidates to promise everything to the populous Eastern megalopolis, or to promise everything to white Christians, or to suburbanites who are now half of all the voters. These are formulas for inability to govern or even civil war. And a system, like direct popular election, based on raw unstructured numbers alone rather than on the structuring federal principle, would effectively reduce the influence of minorities who often are the swing votes in closely divided states—groups like farmers who are only 2 percent of national population or blacks who are only 12 percent.

We need to remember that when we change the rules, we change the game and the game strategy and the skills needed to win. Under the federal principle successful candidates must have consensus building skills. The goal of politics in this country is harmony—majority rule with minority consent. But when and why would a minority consent to majority rule? The answer is only if the minority can see that on some occasions and on some vital issues it can be part of the majority. It is irrational to consent to a game in which you can never win anything at all. To gain minority consent, the Framers created many devices to allow minorities to be part of the game, devices that give minorities more influence than their raw numbers would warrant including the state equality principle for representation in the Senate and the state distracting principle for the House of Representatives. (The majority party in the House is often "over-represented" if our measure is raw numbers of votes nationally aggregated.) Then, of course, there is the state equality principle in voting on constitutional amendments. And there is the three-fourths requirement for passage of amendments. Such devices are designed to give minorities an influential voice in defining the national interest. The president is a major player in defining the national interest, and therefore it is necessary that the presidency be subjected to the moderating influence of a federal election system.

An equally important outcome of a state based election system is that it serves to balance local and national interests. It is not just racial, religious, ethnic or occupational minorities that must be protected, there are local minorities whose consent must be sought; the people in small states must be protected against misuse of the phrase "the national interest." My favorite example is the problem of nuclear waste which none of us want in our backyards—not in my state. The rest of us can outvote Utah—so let's turn Utah into our national nuclear waste dump. This is majority tyranny in action. Nuclear waste is a national problem and the burden of solving it should not be placed on the people of one state without their consent. Since the president is a major player in making national policy, it is just as important that he be sensitive to balancing

national and local interests, and the federal election system is designed to make it so. The right winner is a presidential candidate who recognizes the necessity and often the justice in balancing national and local interests. As Jefferson said, "the will of the majority to be rightful must be reasonable." The federal principle even and especially in presidential elections is a device for building reasonable majorities.

The opponents of the electoral vote system are head counters who confuse an election with a census. In a census our goal is mere accuracy. We want to know how many people are married or divorced, or have incomes over or under $20,000, or are Catholic or Protestant etc. In short, we want to break down the population into its multiple individual parts. In an election, especially a presidential election, we want to bring the people together. We want to build consensus, to build the support necessary and sufficient for our president to govern.

The proponents of direct national election think their system solves problems, but in fact it creates problems that are addressed or avoided by the federal election system. Presidential elections have multiple goals. Obviously we want to fill the office with someone who can govern, but we also want a swift, sure decision, and we want to reduce the premium on fraud, and most of us want to support the two party system—a major source of national stability and a consensus, coalition-building system.

From this perspective, the current system has been very successful. Since 1836 with the almost universal adoption of the state unit rule, awarding all of a state's electoral votes to the winner of the popular plurality, we have had never had a contingency election. That's a proven record of 160 years. And we know the reason why: the magnifier effect of the state unit rule, a.k.a. the winner-take-all system. The victor in the popular vote contest for president will have a higher percentage of the electoral vote. The Magnifier effect does not exaggerate the mandate—popular vote percentages are widely reported, not electoral vote percentages. The magnifier effect is not like a fisherman's story in which the size of the fish grows with the telling. Rather it is like the strong fishing line that serves to bring the fish, whatever its size, safely to shore. It supports the moderate two-party system, and balances national and state interests. And it makes the general election the only election.

Of course, there would be no magnifier effect under direct non-federal election, and the result is that contingency elections would become the rule. Under one proposal there would be a national run off if no candidate received 50 percent of the popular vote. This provision would turn the general election into a national primary, proliferate candidacies and weaken or destroy the two-party system. It would also increase the potential for fraud and result in contested general elections with every ballot box in the United States having to be reopened and recounted under court supervision. Even the Left-handed Vegetarians Party could bring a court challenge because 1 percent or less of the popular vote could trigger a runoff election. And there would be a reason to challenge. In a runoff election even candidates who are not in the contest can win something by making a deal with one of the remaining two in return for support in the runoff. Not only would this mean an extended period of uncertainty about who the president will be—a temptation to foreign enemies, but also little time for the orderly transfer of power.

Most proponents of direct election, recognizing that to require a majority of the popular votes would produce these problems, suggest a 40 percent instead of a 50 percent runoff rule. The fact that most supporters of direct election are willing to make this concession indicates the seriousness of the problems attending contingency elections. This is a compromise of their principle—the arithmetical majority principle. Logically, on their principle, whenever no one polls 50 percent plus one vote there should be a runoff election.

And 40 percent is not a magical figure. It could be 42 or 44% with similar result—frequent runoffs. It is true that only one president, Lincoln, (who was not on the ballot in 10 states) failed to reach the 40 percent plurality figure. However, history under the current system cannot be used to support the 40 percent figure because when you change the rules you change the game. Under the current rules we have had 17 minority presidential terms—presidents who came to the office with less than 50 percent of the popular vote. The last two are Clinton's terms. The list includes some of our best presidents, not only Lincoln, but also Wilson (twice), Polk and Truman. Seventeen minority presidential terms out of 42 presidents! The unit rule magnified their popular pluralities into electoral vote majorities because they won states.

But under direct nonfederal election there would be no magnifier effect. Potential candidates would recognize that multiple entries would be likely to trigger a runoff wherein one losing candidate could win a veto promise, another a Supreme Court nomination and a third a special interest subsidy in return for an endorsement in the runoff. And there is no reason to believe all such deals would be struck in the open. There would be no incentive for coalition building prior to the general election. The two major national parties would lose all control over the presidential nomination process—their lifeblood. Factional candidates, single issue candidates, extremist candidates would serve as spoilers. As one commentator noted, on the day prior to the election, the *New York Times* would have to publish a twenty-page supplement simply to identify all the candidates.

Add to this the second chance psychology that would infect voters, and you have the formula for a national ordeal. Second chance psychology arises from the recognition that a popular vote runoff is a real possibility. Many a voter, thinking he will have another chance to vote in a runoff, will use his general election vote to protest something or other—to send a message.

Recounts would be demanded not only to determine who won, but also whether any candidate actually polled the 40% minimum, and if not which two candidates would be in the runoff. Under the unit rule magnifier effect which discourages multiple candidacies, we have already had five elections in which the popular vote margin was less than one percent. In the 1880 election the margin was one tenth of one percent. If such could happen under the current system where it is unlikely to trigger a runoff, it surely will happen under a 40 percent rule with a hair trigger runoff system. Weeks or months could pass with the outcome in doubt. One candidate could claim victory and start naming his cabinet only to be told some weeks later that he would have to participate in a runoff.

Further, the electorate wearies of prolonged elections. Even in the sports world players as well as teams reach a point where they want an end to it, and so accept sudden death rules. It is so important to fill the office on a timely basis that we have even had one president, Gerald Ford, who was not confirmed by a national election. Ford succeeded to the office on the resignation of his predecessor, Richard Nixon, but unlike vice presidents who had succeeded before him, he had been nominated by Nixon and confirmed by congressional vote under the provisions for filling vice presidential vacancies in the Twenty-fifth Amendment.

No election system is perfect, but the current system has borne the test of time. It has never rejected the winner of a popular vote majority. In every case but one it gave the victory to the winner of the popular plurality. And that one case proves the rule. Cleveland, who lost in the electoral vote, won the popular vote while running a sectional campaign. He did not seek to broaden his support; he focused his message on one section of the country. Unintentionally, he thereby sent a message about the current system to all future presidential candidates: Remember 1888! Don't run a sectional campaign! Further, he won the popular vote by only eight tenths of one percent! This was an election that verged on a tie. Since a timely decision is so important, a reasonable tiebreaker is the win states federal principle.

The proposed amendments would deform not reform the Constitution. It is not just the presidency that is at risk here if the federal principle is illegitimate in presidential elections, why isn't it illegitimate for Senate and House elections? Why should a state with half a million people have the same representation in the Senate as a state with twenty million people? Why should every state have at least one representative in the House? Why shouldn't states with very small populations have to share a representative with folks in another state? And why should each state regardless of its population size have an equal vote on constitutional amendments? The Framers knew the answer to these questions—the federal principle. It is true that the electoral vote system did not work out in precisely the fashion that the Framers anticipated, but it did evolve in conformity to the federal principle and the separation of powers. I have no doubt that they would recognize this if they were here today. It evolved in conformity with the federal spirit of the constitution, the "great discovery," the Framers themselves made.

For this, let us turn to Alexis de Tocqueville, who commenting [in *Democracy in America*, 1835] on the federal principle in the Constitution, called it "a wholly novel theory, which may be considered as a great discovery in modern political science." He goes on to explain that combines the best of both worlds. He says that its advantage is to unite the benefits and avoid the weaknesses of small and large societies. He learned this not only from observation, but also from reading James Madison in *Federalist 39*, who said that our form of government "is, in strictness, neither a national nor a federal Constitution, but a combination of both."

Madison's word "combination" is the key. The federal principle is a "great discovery," because it is a combination like an alloy—my term not his. We create alloys because we want to combine the advantages and avoid the weakness of two different things. We fuse copper and zinc to create brass because brass is harder, more malleable and more ductile than copper. We create steel alloys for the same reason. The federal system is an alloy. It not only makes us strong as a nation, it also allows us to be diverse and flexible, to experiment. It thereby increases our freedom without destroying our national unity. Tocqueville was right; it was a "great discovery" of modern political science. Let us preserve it.

THE CONTINUING DEBATE:
The Electoral College

What Is New

The country reacted mildly to the oddities of the 2000 election. When one poll asked Americans about their reaction, 51% said the outcome was "fair," 46% thought it "unfair," and 3% were unsure. Thus Americans were willing to abide by the rules. However, Americans favor changing the rules. A 2007 poll found about 72% of respondents in favor of the direct popular election of the president. There is a new movement at the state level to get around the difficulties of amending the Constitution to abolish the Electoral College. Instead, advocates are pressing states to agree to cast all their electoral votes for the winner of the national popular vote no matter how the vote within the state came out. Maryland enacted such a law in 2007, and several other state legislatures are considering similar actions.

Where to Find More

An edited book in which contributors discuss various alternatives to the Electoral College and the implications of each is Paul D. Schumaker and, Burdett A. Loomis, *Choosing a President: The Electoral College and Beyond* (Chatham House, 2002). For a defense of the Electoral College, read Gary L. Gregg's edited volume, *Securing Democracy: Why We Have an Electoral College* (Westview, 2001). A valuable Web site for further research is that of the Office of the Federal Register in the National Archives at www.archives.gov/federalregister/. The site even has an interactive function that you can use to try to predict the electoral vote count in the next presidential election. For a group advocating the popular vote option, go to the site of National Popular Vote at www.nationalpopularvote.com/.

What More to Do

Calculate your state's percentage of the national population and its percentage of the electoral vote. Based on this equation, would your state gain or lose political advantage if the Electoral College were to be abolished?

In addition to debating the future of the Electoral College, it is important to consider the alternatives. If the Electoral College were abolished, how would you determine who is on the ballot? That is now governed by state law, and the candidates vary from state to state. In 2004, there were 20 candidates on one or more state ballots. Some were one-state candidates, such as the Prohibition Party's Earl Dodge, who received 208 votes in Colorado. A national ballot qualifying procedure that was too difficult would restrict democratic choice. A standard that was too easy might replicate the gubernatorial recall election in California in 2003, with 135 candidates on the ballot. Then there is the question of what to do in races with three or more contenders. Does the candidate with the most votes win, even if that is less than 50.1%, or should there be a run-off system to eventually achieve a majority vote? Just since World War II, no presidential candidate has received a majority in 6 (1948, 1960, 1968, 1992, 1996, 2000) of the 14 presidential elections. So, if not the Electoral College, then what?

11

CONGRESS

CONGRESSIONAL TERM LIMITS:
Promoting Choice *or* Restricting Choice?

PROMOTING CHOICE

ADVOCATE: Paul Jacob, Executive Director, U.S. Term Limits

SOURCE: Testimony during hearings on "Limiting Terms of Office for Members of the U.S. Senate and U.S. House of Representatives," U.S. House of Representatives, Committee on the Judiciary, Subcommittee on the Constitution, January 22, 1997

RESTRICTING CHOICE

ADVOCATE: John R. Hibbing, Professor of Political Science, University of Nebraska

SOURCE: Testimony during hearings on "Limiting Terms of Office for Members of the U.S. Senate and U.S. House of Representatives," U.S. House of Representatives, Committee on the Judiciary, Subcommittee on the Constitution, January 22, 1997

One way this debate could have been entitled was with a riddle: "When Does Restricting Voter Choice Improve Democracy?" An alternative riddle/title might have been, "When Does Unrestricted Voter Choice Diminish Democracy?" Those who advocate limiting the number of terms members of Congress may serve argue that incumbents have advantages that make it nearly impossible for challengers to unseat them, thereby limiting the "real" choice of voters. Opponents counter that, among other drawbacks, term limits abridge the voters' democratic right to choose whomever they wish to represent them for as long as they wish.

What is certain is that once someone gets elected to Congress they have an extraordinarily good chance of being reelected again. Between 1980 and 2006, about 90% of all incumbent members of Congress sought another term. Of those who did, voters returned 93% of the representatives and 88% of the senators. Moreover, most incumbents win by large margins, especially in House races. From 2002 through 2006, only 10% of all house races were "fully contested," decided by less than a 10% margin. By contrast, while 70% were "lopsided," with the winner getting between 55% and 74.9% of the vote; and 20% were "no contest," with a candidate facing no opposition or winning by 75% or more of the vote. Margins are narrower in the more visible Senate races, but even there during the 2002–2006 election, only 32% of the races were fully contested, while 57% were lopsided, and 11% were no contest. Also undisputable is the fact that the average number of years a person spends in Congress has increased over time. Congressional Research Service data indicates that during the 1800s only 3% of representatives and 11% of senators served more than 12 years. Those figures jumped to 27% and 32% during the 1900s, and since 1947 have risen to 35% and 41% respectively.

154

There are numerous reasons why incumbents have an advantage, which, in sum, create a positive view by most people of their individual members of Congress. A 2006 survey found that 56% of respondents approved of the job their members of Congress were doing, only 27% disapproved, and 17% were not sure. This is remarkable given that only 27% of those respondents approved of the job Congress as an institution was doing, with 64% disapproving and 9% unsure.

Term limits have long limited the tenure of many chief executives. The presidency had a two-term tradition until Franklin Roosevelt sought and won four terms. Soon thereafter, the Twenty-Second Amendment (1951) made the two-term limit mandatory. Additionally, 36 states have term limits for governor. Then in an era of increased dismay by Americans over their political system, the idea of also limiting the terms of state and national legislators began to become prominent. California and Oklahoma passed the first such legislation in 1990. It was an idea whose time had come, and soon 20 other states followed suit. Most of these restrictions were enacted by direct democracy techniques, including initiatives and referendums.

Opponents of term limits quickly challenged their constitutionality. In 1995 by a 6 to 3 vote in *U.S. Term Limits, Inc. v. Thornton*, the U.S. Supreme Court struck down the limits that Arkansas (and by implication all other states) had placed on terms in the U.S. Congress. Term limits on state legislatures, by contrast, are matters primarily of state constitutional law, and in this realm, the federal courts and most state courts have upheld term limits.

The Supreme Court decision means that it would be necessary to amend the Constitution in order to limit the number of terms that members of the U.S. Senate and House of Representatives can serve. Numerous proposals to do that have been made. One common scheme would set a limit of two terms (12 years) for senators and 6 terms (12 years) for members of the House. However, none of the proposals have been able to gather the two-thirds vote needed in each house of Congress to send the amendment on to the states for ratification. After all, by supporting such an amendment, many members would be limiting their own service in Congress. Therefore, what many see as the problem of entrenched legislators remains. The senior senator in the 110th Congress, Robert Byrd, has held his seat since 1959 when Dwight D. Eisenhower was president. Dean of the House, John Dingell, Jr. began 1955 when the current president, George W. Bush was nine years old. Dingell's father, John, Sr., held the seat for the 22 years before that.

POINTS TO PONDER

➤ Consider term limits in the larger context of the balance of power between the president and Congress. Would term limits enhance or diminish Congress' relative power?

➤ Advocate John Hibbing notes that more senior members of Congress are more effective in terms of getting legislation passed. Do you think this is this because they gain expertise and political skill or because they use the power structure to limit the role of junior members?

➤ What impact do you think term limits would have on the proportion of under-represented groups (such as women and racial and ethnic minorities) in Congress?

Congressional Term Limits:
Promoting Choice

PAUL JACOB

America has one clear and decisive advantage over the rest of the world: Our political system.

Our system is a unique democratic republic with constitutional limits on the federal government. It's a system designed to maximize individual freedom and citizen control of government at all levels. Our forebears not only set up this system of protected freedoms, but also recognized the need for change, for continual reform, and for constitutional amendment in order to preserve and enhance our freedom.

George Washington said in his farewell address, "The basis of our political systems is the right of the people to make and alter their constitutions of government." President [Abraham] Lincoln explained: "The country, with its institutions, belongs to the people who inhabit it. Whenever they shall grow weary of the existing government, they can exercise their Constitutional right of amending it." As Thomas Jefferson said to those who object to amending the Constitution, "We might as well require a man to wear still the coat which fitted him when a boy."

The vast majority of Americans today want to amend their Constitution. They want congressional term limits of three terms for House members and two terms for Senators.

EXPERIENCE WITH TERM LIMITS

Term limits is not a new idea. Democracy as far back as Aristotle has known term limits, or rotation in office. Certainly our Founders appreciated rotation in office. John Adams, Ben Franklin, Thomas Jefferson all spoke to the need for limited tenure in public office. Today, term limits are the law of the land for the President, 40 state governors, 20 state legislatures and thousands of local elected officials including many large cities most notably New York and Los Angeles. Americans support congressional term limits not only for what they hope it will do to the culture in Congress, but for what it has already done at other levels of government.

According to Jody Newman, former head of the National Women's Political Caucus, "Our political system is tremendously biased in favor of incumbents." While this has slowed the progress of women and minorities into elected office, term limits are helping to bring more women, minorities and people from all walks of life into politics. This has been the case in cities like New Orleans and Kansas City where record numbers of minorities now hold office as well as the legislature in California which, according to the *Los Angeles Times*, now includes "a former U.S. Air Force fighter pilot, a former sheriff-coroner, a paralegal, a retired teacher, a video store owner, a businesswoman-homemaker, a children's advocate, an interior designer...and a number of businessmen."

Term limits are bringing more competition, and arguably fairer competition. A recent study by Kermit Daniel of the University of Pennsylvania and Joan R. Lott of the University of Chicago concluded: "California's legislative term limits have dramatically reduced campaign expenditures, while at the same time that more candidates are running for office and races are becoming more competitive. The changes are so large that more incumbents are being defeated, races are closer, more candidates are running, and there are fewer single candidate races than at any other time in our sample."

In Ohio, state legislative term limits were credited with helping pass serious ethics reform. "Term limits established a kind of public-interest momentum" according to Ohio Common Cause executive director Janet Lewis, whose group had led the fight against term limits. Robert McCord, a columnist with the *Arkansas Times* declared "the Arkansas House of Representatives has been reborn" after the state's voters enacted a six-year House limit and representatives were quick to dismantle the seniority system.

Anecdotal and empirical evidence abounds that term limits have reduced partisanship, gridlock, and special interest influence. At the same time, more people are running for office, additional reforms are following in the term limits wake, and the disastrous predictions of opponents are being quietly forgotten.

Unfortunately, Congress continues to be locked in partisan warfare, ethics problems, and largely uncompetitive elections. Congress needs term limits.

CONGRESS HAS A CONFLICT OF INTEREST

When the amendment process of the Constitution was originally debated [in 1787], delegate George Byron of Pennsylvania had tremendous vision. He saw the potential of a congressional conflict of interest and warned, "We shall never find two-thirds of a Congress voting for anything which shall derogate from their own authority and importance."

Even with consistent and overwhelming public support, about three out of four Americans believe Congress will refuse to propose a constitutional amendment for term limits. Why? Because Congress has a clear conflict of interest. Term limits is

about limiting your personal power and the power of any individual who takes your place in our system.

Most members of Congress do support the concept of term limits and have for some time. After all, Congress voted by two-thirds of both Houses to propose the Twenty-Second Amendment limiting the President to two terms, eight years, in office. More recently (in the 104th Congress) [1995–1996], 355 members of the House voted to limit committee chairs to three terms. Yet, while supporting and imposing the concept on others, many members do not want limits to apply to them personally.

The congressional conflict of interest results in many members of Congress favoring limits twice as generous as most voters, that is, if they favor any limits at all. Congress has also shown a tremendous ability for political maneuvering on the issue.

Last Congress, the House of Representatives failed to represent their constituents as term limits were defeated by outright opponents and "loved to death" by some questionable friends. The three-term House limit enacted by 15 states and supported by gigantic percentages of voters was opposed by a majority of Republicans, as well as Democrats. Only the freshman Republicans were in sync with the wishes of the American people 72 percent voting for a three-term limit, a constitutional majority itself demonstrating the benefit of regular rotation in office.

This conflict also can be found in some members' demand that Congress, rather than the voters, set the limits. As David Mason of the Heritage Foundation wrote, "At a February 28 [1995] House Judiciary Committee mark-up session on these proposals, a coalition of opponents and wavering supporters amended the McCollum bill, so that it…explicitly would preempt state term limit laws (the original bill was silent on state powers)." What Mr. Mason didn't report was Representative McCollum proposed this amendment to his own bill that would have specifically struck down the shorter term limit imposed on him by the voters of Florida. That the House GOP's point-man on the issue would seek to preempt his own state's term limit law passed by a 77 percent vote is a striking example of his conflict of interest.

The commitment of the House Republican Leadership, especially Speaker Newt Gingrich, has been the subject of much doubt. Television producer Brian Boyer, who spent a great deal of time with Gingrich while filming a 1995 documentary, said, "It was very surprising, and this was, remember, from very long conversations with Gingrich, to learn that he personally is not in favor of term limits." Gingrich's spokesperson Tony Blankley told the *American Spectator* in July of 1994 that term limits was "something conceptually [Newt] doesn't like." Columnist Robert Novak wrote in the *Washington Post*, "Republican leaders profess to want 12 years, but it is clear they prefer no limits at all."

A number of Republicans in the leadership voted against every term limit bill as did five committee chairs. Only one member of the leadership, Majority Leader Dick Armey, and only one committee chair voted for the three-term House limit passed by most states. Yet while Mr. Armey said he would have stripped a member of a committee chairmanship had they like Senator Mark Hatfield voted against the Balanced Budget Amendment, there was no such pressure brought to bear for term limits.

Freshman Michael Forbes of New York told the *New York Times* after the failed House vote, "Candidly, this leadership didn't want [term limits] anymore than the old leadership did." But the American people were not fooled—a *Washington Post*/ABC News poll found close to two-thirds believe neither Republicans nor Democrats in Congress really tried to pass term limits.

THREE TERMS VS. SIX TERMS

The question as to the proper length of the term limits is not merely: What should the limits be? Rather, the essential question is: Who should set the limits? U.S. Term Limits is dedicated to the proposition that the people, not Congress, should set the limits.

Some observers of the battle in Congress over whether House terms should be limited to three terms or six terms have posited that the term limits movement is split. This is simply not the case. The term limits movement is strongly united behind three terms. Only in Congress (and especially among longtime members whose support for any limit whatsoever is questionable) is there significant approval of six terms and fierce opposition to three terms.

Throughout the rest of America, support for three terms far surpasses support for six terms. The American people, pro-limits scholars and virtually every state term limit group in the country supports a three-term limit in the House and a two-term limit in the Senate. Poll after poll demonstrates public support for three terms over six. A 1996 Fabrizio-McLaughlin poll of 1,000 adults nationally found supporters favored three terms 81 percent to 16 percent over six terms.

Not surprisingly, election results bear this out. In every head to head vote three terms has won over six terms. Colorado voters went to the polls in 1994 and voted to lower their limits from six terms to three terms. The arguments in favor of a six-term House limit are so barren, that one such Beltway advocate brazenly and erroneously claims this is "compelling" evidence of support for the longer limit.

ONLY IN WASHINGTON

South Dakota has voted on both a 12-year House limit and a 6-year House limit in separate elections where one would not replace the other. The 6-year limit received 68 percent of the vote to 63 percent for the 12-year limit. After the Wyoming legislature voted to double its state House limits from three terms to six, voters said keep the three-term limit 54 to 46 percent. This even after the sitting governor and three former governors came out in favor of the longer limits.

In fact, the latest trend for politicians opposed to term limits is to pretend to favor term limits, but only longer ones like 12 years. In New York City, Peter Vallone, Council President and adamant term-limit opponent, was unsuccessful in his attempt to defeat term limits in 1993. Just this past election, he sought to extend the limits from eight years to twelve years. Even with a purposely slanted and misleading ballot title, the voters saw through the council's scheme and rejected this term extension. The same effort to claim support for the term limits concept in order to extend the limits has been and is being repeated in many cities and states with term limits. The voters continue to oppose these term extensions.

The intellectual support for a shorter House limit is also very substantial. A working group of 31 scholars formed by Empower America in December of 1994 studied the term limits issue and concluded, "We put term limits on our agenda, and would even go so far as to favor the specific proposal to limit terms to 6 years in the House and 12 in the Senate."

Mark Petracca, a professor at the University of California-Irvine and a leading scholar on limits, told Congress "my preference is strongly for a limit less expansive than 12 years or 6 terms in the House....A six-term or 12-year limit in the House...won't do much to deprofessionalize the House. Neither may it do much to remedy the other exigencies driving the term limits movement."

David M. Mason of the Heritage Foundation points to "Senate-envy" as the number one reason House members favor the much longer six-term limit and reminds us, "The incumbents' plea for experience only echoes arguments of term limits opponents."

Senator Fred Thompson of Tennessee pointed out one of the reasons people oppose a six-term limit and support three terms. In his 1995 House and Senate testimony, he stated, "Limiting House Members to six terms, instead of the three terms as I have proposed, would leave the seniority system intact and do little to level a playing field that has huge advantages for incumbents." Missouri Senator John Ashcroft recognizes a three-term limit would reduce the incentive for gerrymandering congressional districts for the benefit of incumbents, stating, "it would be one of several benefits exclusive to the 3/2 term proposal..."

Of the major Republican candidates for president in 1996, Lamar Alexander, Pat Buchanan, Steve Forbes, Phil Gramm, and Alan Keyes all supported a limit of three House terms. As Pat Buchanan told the Senate, "Now, what about this 12-year proposal? Well, let me associate myself with what...Lamar Alexander...said. I am unalterably opposed to 12 years. I am for 6 years and out. I know that folks say let's treat both Houses the same way. But the Founding Fathers did not treat both Houses the same way."

There are a plethora of other important policy reasons for enacting a three-term limit as opposed to six terms. Three-term limits will mean greater turnover, more competitive elections, more and quicker campaign reform, and a larger dose of fiscal sanity.

The "Legislative Backgrounder" attached as an appendix to this testimony details further evidence of the public policy benefits associated with a three-term rather than six-term limit.

In reality, many in Congress supposedly favoring a six-term limit appear to not support term limits at all. Representative Bill Barrett of Nebraska has supported the six-term McCollum bill, but wrote in 1995, "I understand voters are frustrated and dissatisfied with the performance of Congress, but I doubt term limits are the answer." Another cosponsor of the McCollum bill is Representative David Camp of Michigan who like Barrett voted against the three-term limits passed in his state. Camp told the *Michigan Midland Daily News* [May 23, 1995], "Voters understand that if they want to limit a member of Congress' term, they can vote for the opponent." These are not the statements of term limit enthusiasts.

In the face of popular and intellectual reasons that three-term limits are superior, the main argument advanced by the longer limit advocates in Congress is that they will simply refuse to support any limits shorter than 6 terms regardless of any support or rationale evidenced against them. This is presented as realism and practicality, but at its core it's the intellectual integrity of a hijacker. Congress in such a case is saying, "The people may have right on their side, but we have the power to ignore them."

INFORMED VOTER LAWS

Nobel prize-winning economist Milton Friedman recognizes the congressional conflict, but also appreciates the ingenuity o f the American people in declaring, "Congress is never, not in a million years, going to impose term limits on itself unless it has to."

After the vote in the House in 1995, the American people understood they would have to take matters into their own hands, and they did. The result? In 1996, nine states passed Informed Voter Laws sometimes called Term Limits Accountability Laws. These states are Alaska, Arkansas, Colorado, Idaho, Maine, Missouri, Nebraska, Nevada and South Dakota.

The laws are very simple. First, they instruct members of Congress to support a specific 3/2 term limits amendment written precisely in the initiative. With differing opinions among members of Congress in the past, and the built-in conflict of interest, the voters of these states seek to make the term limits amendment they want explicitly clear.

Secondly, these laws create a procedure for informing the voters if their instructions on term limits are simply disregarded. If members from these states fail to support the 3/2 amendment or attempt to enact watered-down limits longer than 3/2, the Secretary of State will inform the voters by printing "DISREGARDED VOTER INSTRUCTION ON TERM LIMITS" next to the incumbents' names on the ballot.

Candidates who are not incumbents are allowed to sign a pledge to abide by the voters' instructions when they file for the office. If they do not so pledge, the voters will again be informed by the Secretary of State printing "DECLINED TO PLEDGE TO SUPPORT TERM LIMITS" next to their name on the ballot.

Some will argue these laws are unconstitutional. The opponents of term limits have long used the lawsuit as their primary weapon. Already the voters are being sued by special interests and politicians in a number of states trying to overturn the people's vote. But let me suggest the courts will not save politician-kind this time.

Prior to the 1996 election, the Arkansas Supreme Court declared the state's Informed Voter Initiative unconstitutional and removed it from the ballot. The state court argued the measure would cause "potential political deaths" if elected officials did not heed the instructions of an informed public. To this end, I can only say I certainly hope so. But the U.S. Supreme Court did not allow the Arkansas court to deny the people a vote on this measure. In a highly unusual move, the High Court 7 to 2 issued an emergency stay of the state court decision and the voters got their opportunity to cast ballots for or against the Informed Voter Law.

On November 5, more than 60 percent of Arkansans voted to add the Term Limits Informed Voter amendment to their state constitution. Now the U.S. Supreme Court has been petitioned to take the case, and we believe the people of Arkansas will prevail on the merits.

The response to these Informed Voter Laws has been universal shock and horror from the political establishment. What is there to cause such objection? These laws offer congressmen non-binding instructions from the people they work for and are charged with representing. The republican right of instruction is nothing new and surely no elected official could object to his or her constituents making their desires known regarding their government and their very own representative.

The informational aspect of the initiative has been attacked as the Scarlet Letter. Yet term limit enemies do not argue the information is anything but accurate. Their claims that such an "instruct and inform" tactic is coercive are all predicated on their understanding that the public deeply favors term limits and will likely use the accurate information to oppose those not representing their position. Do incumbents have a right to block truthful information harmful to them from the voting public? If citizens are free to make their instructions known, are they to be denied any knowledge as to how their elected representatives have acted? There is no public good in promoting public ignorance on term limits.

Some have argued that the voters will demand similar information on a whole host of issues. They imagine ballot information such as "VOTED TO RAISE TAXES" or "SUPPORTED CONGRESSIONAL PAY RAISE" next to candidates' names. What if it were so? Isn't public education a good thing? If the voters want more information, then they should have it. Yet, similar voter instructions were given and ballot notations used 90 years ago by the Progressives in pursuit of the Seventeenth Amendment for popular election of U.S. Senators and not until now on term limits have citizens returned to this device. The reasons are obvious. Voters understand they must call the tune if they can hope to overcome the political self-interest of members on the issue.

Harry Truman was called "Give 'em Hell Harry." But Truman remarked, "I never did give anybody hell. I just told the truth and they thought it was hell." These Informed Voter Laws likewise only tell the truth, and while they have popular support, term limits opponents will think they're hell. With public knowledge, politicians lose their wiggle-room on an issue that truly matters to voters.

The American people want a constitutional amendment for a three-term limit in the House and a two-term limit in the Senate. The sooner this body proposes such an amendment, the sooner Congress can be reconnected to this great country. For as the great Englishman Edmund Burke said: "In all forms of Government the people [are] the true legislator."

I ask you to put aside all political games and offer a proposal the American people have endorsed. If this Congress chooses to vote it down, so be it. At least the people will have a clean vote on real term limits.

Congressional Term Limits:
Restricting Choice

John R. Hibbing

I urge you to do what you can to keep the terms of members of Congress from being limited to a set number. I will organize my case against term limits around three points: the value of congressional experience, the uncertain consequences of term limits for representation, and the inability of term limits to improve the public's opinion of Congress.

CONGRESSIONAL EXPERIENCE

The term limit movement believes it is important to have a constant infusion of "new blood" in Congress lest the body become stale and set in its ways. Opponents of term limits worry that too much new blood would lead to a decrease in both legislative quality and institutional memory as inexperienced members wrestle with devilishly complex issues. Which side is correct? What is the optimal level of membership turnover for an institution like Congress? Most of the debate on these questions has proceeded without any firm evidence for the value of congressional experience. I would like to interject some evidence now.

About 10 years ago, I attempted to determine the manner in which members of this house changed as their careers in Congress unfolded. I found that, with a few exceptions of course, most members did not change much ideologically. Liberals stayed liberal and conservatives stayed conservative. Early career roll call patterns were good predictors of late career roll call patterns. Surprisingly, perhaps, early career electoral results were also good predictors of late career electoral results. It is not the case

that many members transform marginal seats into safe seats. The chances of losing office because of an election are nearly as great for senior members as they are for junior members. Attention to the district, as measured by the number of trips home, diminishes with increasing tenure but only by a little. Most senior members work quite hard at maintaining a presence in the district. Finally, the odds of a member being involved in some type of scandalous behavior do not increase with tenure. Junior members are just as likely as senior members to be scandal-ridden. The popular vision of an inert, uncaring, corrupt, and electorally unchallengeable senior member is simply inaccurate. On each of these counts, senior members are almost no different from junior members.

This statement does not apply, however, when attention shifts to legislative activity, that is, actually formulating and passing legislation. Here I found substantial differences between junior and senior members. Senior members, it turns out, are the heart and the soul of the legislative process. They are more active on legislation (giving speeches, offering amendments, and sponsoring bills), they are more specialized (a greater portion of their legislative attention goes to a focused substantive area), and they are more efficient (a greater percentage of their legislation becomes law). These patterns, I might add, persist even when senior members do not become leaders on committees or subcommittees, so it is not just that member activity reflects the positions of power that some senior members hold. The reasons for altered legislative contributions are broader than that and have to do, simply, with increased legislative experience.

Now, I will be the first to admit that many of these indicators of legislative involvement are badly flawed. It is impossible to measure quantitatively a representative's overall legislative contribution. As members know better than anyone, the legislative process is too rich and subtle to be captured by counting speeches or calculating legislative batting averages. But we must try to understand the relative contributions of senior members if we are to know the consequences of statutorily prohibiting the service of senior members, and here it can be said with some confidence that senior members have more active, focused, and successful legislative agendas. Junior members tend to introduce bills on topics about which they know very little. The subject matter of these bills is all over the map and the bills have precious little chance of making it out of committee let alone becoming law. These are empirical facts. We need more senior members; not fewer.

UNCERTAINTY ABOUT CONSEQUENCES

Many people support the term limit movement because they believe it would make members more responsive to the people. The argument is that Congress has grown out of touch and that if members served only short time periods, along the lines of the citizen legislatures of old, they would be more in touch with the needs and concerns of ordinary people. But there are others who support the term limit movement for exactly the opposite reason. [Columnist] George Will is probably the best-known proponent of the position that term limits should be enacted in order to make Congress less sensitive to the desires of ordinary people. Will and others believe that mandatory term limits would embolden representatives, giving them the nerve to go against public opinion. Only when members know their stint in Congress will soon end, the argument is, will members stop pandering to unrealistic public demands for both lower taxes and more government services. I do not know which side is correct about the consequences of term limits for the proximity of Congress to the people but I do know that the inability of those in the term limit movement to agree amongst themselves on whether Congress is too close or not close enough to the people together with their inability to know whether term limits would in actuality reduce or increase the distance between the people and their Congress should give us pause. Before we enshrine a reform in the Constitution of the United States, should we not at least expect the champions of that reform to know what they want to accomplish?

Public Opinion of Congress

My current research interests have to do with the reasons the public tends to be displeased with Congress. People believe Congress has been captured by special interests, extremist parties, and professionalized politicians and that ordinary folks have been lost in the shuffle. They want changes that would restore the public's role in the process. The only way we can restore public confidence in Congress, some reformers argue, is to enact measures, like term limits, that are central to the public's populist agenda.

It is my belief that term limits would not improve the public's opinion of Congress in the long run. Much public unrest stems from the belief that Congress creates conflict. The common notion is that agreement exists among the masses but that when special interests, parties, and ambitious politicians come together in Congress they manage to construct disagreement where it need not exist. But the truth of the matter is that, while interest groups, parties, and politicians sometimes create conflict, most of the time they only reflect the people's diverse views. Survey research indicates clearly that people are deeply divided over how to solve almost every major societal problem. This disagreement would exist whether or not term limits were enacted. In fact, I contend the public would be even more disillusioned than they are currently once they saw political conflict continuing unabated long after term limits were enacted.

The real solution is to educate people on the extent of their own disagreements and on the difficulties faced by elected officials in moving from these disagreements to responsible, brokered solutions to problems. People harbor beliefs that reforms such as term limits will be able to reduce conflict and the accompanying deliberation (bickering) and compromise (selling out) that they find so objectionable. Nothing could be further from the truth. Rather than pretending there is a magic solution to political conflict, we need to educate the people on the necessity of having learned, experienced legislators who can work their way through the challenging assignment of coming to agreement in the face of public ignorance and uncertainty.

THE CONTINUING DEBATE:
Congressional Term Limits

What Is New

The 2006 elections demonstrate the relative safety of incumbents. Even though the elections were something of a political earthquake, with the Republican losing control of both Houses of Congress to the Democrats, the vast majority of incumbents ran for reelection and won. In the House, 92% of the incumbents ran, and of them, 94% were reelected. Among the 33 senators whose terms were expiring, 88% ran again, 79% were reelected. Moreover, the individual races were only marginally more competitive than their usual low norm, with only 26% of the U.S. Senate elections and 15% of the House races decided by less than a 10% margin. Furthermore, even after the influx of 79 new members of the House and 10 new senators, the average member of the House has 10 years service, and the average Senator has 13 years. Thus if the 10-year House limit and 12-year Senate limits were put into place, most members of both chambers would not be eligible to run again in 2008.

In recent years, term-limit advocates had more defeats than victories. The "informed voter measures" favored by advocate Paul Jacobs did not withstand the test of constitutionality. Those in Missouri were challenged and ruled unconstitutional by the U.S. Supreme Court in *Cook v. Gralike* (2001). As for term limits on state legislators, the number of states with them has decreased to 15 since 1997. Four state supreme courts (Massachusetts, Oregon, Washington, and Wyoming) struck them down as violating their respective state constitutions. Idaho's legislature repealed limits in 2002, and Utah's legislature followed suit in 2003. The last states to hold a referendum on term limits were Mississippi in 1999 and Nebraska in 2000. In Mississippi, 55% of the voters rejected term limits, making the state the first to do so by direct democracy. Taking the opposite stand, 56% of Nebraska's voters supported term limits. A final note is that the concept remains popular with the public. When a 2003 survey asked about them for state elected officials, 67% of the respondents said term limits were a "a good idea," 27% thought them a "bad idea," 3% replied "it depends," and 4% were unsure.

Where to Find More

A good new study that presents a series of empirical studies of the impact of term limits on state legislatures is Rick Farmer, John David Rausch, Jr., and John C. Green (eds.), *The Test of Time: Coping with Legislative Term Limits* (Lexington, 2003). U.S. Term Limits, the group represented by advocate Paul Jacob, has a helpful Web site at www.ustl.org/. You can also find good information on the site of the National Conference of State Legislators at www.ncsl.org/programs/legman/about/termlimit.htm.

What More to Do

Apply the abstract idea of terms limits to the current Congress by assuming a 10-year limit for members of the House and a 12-year limit for senators. Consider your two senators and one member of the House and also identify one or more other members of Congress whom you admire or who, because of their seniority, are powerful advocates of positions you support. If these people were at or over the term limit at the next election in 2008, would you want them to be forced to retire because of term limits?

12 PRESIDENCY

COMMUTING THE PRISON SENTENCE OF "SCOOTER" LIBBY:
Justice Served *or* Abuse of Power?

JUSTICE SERVED

ADVOCATE: David B. Rivkin, Jr., Partner, Baker Hostetler, LLP and former member, White House Counsel's Office

SOURCE: Testimony during hearings on "Use and Misuse of Presidential Clemency Power for Executive Branch Officials" before the U.S. House of Representatives, Committee on the Judiciary, July 11, 2007

ABUSE OF POWER

ADVOCATE: Douglas A. Berman, William B. Saxbe Designated Professor of Law, Moritz College of Law, The Ohio State University

SOURCE: Testimony during hearings on "Use and Misuse of Presidential Clemency Power for Executive Branch Officials" before the U.S. House of Representatives, Committee on the Judiciary, July 11, 2007

One of the lesser-known powers of the president is the ability to intervene in the judicial process by reducing or even nullifying fines and prison sentences. The authority to do so is based on Article II, Section 2 of the Constitution, which empowers the president to "grant reprieves and pardons for offenses against the United States, except in cases of impeachment." Pardons wipe out a person's guilt and criminal record. Reprieves shorten or eliminate a sentence. They are collectively referred to as clemency. Note that pardons and reprieves apply only to criminal cases (and not to civil cases) and only to federal cases (and not state and local cases). Also, pardons can only be issued for acts that have already occurred. That is they cannot be issued to exempt someone from prosecution for a criminal act they have not yet committed. However, pardons do not require trial and conviction. They can be granted any time after an act, even if no changes have been filed. In perhaps the most famous pardon in history, President Gerald Ford pardoned former President Richard Nixon "for all offenses against the United States which he, Richard Nixon, has committed or may have committed or taken part in during the period from January 20, 1969 through August 9, 1974," the period in which Nixon was president. Oddly, this means you can be pardoned for something you presumably did not do under the "innocent until proven guilty" standard.

Historically, presidents have granted clemency in over 28,000 cases, an average of almost 200 a year, with pardons much more common than reprieves. In recent decades, though, an emphasis on being tough on crime has greatly reduced the incidence of clemency. President Harry Truman averaged 265 acts of clemency each year; Jimmy Carter averaged 141, and Bill Clinton averaged 54. The two Presidents Bush have been by far the least forthcoming with clemency since World War II. Both average only 19 grants, with the younger Bush's record reflecting 2001–2006.

Most pardons are given to people who committed minor crimes long ago and have lived exemplary lives since then. But some pardons have been politically important and even controversial. For example, 54% of Americans opposed Jimmy Carter's clemency for those who had evaded the draft during the Vietnam War, and 60% of Americans disapproved of the pardon that Gerald Ford gave to Richard Nixon.

The act of clemency at issue in this debate was given by President George W. Bush to I. Lewis "Scooter" Libby after he received a 30-month sentence for committing perjury before a grand jury, for lying to FBI agents, and for obstructing a federal investigation, and after the courts rejected Libby's attempt to remain free pending an appeal of this conviction. Bush's commutation wiped away the prison sentence but left in place a $250,000 fine. Until 2006, Libby had been chief of staff to Vice President Richard Cheney. A Yale Law School graduate, Libby also served in various positions in the Departments of State and Defense.

The background to Libby's cased began in 2003 when retired diplomat Joseph Wilson charged in a *New York Times* article that the Bush administration had exaggerated the possibility of an Iraqi nuclear weapons program in order to justify the invasion. Stories soon surfaced in the press identifying Wilson's wife, Valerie Plame, as a Central Intelligence Agency (CIA) operative. Many suspected that White House officials had leaked Plame's status to get back at Wilson. Whatever the motive, disclosing an intelligence agent's name violates federal law. Therefore, the Department of Justice began a grand jury probe led by Special Prosecutor Patrick Fitzgerald, a U.S. Attorney from Chicago.

Libby was not convicted for having disclosed Plame's position, but rather for repeatedly claiming he had first heard about Plame's CIA connection from a journalist, when, in fact, he learned about it from Vice President Cheney. Oddly no one was charged for leaking Plame's name even though it is clear that at least one official, Deputy Secretary of State Richard Armitage, and perhaps others, including White House counselor Karl Rove, had done so. Indeed the only person to go to jail regarding the case was *New York Times* reporter Judith Miller. She had reported that Plame was connected to the CIA, and served 12 weeks in jail for contempt of court for refusing to identify her source—Libby—until he released her from her pledge of confidentiality.

POINTS TO PONDER

➤ What are the arguments for and against giving presidents the unchallengeable authority to pardon criminal for their acts.

➤ What impact, if any, should a convicted felons earlier "good works," such as long service in government, have on their sentence?

➤ Do you find any validity with the charge by some that in prosecuting Libby, the special prosecutor was trying to save face in light of the fact that he could not gather enough evidence to meet his main goal of charging those who disclosed Plame's CIA connection?

Commuting the Prison Sentence of "Scooter" Libby: Justice Served

DAVID B. RIVKIN, JR.

I want to express my gratitude to [the committee's leaders] for inviting me to appear before you today to participate in the hearing on President Bush's use of his pardon power to commute the prison sentence of the former chief of staff to Vice President Cheney, Scooter Libby. Let me say at the outset that nobody can seriously argue that, with the single exception of impeachment cases, the president's pardon power is not absolute on its face or that it cannot be exercised by the president in any and all policy contexts, so long as the underlying offense involves violations of federal law. Indeed, the concerns that have been expressed about this commutation are primarily of a policy nature and go to the propriety of the commutation of Mr. Libby's prison sentence and the context in which it was issued. My bottom line view is that, given all the facts and circumstances involved in [special prosecutor] Patrick Fitzgerald's investigation and prosecution of Mr. Libby, the commutation of his sentence at this time by the president is entirely appropriate. Indeed, it is my hope that, in due course, the president will take the next step and issue a full pardon to Mr. Libby.

Let me go through the policy arguments that have been raised against the president's action and outline for you some suitable rebuttals. First, let's take the issue of timing of the commutation, since many critics have suggested that it was premature. The simple answer is that, following [U.S. District Court] Judge [Reggie B.] Walton's decision not to allow the continuation of bail for Mr. Libby

[while] his appeal [was pending before D.C. Circuit of the U.S. Federal Courts of Appeals], and the rejection by the D.C. Circuit of Mr. Libby's challenge to this decision, he was subject to an immediate incarceration. In this regard, I recognize that Judge Walton's decision was entirely within his discretion—there is no constitutionally-protected right to bail following conviction. Accordingly, the D.C. Circuit's affirmation of this decision is also quite legally correct. Nevertheless, in my view, it was unnecessarily harsh.

Second is the criticism that the commutation of Mr. Libby's sentence, imposed after the jury found him guilty of perjury and obstruction of justice, somehow evinces disregard for the rule of law or, at the very least, trivializes what are properly considered to be serious violations of federal law. Let me stipulate that perjury and obstruction of justice are indeed major transgressions and ought to be taken seriously. By the same token, the very nature of the pardon power presupposes the president's ability to pardon individuals convicted of serious violations of federal law; there is no suggestion in the Constitution that only minor offenses ought to be a proper subject for the exercise of the pardon power.

More fundamentally, I believe that the pardon power, when properly deployed, advances the cause of justice. The Framer's understood that justice under the law, the justice of rules, procedures and "due process," while important to our system of "ordered" liberty, is not the only conceivable form of justice. They wanted the political branches to render a different kind of justice, driven by the considerations of equity and not by rules. It is the closest we come today to what the founders [of the country] would have called the natural law-driven justice. The president's pardon power is one example of such justice; the ability of Congress to pass private bills, which sidestep the rules governing immigration or land acquisition, is another.

The pardon power is, of course, inherently selective—it does critics no good to complain that thousands of people seek it, but only a few obtain favorable results. It is inherently discretionary, and is an extraordinary remedy to advance what the president exercising it believes to be in the best interests of justice. The fact that somebody was prosecuted and convicted by the jury of his peers, in accordance with the established evidentiary and other judicial procedures, suggests, in most instances, that justice was done. Unfortunately, there are some instances where this is not the case.

This is not, by the way, to criticize our criminal justice system, which is, probably, the fairest and most defendant-friendly system in today's world. However, any rule-based system, no matter how well-managed and operated, inevitably, albeit very occasionally, produces less than perfect results. There are instances where obviously guilty individuals go free, and there are occasions where individuals, who should not have been prosecuted at all, end up being convicted.

In my view, there are several reasons why the entire prosecution of Mr. Libby did not evolve in a way that could have promoted justice or ended up promoting justice. This, incidentally, is not meant to impugn the integrity of any of the participants in what, in my view, became a rather tragic process. Prosecutor Fitzgerald is undoubtedly an honorable man, and, by

all accounts, does not have a partisan bone in his body. The same is true about Judge Walton, and I have no doubt that the jury was fair and conscientious in its deliberations. The problems reside elsewhere.

The most important and consequential problem was the decision to appoint a special counsel to investigate this matter in the first place. This step was particularly regrettably, since the senior DOJ [Department of Justice] officials knew, prior to tapping Mr. Fitzgerald, that the leak of Valerie Plame's name to the columnist Robert Novak—the ostensible basis of the CIA's referral of the matter to the Department of Justice—was effected by the Deputy Secretary of State Dick Armitage and that Mr. Fitzgerald either learned about this fact at the time he was appointed and likewise. Also, it appears that shortly after his appointment, Mr. Fitzgerald knew that the very reason for his appointment—alleged violation of IIPA [Intelligence Identities Protection Act of 1982]—was in error, since Ms. Wilson was not a covert agent within the meaning of the IIPA. More generally, as I have written and argued on other occasions, the appointment of a special or independent counsel, no matter the probity and virtue of the individual involved, invariably skews the exercise of prosecutorial discretion and is virtually guaranteed to produce less than optimal results. It fosters time and again a "leave no stone unturned," protracted, costly, and Inspector Javier-like pursuit of the individual being investigated. Yet, doing justice is not a mechanical process and it must always be informed by a sound exercise of prosecutorial discretion. [The reference to Inspector Javier is unclear, but it may refer to Inspector Jefe Javier Falcón, the main character is the Robert Wilson's murder mystery novels such as *The Vanished Hands* and *The Hidden Assassins*.]

Here, we have a situation where a special counsel spent several years and millions of taxpayer dollars all because he believed that Mr. Libby might have lied to him or to his investigators when they investigated a "crime" they already knew had not been committed. In the process, the special counsel caused a great deal of harm to the ability of reporters to ply their business—which is a core element of our body polity's overall system of political and institutional checks and balances. I emphasize the word "might" because, quite aside from the frailties of human memory, Mr. Fitzgerald could not have known for sure at the time he went after Judith Miller (a *New York Times* reporter), Matt Cooper [of *Time* magazine], and other media figures that Mr. Libby's account of having heard first from reporters of Ms. Plame's work and her alleged role in organizing her husband's trip to Niger was false. That conclusion on his part necessarily had to await until he successfully coerced the reporters involved. Ask yourself whether a regular DOJ prosecutor, not wearing a special counsel hat, would have done this.

And, to those who say that, given Mr. Libby's high-government position, a regular government prosecutor would have been just as relentless as Mr. Fitzgerald, my response is look at how the Department of Justice's career attorneys (in the Public Integrity section) treated another high-ranking official, President Clinton's former National Security Advisor, [Samuel R.] Sandy Berger. There is no dispute about what Mr. Berger has done, since he admitted, after some time lapsed, to such transgressions as stealing highly classified documents from the National Archives, destroying at least some of them, and lying about it to executive branch officials. What he did certainly amounted to an obstruction of justice, providing misleading and

false information to Executive branch officials, and several other serious criminal law transgressions. The only reason perjury is not on my list is because Mr. Berger was not put in the position where he had to testify under oath.

Yet, presented with all of these facts, the career attorneys in the Department of Justice decided not to prosecute him and settled for the imposition of a fine on Mr. Berger, as well as the forfeiture for a period of years of his security clearance. My point here is not to suggest that Mr. Berger was treated too leniently; rather it is to suggest that Mr. Libby was treated too harshly. In my view, when two senior government officials, who have been accused or suspected of having engaged in a substantially similar conduct—in neither case was personal enrichment or any other pecuniary consideration an issue—receive a dramatically different treatment from our criminal justice system, we cannot say that justice was done.

This brings me to my last point, which has been trumpeted by the critics of the president's commutation of Mr. Libby's sentence—why wasn't he exonerated by the jury, since juries are often swayed by arguments that a particular defendant was treated overly harshly by the government or was made a scapegoat for the transgressions of others. Indeed, Mr. Libby's lawyers have tried to deploy some arguments along these lines and yet, did not succeed. In my view, the reason for this has to do with how Mr. Fitzgerald chose to present his case to the jury. He did so ably, and without violating his ethical obligations; yet, in my view, it was done in a way that was fundamentally unfair and sealed Mr. Libby's fate with the jury.

Jurors are human beings and as human beings want to understand a defendant's motivations. As a result, the overall narrative provided by the prosecutor, the context if you will, is extremely important. In Mr. Libby's case, Mr. Fitzgerald presented the jury the following damning narrative—there was a nefarious effort in the White House to destroy Joe Wilson's reputation and even to punish him, by allegedly hurting the career of his wife Valerie Plame; these activities were a part and parcel of the broader effort to sell the Iraq war to the American people. While I believe this narrative to be fundamentally false, it proved successful with the jury.

The fact that the critics of the president's decision to commute Mr. Libby's sentence invariably invoke the broad narrative of the alleged White House Iraq war-related nefarious activities, underscores how unfair and politicized this whole exercise has been.

To summarize, since, in my opinion, Mr. Libby's prosecution led to a fundamentally unjust result, the use of the pardon power to remedy the injustice, if only partially at this time, was an entirely correct and proper exercise of the president's powers.

Commuting the Prison Sentence of "Scooter" Libby: Abuse of Power

Douglas A. Berman

Thank you for this opportunity to share my perspective on President George W. Bush's sudden and surprising decision to commute entirely the prison term of I. Lewis "Scooter" Libby.

As I will explain, President Bush's commutation was fundamentally a sentencing decision—a sentencing decision that is peculiar and suspect on its own terms, and a sentencing decision that is inconsistent with the Justice Department's stated sentencing policies, with arguments federal prosecutors make in courts across the nation every day, and with the equal justice principles Congress has pursued in modern sentencing reforms....[B]ecause the president's commutation shines light on some troublesome consequences of peculiar use of the clemency power, I urge this Committee to seize this unique political moment to consider ways Congress might improve the process of, and public respect for, executive clemency decision-making.

I. THE COMMUTATION IS A PECULIAR AND SUSPECT SENTENCING DECISION.

President Bush's official statement which accompanied his clemency decision sets out some reasons for his decision to commute entirely the prison term of Mr. Libby. [Presidential Press Secretary] Tony Snow and other White House officials have subsequently provided additional details about the president's thinking and the nature of his decision. These explanations make clear that the president's commutation is fundamentally a sentencing decision. But, upon careful review, the commutation is revealed to be a peculiar and suspect sentencing decision given the president's own statements about the Libby case and U.S. District Judge Reggie Walton's determination that Mr. Libby should receive a significant term of imprisonment for his crimes.

A. The President's explanation for commuting Mr. Libby's prison term

President Bush's official statement notes the "serious convictions of perjury and obstruction of justice" in Mr. Libby's case. The statement stresses the importance of the investigation into the leaking of Valerie Plame's name and describes Special Counsel Patrick Fitzgerald as "a highly qualified, professional prosecutor who carried out his responsibilities as charged." President Bush's statement also expresses "respect" for the jury's verdict and asserts that "if a person does not tell the truth, particularly if he serves in government and holds the public trust, he must be held accountable." President Bush emphasizes that "our entire system of justice relies on people telling the truth." Taken together, these statements indicate that the president has no public concerns about either the investigation or the prosecution that led to Mr. Libby's "serious convictions."

Though lauding Mr. Fitzgerald's investigation and prosecution and the jury's work, President Bush's statement criticizes U.S. District Judge Reggie Walton's sentencing decision. The president's statement asserts that "the district court rejected the advice of the probation office," which apparently suggested a sentence in the range of 15–21 months' imprisonment. The president then explains that he has "concluded that the prison sentence given to Mr. Libby is excessive" and has decided to commute the 30-month prison term imposed by Judge Walton.

Seeking to justify this decision, the president claims that Mr. Libby is still subject to "a harsh punishment" because his commutation leaves in place the fine and supervision term ordered by Judge Walton. President Bush's statement also stresses collateral consequences—the damage to his reputation and his family's suffering—from Mr. Libby's convictions.

Providing a further account of the president's commutation decision, White House spokesman Tony Snow made these points in a July 5th *USA Today* commentary:

> The president believes pardons and commutations should reflect a genuine determination to strengthen the rule of law and increase public faith in government....In reviewing the case, the president chose to rectify an excessive punishment, and at the same time, the president made clear that he would not second-guess the jury that found Libby guilty.

B. Peculiar and suspect aspects of the President's sentencing decision

The president's stated reasons for commuting all of Mr. Libby's prison are hard to understand and harder to justify. Mr. Libby's prison term was set at the bottom of the sentencing range suggested by the federal guidelines created by the U.S. Sentencing Commission; this prison term was recommended by an experienced prosecutor and selected by an experienced federal district judge. In other words, the

president's conclusion that Mr. Libby's prison term was "excessive" contradicts the recommendation of an expert sentencing agency and the determinations of the prosecutor and judge most familiar with the details of Mr. Libby's criminal offenses and personal circumstances. Notably, under existing precedents, the U.S. Court of Appeals for the D.C. Circuit would have considered Mr. Libby's 30-month prison term—and even a longer within-guideline term—"presumptively reasonable" on appeal.

Unlike some other high-profile cases which have led to calls for the president to exercise his clemency powers, the prison sentence in Mr. Libby's case was not the product of a mandatory sentencing provision. Rather, under federal statutes, Judge Walton could have imposed a lower sentence or a sentence as high as the statutory maximum of 25 years' imprisonment. In the exercise of his discretion, however, Judge Walton was obliged to consider the guideline range of 30–37 months' imprisonment and was required to select a sentence he judged "sufficient, but not greater than necessary" to achieve the purposes of punishment Congress has set forth in [law].

Judge Walton reached his sentencing decision after reviewing a detailed pre-sentencing report, lengthy sentencing memoranda from the parties, and hundreds of letters from interested persons. Judge Walton also held a sentencing hearing in which he heard arguments from the parties and provided Mr. Libby an opportunity to address the court directly. Judge Walton thereafter determined that a 30-month prison sentence for Mr. Libby, in addition to a sizeable fine and a post-imprisonment term of supervision, was appropriate in light of federal sentencing law and policy

Judge Walton's sentencing determinations would appear to vindicate President

Bush's stated view that "serious convictions of perjury and obstruction of justice," especially when committed by a person who "serves in government and holds the public trust," call for "a harsh punishment." Moreover, Judge Walton's selection of a prison term at the very bottom of the calculated guideline range suggests that he was attentive to collateral personal consequences that Mr. Libby's prosecution and convictions necessarily produce. Nevertheless, Judge Walton still concluded that a 30-month prison term was "sufficient, but not greater than necessary" to achieve the punishment goals Congress set out in [law].

Of course, defendants and their attorneys often complain that sentences imposed within guidelines ranges are excessive, and they frequently appeal within-guideline sentences claiming that they are unreasonably long. In thousands of such appeals in recent years, however, no federal appellate court has declared a single within-guideline sentence to be unreasonably long. Indeed, since the Supreme Court's 2005 decision in *United States v. Booker*, the vast majority of sentences imposed above the guidelines have been declared reasonable by federal circuit courts, and many sentences below the guidelines have been declared unreasonable in light of congressional sentencing purposes and policies. [In *United States v. Booker* (2005), the Supreme Court held that that U.S. Sentencing Guidelines enacted by Congress violated the Sixth Amendment by, among other things, imposing mandatory, rather than advisory rules on federal judges related to sentencing convicted felons.]

Given that Mr. Libby faced a statutory maximum sentence of 25 years' imprisonment and a calculated guideline range of 30–37 months' imprisonment, Judge Walton's imposition of a prison term of only 30 months was arguably merciful. As noted above, this prison term would have been considered presumptively reasonable by the U.S. Court of Appeals. Against this legal backdrop, the president's conclusion that Mr. Libby's prison term was "excessive" is curious, to say the least.

Even if one accepts the president's assertion that a 30-month prison term for Mr. Libby was excessive, it is hard to justify or understand the president's decision to commute Mr. Libby's prison sentence in its entirety. It is particularly difficult to see how, in Tony Snow's words, "the rule of law" and "public faith in government" have been served by enabling Mr. Libby to avoid having to serve even one day in prison following his "serious convictions of perjury and obstruction of justice." Indeed, the conclusion to the prosecution's sentencing memorandum submitted to the District Court in this case spotlights why a term of imprisonment for Mr. Libby seemed essential—and certainly not "excessive"—to both Mr. Fitzgerald and Judge Walton:

> Mr. Libby, a high-ranking public official and experienced lawyer, lied repeatedly and blatantly about matters at the heart of a criminal investigation concerning the disclosure of a covert intelligence officer's identity. He has shown no regret for his actions, which significantly impeded the investigation. Mr. Libby's prosecution was based not upon politics but upon his own conduct, as well as upon a principle fundamental to preserving our judicial system's independence from politics: that any witness, whatever his political affiliation, whatever his views on any policy or national issue, whether he works in the White House or drives a truck to earn a living, must tell the

truth when he raises his hand and takes an oath in a judicial proceeding, or gives a statement to federal law enforcement officers. The judicial system has not corruptly mistreated Mr. Libby; Mr. Libby has been found by a jury of his peers to have corrupted the judicial system.

II. THE COMMUTATION IS CONTRARY TO THE BUSH ADMINISTRATION'S SENTENCING POLICIES AND PRACTICES, AND TO PRINCIPLES OF THE SENTENCING REFORM ACT.

Though peculiar and suspect on its own terms, President Bush's decision to commute entirely the prison term of Mr. Libby is especially puzzling and troubling in light of the Bush Administration's stated sentencing policies and practices. The president's commutation also undermines principles of modern federal sentencing reform reflected in the Sentencing Reform Act of 1984 and sentencing policies stressed by members of Congress from both political parties.

A. The Justice Department's modern vigorous advocacy for within-guidelines prison sentence for white-collar offenders

In testimony to Congress and the U.S. Sentencing Commission and in other policy advocacy, the Justice Department during the Bush Administration has repeatedly and vigorously argued for certain and stiff punishment for white-collar offenders. In addition, throughout the Bush Administration, federal prosecutors in courts nationwide have repeatedly and vigorously argued against judges reducing sentences below the guidelines based on the kinds of personal considerations mentioned in President Bush's commutation statement.

Policy advocacy. The Justice Department during the Bush Administration has consistently urged Congress and the Sentencing Commission to support and strengthen sentencing laws to ensure that white-collar offenders receive serious punishments including terms of imprisonment. Here are a few notable excerpts taken from written testimony and speeches from various Justice Department officials:

- In 2001, then-Acting Deputy Attorney General Robert Mueller testifying before the U.S. Sentencing Commission stressed the importance of equal and severe punishment for privileged defendants:

  > When [successful professionals] break the law, they should not be excused from serving a prison sentence simply because they did not commit crimes of violence. The public has a right to expect that people with privileged backgrounds who commit crimes will not be exempt from the full force of the law and will not be treated with inappropriate leniency.

- In 2002, then-U.S. Attorney James Comey echoed similar points when testifying before the United States Senate:

  > [T]he real and immediate prospect of significant periods of incarceration is necessary to give force to law. Nothing erodes the deterrent power of our laws—and breeds contempt for obeying the law—more quickly than if certain criminals appear to receive punishment not according to the gravity of the offense, but according to their social or economic status.

- In 2003, the Justice Department's ex officio member of the U.S. Sentencing Commission expressed the Justice

Department's concerns about the Commission's failure to address "the increasingly severe problem of federal judges ignoring the existing guidelines to grant lenient sentences or even probation to wealthy, well connected criminals."

- In a 2005 speech, Attorney General Alberto Gonzales advocated responding to the Supreme Court's *Booker* decision through "the construction of a minimum guideline system" in order to create "a system of tougher, fairer, and greater justice for all." Here are some of Attorney General Gonzales' points in support of his proposal to limit judicial authority to reduce sentences below calculated guideline ranges:

> In the 17-plus years that they have been in existence, federal sentencing guidelines have achieved the ambitious goals of public safety and fairness set out by Congress....[because] increased incarceration means reduced crime....Federal sentencing guidelines have helped keep Americans safe while also delivering on their promise to reduce unwarranted disparities in sentences....

For 17 years, mandatory federal sentencing guidelines have helped drive down crime. The guidelines have evolved over time to adapt to changing circumstances and a better understanding of societal problems and the criminal justice system. Judges, legislators, the Sentencing Commission, prosecutors, defense lawyers, and others have worked hard to develop a system of sentencing guidelines that has protected Americans and improved American justice.

Interestingly, in his 2005 speech calling for a legislative response to Booker, Attorney General Gonzales expressed particular concern about defendants "receiving sentences dramatically lower than the guidelines range...on the basis of factors that could not be considered under the guidelines." Attorney General Gonzales singled out for criticism below-guideline sentences given to white-collar offenders: he assailed one judge's decision to impose only a term of probation due to the collateral harms suffered by the defendant; he attacked another judge's decision to reduce a prison term based in part on the defendant's advanced age and his need to help care for his severely ill wife.

Court advocacy. The Justice Department's vigorous advocacy for within-guidelines prison sentences for white-collar offenders takes place in courtrooms as well as in testimony and speeches. In response to defense arguments for reduced prison terms, federal prosecutors regularly argue to sentencing judges and appellate courts that terms of imprisonment, and not merely fines and probation, are essential to achieve the goals of punishment and deterrence stressed by Congress in the Sentencing Reform Act. Especially in white-collar cases involving first-offenders—whether involving economic crimes such as those that led to convictions in the Enron and WorldCom prosecutions, or involving high-profile defendants such as Martha Stewart and the rapper Lil' Kim convicted for perjury and obstruction like Mr. Libby—federal prosecutors consistently encourage judges to disregard defense arguments for lower sentences because of the collateral harms that prominent and privileged defendants necessarily suffer as a result of a federal prosecution.

Perhaps the most telling recent court advocacy relevant here comes from the Justice Department's successful arguments before the Supreme Court in support of the reasonableness of a 33-month sentence received by Victor Rita for perjury and obstruction of justice. Mr. Rita, a highly decorated military veteran who suffers significant medical ailments, was peripherally involved in a federal investigation of InterOrdinance, a firearms company. Based on a misrepresentation about his dealings with InterOrdinance, Mr. Rita was prosecuted and convicted of perjury and obstruction of justice, and he was given a within-guideline sentence of 33-months' imprisonment.

In response to Mr. Rita's claims on appeal that his sentence was unreasonably long given his distinguished military and government service and his poor health, the Department of Justice argued to the Fourth Circuit and then to the Supreme Court that a 33-month prison term for Mr. Rita was "reasonable." The Department supported its reasonableness claims by stressing that Mr. Rita's sentence was at the bottom of the calculated guideline range, that Mr. Rita committed his crimes while serving as a federal government employee, and that Mr. Rita failed to accept responsibility for his crimes.

In its 8–1 decision in *Rita v. United States* (2007)—which was handed down just days before President Bush called Mr. Libby's 30-month prison "excessive"—the Supreme Court declared Mr. Rita's 33-month prison sentence reasonable. The majority opinion in Rita stresses that it was sensible to afford within-guideline sentences a "presumption of reasonableness" because in such cases "both the sentencing judge and the Sentencing Commission will have reached the same conclusion as to the proper sentence in the particular case [which] significantly increases the likelihood that the sentence is a reasonable one." The majority opinion also concluded that "Rita's lengthy military service, including over 25 years of service, both on active duty and in the Reserve, and Rita's receipt of 35 medals,

awards, and nominations," even when considered together with other personal suffering and circumstances, did not create "special circumstances [that] are special enough" to call for a lower prison sentence. Notably, in a separate concurrence, Justice Antonin Scalia (joined by Justice Clarence Thomas) described Victor Rita's 33-month prison term for perjury and obstruction of justice as a "relatively low sentence."

Because I personally believe that a long and distinguished military career should be considered an important mitigating factor at sentencing, I was somewhat disappointed and a bit surprised that only one member of the Supreme Court expressed serious concern about the reasonableness of Mr. Rita's 33-month prison sentence for perjury and obstruction of justice. But I was more disappointed and surprised that President Bush decided Mr. Libby should not have to serve even a single day in prison for the same crimes that his Justice Department and the Supreme Court believed reasonably required Mr. Rita to serve 1000 days in prison. Moreover, the important nature of the underlying investigation that Mr. Libby obstructed, as well as his background as a lawyer and as a high-ranking government official, arguably makes Mr. Libby's crimes even more serious than Mr. Rita's.

B. Congress's long-standing interest in achieving equal justice and respect for the law through modern sentencing reforms.

In 1984, Congress enacted the landmark Sentencing Reform Act ("SRA") which sought to remedy a perceived "shameful disparity in criminal sentences" that created "disrespect for the law." The SRA was the result of more than a decade of reports and hearings and it passed with broad bipartisan support.

Throughout the last two decades, members of Congress from both parties have restated their belief and reaffirmed the vitality of the principles of equal justice reflected in the Sentencing Reform Act.…In [an amicus curiae] brief submitted this year to the Supreme Court [in the *Booker* case], Senators Edward Kennedy (D-MA), Orrin Hatch (R-UT), and Dianne Feinstein (D-CA) urged the Court to vindicate "the basic goals of the Sentencing Reform Act, including transparency, the elimination of unwarranted disparity, and fair and proportional sentences," and stressed that Congress has long sought to "remove politics, prejudice, and subjectivity from sentencing."

As evidenced by the public and media reaction, the president's commutation of the entirety of Mr. Libby's prison sentence is not viewed as a paragon of "fairness and equality." Indeed, notwithstanding spokesman Tony Snow's claims to the contrary, the president's commutation decision seems likely to weaken the rule of law and to decrease public faith in government. Moreover, the president's commutation decision is certain to complicate the important work of federal prosecutors and federal judges who seek to advance the principles of equal justice and fairness reflected in the Sentencing Reform Act.

Many academic commentators and media stories have noted that defense attorneys are certain to start filing in many federal sentencing proceedings what is being called the "Libby Motion." Here is how Professor Ellen Podgor has explained the challenges that the president's commutation decision present for those working within the federal criminal justice system:

Every criminal defense lawyer who practices in the white collar arena is asking him or herself—why shouldn't my client have this same privilege? After all the client may

have been convicted of a perjury or obstruction charge, may have children, may be suffering the collateral consequences of the loss of a law license, may have served their country—perhaps in war, and may be a first offender. Should they not receive the same sentence of "no time."

One should expect that there will be Libby Motions made, and/or motions that contain this language in a request for a departure from the guidelines. The motion will likely include a comparison to the client's circumstances with that of Libby. It will probably also contain language from the U.S. Sentencing Guidelines that speaks to a basic policy consideration of the guidelines being to obtain "reasonable uniformity in sentencing by narrowing the wide disparity in sentences imposed for similar criminal conduct." And after all, the guidelines permit departure for factors that were not considered by the U.S. Sentencing Commission. Did the Commission consider that a president would take an entire sentence and commute it prior to the individual even seeing one day in jail? And understanding that the U.S. Sentencing Commission did not consider this, should a departure therefore be allowed?

And the judges, what will they do with these motions? The activist ones might follow the activist executive and say—yes this is grounds for departure. But more likely we will see judges continue to follow the flow of the guidelines and sentence individuals as if the Libby case did not exist. And we law professors will be left to try and explain this to students.

Professor Podgor's comments spotlight how defense attorneys and judges will likely respond to President Bush's commutation, but I think federal prosecutors may now be placed in the most difficult of all positions. Nationwide, federal prosecutors must return to all the courtrooms in which they have argued that within-guideline sentences are always reasonable and now somehow explain why their boss concluded that Mr. Libby's within-guideline sentence was "excessive."

III. THIS COMMITTEE SHOULD EXPLORE POSSIBLE WAYS TO ENHANCE THE PROCESS AND IMPROVE PUBLIC APPRECIATION FOR THE EXERCISE OF HISTORIC EXECUTIVE CLEMENCY POWERS.

There is a sad personal irony to my criticism of President Bush's decision to commute Mr. Libby's entire prison sentence. Almost exactly a decade ago, I was critical of then-Governor Bush's decision not to commute the death sentence of one of my clients, Terry Washington. Mr. Washington was a poor, African-American man who suffered from mental retardation and was sentenced to death in Texas after his conviction for killing a co-worker. Along with other lawyers at a large law firm, I served as Mr. Washington's pro bono appellate lawyer, and I drafted a clemency petition on Mr. Washington's behalf. In addition to noting the mistakes of Mr. Washington's appointed trial lawyer, the clemency petition stressed the severe abuse that Mr. Washington suffered as a child and his significantly diminished mental capacities. In May 1997, then-Governor Bush denied our request to commute Mr. Washington's sentence to life in prison, and the state of Texas executed Mr. Washington.

According to a 2003 *Atlantic Monthly* article by Alan Berlow, then-Governor Bush focused only on the facts of Mr. Washington's crime and never seriously considered the significant personal considerations that arguably justified commuting Mr. Washington's death sentence. Needless to say, Mr. Washington's personal life story could not have been more dif-ferent than Mr. Libby's. But, after seeing the president's obvious compassion for Mr. Libby's fate in his commutation statement, I cannot help but have some sadness about the president's failure to show similar compassion for Mr. Washington and the great majority of criminal offenders whose personal suffering perhaps can never be fully understood by those who are more fortunate.

Executive clemency power has a rich and distinguished history. The Framers of our Constitution robustly championed executive clemency power. At the time of founding, Alexander Hamilton stressed the importance of clemency in the Federalist Papers, emphasizing that "[t]he criminal code of every country partakes so much of necessary severity that without an easy access to exceptions in favor of unfortunate guilt, justice would wear a countenance too sanguinary and cruel." Similarly, James Iredell of North Carolina championed the crucial nature of the executive clemency power, explaining that "there may be many instances where, though a man offends against the letter of the law, yet peculiar circumstances in his case may entitle him to mercy. It is impossible for any general law to foresee and provide for all possible cases that may arise; and therefore an inflexible adherence to it, in every instance, might frequently be the cause of very great injustice."

Of course, one need not look back hundreds of years to find praise for the executive power of clemency. The late Chief Justice William Rehnquist, writing for the Supreme Court, spotlighted that executive clemency power is "deeply rooted in our Anglo-American tradition of law, and is the historic remedy for preventing miscarriages of justice." Such a power is essential, continued Chief Justice Rehnquist, because "[i]t is an unalterable fact that our judicial system, like the human beings who administer it, is fallible" and thus executive clemency provides "the 'fail safe' in our criminal justice system."

Unfortunately, in modern times, the "fail safe" of executive clemency has been failing to effectively serve the ends of justice that the Framers emphasized. Perhaps because only the most troublesome grants of clemency generate media attention and legislative hearings, executive officials often sensibly conclude that they will never face serious criticisms for failing ever to exercise their historic clemency powers, but will always face scrutiny for exercising this power. These political realities have led a Supreme Court Justice and leading scholars to lament that the clemency process has "been drained of its moral force" and that the important concept of mercy has lost its resonance in modern times. The diminished state and perception of executive clemency is quite unfortunate, especially because I believe the Framers would view an executive's record of denying all clemency requests to be a matter of embarrassment rather than a point of pride.

For these reasons, I sincerely hope that this hearing and the work of this Committee will not begin any effort to limit or diminish executive clemency power, but rather will result in efforts to revive and restore this power to its historically important and respected status. To this end, let me close my testimony by making one suggestion as to how Congress might start down this path. Specifically, I urge this Committee to begin work on the creation of a "Clemency Commission."

My vision of this proposed "Clemency Commission" is very much in the model of the U.S. Sentencing Commission. A Clemency Commission could and should be a special administrative body, perhaps placed in the judicial branch, which would be primarily tasked with helping federal officials (and perhaps also state officials) improve the functioning and public respect for executive clemency as, in Chief Justice [William] Rehnquist's words, "the historic remedy for preventing miscarriages of justice." Though the structure and staffing and mandates of a Clemency Commission could take many forms, I envision it as having personnel with expertise about the nature of and reasons for occasional miscarriages of justice in the operation of modern criminal justice systems. The Commission could study the causes of wrongful conviction and "excessive" sentences and overzealous prosecutions and make recommendations to the other branches about specific cases that might merit clemency relief or about systemic reforms that could reduce the risk of miscarriages of justice. In addition, the Commission could be a clearing-house for historical and current data on the operation of executive clemency powers in state and federal systems, and could serve as a valuable resource for offenders and their families and friends seeking information about who might be a good candidate for receiving clemency relief.

Despite constitutional limitations on significant legislative interference with the president's clemency powers, there are certainly various ways this Committee could seek to improve the transparency and understanding of the exercise of this historic executive power. Though the creation of a Clemency Commission would be an ambitious endeavor, I am quite confident that the effort could pay long-term dividends for both the reality and the perception of justice and fairness in our nation's criminal justice systems.

THE CONTINUING DEBATE:
Commuting the Prison Sentence of "Scooter" Libby

What Is New

Bush's action set off barrage of attacks and defenses, largely along partisan lines. Among the Democrats who were then already maneuvering for 2008 Democratic nomination for president, former North Carolina Senator John Edwards charged, "Only a president clinically incapable of understanding that mistakes have consequences could take the action he did today." Taking the opposite view, possible Republican presidential contender, former Tennessee Senator Fred D. Thompson claimed that Bush's action "will allow a good American who has done a lot for his country to resume his life." Joseph Wilson, who set off the chain of events leading to Libby's conviction, told reporters that he and his wife, Valerie Plame, were "deeply disappointed" by Bush's action and castigate Libby for "not only endanger[ing] Valerie and our family, but also our country's national security." As for President Bush, he defended his action on the grounds that the 30-month prison sentence was "excessive" in light of Libby's "exceptional public service," his lack of a prior criminal record, and because his reputation "is forever damaged." Most Americans disagreed, with only 19% supporting the commutation, 66% opposing it, and 15% unsure.

Where to Find More

The U.S. Department of Justice Web site at www.usdoj.gov/usao/iln/osc/ has Libby's indictment, a wide range of evidence, documents, and other items related to the case. The president's full statement on the commutation of Libby's sentence is available by going to the White House site for new releases at www.whitehouse.gov/news/releases for 2007, then to the July 2 statement. More generally, clemency regulations and procedures, recent clemency recipients, clemency statistics, and other information can be found on the Web site of the Department of Justice's Office of Pardons at listed at www.usdoj.gov/pardon/. Some of the variables that influence presidential clemency decisions are found in Andrew B. Whitford and Holona L. Ochs, "The Political Roots of Executive Clemency," *American Politics Research* (2006). For how the bureaucracy can limit the president's discretion in the area of clemency, read H. Abbie Erler, "Executive Clemency or Bureaucratic Discretion? Two Models of the Pardons Process," *Presidential Studies Quarterly* (2007).

What More to Do

The case of Scooter Libby was neither the first nor will it be the last highly controversial extension of presidential clemency. Debate whether you would somehow restrict this presidential power, either by specific limits on the circumstances for its use or by placing a check, such as the possibility of being overturned by Congress, on it.

13 BUREAUCRACY

VIEWS OF U.S. GOVERNMENT SCIENTISTS ON GLOBAL WARMING:
Stifled Politically *or* Fairly Presented?

STIFLED POLITICALLY

ADVOCATE: James E. Hansen, private citizen and Director, NASA Goddard Institute for Space Studies

SOURCE: Testimony during hearings on "Political Interference with Government Climate Change Science" before the U.S. House of Representatives, Committee on Oversight and Government Reform, March 19, 2007

FAIRLY PRESENTED

ADVOCATE: Roy W. Spencer, Principal Research Scientist, Earth System Science Center, The University of Alabama in Huntsville and former Senior Scientist for Climate Studies, NASA's Marshall Space Flight Center

SOURCE: Testimony during hearings on "Political Interference with Government Climate Change Science" before the U.S. House of Representatives, Committee on Oversight and Government Reform, March 19, 2007

This debate exists at two levels. One relates to the science of global warming. How certain are we the significant global warming is occurring, is mostly or completely being caused by human activity, and constitutes a threat to humanity? The second relates to the interaction between, on the one hand, the president and his political appointees who head the executive branch and are its policymakers and chief administrators, and, on the other hand, the career employees that staff the government's many departments and agencies.

Global Warming: This much seems pretty clear: The burning of fossil fuels gives off carbon dioxide (CO_2) into the atmosphere, and these discharges have been increasing at an ever-faster rate since the mid-1700s and, even more, since the 1950s. Many experts argue this buildup of CO_2 is causing global warming, an increase in the Earth's average temperature, because the accumulated CO_2 creates a blanket effect by preventing the nightly cooling of the Earth. Certainly there also seems to be evidence of rising temperatures. Earth's temperature has increased about 1.3° Fahrenheit since the late 1800s; the 1990s were the warmest decade since temperature records were first kept in the mid-1800s, and the first decade of the 2000s is now almost certain to be even warmer.

Many, including James Hansen in the first reading, worry that this warming is causing and will increasingly cause dramatic shifts in precipitation, wind currents, the frequency and severity of storms, and other climactic patterns in sometimes destructive ways, such as causing the polar icecaps to melt and sea levels to rise, inundating coastal areas.

However, others, including Roy Spencer in the second reading, disagree with some or all these scenarios. These scientists challenge the accuracy of measurements, believe that whatever warming is occurring is solely or mostly due to natural trends in the Earth's warming and cooling process, and/or think that temperature increases will be marginal and not threatening.

The Independence of Bureaucrats: An issue that has long bedeviled the United States, and indeed every country, is how much control elected executive officials, such as presidents and prime ministers and their appointed subordinates, should have over career officials. What should be the balance between civil servants closely following the political direction of democratically elected officials, those who presumably represent the people, and civil servants, who represent no one, having the ability to publicly disagree with the elected heads of the executive branch and advocate policy that is at odds with the policy of the president. the agency they work for, and to even shape policy based on their expertise, even if that policy is at cross-purposes with the and the day-to-day exigencies they encounter while implementing policy?

As you think about this issue, be careful to focus on the principle and to avoid deciding what you think based on the immediate case at hand. For example, in the following debate you might find yourself agreeing that global warming is a growing menace and, therefore, also taking the position that the Bush administration was being abusive when it required one of its career staff members, James Hansen, a scientist with the National Aeronautics and Space Administration and the advocate in the first reading, to tailor his public statements about global warming to avoid too overt a clash with the views and policy of his agency and the administration. However, be careful of the specific-to-general inductive reasoning. It can put you in a position of having a position that contradicts your preferences in a different matter and another agency. For example, if Hansen was justified for opposing his agency and the president in this debate, then do you also support the actions during the Korean War of the U.S. commander, General Douglas A. MacArthur? President Harry S. Truman wanted to confine the war to the Korean peninsula, but MacArthur wanted to attack China and lobbied Congress to do so. Truman insisted on civilian control of the military and fired the highly decorated and immensely popular MacArthur for insubordination in 1951. Was this one of the presidency's finest moments, or was Truman abusing his power?

POINTS TO PONDER

➢ What do you make of the evidence that global warming is occurring, is mostly or wholly caused by human activity, and presents a "clear and present danger" to Earth's future?

➢ Is Hansen a hero for trying to tell the truth despite the pressures from above, or, as Spence implies, is Hansen a disgruntled employee who is angry at not being able to present his version of reality and to present it as fact?

➢ Is it always right or always wrong for public employees to criticize the policy stands of elected officials? If not "always" either way, then what standards should determine when it is acceptable and when it is not?

Views of U.S. Government Scientists on Global Warming: Stifled Politically

JAMES E. HANSEN

I provide this testimony because I believe that my experiences illustrate flaws that have developed in the functioning of our democracy. And I will use part of my presentation to compare the benefits of early actions to defuse the building climate crisis with the dangers of continued business-as-usual fossil fuel emissions.

I claim no expertise in legal matters or politics. My approach is to try to imagine how our forefathers would have viewed our present situation and how they may have dealt with the climate change issue. A well-informed educated public was and is a premise of our democracy; it is easy for me to imagine Benjamin Franklin presenting an objective discussion of climate change that would be thoughtfully received. Another fundamental tenet of our democracy, separation of powers within our government, with checks and balances, is brought into focus by the climate crisis.

MY EXPERIENCE

A. White House Approval and Editing of Congressional Testimony

During the past 25 years I have noticed an increase in the degree of political interference with scientific testimony to Congress. My first testimony was to a United States House of Representatives hearing organized by Representative Al Gore in early 1982. I do not recall whether White House approval of that testimony was required, but in any case there were no objections to the content of that testimony.

I testified to the United States Senate about climate change at least three times in the period 1984–1988. These testimonies required approval by the White House Office of Management and Budget (OMB). I did not have direct contact with people in OMB, rather NASA [National Aeronautics and Space Administration] Headquarters (usually the NASA Office of Legislative Affairs) was an intermediary between the scientist (me) and OMB. In one case I strongly objected to changes that OMB made to my testimony, because I felt that the changes substantially altered the conclusions of our research and served to reduce concern about possible human-made climate change.

In this case the NASA intermediary in the Office of Legislative Affairs volunteered the information that I had the right to testify as a private citizen and present my testimony with the wording that I preferred. I took advantage of that right, testifying as a private citizen, and never felt any repercussions for doing so.

In 1989, after climate change had become of greater public and political concern, the constraints on communication via congressional testimony became stricter, at least in my experience. When I submitted written testimony to NASA Headquarters in 1989 for presentation to a Senate Committee chaired by Senator Gore, my secretary was instructed by NASA Headquarters to send the original typescript to NASA Headquarters so that they could insert several changes that were required by the White House OMB. When I was informed of this I was angered, intercepted the typescript, and insisted that any changes had to be made in my office. Several acceptable rewordings were negotiated (NASA Headquarters being the intermediary between OMB and me), but three changes that OMB required were unacceptable to me. The three changes were:

(1) addition of a caveat after my discussion of expected climate changes due to increasing greenhouse gases that "these changes should be viewed as estimates from evolving climate models and not as reliable predictions"; this change negated much of the testimony, in which I argued, on heuristic grounds with support from models, that global warming would lead to increases in the extremes of the hydrologic cycle, i.e., more intense heat waves and droughts but also heavier rainfalls and floods;

(2) addition of a suggestion that the increases of greenhouse gases could be partly or largely due to natural processes; again this was misleading because we were aware that the greenhouse gas increases are primarily of human origin;

(3) addition of a statement that "any policy options which should reduce atmospheric CO_2 growth rates should make good economic and environmental sense, independent of concerns about an increasing greenhouse effect; although the meaning of this statement was unclear, it seemed to say that the greenhouse effect (global warming) should not have any effect on policies. Although some other scientists agreed with the White House OMB edits to my testimony, it was supposed to be my testimony.

Unlike the case earlier in the 1980s, I was told by NASA Headquarters that I needed to accept the changes or not testify. I agreed to accept the changes, but I then sent a fax to Senator Gore requesting that he ask me during the hearing about those specific statements, because I wanted to make clear that they were the opinion of the White House OMB, not my opinion. (This exchange was briefly shown in the documentary *An Inconvenient Truth*.)

Review and editing of scientific testimony by the White House OMB seems to now be an accepted practice. The explanation I was given for why budgetary people should be allowed to review and edit scientific testimony was that NASA plans need to be consistent with the Administration's budget. Discussion with NASA personnel in Legislative Affairs and in Science program offices suggests that people at NASA Headquarters believe that NASA must "play ball" with OMB if it wishes to be treated well in its annual funding. It seems to me that this raises constitutional questions, because it is my understanding that the Constitution provides the power of the purse strings to Congress, not the Executive Branch of our government. I return to this issue in Section 4 below, after discussing in Section 3 the practical impacts of this political interference in climate science.

B. Communication Constraints by NASA Office of Public Affairs

The Office of Public Affairs in science agencies such as NASA exists for the purpose of helping communicate scientific results to the public. During my career I have noticed an increasing politicization of Public Affairs at the Headquarters level, with a notable effect on communication from scientists to the public. I refer not to the professionals in the Public Affairs offices at the NASA science centers, but to Public Affairs at NASA Headquarters, which is in charge overall and is generally headed by a political appointee. Interference with communication of science to the public has been greater during the current Administration than at any time in my career.

The effect of the filtering of climate change science during the current Administration has been to make the reality of climate change less certain than the facts indicate and to reduce concern about the relation of climate change to human-made greenhouse gas emissions. For example, one of my staff members submitted a story based on his paper that found the ocean was less effective at removing human-made CO_2 [carbon dioxide] than had previously been estimated. Public Affairs decided that this story should not be provided to the media. Another staff member had to attend a 'practice' press conference, in which he was asked whether anything could be done to stem accelerating loss of sea ice. When he suggested, "We could reduce emissions of greenhouse gases," he was told sternly, "That's unacceptable!", with the explanation that scientists are not allowed to say anything that relates to policy.

An important example of political interference with the public's right to know has occurred with press releases relating to global warming science that have gone from NASA Headquarters to the White House for review, approval or disapproval, and editing. That this practice is inappropriate, if not illegal, is indicated by the response from NASA Public Affairs when I made note of this practice in a public talk. The NASA Assistant Administrator for Public Affairs traveled from Headquarters to Goddard Space Flight Center to deliver an oral "dressing down" of the professional writer at Goddard Public Affairs who had informed me about this practice. The writer was admonished to "mind his own business." This dressing down was delivered in front of the writer's boss. Such reprimands and instructions are delivered orally. If NASA Headquarters Public Affairs is queried by media about such abuses, they respond, "That's hearsay!", a legal term that seems to frighten the media. My suggestion for getting at the truth is to question the relevant participants under oath, including the then NASA Associate Administrator for Earth Sciences, who surely is aware of who in the White House was receiving and reviewing press releases that related to climate change.

Communication constraints by NASA Headquarters Public Affairs came to light in December 2005, after some of the instructions by Headquarters Public Affairs were written down in memos and e-mails. This occurred shortly after my talk at the American Geophysical Union meeting in San Francisco and the release within a week thereafter of our (GISS, Goddard Institute for Space Studies) analysis of global temperature, which showed record global temperature in 2005. NASA Headquarters Public Affairs was furious about the media attention, their anger being sparked by a call from the White House objecting to the publicity on global warming. The consternation, expressed during several three-way telecons [teleconferences] between Headquarters-GSFC/Greenbelt-GISS/New York, was described by a participant as a "shit-storm." The upshot was a new explicit set of constraints on me, including requirement that any media interviews be approved beforehand and that Headquarters have the "right of first refusal" on all interviews, that I provide my calendar of all planned talks and meetings, and that I obtain prior approval for every posting on the GISS web site.

These orders were delivered orally, as usual, as was a threat of "dire consequences" if I did not comply. However, a new young political appointee at Public Affairs, apparently was not well-schooled in the rules and left a paper trail, including a description of a specific instance in which Public Affairs barred me from speaking to NPR [National Public Radio], offering the Associate Administrator in my stead. These indiscretions were perhaps the primary reason for his departure from NASA, rather than the fact that his resume failed to show that he was one course short of the university degree that he claimed. However, he was not acting on his own or affecting communication with the public in a way contrary to the wishes of his bosses. The paper trail that he left showed that the problem starts at the top, the decision to bar me from speaking with NPR being made "on the ninth floor" of Headquarters.

It became clear that the new constraints on my communications were gong to be a real impediment when I was forced to take down from our web site our routine posting of updated global temperature analysis. At that time I decided to write down the constraints that I had been placed under and to inform the media. An article appeared in the *New York Times*. To NASA's credit, the Administrator promptly issued an unequivocal statement in support of scientific openness.

However, in no way has the impact of deception of the public about climate change been undone by NASA's forthright decision in favor of scientific openness. There remains a vast gap between what is understood about global warming, by the relevant scientific community, and what is known about global warming by those who need to know, the public and policymakers. This gap should be of concern to the Committee on Oversight and Government Reform, because it relates in part to ways in which the functioning of our government is departing from the intentions of our forefathers. Of special

relevance is the usurpation of congressional prerogatives by the executive branch, especially via increased control of the purse strings.

C. Executive Control of Purse Strings

The American Revolution launched the radical proposition that the commonest of man should have a vote of equal weight to that of the richest, most powerful citizen. Our forefathers devised a remarkable Constitution, with checks and balances, to guard against the return of despotic governance and subversion of the democratic principle for the sake of the powerful few with special interests. They were well aware of the difficulties that would be faced, however, placing their hopes in the presumption of an educated informed citizenry, an honestly informed public.

I have sometimes wondered how our forefathers would view our situation today. On the positive side, as a scientist, I like to imagine how Benjamin Franklin would view the capabilities we have built for scientific investigation. Franklin speculated that an atmospheric "dry fog" produced by a large volcano had reduced the sun's heating of the Earth so as to cause unusually cold weather in the early 1780s, as he noted that the enfeebled solar rays when collected in the focus of a "burning glass" could "scarce kindle brown paper." As brilliant as Franklin's insights may have been, they were only speculation as he lacked the tools for quantitative investigation. No doubt Franklin would marvel at the capabilities provided by earth-encircling satellites and super-computers that he could scarce have imagined.

Yet Franklin, Jefferson and the other revolutionaries must be distraught by recent tendencies in America, specifically increasing power of special interests in our government, concerted efforts to deceive the public, and arbitrary actions of government executives that arise from increasing concentration of authority in a unitary executive, in defiance of the aims of our Constitution's framers. These tendencies have dramatic impact on the global warming story.

Last year, about one month after the media hubbub about NASA Public Affairs' censoring of science, the mission of NASA was altered surreptitiously by executive action and the budget for Earth Science Research and Analysis was slashed retroactively to the beginning of the fiscal year, thus subverting constitutional division of power. Many people are aware that something bad happened to the NASA Earth Science budget last year, yet the severity of the cuts and their long-term implications are not universally recognized. In part this is because of a stealth budgeting maneuver, which I suspect most members of Congress are not aware of.

When annual budgets for the coming fiscal year are announced, the differences in growth from the previous year, for agencies and their divisions, are typically a few percent. An agency with +3 percent growth may crow happily, in comparison to agencies receiving +1 percent. Small differences are important because every agency has fixed costs (civil service salaries, buildings, other infrastructure), so new programs or initiatives are strongly dependent upon any budget growth and how that growth compares with inflation.

When the administration announced its fiscal 2007 budget, NASA science was listed as having typical changes of 1 percent or so. However, Earth Science Research and Analysis actually had a staggering reduction of about 20 percent from the 2006 budget that Congress had passed. How could that be accomplished? Simple enough: reduce the 2006 research budget retroactively by 20 percent! One-third of the way into fiscal year 2006, NASA Earth Science was told to go figure

out how to live with a 20-percent loss of the current year's funds.

The Earth Science budget was further tightened in 2007 and is almost a going-out-of-business budget. From the taxpayers' point of view it makes no sense. An 80 percent budget must be used mainly to support infrastructure (practically speaking, you cannot fire civil servants; buildings at large facilities such as Goddard Space Flight Center will not be bulldozed to the ground; and the grass at the centers must continue to be cut). But the budget cuts wipe off the books most planned new satellite missions (some may be kept on the books, but only with a date so far in the future that no money needs to be spent now), and support for contractors, young scientists, and students disappears, with dire implications for future capabilities.

Bizarrely, this is happening just when NASA data are yielding spectacular and startling results. Two small satellites that measure the Earth's gravitational field with remarkable precision found that the mass of Greenland is now decreasing by about 150 cubic kilometers of ice per year and West Antarctica by a similar amount. The area on the ice sheets with summer melting has increased markedly, major ice streams (portions of the ice sheet moving most rapidly toward the ocean and discharging icebergs) have increased doubled in flow speed, and the area in the Arctic Ocean with summer sea ice has decreased 20 percent in the last 25 years.

One way to avoid bad news: stop the measurements! Only hitch: the first line of the NASA mission is "to understand and protect our home planet." Maybe that can be changed to "...protect special interests' backside."

I should say that the mission statement used to read "to understand and protect our home planet." That part has been deleted—a shocking loss to me, as I had been using that phrase to justify speaking out about the dangers of global warming. The quoted mission statement had been constructed in 2001 and 2002 via an inclusive procedure involving representatives from the NASA Centers and e-mail interactions with NASA employees. In contrast, elimination of the "home planet" phrase occurred with no fanfare in a spending report delivered to Congress in February 2006, the same report that retroactively slashed the Earth Science research budget. In July 2006 I asked dozens of NASA employees and management people (including my boss) if they were aware of the change. Not one of them was. Several expressed concern that such management changes by fiat would have a bad effect on organization morale.

These budgetary goings-on in Washington were noted in [two June 2006] editorials of *The Boston Globe*, both decrying the near-termination of Earth measurements. Of course, the *Globe* might be considered "liberal media." But it is conservatives and moderates who should be most upset, and I consider myself a moderate conservative. When I was in school we learned that Congress controlled the purse strings; it is in the Constitution. But it does not really seem to work that way, not if the Administration can jerk the science budget around the way they have....My impression is that conservatives and moderates would prefer that the government work as described in the Constitution, and that they prefer to obtain their information on how the Earth is doing from real observations, not from convenient science fiction.

PRACTICAL IMPACT OF POLITICAL INTERFERENCE WITH CLIMATE CHANGE SCIENCE

There is little doubt that the Administration's downplaying of evidence about global warming has had some effect on public perception of the climate change issue. The impact is to confuse the public about the reality of global warming, and about whether that warming can be reliably attributed to human-made greenhouse gases.

However, I believe that the gap between scientific understanding of climate change and public knowledge about the status of that understanding probably is due more to the impact of special interests on public discourse, especially fossil fuel special interests, rather than political interference with climate change science.

I have no knowledge of whether special interests have had a role in political interference with climate change science. Nevertheless, it is my personal opinion that the most fundamental government reform that could be taken to address climate change and government accountability in general would be effective campaign finance reform.

ISSUES AND QUESTIONS RAISED

A. Propriety of Filtering Congressional Testimony

What is the basis, what is the rationale, by which Congress allows the Administration to filter, edit and alter scientific testimony of government scientists delivered to Congress? Is this behavior a right that is granted to the Executive branch by the Constitution or authorized by other official instruments?

Presumably there is basis for this practice or it would not be tolerated. However, based on my experiences, discussed in part above, it seems to me that the practice is detrimental to the functioning of our democracy. The taxpayers foot the bill for most of the research by government and academic scientists. Thus the public should not be denied the full benefit of knowledge that derives from that research.

B. Politicization of Public Affairs Office

The problem stems from the fact that Public Affairs offices at the headquarters level of the science agencies are headed by political appointees. The inevitable result is a pressure for science to show the answers that the party in power prefers to see. This is true independent of which party is in power. Any such pressure contradicts the nature of scientific investigation, which relies on unprejudiced evaluation of all alternatives.

The best solution to this problem would be to have the Public Affairs offices professionally staffed, with no political appointees. If this is not possible, they should be renamed as Offices of Propaganda.

C. Executive Control of the Purse Strings

When I came to NASA 40 years ago as a 25 year old post-doc it seemed to me that the NASA approach was to focus on excellence in science and engineering. It was expected that Congress and the White House would provide funding based on merits. Perhaps I was naïve. But I did not get any sense that NASA was working for the White House. There has been a huge change between then and now.

The Executive branch seems to be exercising greater control in the functioning of our government, in ways that our forefathers probably did not imagine and almost certainly would not approve. This includes White House control of testimony to Congress, White House control of information that scientists provide to the public through Public Affairs, and most decidedly through control of the purse strings.

Control of the purse strings is the most powerful of the tools in the hands of the Executive branch. It has a tremendous effect on information that is provided to Congress and to the public. You may think that a government scientist can easi-ly exercise his right of free speech, to speak as a private citizen as I am today. But how many will do so, when the power of the purse strings is held by the Executive branch? You may think that there are plenty of government scientists who are confident of their ability to get a job elsewhere or would not mind being sent off to pasture. But it is not so simple as that. With the purse strings the Executive branch holds hostage your "children," your science programs, and your colleagues' livelihood. It is not easy to face your colleagues when they feel that you are damaging their support.

SUMMARY IMPLICATIONS OF CLIMATE CHANGE SCIENCE

A. Status of Science

Progress in climate science during the past several years has increased our understanding of how sensitive the Earth's climate is to forcings, such as human-made emission of gases into the atmosphere by burning fossil fuels. This understanding derives especially from the Earth's history, which shows how the Earth responded to changing forcings in the past.

The data show that the Earth's climate has considerable inertia, due especially to the massive oceans and ice sheets. Yet the climate can change dramatically on century time scales, and even on decadal and shorter time scales.

The evidence confirms a predominance of positive feedbacks that amplify climate response on short time scales, these feedbacks including increasing atmospheric water vapor and decreasing sea ice cover as the planet becomes warmer. However, the data also indicate the presence of feedbacks on decadal, century and longer time scales. These feedbacks include movement of forests and other vegetation poleward as the climate warms, increased net emission of greenhouse gases from the ocean and biosphere, and decrease in the area and brightness of ice sheets.

The predominance of positive feedbacks, along with the inertia of the oceans and ice sheets, has profound practical implications. It means that if we push the climate system hard enough it can obtain a momentum, it can pass tipping points, such that climate changes continue, out of our control. Unless we begin to slow down the human-made climate forcings, there is the danger that we will create a different planet, one far outside the range that has existed in the course of human history.

It is because of these climate feedbacks and the inertia of the ocean and ice sheets that the global warming problem differs fundamentally from the problem of conventional air pollution. By the time that the public can clearly see the existence of climate change, there is momentum in the system for a great deal of additional change. As a result we are probably already very near, if not beyond, the dangerous level of interference with atmospheric composition. I have discussed the possibility of drawing down atmospheric CO_2 by burning biofuels in power plants and capturing and sequestering the CO_2. However, by far the most effective actions at this time would be to slow current emissions to the atmosphere, while better understanding and improved technologies are developed.

Impact of Political Interference on Quality of Decision Making

Political interference in transmittal of information about climate change science to the public has deleterious effects on the quality of decision making. Science cannot make decisions for the public. The public and policy makers must consider all factors in making decisions and setting policy. But these other factors should not influence the science itself or the presentation of science to the public.

One consequence of political interference is that the public is not yet well-informed about the nature and scale of actions that will be needed to address climate change. This is important because it will take time for the public and their policy makers to thoughtfully consider these matters. As an example of the nature and scale of actions that I believe will be needed to address climate change, I list in the following section some specific recommendations that I discussed at a recent presentation in Washington. Congress needs to address the public's right to unfiltered information, including congressional testimony free of political interference, and Public Affairs (public information) offices that are staffed by professionals not by political appointee.

Views of U.S. Government Scientists on Global Warming: Fairly Presented

Roy W. Spencer

I would like to thank the committee for the opportunity to provide my perspective on the subject of political interference in government-funded science, as well as on the science of global warming.

I have been performing NASA-sponsored research for the last twenty-two years. Prior to my current position as a principal research scientist at the University of Alabama in Huntsville, I was Senior Scientist for Climate Studies at NASA's Marshall Space Flight Center. I am also the U.S. Science Team Leader for the Advanced Microwave Scanning Radiometer-E flying on NASA's Earth-observation satellite Aqua.

POLITICAL INTERFERENCE IN GOVERNMENT CLIMATE CHANGE SCIENCE

During my fifteen years as a NASA employee, I was well aware that any interaction between scientists and the press was to be coordinated through NASA management and public affairs. Understandably, NASA managers do not appreciate first reading of their scientists opinions in the morning newspaper. I understood that my position as a NASA employee was a privilege, not a right, and that there were rules I was expected to abide by. Partly because of those limits on what I could and couldn't say to the press on the subject of global warming, I voluntarily resigned from the government in the fall of 2001.

Some level of political influence on government-funded climate science has always existed, and likely always will exist. The influence began many years ago when the government climate research programs were first established. For instance, I once heard a high-level government official say that his success at helping to formulate the Montreal Protocol restricting the manufacture of ozone-depleting chemicals was an example of the kind of success that global warming research could achieve to help restrict fossil fuel use. This is clearly a case of political and policy biases driving a scientific research agenda.

On the individual scientist level, if a government scientist wants to issue a press release addressing the theoretical possibility of catastrophic climate change in the future, and entitles it, "Global Warming to be Much Worse than Previously Thought," should the scientist's supervisors have the authority to intervene if they believe the title of the press release can not be justified by the research? What if the title reads, "Global Warming Could Destroy Most of Humanity in the Next Five Years"? Could managers intervene then? At some point, the agency for which the government scientist works must bear some responsibility for what that scientist, in his official capacity, says to the public and press. Managers can not simply give blanket approval to whatever the scientist wants to say just to avoid the impression of "muzzling the science." This is one reason why agencies like NASA and NOAA need to retain some level of control over how their employees portray their science to the public.

Political influences on climate research have long pervaded the whole system. Both government funding managers and scientists realize that science programs, research funding, and careers depend upon global warming remaining a serious threat. There seems to be an unspoken pressure on climate scientists to find new ways in which mankind might be causing a climate catastrophe—yet no emphasis at all on finding possible climate stabilizing mechanisms.

Even the climate researchers themselves have biases that influence the direction they take their research. In psychology this is called "confirmation bias," and in my experience this is not the exception, but the rule. Researchers tend to be more accepting of data that confirms their preconceived notions or political or societal predilections. After all, what scientist would not want to be the one to discover an impending environmental disaster that awaits humanity…to "save the Earth"? Or, if one believes that modern technology is inherently evil, would not one then want to find sufficient evidence to put the fossil fuel industry out of business? If one has socialistic tendencies, then carbon permit trading provides an excellent mechanism for a redistribution of wealth from the richer countries to the poorer countries.

In my own case, I would rather be the researcher who discovers that global warming will be relatively benign—after all, what sane person could wish catastrophic global warming upon humanity for selfish political or social engineering reasons?

Bias in the expectation of policy outcomes was even shown in this committee's last hearing on this subject. On January 30, 2007, Rick Piltz, the Director of Climate Science Watch Government Accountability Project, told this committee, "Climate Science Watch engages in investigation, communication, and reform advocacy aimed at holding public officials accountable for using climate research with integrity and effectiveness in addressing the challenge of global climate change."

"Reform advocacy" and the phrase "addressing the challenge of global climate change" clearly presume that climate change is "a challenge" worthy of great worry and strong policy action. But based upon my own experience, it would have been at least as appropriate to have a separate advocacy group "addressing the challenge of unwarranted exaggeration of global climate change."

There is a way to reduce the impact of such biases in government-funded climate research programs. Years ago, the Department of Defense recognized the dangers of "group-think" and "tunnel-vision" when developing new defense systems. They formally instituted a "Red Team" approach where people are tasked with finding holes in the prevailing wisdom and consensus of how things should work. In my opinion, a Red Team approach to government funding of global warming research, especially in the climate modeling arena, would be very valuable.

So, rather than trying to eliminate political influence on the direction of government-funded research, this committee could help to at least balance those influences. After all, the science doesn't care what the answer is to the question of how much warming will occur in the future. And in my experience, the taxpayers would welcome a less biased approach to the spending of their money.

This committee now has the unique opportunity to help level the playing field for the scientific minority, and make sure that research programs are not biased by desired political outcomes. If only because scientists are human, political influence and biases will always exist in scientific research. But this committee can help by making sure that government is not contributing to the problem.

THE SCIENCE OF GLOBAL WARMING

Even though globally averaged temperatures in recent decades have been unusually warm, there is no compelling evidence that they are either unprecedented in the last 1,000 years, or attributable to human greenhouse gas emissions. Given the extreme cost to humanity (especially the poor) that most economists claim will result from the restricting or otherwise penalizing the use of fossil fuels, a guiding principle for accepting claims of catastrophic global warming should be: Extraordinary claims require extraordinary evidence. Let us examine whether such extraordinary and compelling evidence exists.

Current Warmth in Its Historical Context

In June 2006, a National Research Council report (NRC, 2006) requested by Congress examined claims that globally averaged temperature are warmer now than anytime in the last 1,000 years. That panel concluded that high confidence could only be given to the statement that we are now the warmest in 400 years—not 1,000 years. We should be thankful for this, since much of the last 400 years was enveloped in the "Little Ice Age"—a period that was particularly harmful to mankind. Furthermore, actual temperature measurements (not proxies) in Greenland boreholes reveal the Medieval Warm Period (MWP) to be warmer than today. The GRIP (Greenland) borehole temperature record is not a proxy, but a direct measure of temperature. It shows that current warmth is not unusual in the context of the last 2,000 years. A similar result for the last 1,000 years has also been obtained from borehole temperatures in the Ural Mountains.

In summary, the evidence for today's global warmth being unusual for inter-glacial conditions is neither extraordinary nor compelling.

Attribution of Current Warmth to Mankind

Some have found it effective to use the close relationship between ice core-inferred temperatures and carbon dioxide variations to imply that we will see similar relationships from anthropogenic CO_2 emissions. But this interpretation of ice core data is, at best, controversial. If indeed these measurements are what they are claimed to be (estimates of global temperature and carbon dioxide concentrations), then virtually all of the evidence points to the temperature changes leading the carbon dioxide changes—not the other way around—by at least 100 years. The Earth's carbon dioxide budget is still poorly understood, with huge sources and sinks of carbon in the oceans and land, and so it is entirely possible that the carbon dioxide changes were the result of biogeochemical changes resulting from the temperature changes. Since the cause-and-effect relationships in these ice core records appear to be the reverse of what we expect with anthropogenic global warming, I believe that ice cores should not be used to promote any quantitative estimates of how much warming a given amount of extra carbon dioxide will "cause."

Nevertheless, it is indeed possible to construct a possible scenario of radiative forcing wherein carbon dioxide causes the warming we have seen over the last few decades. But this in no way constitutes extraordinary and compelling evidence that greenhouse gas changes caused the warming—it is merely one possible explanation. A small decrease in low level cloudiness or a small increase in high level cloudiness—too small to be reliably measured with current satellite technology—could also explain our current warmth.

Detailed estimation of radiative imbalances from a wide variety of manmade greenhouse gases and aerosols are popular activities, but those radiative imbalances are theoretically calculated, not measured. They are still too small to be reliably measured with our satellite systems. What we do know is that substantial natural fluctuations in the Earth's radiation budget do occur which are much more abrupt and larger than those due to manmade greenhouse gases. It seems that since science can measure atmospheric carbon dioxide changes much more accurately than small variations in global cloud amounts and other natural processes, science then tends to ignore the possibility that recently global warming could be more due to natural causes than manmade ones.

It is often stated (usually with grave concern) that atmospheric carbon dioxide concentrations are higher now than they have been for hundreds of thousands of years (or more). But objectively, one must ask: so what? [In fact,] carbon dioxide concentrations in the atmosphere are extremely low, and even two or three times an extremely small number is still an extremely small number. The fact that carbon dioxide concentrations could "double" in this century might sound scary, but we need to first examine what processes determine Earth's natural greenhouse effect. In absolute terms, the increase in carbon dioxide concentrations since 1958 has been extremely small, [growing] to only 0.1% of the atmosphere.

What Causes the Earth's Greenhouse Effect?

To understand what effect anthropogenic greenhouse gas emissions might have on global climate, we must first understand what causes the Earth's natural greenhouse effect. The atmosphere's greenhouse effect is mostly due to water vapor and clouds. Many climate modelers and researchers suggest that there is some sort of 'delicate balance' between the sunlight that the Earth absorbs (energy in), and the greenhouse-influenced infrared radiation that the Earth emits to outer space (energy out), but this "delicate balance" view has no observational support, and reflects too simplistic a view of the role of weather in the climate system.

It is grossly misleading to say that the Earth's surface temperature is the "result" of a balance between absorbed sunlight and emitted infrared light, as it confuses cause and effect. Sunlight is what causes (energizes) our weather, but it is the weather that then largely "decides" how much greenhouse effect there will be. Simply put, the greenhouse effect is mostly the result of surface temperature-driven weather; it is not the cause of weather and surface temperatures.

While such conceptual distinctions are not important if the climate models contain the correct physics, it is our conceptual view that determines what physical processes we decide to include in a climate model. So, it is more than a little ironic that the atmospheric process which likely has the single strongest control over climate is the one that is understood the least: precipitation.

It seems that even many climate modelers do not realize that precipitation systems either directly or indirectly determine most of the Earth's greenhouse effect. Changes in precipitation efficiency, while poorly understood, are known to have a controlling effect on climate. As tropospheric air is continuously recycled through rain and snow systems, precipitation processes remove excess water vapor, and the air flowing out of them contains varying amounts of water vapor and clouds: the dominant contributors to the natural greenhouse effect. For example, the dry air sinking over the world's deserts was dehumidified in precipitation systems. Similarly, the dry air that rapidly cools in wintertime high pressure areas was dehumidified by rain or snow systems. Deep layers of water vapor in the vicinity of precipitation systems might locally enhance greenhouse warming, but this extra heating helps maintain the circulation—which then removes water vapor.

And the role of precipitation systems on the Earth energy budget does not end there. The change of tropospheric temperature with height is also under the control of these systems, and that vertical temperature structure affects cloud formation elsewhere. For instance, air sinking in response to the heat release in precipitation systems helps create a temperature inversion on top of the boundary layer, underneath which vast expanses of marine stratus and stratocumulus clouds form. These clouds have strong cooling effects on the climate system, and any change in them with warming is thus partly controlled by precipitation system changes. Modelers agree that changes in these low-level cloud decks with warming is still an open question; what I am pointing out is that precipitation systems are integral to the maintenance of those cloud decks.

Precipitation systems are indeed nature's "air conditioner." Since weather processes have control over the greenhouse effect, it is reasonable to assume that the relative stability that globally averaged temperatures exhibit over many years is due to natural negative feedbacks in the system which are, quite likely, traceable to precipitation systems. Since climate models have a history of temperature drift, it is clear that they have not contained all of the temperature-stabilizing influences that exist in nature. And the stronger those stabilizing influences, the less warming we

can expect from anthropogenic greenhouse gas emissions.

Positive or Negative Feedbacks?

It is certainly true that (1) greenhouse gases warm the lower atmosphere, (2) carbon dioxide is a greenhouse gas, and so (3) increasing carbon dioxide concentrations can be expected to warm the surface. But one must ask: To what extent?

Climate modelers know that the direct surface warming effects of even a doubling of carbon dioxide concentrations would be very small—only about 1 deg. F, probably sometime late in this century. The greatest concern, then, centers around the positive feedbacks exhibited by climate models which amplify this small warming tendency. But just how realistic are these positive feedbacks? The latest published comparison of the sensitivity of climate models to changes in radiation reveal that all climate models tested are more sensitive than our best available radiation budget satellite data suggest. Taken at face value, this means that all the models produce too much global warming.

Most researchers who believe in substantial levels of global warming claim that water vapor feedback is surely positive, and strong. They invariably appeal to the fact that a warming tendency from the extra carbon dioxide will cause more water vapor to be evaporated from the surface, thus amplifying the warming. But again we see a lack of understanding of what maintains tropospheric water vapor levels. While abundant amounts of water vapor are being continuously evaporated from the Earth's surface, it is precipitation systems that determine how much of that water vapor is allowed to remain in the atmosphere—not the evaporation rate. This, then, is one example of researchers' bias toward an emphasis on warming processes (water vapor addition), but not cooling processes (water vapor removal). The fact that warmer air masses have more water vapor is simply the result of the greater amounts of solar heating that those air masses were exposed to; it is not evidence for positive water vapor feedback in response to increasing carbon dioxide levels.

I also see widespread bias in the way researchers talk about the Earth's greenhouse effect, i.e. that it "keeps the Earth habitably warm." They totally ignore the fact that at least 60% of the surface warming that the greenhouse effect "tries" to cause never happens because of the cooling effects of weather (evaporation, convection, cloud formation, etc.). Thus, it is quantitatively more accurate to say that "the cooling effects of weather keep the Earth habitably cool," than it is to say, "the greenhouse effect keeps the Earth habitably warm." So again, we see a "warm" bias in the way many climate researchers talk about climate change.

Validation of Climate Models

Climate models are usually validated by comparing their average behavior, such as the monthly average temperature at different locations, to observations of the real climate system. But recently, it has been persuasively argued that meaningful validation of climate models in the context of their feedbacks can only be made by comparing the instantaneous relationships in climate models and observations. For instance, daily changes in clouds, radiation, and temperature can be measured by satellites during interannual variations in the climate system. This makes physical sense, since it is at daily time scales where most weather action takes place.

At UAH [University of Alabama, Huntsville], we have begun doing just that, and we have documented a negative feedback due to changes in precipitation systems. As rain system activity and tro-

pospheric warmth reach peak levels during tropical intraseasonal oscillations (ISOs), we measured an increase in outgoing infrared radiation, which was traced to a decrease in cirrus cloudiness. This evidence, at least at the intraseasonal time scale of the ISO, supports Lindzen's controversial "infrared iris" hypothesis of climate stabilization.

CONCLUSION

Political Interference in Climate Change Science

Government agencies and their managers have a long history of requiring employees to coordinate research results with management and public affairs officials before talking to the press. As a NASA employee of fifteen years I accepted this as part of my responsibility to support NASA's mission as a "team player" in support of overarching agency goals, and I believe there are good reasons for maintaining such a practice.

A much bigger political influence problem is the governmental bias towards a specific type of climate research that supports specific political or policy outcomes. This research is almost always biased toward the finding of climate destabilizing mechanisms, rather than climate stabilizing mechanisms. Because it takes a higher level of complexity in any physical system to produce self-regulation and stabilization, such findings do not naturally flow out of the existing research. An active effort, analogous to the Department of Defense "Red Team" approach, could be utilized to alleviate this inequity. Given the immense cost (especially to the poor) of proposed carbon control policies that most economists foresee, it is not helpful for tax dollars to be funneled in a research direction that unfairly favors certain political or policy outcomes.

Global Warming Science

I believe that there is good theoretical and observational support for the view that how precipitation systems respond to warming is the largest source of uncertainty in global warming predictions by climate models. There is good reason to believe that the models still do not contain one or more negative feedbacks related to cloud and precipitation changes associated with warming. Therefore, it is imperative that critical tests of model processes with satellite observations be carried out before warming predictions from those models be given much credence. Only through a large dose of either faith or ignorance can one believe current climate models' predictions of global warming.

THE CONTINUING DEBATE:
Views of U.S. Government Scientists on Global Warming

What Is New

The Bush administration has eased its position on global warming to at least tacitly conceding that it is occurring, but the White House continues to resist the idea that the United States should adhere to the 1997 Kyoto Protocol to the United Nations Framework Convention on Climate Change (1992). The protocol requires industrialized countries to make significant reductions in their emissions of CO_2 and other greenhouse gases. Instead, Bush called in 2007 for a meeting of countries to discuss voluntary limits. Surveys show that most Americans see global warming as a problem and think Bush should do more, but they are less alarmed about it than people in most countries. Similarly, when presented with a list of issues, most Americans prioritize global warming below the war in Iraq, terrorism, the economy, education, and some other concerns. Moreover, Americans favor tax breaks to encourage lowering CO_2 discharges, but oppose most requirements to do so or paying higher energy taxes to discourage consumption. This latter idea leaves Americans especially cold, with 2007 polls finding 58% against increasing gasoline taxes and 79% against increasing electricity taxes. As for the scientific debate, only a bit more than half of all Americans (54%) in 2007 believed both that global warming was occurring and caused by human activity. Another 20% thought global warming to be a natural phenomenon, 22% considered global warming an unproven theory, and 4% were unsure.

Where to Find More

A worthwhile Internet site on global warming is at The U.S. Environmental Protection Agency at yosemite.epa.gov/oar/globalwarming.nsf/. For a site that takes a skeptical view of the alarm over global warming, go to www.globalwarming.org/. Taking the opposite view is the Union of Concerned Scientists at www.ucsusa.org/. A warning about global warming and a plea to address the issue is given by former Vice President Al Gore in the documentary, *An Inconvenient Truth* (2006). The film is criticized in "The *Real* 'Inconvenient Truth'," at www.junkscience.com/Greenhouse/. On the issue of bureaucracy in a democracy, read Willliam T. Cormley Jr. and Steven J. Balla, *Bureaucracy and Democracy: Accountabilitly and Performance* (CQ Press, 2004); and Glen Hahn Cope, "Bureaucratic Reform and Issues of Political Responsiveness," *Journal of Public Administration Research and Theory* (1997).

What More to Do

Look for other examples of what some argue are abusive intervention by the White House in the bureaucracy and see whether you agree to disagree with what occurred. The controversy in 2007 over the dismissal of a number of U.S. Attorneys by the Bush administration is a good place to start. Also look at the claims of various U.S. Surgeons General that their view have been oppressed by various presidents including Ronald Reagan, Bill Clinton, and George W. Bush.

14   JUDICIARY

THE IDEOLOGY OF THE SUPREME COURT:
Radical Rightward Swing *or* Moderate Conservative Tilt?

RADICAL RIGHTWARD SWING

ADVOCATE: Jeff Lincoln, "Supreme Court Term Marks Shift to the Right"
SOURCE: World Socialist Web Site, July 14, 2007

MODERATE CONSERVATIVE TILT

ADVOCATE: Jonathan H. Adler, Professor of Law and Director, Center for Business Law & Regulation, Case Western Reserve University School of Law
SOURCE: *National Review* online, July 5, 2007

An intriguing fact about the U.S. Constitution is that while it is the cornerstone of the vast and complex U.S. governmental system, it is also shorter than the constitution of any of the 50 states. This is not simply a bit of trivia. One ramification of the brevity of the Constitution is that it is frequently vague. For example, Debate 1 on the Second Amendment and gun ownership highlights the controversy over the meaning of the amendment's words "the right of the people to keep and bear arms shall not be infringed," especially in light of the amendment's introductory clause, "A well regulated militia, being necessary to the security of a free state."

Scores of similar examples of constitutional controversy exist and are endlessly debated. In the end, though, it is often only the opinions of nine individuals that count. Those nine people are the justices of the U.S. Supreme Court. The reason, as Chief Justice Charles Evans Hughes once put it, is, "We are under a Constitution, but the Constitution is what the judges say it is." This ability of the justices to decide what the often-uncertain wording of the Constitution means and to make that understanding the law of the land has two sources. One is the power of interpretation, the ability to find meaning in the words of the Constitution and legislative acts. In doing so, judges to a degree follow "original intent": what the authors of the Constitution, its amendments, or specific legislative acts meant. The current justices also pay attention to precedent: what earlier justices have ruled in cases similar to the ones before the current court. It is also the case, though, that every justice brings a degree of ideological perspective to the court. This is not surprising since the judges are products of the U.S. political system, have developed an ideological perspective prior to becoming judges, have often served in elected or appointed political office, and have been appointed by the president and confirmed by the Senate in what is usually a very political, even partisan, process. It is not surprising then that Democratic presidents appoint Democratic judges, and Republican presidents appoint Republicans to the bench. Indeed, every justice but one since 1945 has been a member of the political party of the president who appointed him or her. The only exception was Lewis F. Powell, a conservative Democrat nominated by Richard Nixon. Given the ideologies of the respective parties, it is also not surprising that justices appointed by Democratic presidents tend to take liberal positions on the bench, and Republican-appointed judges most often make conservative rulings.

President George W. Bush had an extraordinary opportunity in 2005. Within a few months of one another, two Supreme Court vacancies occurred when Justice Sandra Day O'Connor retired and Chief Justice William H. Rehnquist died. More than 30 years had elapsed since the last time a president been able to nominate two Supreme Court justices in the same year.

Of the remaining justices, two (Antonin Scalia, Clarence Thomas) were solidly conservative, one (Anthony M. Kennedy) had a moderate to slightly conservative voting record on the court, and four (Stephen G. Bryer, John Paul Stevens, David H. Souter, and Ruth Bader Ginsburg) had somewhat liberal records. Debate raged over what kind of individuals Bush should pick. Some wanted him to name staunch conservatives; others favored moderate jurists modeled after O'Connor. In the end, the two new justices were Chief Justice John G. Roberts, Jr. and Associate Justice Samuel A. Alito, Jr. Critics argued that the two along with Scalia, Thomas, and (usually) Kennedy would move the Supreme Court distinctly rightward ideologically. Many supporters of Roberts and Alito also believed that would be true. To a large degree, what separated these critics and supporters was how they evaluated the potential shift. Liberals were appalled; conservatives cheered.

Not everyone agreed that the shift would occur, however. It was uncertain how much Roberts or Alito would be willing to make ruling that overturned precedent. Also, some judges shift their ideological views once on the court. Justice Souter was appointed in 1990 by President George H. W. Bush yet has been much more liberal than projected. There was also disagreement over whether Justice Kennedy was a conservative, giving them a 5 to 4 majority on the court or more of a moderate as O'Connor had been, leaving Kennedy as the "swing vote," on a court split with 4 conservatives and 4 liberals. In the following two readings, Jeff Lincoln and Jonathan H. Adler debate the degree of the ideological shift based on the record of the court during its first full term (normally October through June) with Roberts and Alito on the bench.

POINTS TO PONDER

➢ Do Lincoln and Adler really disagree on the how extensive the ideological shift has been, or are they merely labeling it differently?

➢ Lincoln characterizes Justice Kennedy as part of the conservative block. Adler sees Kennedy as a swing justice. Which is closer to reality?

➢ What does it say about American democracy when what the Constitution says about the government process and policy depends significantly on the ideological views of nine justices, who serve unlimited terms and are answerable to no one?

The Ideology of the Supreme Court: Radical Rightward Swing

JEFF LINCOLN

June 28[, 2007] marked the completion of the first full term of the United States Supreme Court of Chief Justice John G. Roberts, Jr., replete with decisions demonstrating a dramatic shift to the right in constitutional doctrine. The court handed down decisions removing restrictions on the operations of large business and financial concerns while sharply curtailing access to the courts for average working Americans seeking relief from their depredations, at the same time opening the population up to antidemocratic attacks by the state.

A review of the voting patterns of the individual justices reveals that a clear right-wing majority bloc exercises control over decisions. The *New York Times* on July 1 pointed out that one third of the decisions this term were decided 5 to 4, more than in any recent period. Of these cases, the four most conservative justices—Antonin Scalia, Clarence Thomas, Samuel A. Alito, Jr., and Roberts—prevailed about 70 percent of the time, while the four more liberal justices—John Paul Stevens, David H. Souter, Ruth Bader Ginsburg, and Stephen G. Breyer—prevailed in less than one third of the cases.

The victories for the conservative group are due to so-called "swing" justice Anthony M. Kennedy, who voted with the right-wingers overwhelmingly, only breaking ranks in a few cases. In fact, the *Times* article notes that the person whom Kennedy voted with most often was Alito, the two of them agreeing in 87 percent of all non-unanimous cases. That Kennedy is now considered the "center" of the Supreme Court, a position previously shared with Sandra Day O'Connor—another [President Ronald W.] Reagan appointee—speaks volumes about the political composition of the court.

The Supreme Court decided only 68 cases this term—the fewest in over 50 years, and an unusually high percentage of them involved damage suits against corporations. Each case was decided in favor of the corporation, indicating the court's decisive turn in a pro-business, anti-consumer direction. The term also included a number of significant rulings limiting First Amendment speech and Establishment [of religion] Clause protections, restricting abortion rights, prohibiting school desegregation efforts, and restricting the ability of criminal defendants to appeal.

To put the direction of the court into perspective, it is worth drawing a balance sheet of the major cases of the term.

In *Gonzales v. Carhart,* the Supreme Court upheld the Partial Birth Abortion Act of 2003, which imposes harsh fines and prison sentences on doctors who perform dilatation and extraction abortions. The law allowed no exception even for the health of the mother and is likely to impose significant hardships on women seeking abortions for medical reasons during their second or third trimester. The five-justice majority opinion was authored by Kennedy and marks the first time that a complete ban on a specific abortion procedure has been upheld by the Supreme Court. Besides calling into question the constitutional right to an abortion, the right-wing justices ignored limits on federal power they used in the past to strike down state civil rights laws and environmental protections.

This term also saw the court reverse much of the progressive advances embodied in the landmark *Brown v. Board of Education* decision. In *Parents Involved in Community Schools v. Seattle School District*, the court ruled that voluntary racial integration efforts by school districts were unconstitutional, even if intended to prevent resegregation. The decision is a sweeping repudiation of the sentiments that motivated broad masses of working people, both black and white, to mobilize for the advancement of civil and democratic rights under the banner of equality.

The Court dealt a blow to workers who find themselves the victims of pay discrimination. In *Ledbetter v. Goodyear Tire and Rubber Company*, the court dismissed the claim of a female employee who worked for 20 years at Goodyear and was unfairly paid a significantly lower salary than her male counterparts. She won a jury verdict it overturned on appeal. The court's decision held that a person must file a complaint within 180 days of the discriminatory act or the claim will be dismissed. This contradicts the longstanding position of the Equal Employment Opportunity Commission that an employee has a new chance to bring a claim every time he or she receives a paycheck with lower pay as a result of discrimination. The new rule makes payment discrimination suits virtually impossible as such discrimination often takes years to discover. *Ledbetter*, like many of the decisions this term, is one in which the majority worked backward from its desired result, utilizing specious reasoning to deny persons the right to have their case decided by a jury.

In two other 5–4 decisions, the court lessened the guarantees of a criminal defendant to a fair trial by an impartial jury and to have a meaningful review of their trial procedure on appeal. In *Brown v. Uttecht*, the Supreme Court upheld a trial court's decision to strike a juror who expressed a moral opposition to the indiscriminate use of the death penalty. The majority opinion noted that the state has a strong interest in packing a jury with people who are willing to have people executed. The *Bowles v. Russell* decision denied a criminal defendant's right to appeal because it was filed three days too late despite the fact that he was following the directions given to him by the trial judge.

In a serious erosion of the separation of church and state, the court threw out a case brought by an atheist challenging the use of executive department funds to promote the Bush administration's "faith-based" initiatives. In *Hein, Director, White House Office of Faith-Based and Community Initiatives v. Freedom From Religion Foundation, Inc.*, the court held that citizens have no general taxpayer standing to sue if the government is using funds for religious purposes as long as Congress did not expressly authorize the spending. The distinction is absurd, as the legislative branch allocated the money to the executive, and it makes presidential violations of the Establishment Clause immune from judicial review.

In two decisions dealing with other First Amendment issues, the court held that students may be disciplined for speech but that the government cannot limit the ability of wealthy individuals and corporations to influence elections. In *Morse v. Frederick*, the court held that a school principal could not be sued for suspending a student who displayed a banner with the words "Bong Hits 4 Jesus" at an Olympic torch parade near school grounds, gutting an earlier ruling that students do not shed their First Amendment rights at the school house gate. On the other hand, in *Federal*

Election Commission v. Wisconsin Right to Life Inc., the court struck down any limits on the financing of electioneering broadcasts by organizations that act as mouthpieces for the interests of large corporations as a violation of free speech.

In these decisions, largely dealing with the rollback of democratic rights and protections against the prosecutorial power of the state, certain divisions within the court emerge, both between and within the various groups of justices, with dissenting opinions sometimes vituperative.

In an unprecedented move for her, Ginsburg read aloud two dissents from the bench. Other justices noted in their dissents that the decisions of the court were the outcome of changing justices rather than developments in legal doctrine. Breyer wrote in the school desegregation case that "It is not often in the law that so few have so quickly changed so much." In his dissent to that decision, Stevens, the most senior justice, noted that "no member of the Court that I joined in 1975 would have agreed with today's decision."

These sentiments reflect growing concern among the more liberal justices that the reckless path taken by the conservative majority ignores the social and political ramifications of such a dramatic change in constitutional jurisprudence.

Within the conservative majority, there is a divide between Roberts, Alito, and Kennedy—whose modus operandi is to distinguish on trivial grounds or carve out exceptions to prior decisions, effectively overturning precedent while paying it lip service—and Scalia and Thomas, who have abandoned all pretense of upholding precedent and want to plow ahead overruling anything they find inconvenient.

Despite disagreements among the justices about how to proceed regarding these social issues, one thing is clear: when it comes to defending the interests of big business, there is a definite consensus as the following cases confirm:

In *Credit Suisse Securities (USA) LLC v. Billing*, the court decided in a 7-to-1 decision to dismiss a shareholder's antitrust suit against several investment banks that colluded to fix the prices for their initial public offerings. The result of the decision is that investment banks will effectively be immune from antitrust liability.

Likewise, in *Tellabs Inc. v. Makor Issues & Rights Ltd.*, the court ruled 8 to 1 that persons alleging that companies are engaged in securities fraud or manipulation must show "compelling evidence" of an intent to defraud before they can proceed or their lawsuit will be dismissed.

In a pair of unanimous decisions, the court sided with large companies against the interests of employees and consumers. In *Safeco Insurance of America v. Burr*, the court created exemptions for insurance companies for notifying customers if they deny or cancel coverage, an action required under the Fair Credit Reporting Act. In *Long Island Health Care at Home v. Coke*, the court extended an exemption under the Fair Labor Standards act to home companion care workers employed by large agencies so that those agencies would not be required to abide by minimum wage and overtime requirements.

These outrageous pro-business decisions were either reached unanimously or with a lone dissenter; all were authored by the court's "liberal" justices. The *New York Times* reported that the business community was "gleeful," quoting an attorney who handles Supreme Court cases for the Chamber of Commerce (Roberts's former assignment): "It's our best Supreme Court term ever."

The Democratic Party played the key role in the current state of affairs by refusing to block the appointments of Roberts and Alito and the consolidation of the right-wing majority. There was never any question about the views of either justice, as each had a long pedigree of right-wing judicial positions. Although the implications of a right-wing majority were clear, there was no serious attempt to oppose the appointment of either justice. With the Republican majority that existed at the time in the US Senate, the only means the Democrats had to stop either nominee's confirmation was the filibuster. For Alito, only a half-hearted attempt to filibuster was mounted at the last minute, and only after it was clear that such an attempt would not succeed. The Senate then voted 72 to 25 for cloture—41 votes would have defeated the motion—leading the way to his lifetime appointment. In the case of Roberts, not only was no filibuster even attempted, but he was confirmed with half of the Democrats in the Senate voting in his favor.

These most-recent decisions by the Supreme Court underscore a sharp turn to right. The legal opinions rendered by the court are designed to roll back the expansion of democratic rights that it recognized in a previous era, strengthening the repressive powers of the state apparatus, indicating the turn by the ruling elite toward more authoritarian forms of rule. Likewise, the goal of all the justices is to remove any restrictions that may hamper the profit-pursuing operations of corporations and the super-rich, largely by limiting access to the courts by average individuals who seek to challenge the dictates of big business.

When viewed in its historical context, the actions of the current court constitute a wholesale judicial counteroffensive against the [Chief Justice Earl] Warren Court (1953–1969) and its legacy of democratic legal reforms. Whatever differences exist among the right-wing judges are merely over tactics and degrees. They agree that the constitutional doctrine developed in the postwar period, based on the concepts of individual privacy, secularism, and the right to seek redress in the courts, all of which are embodied in the US Constitution, stands as an intolerable restraint on the ruling elite's ability to further its own interests.

While there have been periods where the Supreme Court has resisted change and acted as a brake on progressive struggles—most notably during the early years of [President] Franklin D. Roosevelt's "New Deal"—this is the first time since the decades following the end of Reconstruction that the court has taken a leading role in dismantling gains won in an earlier period. The failure of the Democratic Party to oppose this trend indicates that there is no constituency within the ruling elite that is dedicated to the defense of fundamental democratic rights. Such a defense can only be undertaken by an independent movement of the working class based on a socialist perspective.

The Ideology of the Supreme Court:
Moderate Conservative Tilt

JONATHAN H. ADLER

It was perhaps inevitable that Linda Greenhouse of the *New York Times* would proclaim the Supreme Court has become the "Court that conservatives had long yearned for and that liberals feared." The replacement of Justice Sandra Day O'Connor, a moderate and increasingly inconsistent pragmatist justice, with conservative minimalist [Justice] Samuel [A.] Alito[, Jr.] ensured a modest change across many areas of legal doctrine. Yet it is an exaggeration to report a "steady and well-documented turn to the right" during the [Supreme Court's] 2006–07 term, as did the *Washington Post* in an end-of-term review.

The replacement of Justice O'Connor with Justice Alito has shifted the Supreme Court slightly to the right, but there is no conservative legal revolution in the offing. If anything, the pattern of the Court's decisions somewhat reflects Justice [Anthony M.] Kennedy's somewhat conservative jurisprudence—moderately conservative and generally resistant to dramatic shifts in established doctrine. On many issues, Kennedy is in line with the minimalist approach of the chief justice and Justice Alito, yet on many others he is willing to be significantly more aggressive and depart from conservative principles. The swing justice has a soft spot for sweeping moral arguments, such as claims about personal autonomy or the nature of deliberative democracy

Some feign surprise at the voting pattern of the Court's two newest justices, Chief Justice [John G.] Roberts[, Jr.] and Justice Alito. Yet both justices have performed as advertised. President Bush promised Supreme Court nominations in the mold of Justices [Antonin] Scalia and [Clarence] Thomas, and there was never much doubt that Roberts and Alito would join the conservative side of the court. They are both "conservative minimalists"; they read legal texts fairly but narrowly, resist the creation or recognition of new legal rights, show respect for precedent, and avoid announcing legal rules broader than necessary to decide a given case. If anything, some conservatives may think President [George W.] Bush over-promised, as Roberts and Alito are more reluctant to reverse prior cases than either Scalia or Thomas. Indeed, Alito and Roberts are less prone to overturn prior precedent than *any* of their colleagues on the Court.

The two newest justices have undoubtedly had an impact, however. Both Bush nominees bring powerful intellects and strong principles to the Court. Chief Justice Roberts has much in common with his mentor, the late Chief Justice William Rehnquist, but Justice Alito is both more conservative and consistent than was Justice O'Connor. Nonetheless, the change has been anything but revolutionary. Most of the [Chief Justice Earl] Warren and [Chief Justice Warren E.] Burger Court precedents that most stoke conservative ire remain on the books.

In many respects, this year saw the emergence of the "Kennedy Court," with all that implies. As the swing justice, Justice Kennedy was able to dictate the outcome in many cases. He voted with the majority in every one of this term's 5–4 decisions, even those that were not decided along ideological lines. But even when he did not cast the deciding vote, Justice Kennedy was almost always in the majority. The Court decided 68 cases after oral argument this term, and Justice Kennedy dissented *only twice*, according to end-of-term statistics compiled by the folks at SCOTUSBlog. Chief Justice Roberts, by comparison, dissented eight times, and Justice Alito ten, whereas Justices Thomas and Souter each had 16 dissents. Justice Stevens was the most frequent dissenter, voting with the minority 26 times.

This term's docket [cases heard] included many cases in which Justice Kennedy joined the four more conservative justices in many high profile cases, but a single term does not produce a representative sample. A different mix of cases would likely produce quite different results. On questions from sexual privacy to capital punishment to executive authority in the war on terror, Justice Kennedy often joins the more liberal members of the Court. On still other issues, including federal pre-emption and state regulatory authority over interstate commerce, the Court is closely divided, but not on traditional ideological lines.

Justice Kennedy is the least likely member of the Court to uphold government restrictions on speech. Thus, he joined Justices Scalia and Thomas in urging the Court to overturn portions of the Court's 2003 decision in *McConnell* v. *FEC* and void federal limits on political advertising adopted as part of the McCain-Feingold campaign finance reforms [Senator John McCain (R-AZ) and Senator Russ Feingold (D-WI)], rejecting the incremental approach adopted by Chief Justice Roberts that would have preserved the recent precedent. He also joined Justice Alito's concurrence in the "Bong hits 4 Jesus" case, to ensure the Court's ruling would not permit limits on political speech by students [in the case *Morse v. Frederick, 2007*].

If Roberts and Alito are consistent minimalists, Justice Kennedy has a "maximalist" streak. Kennedy joined Justice Stevens' opinion for the Court in *Massachusetts* v. *EPA*, effectively ordering the Environmental Protection Agency to regulate greenhouse gas emissions from motor vehicles. This decision could have profound implications, particularly for the law of "standing." It invented a new doctrine of "special solicitude" for state attorneys general who wish to sue the federal government. He also wrote the majority opinion in *Leegin Creative Leather Products* v. *PSKS, Inc.*, overturning a decades-old antitrust precedent, and another in *Panetti* v. *Quarterman* adopting an innovative and expansive interpretation of federal law allowing convicted criminal defendants to file additional habeas corpus petitions.

Many commentators suggest that there was an unusual level of rancor and division in the Supreme Court this year. Simon Lazarus complained of "an unprecedented avalanche of 5–4 end-of-term Supreme Court decisions," in *The American Prospect* and the *Washington Post* editorialized that the Court "seemed more fractured than ever." Such claims, like the proclamations of a conservative ascendancy, are overstated.

Only one-in-four decisions was unanimous, and one-in-three was decided 5–4. This is hardly an unprecedented level of division, however. The level of unanimity was even lower during the 2004–05 session. That term the number of 5–4 decisions also reached 30 percent (as it did in the 2001–02 session). If anything was unprecedented it was the unusually high percentage of unanimous rulings (45 percent), and low number of 5–4 decisions (13 percent) during Chief Justice Roberts's first term that inflated expectations. The 2005–06 unanimous rulings in cases challenging abortion restrictions and the Solomon Amendment were more unusual than the split decisions of the term just past.

This is not to deny the very real doctrinal divisions on the Court. The justices are closely split on many issues, ranging from criminal procedure and federalism to race and the status of unenumerated rights. SCOTUSBlog's analysis of the "rate of dissension"—a measure of the number of dissents per case—found the 2006–07 term the most divided in recent years, barely edging out the 2001–02 term, 1.82 dissents per case to 1.81. This and other measures of the Court's may be magnified by the Court's ever-shrinking docket, however. Where once the High Court heard 100 cases a term, the justices only accepted 72 for 2006–07. As the Court grants fewer cases, those that remain on the docket may be more difficult, contentious, and closely fought on the mar-

gin. The oral statements from Justices [Ruth Bader] Ginsburg and [Stephen G.] Breyer delivering dissents in high-profile cases may have been unusual, but they were decidedly mild compared to some of the fiery statements from prior years, as when the Court handed down its decisions in two abortion-related cases, *Stenberg* v. *Carhart* and *Colorado* v. *Hill*.

Last Friday, after the term ended, the Court agreed to hear another case concerning the legal rights of Guantanamo Bay detainees in the 2007–08 term. This was unusual because it required the Court to reverse course, granting rehearing of a petition the Court had already denied earlier this year. This means that at least five justices were willing to hear the case—as opposed to the usual four. It may also indicate that five justices are skeptical of the Bush administration's legal arguments. If so, this is another sign that reports of a conservative judicial revolution are a bit premature and that this remains a Court worth watching.

THE CONTINUING DEBATE:
The Ideology of the Supreme Court

What Is New

One way to calculate voting blocs on the current justices is to look only at the most narrowly decided cases, those with a 5 to 4 vote, and see how often various justices agreed with the opinion of Clarence Thomas, probably the court's most conservative justice. The other justices and their level of agreement with Thomas during the 2006–2007 term were Scalia (100%), Roberts (91%), Alito (83%), Kennedy (61%), Ginsburg (8%), Beyer (4%), Souter (4%), and Stevens (4%). Thus Thomas, Scalia, Roberts, and Alito were a conservative block; Ginsburg, Beyer, Souter, and Stevens a liberal bloc; and Kennedy was between the two, siding with the conservatives a bit more often than with the liberals. These two blocks voted cohesively on 20 of the 23 decision decided 5 to 4, with Kennedy voting 7 times with the liberals and 13 times with the conservatives. It is important to remember, though, that only about a third of all the cases in the 2006–2007 term were decided 5 to 4. If all the cases were considered, then the blocs still exist but are less tightly. On all 72 decisions, for example, Justice Stevens, perhaps the court's most liberal justice, voted with Justice Thomas 52% of the time.

Where to Find More

For current court information, including voting patterns, go to the Supreme Court of the United States blog (SCOTUSBLOG) at www.scotusblog.com/. *The Harvard Law Review* also publishes annual data on cases, voting, and other matters, usually in its *November* issue. Visit the Supreme Court's Web site at www.supremecourtus.gov/, especially for the cases on its docket for the them beginning in October 2007. Another good site, one which contains visual and audio material as well at www.oyez.org/. For the selection of justices, read Christine L. Nemacheck, *Strategic Selection: Presidential Nomination of Supreme Court Justices from Herbert Hoover through George W. Bush* (University of Virginia Press, 2007). A study of the respective impacts of jurisprudence and politics on court decisions is Stephen M. Feldman, "The Rule of Law or the Rule of Politics? Harmonizing the Internal and External Views of Supreme Court Decision Making," *Law and Social Inquiry* (2005).

What More to Do

For either the 2006 or, if available, the 2007 term, pick 10 consecutive cases decided by a 5 to 4 vote and analyze them for the voting pattern that emerged among the justices. Also see whether the cases seem to be a liberal-conservative matter. Many are not or can be misleading. For example, the press widely portrayed the courts decision in *Federal Election Commission v. Wisconsin Right to Life* (2007) as conservative, yet the prevailing side was supported by not only conservative groups such as Wisconsin Right to Life but also by liberal groups like the American Civil Liberties Union. So beware of easy conclusions about who supports what.

15 STATE AND LOCAL GOVERNMENT

POLICE CRUISERS RAMMING FLEEING VEHICLES:
Violation of the Fourth Amendment *or* Justifiable Tactic?

VIOLATION OF THE FOURTH AMENDMENT

ADVOCATE: Craig T. Jones, Edmond & Jones, and Andrew C. Clarke, Borod & Kramer, Counsels for Respondent Victor Harris

SOURCE: Brief for the Respondent to the U.S. Supreme Court in *Scott v. Harris* (2007)

JUSTIFIABLE TACTIC

ADVOCATE: Orin S. Kerr, attorney at law and Philip W. Savrin and Sun S. Choy, Freeman Mathis & Gary, Counsels for Plaintiff Timothy Scott

SOURCE: Brief for the Plaintiff to the U.S. Supreme Court in *Scott v. Harris* (2007)

State and local governments in the United States have considerable authority in many areas, including police procedures. Nevertheless, the U.S. Constitution is the supreme law of the land, and in the U.S. federal system, state and local authorities have to act with the boundaries of, among other things, Americans' constitutional rights. The circumstances in which the Fourth Amendment circumscribes the police are at issue here.

This debate begins with a high-speed police pursuit much like those seen frequently on *Cops* and other reality-based television programs. Just before 11 at night on March 29, 2001, Coweta County (Georgia) Deputy Sheriff Clinton Reynolds clocked 19-year-old Victor Harris driving 73 mph in a 55 mph zone and set out in pursuit. Harris refused to stop, and an extended chase ensued. Another deputy sheriff, Timothy Scott, soon joined the pursuit. The details of the chase and how much of a threat to the community Harris's attempt to flee constituted are part of the dispute and are detailed during the following readings by the attorney representing Harris and Scott. What is not in dispute its that after a time, Scott attempted to use a PIT (pursuit intervention technique) maneuver to stop Harris. A PIT maneuver involves a police cruiser striking a fleeing vehicle a glancing blow on the side behind its rear wheels sufficient to cause the car to "spin out," thereby hopefully ending the chase. In this case, the impact of Scott's police cruiser with Harris's car forced it off the roadway, where it flipped going down an embankment and crashed into a telephone pole. Harris, who was not wearing a seatbelt, sustained injuries that left him a quadriplegic.

Harris subsequently sued Scott for violating his rights under the Fourth Amendment. Among other things, that amendment guarantees individuals the right "to be secure in their persons" from "unreasonable search and seizures" except "upon probable cause." Within the meaning of the amendment, seizure of a person includes the way that police take custody of alleged criminals. Harris asserted that a PIT maneuver constituted "deadly force," and that he had done nothing to justify Scott's use of such an extreme measure. Harris also contended that well-established law and practice should have made it clear to Scott that his actions were excessive. Harris further argued that Scott had no training in using a PIT maneuver, making his use of the tactic especially reckless.

Scott replied by asking the courts to reject Harris's case on the grounds that police officers and other government agents are immune from being sued by individuals for acts committed by the officers as part of their official duties. Police only lose this immunity, according to the Supreme Court in *Saucier v. Katz* (2001), if they (1) violate a constitutional right and (2) should reasonably have known at the time that their actions constituted a constitutional violation. Scott argued that he violated neither of these standards because Harris's action presented a threat to the community and that he had ignored sirens and other repeated, less aggressive indications to stop. Denying Harris's depiction of a PIT maneuver as "deadly force," Scott further responded that he acted within the rules set by his department and with the express permission to exercise PIT maneuver by a supervising officer.

In the first round of the case, a U.S. District Court in Georgia ruled in favor of Harris. Scott appealed to the 11th Circuit Court of Appeals in Atlanta, but it sustained the ruling of the district court. That set the stage for this debate, with the reading made up by the briefs filed with the U.S. Supreme Court by the lawyers for, first, Victor Harris, the respondent, then Timothy Scott, the petitioner.

As you read the briefs, you will see that three earlier Supreme Court cases play a major role. In *Tennessee v. Garner* (1985), which involved a police officer killing a fleeing, unarmed burglar as he tried to climb a fence, the court ruled that police can only use deadly force to apprehend a fleeing unarmed suspect if they have probable cause to believe that the suspect poses a substantial threat of death or serious physical injury to them others. The second case is *Graham v. Connor* (1989). It occurred after police roughly arrested Graham on suspicion of holding up a convenience store even though, it turned out, no crime had been committed. The court rejected Graham's suit, arguing the standard of "probable cause" should be judged according to what a reasonable officer on the scene might conclude or do. *Brower v. County of Inyo* (1989) is the third case. It began when a fleeing suspect was killed after hitting a trailer truck that police had placed as a roadblock in such a way (around a sharp turn, with lights from police cruisers shining in an approaching driver's eyes) as to reasonably preclude any outcome other than a crash. The court applied a three-prong standard of "objective reasonableness," measuring the force used versus (1) the severity of the offense; 2) the level of threat posed by a suspect to police or civilians, and 3) whether the individual resisting or trying to escape. In this case, the court found the police had failed to meet the objective reasonableness standard.

POINTS TO PONDER

➤ At what level of likelihood should an action like a PIT maneuver, that might kill a suspect, but usually does not, be considered "deadly force"?

➤ What standards should determine whether police can deem a fleeing suspect an immediate and substantial threat to themselves and to the citizenry?

➤ To what degree are suspects encouraged to flee and allowed sometimes to escape arrest if police are limited in their ability to pursue them and sometimes use strong measures to arrest them?

Police Cruisers Ramming Fleeing Vehicles: Violation of the Fourth Amendment

CRAIG T. JONES AND ANDREW C. CLARKE

STATEMENT OF THE CASE

On March 29, 2001, at approximately 10:42 p.m., Deputy Clinton Reynolds of the Coweta County Sheriff's Department (CCSD) was stationed on Highway 34 when he clocked Harris' vehicle traveling 73 mph in a 55 mph zone. Deputy Reynolds flashed his blue lights to attempt to get Harris to slow down. Deputy Reynolds testified that if Victor Harris had slowed down, Deputy Reynolds would not have even initiated a traffic stop. As Harris' vehicle passed by Deputy Reynolds' police car, it "was still doing seventy three miles per hour." Based solely on the traffic offense of speeding 73 mph in a 55 mph zone, Deputy Reynolds decided to pursue Victor Harris.

Shortly after commencing the pursuit, Deputy Reynolds obtained Harris' vehicle's license plate number and broadcast this information to his dispatcher. The vehicle that Victor Harris was driving was registered in his name and at his proper address. However, Deputy Reynolds failed to broadcast any information concerning the underlying charge that precipitated the pursuit (which was speeding).

Scott neither knew nor requested any information pertaining to the underlying basis for the pursuit until the pursuit was concluded. Pursuant to the CCSD's pursuit policy, officers should not have engaged in this pursuit as the offense which precipitated the pursuit was only speeding and they had Harris' license plate number which would have allowed the officers to apprehend Harris at a later date. At some point during the pursuit, Deputy Reynolds' dash-mounted video camera activated. There are four police videotapes which captured portions of the pursuit. There are two videotapes from CCSD deputies Reynolds and Scott [and two by Peachtree City officers Ercole and Sgt. Brown]. The pursuit began in Coweta County, Georgia and ended at Peachtree City in Fayette County, Georgia near Harris' home.

Despite not being requested to join the pursuit and having no information regarding the basis for the pursuit, Scott unilaterally decided to assist Deputy Reynolds in his pursuit of Harris. In Scott's overzealousness to join the pursuit, it appears that he drove his patrol car at speeds well over 100 mph and actually forced motorists off the road.

After Harris entered Peachtree City, Harris slowed his vehicle, turned on his blinker and entered an empty drug store parking lot. When Harris turned into the parking lot, there were two Peachtree City Police Department (PCPD) officers in their squad cars in the parking lot. The Peachtree City officers were not informed that a pursuit was heading into their jurisdiction. This is important because Peachtree City police officers are equipped with "stop sticks" which can be placed across the roadway to flatten a vehicle's tires slowly to safely terminate a pursuit. Had the PCPD been apprised of the pursuit, they could have attempted to deploy the stop sticks. Deputy Reynolds followed Harris into the parking lot. Harris drove through the parking lot towards Highway 74.

Harris was traveling through the parking lot, there was no vehicular or pedestrian traffic present that would have been endangered by the pursuit. Scott was traveling too fast to make the turn into the parking lot. After missing the entrance to the parking lot, Scott turned right at the next corner and sped around the other side of the parking lot, where he attempted to block Harris from exiting onto Highway 74 by driving his vehicle directly into the path of Harris' vehicle. Peachtree City officers were not involved in any manner in attempting to stop Harris from exiting the parking lot.

As Harris was attempting to exit the parking lot onto Highway 74, Scott drove his vehicle directly into Harris' lane of traffic. The police videos indicate that: 1) Scott drove his vehicle directly into Harris' lane of traffic; 2) Harris turned his vehicle to the left to avoid contact with Scott's vehicle; 3) Scott turned his police vehicle to the right in an effort to "box in" Harris; and 4) minor contact occurred between Harris' and Scott's vehicles. Peachtree City's Sgt. Brown observed this incident and noted in his official report that he saw "one Coweta County unit ram the Cadillac."

After the pursuit left the parking lot, Sgt. Brown and the PCPD officers did not join the pursuit because they were not informed of the underlying reason for the pursuit. Sgt. Brown testified that a pursuit for a speeding violation would be in violation of the PCPD Pursuit Policy which only allows pursuits for violent felonies. After leaving the parking lot, the Peachtree City police officers simply followed the pursuit from a distance in an effort to assist the pursuing officers and clear the intersections in the path of the pursuit. Sgt. Brown ordered his fellow Peachtree City officers to block all intersections on the pursuit route. The Peachtree City police officers followed Sgt. Brown's orders and immediately blocked off the intersections on the pursuit route which significantly reduced any danger from the pursuit.

After the pursuit left the parking lot, Scott requested to be the primary pursuing unit stating over the radio, "Let me have him 78 [Reynolds], my car's already tore up." Harris denies that Scott's vehicle was "tore up" as there was little, if any, visible damage to his vehicle. Scott then took over as the lead pursuing vehicle by passing both Deputy Reynolds and PCPD Officer Ercole. After becoming the lead pursuing vehicle, Scott requested permission from his supervisor, Sgt. Fenninger, to use a PIT maneuver on Harris.

The Court of Appeals' opinion notes that the PIT maneuver is "a driving technique designed to stop a fleeing motorist safely and quickly by hitting the fleeing car at a specific point of the vehicle, which throws the car into a spin and brings it to a stop." This definition assumes that the maneuver will be executed at lower speeds by properly trained officers, and therefore can terminate a flight "safely."

Significantly, neither Scott nor Sgt. Fenninger had any training on the use of the PIT maneuver. Scott claims that he learned about the PIT maneuver by talking informally with other members of the CCSD who had received the training prior to this incident. However, this testimony is disputed because Sheriff Yeager confirmed that no one from the CCSD had been trained or certified in the use of the PIT maneuver prior to this incident. Scott's own expert, Michael Brave, testified that a PIT maneuver cannot be used at speeds of 80–100 mph and that there is no question that Scott did not attempt a PIT maneuver on Harris. Sgt. Fenninger was monitoring a different radio frequency when the pursuit began. After another officer advised Sgt. Fenninger of the pursuit, Sgt. Fenninger began to monitor the pursuit. Sgt. Fenninger responded to Scott's request for permission to PIT by stating over the radio, "Go ahead and take him out. Take him out." Sgt. Fenninger testified that when he told Scott to "take out" Mr. Harris, Sgt. Fenninger was authorizing Scott to use deadly force to terminate the pursuit. After Sgt. Fenninger told Scott to "take out" Harris, Deputy Reynolds broadcast over the radio, "We're running about 90 now."

At the time of these transmissions, the pursuit was traveling southbound on Highway 74,. a two-lane highway without a shoulder and with steep embankments or culverts on either side of the road. At the time of the pursuit, the road was wet. Scott judicially admits that there were no motorists in the area who were in danger from the pursuit. Despite these conditions, Scott sped up his patrol car and rammed it into Harris' vehicle.

It is undisputed that Scott did not perform a PIT maneuver, and that he could not have performed a PIT maneuver under these conditions even if he had received PIT training. It is probable that Scott never attempted to perform a true PIT maneuver since he was never trained in its application. To any objectively reasonable officer trained in the PIT maneuver, it would have been readily apparent that it could not be performed under the circumstances: i.e., while traveling at high speeds on a wet, two-lane highway with no shoulders, and with deep culverts or embankments on each side. As a result of being rammed by Scott, Harris' vehicle left the roadway and flew off an embankment, flipped and came to rest against a telephone pole, causing severe and permanent injuries to Victor Harris. Immediately after Scott rammed Harris' vehicle, Deputy Reynolds notified dispatch that "it's going to be a bad 10–50 [car accident], get them to start an ambulance."

Sgt. Mark Brown of the PCPD was following the pursuit and arrived on the scene within seconds of the wreck. Sgt. Brown's initial reaction to Scott's ramming of Harris illustrates the egregiousness of this conduct to a reasonable police officer. Upon witnessing the ramming, Sgt. Brown exclaimed into his microphone: "Jesus Christ, what the…?" and "Fucking, they rammed him!" After this incident, Deputy Reynolds filed an Application for Criminal Arrest Warrant for: 1) speeding—73 mph in a 55; 2) fleeing and attempting to elude; and 3) reckless driving. Despite the fact that warrants were issued for these traffic violations, Harris was never prosecuted for these or any other offenses. While Harris admits that he violated traffic laws during the pursuit, Harris denies that he drove in such a reckless manner as pose a clear and present danger to the public as he was in control of his vehicle until it was rammed off the road by Scott.

During the course of the pursuit, Harris did pass some vehicles on a double yellow line in violation of the traffic laws. However, at least eight (8) times during the pursuit, Harris utilized his blinkers while passing or making turning movements. Harris admits he ran a red light at the intersection of Highway 34 and Fisher Road. However, there were no vehicles attempting to cross the intersection when he proceeded through it. While Harris exceeded the speed limit during the pursuit, Harris stayed in control of his vehicle. After entering Peachtree City, Sgt. Brown ordered his officers to block intersections on Highway 74 which significantly diminished the risks to the public. Harris slowed his vehicle at the intersection of Highway 74 and Kelly. After this intersection, there were no other motorists in the path of the pursuit. Significantly, at no time during the course of the pursuit did Harris ever use his vehicle offensively in an attempt to assault or strike the officers or any other motorist.

Incredibly, Scott argues in his brief that reasonable officers would not have known that ramming a vehicle at 90 mph on a wet, narrow, two-lane road bordered by deep culverts and steep embankments constituted the use of deadly force. This argument defies logic and common sense and illustrates Scott's flagrant disregard for the factual record. His own department's Use of Force Policy provided a clearly understandable definition of "deadly force," stating as follows: "Force which, under the circumstances in which it is used, is readily capable of causing death or other serious injury is considered deadly force."

Based on this objective definition, Scott's conduct was an obvious use of deadly force, because it cannot be disputed that ramming a vehicle at high speeds is "capable of" causing death or serious injury. In fact, this conduct is not only "capable of" causing death or serious bodily injury, but is almost certain to cause death or serious bodily injury. Further, Scott unequivocally testified that: 1) he knew that a police vehicle can be used as an instrument of deadly force; 2) when he rammed Harris' vehicle, he knew that it was likely that Harris would be injured or killed; and 3) when he rammed Harris' vehicle, he was utilizing deadly force. More importantly, all members of the CCSD who were questioned about whether Scott's use of his patrol car to ram Harris' vehicle constituted deadly force clearly testified that this conduct amounted to the use of deadly force.

INTRODUCTION TO LEGAL ARGUMENT

The issue presented in this appeal is whether the District Court and the Court of Appeals correctly held that Scott, who admittedly used deadly force against a fleeing traffic offender who did not pose an immediate threat to human life, is not entitled to qualified immunity as a matter of law.

All police officers who testified on the issue acknowledge that deadly force was used against Harris at a time when Harris admittedly posed no immediate threat to any human life. In short, the extraordinary factual record in this case not only authorizes, but demands, a finding that Scott used excessive force in violation of Harris' Fourth Amendment rights. To hold otherwise would immunize from constitutional liability all law enforcement officers who knowingly apply deadly force in circumstances when no life is in immediate danger in order to seize a fleeing traffic offender. Such a grave intrusion into a citizen's constitutional right to be free from the use of excessive and deadly force under the Fourth Amendment has never been tolerated and violates this Court's clearly established precedent and common sense.

SUPREME COURT CASES

This case is governed by a trilogy of decisions by this Court that gave "fair warning" that the conduct which occurred in the case was unconstitutional in the year 2001, and those decisions were correctly applied by the courts below.

In [the first case in the trilogy,] the landmark case of *Tennessee v. Garner* (1985), this Court held that a police officer who uses deadly force to seize a fleeing felony suspect who "poses no immediate threat" to human life violates the Fourth Amendment. In this case, Victor Harris was a teenaged, fleeing traffic offender, not a fleeing felon, so the Court's reasoning in *Garner* is even more compelling.

The Court in *Garner* did recognize that limited circumstances might justify the use of deadly force, to wit: (1) "where the officer has probable cause to believe that the suspect poses a threat of serious physical harm, either to the officer or to others," or "if the suspect threatens the officer with a weapon or there is probable cause to believe that he had committed a crime involving the infliction or threatened infliction of serious physical harm," and (2) if deadly force is "necessary to prevent escape," and, (3) "if, where feasible, some warning has been given." Without meeting all of these conditions, the use of deadly force is constitutionally unreasonable. According to *Garner*, police may not use deadly force to apprehend a fleeing felon unless the suspect poses an immediate threat to the life of the officer or some other person. It is essentially a "defense of life" standard. Scott acknowledges that *Garner* establishes a bright-line rule regarding deadly force applications noting that, "*Garner* applies in special circumstances when it is clear that the force used by an officer amounts to deadly force. In that context, *Garner* accurately translates the general requirement of reasonableness into a specific constitutional rule. However, *Garner's* special rule is not useful when the question of deadly force is open and unclear." In order to avoid complying with the *Garner* preconditions in evaluating whether Scott violated Harris' constitutional rights, Scott simply attempts to argue that Scott, or any reasonable officer for that matter, should not have known that ramming a vehicle at ninety (90) mph constitutes deadly force. The argument that neither Scott nor any objectively reasonable officer would understand that ramming a vehicle at 90 mph is the use of deadly force is a distortion of the record and an affront to any reasonable law enforcement officer. This specious argument lies at the heart of Scott's attempt to manufacture a "hazy border" under which he can claim the protection of qualified immunity, but the facts of this case are clearly governed by the rule set forth in *Garner*.

While *Garner* did not define "deadly force," it is clear that its holding is not limited to firearms but applies to all applications of deadly force. [In the various

U.S. courts of appeals,] deadly force has been uniformly defined as any use of force which creates a substantial likelihood of causing death or serious bodily injury. The uniformity of this definition is reinforced by the fact that it has been widely adopted by modern police agencies, and indeed, Scott's agency, the CCSD, defined deadly force in precisely this manner.

Under this objective definition, Scott's ramming of Harris' car was clearly the use of deadly force since it was substantially certain that death or serious bodily injury would result from contact between the vehicles at high speed, and the testimony in the record is unanimous on that point. Scott unequivocally testified that: 1) he knew that a police vehicle can be used as an instrument of deadly force; 2) when he rammed Harris' vehicle, he knew that it was likely that Harris would be injured or killed; and 3) when he rammed Harris' vehicle, he was utilizing deadly force. More importantly, all members of the CCSD who were questioned about whether Scott's use of his patrol car to ram Harris' vehicle constituted deadly force clearly testified that this conduct amounted to the use of deadly force. Even Scott's expert, Mr. Brave, acknowledged in an article that deliberately ramming a vehicle at high speed constitutes deadly force.

[In the second case in the trilogy,] *Garner's* focus upon reasonableness was expanded by *Graham v. Connor* (1989), which held that all claims resulting from the use of force against a suspect eluding capture—whether involving deadly or non-deadly force—are to be analyzed under the Fourth Amendment's objective reasonableness standard. In short, *Graham* requires what was implicit in *Garner*: that the force used be proportional to the threat. Unless the suspect is posing an immediate threat to human life, there is no justification for the use of force which is likely to kill or cause serious injury to the suspect.

The test of reasonableness under the Fourth Amendment is not capable of precise definition or mechanical application, however, its proper application requires careful attention to the facts and circumstances of each particular case, including the severity of the crime at issue, whether the suspect poses an immediate threat to the safety of the officers or others, and whether he is actively resisting arrest or attempting to evade arrest by flight. In short, *Graham* requires what was implicit in *Garner*: that the force used be proportional to the threat. Unless the suspect is posing an immediate threat to human life, there is no justification for the use of force which is likely to kill or cause serious injury to the suspect.

Finally [in the trilogy's third case,] *Brower v. County of Inyo* (1989), the Court addressed whether a suspect fleeing from police who runs into a "deadman's roadblock" was "seized" under the Fourth Amendment. In holding that a police officer's use of an automobile to create a roadblock to stop a fleeing suspect constituted a "seizure," the Court noted that a seizure occurs "when there is a governmental termination of freedom of movement through means intentionally applied"—regardless of whether the "means intentionally applied" is a bullet, a fist, or a deliberate high-speed collision. *Brower* distinguished the case of a deliberate collision amounting to a seizure from the typical automobile negligence claim as follows:

> Thus, if a parked and unoccupied police car slips its brake and pins a passerby against a wall, it is likely that a tort has occurred, but not a violation of the Fourth Amendment. If, instead of that, the police cruiser had pulled alongside the fleeing car and sideswiped it, producing the crash, then the termination of the suspect's freedom of movement would have been a seizure.

Brower summarily discarded the argument that Brower's flight from police precluded a finding that that Brower was subjected to a Fourth Amendment seizure.

ARGUMENT

Since the 1980s, this trilogy of Supreme Court rulings has defined the contours of the Fourth Amendment in use of force cases. Based on these decisions, it is clear that:

1) The Fourth Amendment is violated when a police officer to uses deadly force to seize a fleeing suspect who "poses no immediate threat" to human life.

2) All claims resulting from the use of force against a suspect—whether involving deadly or non-deadly force—are to be analyzed under the Fourth Amendment's objective reasonableness standard.

3) In analyzing the objective reasonableness of use of force against a suspect, the force must be proportional to the threat.

4) A seizure occurs whenever there is a governmental termination of freedom of movement through means intentionally applied. The use of a police vehicle to sideswipe or ram a vehicle causing it to crash is a seizure which must meet the objective reasonableness standard of the Fourth Amendment.

5) A suspect's flight from police officers does not reduce or eliminate an officer's responsibility for acting reasonably when seizing a suspect.

The Facts of the Case

In applying these bedrock constitutional principles to the case at bar, it is clear that Scott violated Harris' constitutional rights under the Fourth. Scott's contention that there are no genuine issues of material fact as to whether Scott's conduct violated Harris' constitutional rights completely disregards both the record and the factual findings of the District Court.

Despite Scott's argument to the contrary, the undisputed proof in the record indicates that Scott's ramming of Harris was an application of deadly force as it was obvious that this conduct may cause death or serious bodily injury. As such, the *Garner* pre-conditions for the use of deadly force must be considered. Under *Garner*, deadly force could not be utilized against Harris unless:

1) Harris posed an immediate threat to officers or others; or there was probable cause to believe Harris committed a crime involving the infliction, or threatened infliction, of serious physical harm; and

2) deadly force was necessary to prevent escape; and

3) a warning was given, if feasible.

Scott has judicially admitted that the application of deadly force was performed at a time when no other motorists were in the area and Harris was driving away from Scott. Thus it is clear that neither Scott nor any third parties were in immediate danger at the time of the application of deadly force.

Moreover, the underlying crime which precipitated the pursuit was a traffic offense which is not a crime involving the infliction or threatened infliction of serious physical harm. In fact, Harris' crime was so minor that Deputy Reynolds testified that he would not have even initiated a traffic stop if Harris had slowed down after he flashed his blue lights. The fact that traffic offenses are not considered serious enough to justify dangerous police activity is reflected in the growing trend in modern police departments that have specifically precluded high-speed pursuits of traffic offenders and restricted their use to violent felonies only.

While Scott argues that Harris' conduct during the course of the pursuit created the necessity for the use of deadly force, both the District Court and Court of Appeals found, when viewing the record in the light most favorable to Harris, that Harris' conduct during the course of the pursuit did not entitle Scott to use deadly force to apprehend him because:

1) Harris stayed in control of his vehicle;

2) Harris never used his vehicle offensively as a weapon against the officers or anyone else;

3) Harris was not violently resisting, but simply attempting to flee;

4) Harris was driving away from Scott when deadly force was applied; and

5) at the time of the application of deadly force, there was no one in the immediate area who was endangered by Harris' flight.

Ignoring the record and taking Scott's argument to its illogical conclusion, Scott is arguing that deadly force may be used against any person who flees from the police in an automobile—failing to recognize that flight alone does not pose grave dangers to officers or the public in all cases.

Significantly, the CCSD adopted a "violent felony only" policy after this incident in 2002, thereby aligning itself with the majority of modern police departments.

In addition, *Garner* mandates that deadly force only be utilized to apprehend a fleeing suspect when it is necessary. Since the officers had Harris' license plate number, and Scott had "personally observed Harris at very close range," deadly force was not necessary to apprehend Harris at a later time. Based on these facts, Scott could have clearly attempted to apprehend Harris at his home at a later date. Further, the factual record developed in this case clearly indicates that terminating the pursuit would substantially reduce any risks emanating from the pursuit. Under the facts of this case, the use of deadly force was not necessary to apprehend Harris and to diminish the risks of the pursuit to the public.

Scott mistakenly suggests that analyzing the case under *Graham* rather than *Garner* would result in a different outcome. Graham does not overrule the *Garner* pre-conditions to the use of deadly force but simply acknowledges what was implicit in *Garner*: that any use of force must be proportional to the threat. Under *Graham*, to evaluate whether an officer's use of force is reasonable, careful attention must be paid to the facts of each case which includes: the severity of the crime at issue, whether Harris' vehicle was properly registered at his correct home address.

Scott implicitly acknowledges this fact in his brief stating, "It is true that police generally have the option of calling off the pursuit, which in some circumstances may lessen the risk." While implicitly acknowledging that termination would reduce the risks of the pursuit, the factual record fully supports this contention as Harris' expert, Dr. Geoffrey Alpert, has unequivocally testified that research has validated this theory and Scott's expert has failed to provide an opinion refuting this testimony.

Analyzing the *Graham* factors without consideration of the *Garner* pre-conditions results in the same conclusion. The crime which precipitated the pursuit was a traffic offense. Despite Scott's argument that Harris was guilty of a myriad of serious criminal offenses, including felonies, during the course of the pursuit, both the District Court and Court of Appeals properly declined to make that determination as a matter of law. Moreover, Harris was only charged with misdemeanor traffic offenses for which he was never prosecuted, and Scott has judicially admitted that the use of force was applied at a time when no other person was immediately endangered by the pursuit. Most significantly, Harris was merely fleeing—not violently resisting arrest. Under both *Garner* and Graham, there are clearly genuine issues of material fact as to whether Scott's use of force against Harris was excessive and thus prohibited by the Fourth Amendment.

The rules on the use of deadly force established by this Court are so well understood that they are embodied in nationally accepted standards of the law enforcement profession which provide that "forcible stopping maneuvers" like the ramming of a vehicle at high speed "should be used only in those instances where the application of deadly force would be justified." The model pursuit policy of the International Association of Chiefs of Police (IACP) prohibits their use altogether, stating that "officers may not intentionally use their vehicle to bump or ram the suspect's vehicle in order to force the vehicle to a stop off the road or in a ditch."

Based on a proper analysis of the record in the light most favorable to Harris and applying the foregoing precedents, both the District Court and the Court of Appeals correctly found that there are genuine issues of material fact as to whether Scott's actions violated Harris' Fourth Amendment rights. Under the facts in the record, a jury could reasonably conclude that the need to capture a traffic violator does not justify sentencing him to life in a wheelchair, even if that means he gets away, and even if the police are later unable to prove that he was the one driving the car by running his tag number and attempting to arrest him at the house where he has lived his entire life. As reasonable minds can differ as to whether

Scott's use of force was objectively reasonable, this matter is left to the sole province of the jury.

Existing Law When the Incident Occurred

Clearly established law in 2001 gave fair warning to a reasonable police officer that it is a Fourth Amendment violation to use deadly force to terminate a pursuit by ramming the vehicle of a fleeing traffic offender at a time when the offender poses no immediate threat to human life, and when the offender is merely fleeing and has not violently resisted apprehension at any time during the course of the pursuit. Since Harris has shown that there are genuine issues of material fact regarding whether Scott violated his Fourth Amendment rights, the next step in the qualified immunity analysis is to determine whether the law was sufficiently clearly established to provide Scott with fair warning that his conduct violated Harris' constitutional rights.

Therefore, the "salient question" before this Court is whether the contours of the law which existed on March 29, 2001, were sufficiently clear to give a reasonable law enforcement officer "fair warning" that he could be liable for deliberately ramming a police car into a car driven by a fleeing traffic offender when the fleeing offender posed no immediate risk to the life and safety of the officer or others. While Scott argues that the holdings of the *Garner/Graham/Brower* trilogy are couched in general terms which are too vague to clearly establish the law in this case, Harris submits that these cases articulate an unambiguous rule which applies "with obvious clarity" to this case. The Court's rulings in *Garner*, *Graham*, and *Brower* are not limited by their terms to the specific facts of those cases—rather, they clearly and succinctly define the limits of force allowable under the Fourth Amendment.

Harris submits that this Court's rulings in *Garner*, *Graham* and *Brower* clearly establish protections embodied by the Fourth Amendment, to wit:

1) deadly force may not be used to apprehend a fleeing offender unless the offender places the officer or others in immediate danger of death or serious bodily injury; and

2) any use of force by officers—deadly or otherwise—must be proportional to the threat posed by the offender.

These principles apply with obvious clarity to the facts of this case and place Scott on notice that his conduct violated this clearly established law. The undisputed facts in the record reveal that:

1) Harris was being pursued for a simple traffic offense;

2) Scott used deadly force when he rammed Harris in an effort to apprehend him; and

3) at the time that Scott used deadly force, no one was in immediate danger of being harmed.

Scott argues that the only way that Harris could prove that the law was clearly established is to show that, prior to March 29, 2001, a previous case holding an officer liable for violating the Fourth Amendment by finding that making intentional direct contact with a fleeing motorist at high speeds constituted the improper use of deadly force. While Scott does not precisely specify what aspect of the law he contends is not clearly established by the previously cited cases, a more particularized analysis of the case law as it existed on March 29, 2001 reveals that the law was sufficiently clear to place Scott on notice that his conduct violated Harris' constitutional rights as far back as the 1980s.

In arguing that the law was not clearly established, Scott cites a number of cases which ultimately granted qualified immunity to officers who had used deadly force to terminate a chase. However, an examination of these cases reveals that all the cases cited by Scott analyzed the officer's use of deadly force under the *Garner/Graham* analysis discussed herein. Therefore, it is ironic that Scott suggests that this analysis does not apply with obvious clarity to this case. Properly analyzed, the reasoning of the cases cited by Scott all support Harris' argument that Scott's use of deadly force to terminate the chase by ramming Harris' car while no other persons were in immediate danger was unconstitutional under clearly established law.

Harris submits that the cases offered by Scott provide no support for the argument that the law was insufficiently developed to provide Scott with fair warning that his conduct violated the Fourth Amendment. In fact, the reasoning of these cases clearly supports Harris' position that the *Garner/Graham/Brower* trilogy provides the proper analysis of the case at bar—both in determining whether a constitutional violation occurred (under the first prong of Saucier) and whether the law was clearly established (under the second prong). Immunity was granted in the cases cited by Scott—not because of any lack of clarity in the governing law—but because the application of clearly established law to the undisputed facts illustrated that the officers' conduct was reasonable under a *Garner/Graham/Brower* analysis.

Harris submits that these cases illustrate that the state of the law in 2001 was sufficiently developed to provide Scott with fair warning that his conduct violated Victor Harris' clearly established Fourth Amendment rights because these cases all determined that an officer's application of deadly force to terminate a pursuit is governed by

Garner/Graham/Brower. Therefore, this trilogy of cases applies with obvious clarity to this case and clearly establishes the applicable law. At a minimum, these cases serve to further clarify that the holdings of *Garner/Graham/Brower* apply to cases where force is used to terminate a pursuit.

Brower clearly established that using a police vehicle to terminate a pursuit through a roadblock or an intentional sideswiping was a Fourth Amendment seizure. While those...cases held that the officers were entitled to qualified immunity, both courts made this determination based on the fact that *Brower* had not yet been decided, rejecting the argument that *Garner*, standing alone, could clearly establish that a seizure had occurred under the facts of those cases.

Finally, Scott argues that this Court's decision in *Brosseau v. Haugen* (2004) entitles him to qualified immunity as a matter of law. In *Brosseau*, the Court did not discuss whether the officer's conduct violated the Constitution. Instead, the Court went straight to the second prong of *Saucier* and held that the officer was entitled to qualified immunity because it was not clearly established that shooting a violent suspect who was attempting to flee in a vehicle and posed a serious risk to persons in the immediate area was unconstitutional. Again, Scott attempts to latch on to the holding of the cause without any consideration of the factual circumstances of the case. Just as this Court distinguished Both *Garner* and [this] case involve fleeing suspects who were not violently resisting arrest. *Brosseau* is different because it involved a suspect who was violently resisting arrest.

Unlike Harris, the fleeing offender in *Brosseau* was a felony suspect with a no-bail warrant out for his arrest with whom Officer Brosseau had a violent physical encounter prior to the shooting. Believing that the suspect, Mr. Haugen, had entered a Jeep to retrieve a gun, Brosseau broke the windowpane of the Jeep and attempted to stop Haugen by hitting him over the head with the butt and barrel of her gun. Haugen was undeterred, however, and began to take off out of the driveway, without regard for the safety of those in his immediate vicinity

Prior to using deadly force, Brosseau warned Haugen that she would shoot by pointing her gun at the suspect while commanding him to get out of the car, and then using the gun to shatter the glass of the car window and hit him in an attempt to get the keys. In granting qualified immunity, the Court held that *Garner* did not provide a reasonable officer with fair notice of a Fourth Amendment violation in "the situation [Brosseau] confronted: whether to shoot a disturbed felon, set on avoiding capture through vehicular flight, when persons in the immediate area are at risk from that flight."

Those facts are not comparable to this case. There is no comparable evidence that Scott had arguable probable cause to believe that Harris posed an immediate risk of death or serious danger to Scott, other officers, or nearby citizens. Harris was being chased for a traffic violation. Unlike the situation in *Brosseau*, the parties herein were not in close physical proximity nor had they been engaged in a violent, one-on-one struggle. In fact, Scott and the other pursuing officers were following Harris from behind in their squad cars. At the time of the ramming, Harris was driving in a non-aggressive fashion— i.e., without trying to ram or run into the officers or others. Moreover, unlike

Haugen, who was surrounded by officers on foot, with other cars in very close proximity in a residential neighborhood, Scott's path on the open highway was largely clear. The videos introduced into evidence show little to no vehicular (or pedestrian) traffic, allegedly because of the late hour and the police blockade of the nearby intersections by the PCPD. Finally, Scott issued absolutely no warning (over the loudspeaker or otherwise) prior to using deadly force.

While Scott's argument completely disregards the factual record in this case in analyzing his entitlement to qualified immunity as a matter of law, it is clear that both the District Court and the Court of Appeals appropriately determined that genuine issues of material fact exist regarding whether Scott violated Victor Harris' clearly established Fourth Amendment rights. Given the limitations on the use of deadly force that arise under the rule of *Garner* and its progeny—a rule which applies with obvious clarity to the case at bar—the law was sufficiently developed to provide Scott with more than 'fair warning' that his conduct violated Harris' constitutional rights. At the time of this incident, any objectively reasonable officer would have known that ramming a fleeing suspect at high speeds constituted a seizure by deadly force, and accordingly, it could only be justified under circumstances authorizing the use of deadly force against a fleeing suspect. This much was acknowledged by Scott, who simply argues that his use of deadly force was reasonable under the circumstances—despite the fact that he used deadly force against a nonviolent misdemeanant who was merely fleeing.

Police Cruisers Ramming Fleeing Vehicles: Justifiable Tactic

ORIN S. KERR, PHILIP W. SAVRIN AND SUN S. CHOY

SCOTT'S USE OF FORCE WAS CONSTITUTIONAL

Substantively, Fourth Amendment claims "are evaluated for objective reasonableness based upon the information the officers had when the conduct occurred," [according to this court in] *Saucier v. Katz* (2001). This is so because "The 'reasonableness' of a particular use of force must be judged from the perspective of a reasonable officer on the scene, rather than with the 20/20 vision of hindsight," according to *Graham v. Connor* (1989). [Moreover,] "Officers can have reasonable, but mistaken, beliefs as to the facts establishing the existence of probable cause…and in those situations courts will not hold that they have violated the Constitution."

Harris's arguments in this case hinge on the solitary assumption that the legal framework of *Tennessee v. Garner* (1985) applies to Scott's use of force, and clearly so. *Garner* does not supplant *Graham's* "totality of the circumstances" test, but instead applies *Graham's* factors to the unique situation where a police officer shot an unarmed, nondangerous suspect in the back of the head for the sole purpose of preventing his escape. The suspect in that case was on foot and attempting to scale a fence when he was killed. *Garner* resolved that "[a] police officer may not seize an unarmed, nondangerous suspect by shooting him dead." It acknowledged that an "armed burglar would present a different situation," and expressly limited its holding to the facts at issue: "We hold that the statute is invalid insofar as it purported to give [the officer] the authority to act as he did."

A suspect using a vehicle to flee at high speeds presents a completely different challenge to law enforcement than an unarmed suspect on foot. By continuing to flee in a vehicle, the suspect does not merely seek to elude capture, but risks harming the public (intentionally or unintentionally) in the process. As a matter of constitutional doctrine, the limitations on the use of force enunciated in *Garner* simply do not apply to the perils of vehicular flight. Stated otherwise, the risks presented by a driver determined to elude capture in an automobile, at high speeds and in the manner attempted by Harris, present unique exigencies that an officer cannot reasonably anticipate.

Harris insists a jury could find he was nondangerous because he stayed in control of his vehicle and did not try to run anyone off the road, Scott's path was "largely clear," and traffic was relatively light. Essentially, Harris urges that he was a "safe" reckless driver. This argument tracks the [appeals court's] recognition that Harris "slowed for turns and intersections, and typically used his indicators for turns. He did not run any motorists off the road." It also ignores the undisputed facts, shown on the videotape, that there were motorists on the road and that Harris refused to even slow down in face of lawful commands to stop.

When Scott joined the pursuit, Harris had already failed to yield to Deputy Reynolds's flashing lights and siren; had passed motorists by crossing over double yellow traffic control lines at high speeds; and had raced through a red traffic light.

After Scott responded to Reynolds's call for assistance, Harris tried to escape through the parking lot of a strip shopping center. Scott maneuvered his vehicle to block Harris's egress, but was unsuccessful. Once Harris's vehicle collided with his patrol car, Scott then personally witnessed Harris again racing down a two-lane road at high speeds, crossing double yellow control lines, and running a red light. It was only at that point that vehicle contact was made to end the ongoing threat of harm to the public.

By then, Scott had exhausted less intrusive means, such as lights, sirens, engaging Harris in a pursuit, and attempting to block his exit from the drug store parking lot. [This court has said in] *United States v. Montoya de Hernandez* (1985) that, "Authorities must be allowed to graduate their response to the demands of any given situation." Harris was fairly warned that the police would steadily increase the force unless and until he complied with their lawful command for him to stop his vehicle.

Harris's attempt to portray himself as a mere speeder to whom a citation might have been issued ignores *Graham's* sharp admonition that, "The 'reasonableness' of a particular use of force must be judged from the perspective of a reasonable officer on the scene, rather than with the 20/20 vision of hindsight." A reasonable officer in Scott's position would view Harris as someone who had committed numerous offenses, was putting the public at serious risk by driving extremely recklessly on a two-lane road with other vehicles present, and made his unwillingness to stop repeatedly clear.

Harris's assumption that his high-speed vehicular flight is legally indistinguishable from *Garner's* unarmed burglar on foot has no legitimate basis. Even though he did not injure anyone else during his escapade, Harris knowingly created a risk of harm, which is the definition of reck-

lessness. Because the risks of harm in this case cannot be likened to the absence of harm presented by an unarmed burglar on foot, *Garner's* analysis of the use of force does not apply. Instead, *Graham's* more general "totality of the circumstances" test applies, which accords discretion to officers to use force based on objectively reasonable beliefs as to the risks they are confronting.

Harris further assumes that Scott used deadly force, relying on alleged admissions in the [trial] testimonies and, once again, on *Garner*. In relying on testimony, Harris overlooks that (a) [Scott's] defense counsel properly objected to witnesses providing legal opinions; and (b) Scott has repeatedly contended in court documents that he did not use deadly force. Further, Scott did not admit that he used deadly force. The actual question posed to Scott was whether "there was a likelihood that Victor Harris could be seriously injured or in a wreck due to the speed of the vehicles." In his brief before this Court, Harris alters this testimony to contend that Scott "knew that it was likely that Harris would be injured or killed." As explained below, neither of these statements articulates the correct Fourth Amendment standard, a legal matter to which Scott did not, and could not, admit.

Harris's remaining basis for contending that Scott used deadly force is the appellate court's reliance on *Garner*. *Garner*, however, did not define "deadly force," nor did it need to. [In that case the police officer] used a firearm, which is clearly an example of deadly force." Lower courts since *Garner* have struggled with whether to characterize various police tools and instruments as deadly force. An oft-cited case in this context [occurred when] a police dog was dispatched to bite a suspected burglar who was hiding in a darkened building. Even though the suspect died as a result of the bite, [one court of appeals] found no use of deadly force. In reaching that conclusion, the court acknowledged that "the mere recognition that a law enforcement tool is dangerous does not suffice as proof that the tool is an instrument of deadly force."

The Model Penal Code defines a threat of serious bodily injury as presenting a "substantial risk of...serious, permanent disfigurement, or protracted loss or impairment of the function of any bodily member or organ." Yet, dropping an explosive on a roof to gain entry to a building was not "deadly force" under *Garner*. Nor was a dog bite to the suspect's neck considered deadly force, even though dogs are trained to inflict bodily harm, and even though the bite killed the suspect.

What is clear is that Scott [similarly] did not use deadly force. Although Harris's injuries are severe, Scott's conduct was reasonably calculated under the circumstances to stop Harris, not kill him. Scott did not shoot at Harris or his vehicle. Despite the repeated characterizations of Scott's force as a "ramming," Scott did not crash into the car at a high speed differential or push Harris off the road. As the videotape shows, the road where the contact took place appeared (at night) to be level.

Even if Scott's conduct amounted to deadly force and the *Garner* conditions govern, his actions were constitutional. Harris disagrees and suggests that under *Garner*, the harm must be "immediate" before justifying deadly force. By so contending, Harris confuses the immediacy of the threat with the immediacy of the harm. *Garner* requires that the threat be immediate in the sense that the risk of harm is immediately apparent. It does not require that the harm is immediate, in the sense of a split-second away. *Garner* implements the concern that the threat must be immediate by requiring "probable cause to

believe that the suspect poses a significant threat of death or serious physical injury to the officer or others." The officer must have probable cause, which requires the officer to assess the seriousness of the threats that are immediately before him.

Under *Garner*, a catastrophic harm need not be a split second away before the officer can act. A contrary rule would make it difficult (if not impossible) for an officer to comply with the Fourth Amendment when, as here, a use of force takes time for the officer to execute. The officer might start to use force at one time only to find that the immediacy had waned at the moment of contact. Alternatively, the officer might not realize that force was needed immediately until it was too late.

In this case, Harris's reckless driving provided ample probable cause to believe that he presented an ongoing threat of serious physical harm under *Garner*. The threat was immediate: Scott personally observed it in the minutes and seconds leading up to his use of force. Based on what he personally observed, he properly determined that Harris presented an immediate threat of serious physical harm to innocent bystanders. Probable cause does not require 100% certainty; it requires a fair probability based on a common-sense practical judgment.

Harris's driving created a fair probability that he would cause serious physical harm and therefore satisfied *Garner*. Any other conclusion would require law enforcement officers to either make no physical contact with a fleeing suspect at all or wait until a fleeing suspect is seconds away from injuring an innocent person before taking action to neutralize the threat presented. In addition to increasing the threat of harm, such a rule would promote dangerous flight as an efficient means for suspects and their conspirators to shield contraband and other fruits of their criminal enterprise from disclosure.

SCOTT DID NOT VIOLATE CLEARLY ESTABLISHED LAW

If the Court concludes that Scott violated the Fourth Amendment, he would be entitled to qualified immunity because the case law provided no "fair warning"— either in March 2001 or even today—that the use of a vehicle to terminate a pursuit was unconstitutional under the circumstances presented.

Supreme Court Decisions

Harris suggests that the "trilogy" of *Graham-Garner-Brower* [supports his case]. Harris's repeated invocation of *Brower* is puzzling. There, the Court found that a seizure had been alleged where the suspect's vehicle crashed into a police roadblock: "It was enough here, therefore, that, according to the allegations of the complaint, Brower was meant to be stopped by the physical obstacle of the roadblock—and that he was so stopped." [In] *Brower* [this court] did not analyze the reasonableness of the seizure: "the circumstances of the roadblock, including the allegation that headlights were used to blind the oncoming driver, may yet determine the outcome of this case." In contrast, the issue in this case is precisely one of reasonableness; *Brower* cannot clearly establish the law on an issue the Court expressly declined to address.

Thus, Harris is left with *Graham* and *Garner* as Supreme Court cases to resolve the "clearly established" analysis. This Court has admonished that these cases are necessarily cast at a high level of generality to take account for the fact-specific nature of the inquiry and to give allowances for reasonable mistakes as to facts or law that an officer in the field may make:

It is sometimes difficult for an officer to determine how the relevant legal doctrine, here excessive force, will apply to the factual situation the officer confronts. An officer might correctly perceive all of the relevant facts but have a mistaken understanding as to whether a particular amount of force is legal in those circumstances. If the officer's mistake as to what the law requires is reasonable, however, the officer is entitled to the immunity defense. *Graham* does not always give a clear answer as to whether a particular application of force will be deemed excessive by the courts. This is the nature of a test which must accommodate limitless factual circumstances.

This Court's decision in *Brosseau v. Haugen* (2004) is particularly instructive. *Brosseau* found no violation of clearly established law even though the officer shot a suspect from behind, whom she thought was attempting to escape in his vehicle. While Officer Brosseau suspected that Haugen would drive in a dangerous manner based on prior conduct, Scott had probable cause to believe—if not to a certainty—that Harris would continue to drive recklessly unless and until he was stopped.

Law Enforcement Policies

Harris claims that "nationally recognized" law enforcement standards recognize "ramming" as appropriate when deadly force is authorized. Whether or not this statement is true, Scott's use of force in this particular case, and on these particular facts, did not violate this standard. Even then, police departments are free to adopt whatever limits they desire, and often are more restrictive than the Constitution might otherwise allow.

Administrative policies and procedures do not (and cannot) define what is constitutional as a matter of law. That is the function of the courts.

Moreover, Scott followed the policies applicable in Coweta County, [which states:] "Deliberate physical contact between vehicles at any time may be justified to terminate the pursuit upon the approval of the supervisor." And, as the district court found, Scott received the requisite supervisory permission to make contact with Harris's vehicle. Scott's adherence to departmental policy further buttresses the conclusion that he did not violate clearly established law.

THE CONTINUING DEBATE:
Police Cruisers Ramming Fleeing Vehicles

What Is New

In the end, the Supreme Court ruled 8 to 1 for Deputy Scott, reasoning that he had acted "reasonably" and therefore not violated the under the Fourth Amendment. Writing for the majority, Justice Antonin Scalia noted that the justices had watched the videos of the pursuit, which he termed, "a Hollywood-style car chase of the most frightening sort." In such circumstances, Scalia continued, "A police officer's attempt to terminate a dangerous high-speed car chase that threatens the lives of innocent bystanders does not violate the Fourth Amendment, even when it places the fleeing motorist at risk of serious injury or death." The lone dissenting justice, John Paul Stevens argued that Harris's actions were not "a capital offense, or even an offense that justified the use of deadly force rather than an abandonment of the chase."

Police pursuits remain a difficult issue. About 3,250 people a year die in the United States during such chases. Seventy-two percent of the victims are in the fleeing vehicle, 1% are police officers, the rest are occupants in other cars, pedestrians, and other bystanders.

Where to Find More

Just as the Supreme Court did, you can watch the two (car 1, car 2) police videos of the chase at www.youtube.com/watch?v=auw_VAczrTw. The tape can be downloaded from the court's opinion page at www.supremecourtus.gov/opinions/06slipopinion.html. For an organization that campaigns for "safer and smarter police pursuits," go to www.pursuitwatch.org/. A site run by police officers related to pursuits and other driving issues is at www.policedriving.com/. An academic review is Wendy L. Hicks, "Police Vehicular Pursuits: An Overview of Research and Legal Conceptualizations for Police Administrators," *Criminal Justice Policy Review* (2003). More on fatalities from pursuits can be found in H. Range Hutson, et al., "A Review of Police Pursuit Fatalities in the United States From 1982–2004," *Prehospital Emergency Care* (2007).

What More to Do

Find out what the rules of pursuit are for your local police departments, including that of your university, if it has one. Also see what training in pursuit driving, PIT maneuvers, and related tactics the officers in these departments have. Write a model of what the rules for police pursuits should be. Include when pursuits can take place, when they should be aborted, who can engage in them, and when and by whom more aggressive measures, such as a PIT maneuver, can be used.

16 CRIMINAL JUSTICE POLICY

THE DEATH PENALTY:
Fatally Flawed *or* Defensible?

FATALLY FLAWED

ADVOCATE: Stephen B. Bright, Director, Southern Center for Human Rights, Atlanta, Georgia; Visiting Lecturer in Law, Harvard and Yale Law Schools

SOURCE: Testimony during hearings on "An Examination of the Death Penalty in the United States" before the U.S. Senate, Committee on the Judiciary, Subcommittee on the Constitution, February 1, 2006

DEFENSIBLE

ADVOCATE: John McAdams, Professor of Political Science, Marquette University

SOURCE: Testimony during hearings on "An Examination of the Death Penalty in the United States" before the U.S. Senate, Committee on the Judiciary, Subcommittee on the Constitution, February 1, 2006

Murder and capital punishment share four elements. They are: (1) a planned act (2) to kill (3) a specific person who (4) is not immediately attacking anyone. Should then murder and capital punishment be judged just or unjust by the same standard?

The first question is whether killing is ever justified. The doctrine of most religions contain some variation of the commandment, "Thou shalt not kill." For moral absolutists and pacifists, this prohibition is unbendable. They would not kill another person under any circumstances. Most people, however, are moral relativists who evaluate good and evil within a context. They do not condemn as immoral killing in such circumstances as self-defense and military combat.

What about premeditated acts by individuals? Most societies condemn these as murder even if the other person has harmed you. To see this, assume that a murderer has killed a member of your family. You witnessed it and thus are sure who is guilty. If you track down the murderer and execute him or her, by law now you are also a murderer. Yet 67% of Americans favor capital punishment, which is the state carrying out roughly the same act.

Arguably the difference is the willingness of most people to apply different moral standards to individuals acting privately and society acting through its government. This distinction is an ancient one. For example, God may have commanded "Thou shalt not kill" for individuals (Exodus 20:13), but in the very next chapter God details "ordinances" to Moses, including, "Whosoever strikes a man so that he dies shall be put to death" (Exodus 21:12). The point here is not whether you want to accept the words that Exodus attributes to a deity. After all, just two verses later, God also decrees death to "whoever curses his father or his mother." This would leave few teenagers alive today. Instead, the issue to wrestle with is whether and why it is just or unjust for a government, but not an individual, to commit an act with the four elements noted in the first paragraph. For those who see no moral distinction between actions by individuals and a society, capital punishment is wrong no matter how heinous the crime is, how fair the legal system is, or what the claimed benefits of executing criminals are.

There are others, though, who do not argue that capital punishment is inherently immoral. Instead they make a pragmatic case. They begin with the reasonable proposition that executing someone is a drastic step, then argue that there is no evidence of positive effect that would warrant such an extreme act. To think about this point, you have to first decide what it is you want capital punishment to accomplish. One possibility is to deter others from committing similar crimes. The other possibility is punishment as a way of expressing the society's outrage at the act. A great deal of the debate at his level is about whether capital punishment is a deterrent. It is beyond the limited space here to take up that debate, but to a degree it misses the point of why most Americans who favor capital punishment do so. When asked in one poll why they support it, 70% replied it is "a fitting punishment for convicted murders, while only 25% thought, "the death penalty deters crime," and 4% were unsure.

Yet another line of attack on capital punishment is the argument that the system is flawed. Some contend that mistakes get made, and innocent people are sometimes convicted and executed. This view is well represented by Stephen B. Bright in the first reading and disputed by John McAdams in the second reading.

Then there is the argument that, as conducted in the United States, the process from investigation, through trial and sentencing to the carrying out of the death penalty is racially tainted. As evidence, those making this argument point to the fact that the demographic characteristics of those executed are not in proportion to their group's percentage of the society. African Americans (about 12% of the population) made up 40% of those executed in 2006. Among other group, Latinos, 15% of the population, made up 11% of those executed, and Native Americans, 1% of the population, were 2% of those executed. No Asia Americans were put to death judicially in 2006. It is worth noting that all of the 53 prisoners executed in 2006 were men.

POINTS TO PONDER

➤ Before beginning, make a note to yourself about whether or not you favor the death penalty and the most important reason you take that view.
➤ Since no judicial system is perfect, it is safe to assume that at least some of those executed have been wrongly convicted. If you believe that the error rate does not have to be zero to continue capital punishment, then what is the highest acceptable error rate?
➤ What, if anything, would make you change your view on capital punishment?

The Death Penalty:
Fatally Flawed

STEPHEN B. BRIGHT

This is a most appropriate time to assess the costs and benefits of the death penalty. Thirty years ago, in 1976, the Supreme Court allowed the resumption of capital punishment after declaring it unconstitutional four years earlier in *Furman v. Georgia*. Laws passed in response to Furman were supposed to correct the constitutional defects identified in 1972.

However, 30 years of experience has demonstrated that those laws have failed to do so. The death penalty is still arbitrary. It's still discriminatory. It is still imposed almost exclusively upon poor people represented by court-appointed lawyers. In many cases the capabilities of the lawyer have more to do with whether the death penalty is imposed than the crime. The system is still fallible in deciding both guilt and punishment. In addition, the death penalty is costly and is not accomplishing anything. And it is beneath a society that has a reverence for life and recognizes that no human being is beyond redemption. Many supporters of capital punishment, after years of struggling to make the system work, have had sober second thoughts it. Justice Sandra Day O'Connor, who leaves the Supreme Court after 25 years of distinguished service, has observed that "serious questions are being raised about whether the death penalty is being fairly administered in this country" and that "the system may well be allowing some innocent defendants to be executed."

Justices Lewis Powell and Harry Blackmun also voted to uphold death sentences as members of the court, but eventually came to the conclusion, as Justice Blackmun put it, that "the death penalty experiment has failed."

The *Birmingham News* announced in November that after years of supporting the death penalty it could no longer do so "[b]ecause we have come to believe Alabama's capital punishment system is broken. And because, first and foremost, this newspaper's editorial board is committed to a culture of life."

The death penalty is not imposed to avenge every murder and—as some contend—to bring "closure" to the family of every victim. There were over 20,000 murders in 14 of the last 30 years and 15,000 to 20,000 in the others. During that time, there have been just over 1,000 executions—an average of about 33 a year. Sixteen states carried out 60 executions last year. Twelve states carried out 59 executions in 2004, and 12 states put 65 people to death in 2003.

Moreover, the death penalty is not evenly distributed around the country. Most executions take place in the South, just as they did before *Furman*. Between 1935 and 1972, the South carried out 1887 executions; no other region had as many as 500. Since 1976, the Southern states have carried out 822 of 1000 executions; states in the Midwest have carried out 116; states in the west 64 and the Northeastern states have carried out only four. The federal government, which has had the death penalty since 1988, has executed three people. Only one state, Texas, has executed over 100 people since 1976. It has executed over 350.

Further experimentation with a lethal punishment after centuries of failure has no place in a conservative society that is wary of too much government power and skeptical of government's ability to do things well. We are paying an enormous cost in money and the credibility of the system in order to execute people who committed less than one percent of the murders that occur each year. The death penalty is not imposed for all murders, for most murders, or even for the most heinous murders. It is imposed upon a random handful of people convicted of murder—often because of factors such as the political interests and predilections of prosecutors, the quality of the lawyer appointed to defend the accused, and the race of the victim and the defendant. A fairer system would be to have a lottery of all people convicted of murder; draw 60 names and execute them. Further experimentation might be justified if it served some purpose. But capital punishment is not needed to protect society or to punish offenders. We have not only maximum security prisons, but "super maximum" prisons where prisoners are completely isolated from guards and other inmates, as well as society.

THE DEATH PENALTY IS ARBITRARY AND UNFAIR

Justice Potter Stewart said in 1972 that the death penalty was so arbitrary and capricious that being sentenced to death was like being struck by lightning. It still is. As was the case in 1972, there is no way to distinguish the small number of offenders who get death each year from the thousands who do not. This is because prosecutorial practices vary widely with regard to the death penalty; the lawyers appointed to defend those accused are often not up to the task of providing an adequate defense; differences between regions and communities and the resulting differences in the composition of juries; and other factors.

PROSECUTORIAL DISCRETION AND PLEA BARGAINING

Whether death is sought or imposed is based on the discretion and proclivities of the thousands of people who occupy the offices of prosecutor in judicial districts throughout the nation. (Texas, for example, has 155 elected prosecutors, Virginia 120, Missouri 115, Illinois 102, Georgia 49, and Alabama 40). Each prosecutor is independent of all the others in the state.

The vast majority of all criminal cases—including capital cases—are decided not by juries, but through plea bargains. The two most important decisions in any capital case are the prosecutor's—first, whether to seek the death penalty and, second, if death is sought, whether to agree to a lesser punishment, usually life imprisonment without any possibility of parole, instead of the death penalty as part of a plea bargain.

The practices of prosecutors vary widely. They are never required to seek the death penalty. Some never seek it; some seek it from time to time; and some seek it at every opportunity. Some who seek it initially will nevertheless agree to a plea bargain and a life sentence in almost all cases; others will refuse a plea disposition and go to trial. In some communities, particularly predominantly white suburban ones, the prosecutor may get a death sentence from a jury almost any time a case goes to trial. In other communities—usually those with more diverse racial populations—the prosecutors often find it much more difficult, if not impossible, to obtain a death sentence. Those prosecutors may eventually stop seeking the death penalty because of they get it so seldom. And regardless of the community and the crime, juries may not agree to a death sentence.

Timothy McVeigh's codefendant, Terry Nichols, was not sentenced to death by either a federal or state jury for his role in the bombing of the federal building in Oklahoma City that caused 168 deaths. Without being critical of any person or community and without questioning the motives of any of them, it is clear that there is not going to be consistent application of the death penalty when prosecutors operate completely independent of one another.

Because of different practices by prosecutors, there are geographical disparities with regard to where death is imposed within states. Prosecutors in Houston and Philadelphia have sought the death penalty in virtually every case where it can be imposed. As a result of aggressive prosecutors and inept court-appointed lawyers, Houston and Philadelphia have each condemned over 100 people to death—more than most states. Harris County, which includes Houston, has had more executions in the last 30 years than any state except Texas and Virginia.

Whether death is sought may depend upon which side of the county line the crime was committed. A murder was committed in a parking lot on the boundary between Lexington County, South Carolina, which, at the time, had sentenced 12 people to death, and Richland County, which had sent only one person to death row. The murder was determined to have occurred a few feet on the Lexington County side of the line. The defendant was tried in Lexington County and sentenced to death. Had the crime occurred a few feet in the other direction, death penalty almost certainly would not have been imposed.

There may be different practices even within the same office. For example, an Illinois prosecutor announced that he had decided not to seek the death penalty for Girvies Davis after Davis' case was reversed by the state supreme court. However, while the case was pending, a new prosecutor took office and decided to seek the death penalty for Davis. He was successful and Davis was executed in 1995.

As a result of a plea bargain, Ted Kaczynski, the Unabomber, who killed three, injured many others, and terrified even more by mailing bombs to people, avoided the death penalty. Serial killers Gary Leon Ridgway, who pleaded guilty to killing 48 women and girls in the Seattle area, and Charles Cullen, a nurse who pleaded guilty to murdering 29 patients in hospitals in New Jersey and Pennsylvania, also avoided the death penalty through plea bargains, as did Eric Rudolph, who killed a security guard in Birmingham and set off a bomb that killed one and injured many more at the 1996 Olympics. Rudolph was allowed to plead and avoid the death penalty in exchange for telling the authorities where he hid some dynamite in North Carolina. Others avoid the death penalty by agreeing to testify for the prosecution against the other(s) involved in the crime.

Although some serial killers are sentenced to death, most of the men and women on death rows are there for crimes that, while tragic and fully deserving of punishment, are less heinous that the examples mentioned above as well as many other cases in which death was not imposed.

REPRESENTATION FOR THE ACCUSED

Once a prosecutor decides to seek death, the quality of legal representation for the defendant can be the difference between life and death. A person facing the death penalty usually cannot afford to hire a attorney and is at the mercy of the system to provide a court appointed lawyer. While many receive adequate representation (and often are not sentenced to death as a result), many others are assigned lawyers who lack the knowledge, skill, resources—and sometime even the inclination—to handle a serious criminal case. People who would not be sentenced to death if properly represented are sentenced to death because of the incompetent court-appointed lawyers.

For example, Dennis Williams was convicted twice of the 1978 murders of a couple from Chicago's south suburbs and sentenced to death. He was represented at his first trial by an attorney who was later disbarred, and at his second trial by a different attorney who was later suspended. Williams was later exonerated by DNA evidence. Four other men sentenced to death in Illinois were represented by a convicted felon who was the only lawyer in Illinois history to be disbarred twice.

A dramatic example of how bad representation can be is provided by this description from the *Houston Chronicle* of a capital trial:

> Seated beside his client—a convicted capital murderer—defense attorney John Benn spent much of Thursday afternoon's trial in apparent deep sleep. His mouth kept falling open and his head lolled back on his shoulders, and then he awakened just long enough to catch himself and sit upright. Then it happened again. And again. And again.
>
> Every time he opened his eyes, a different prosecution witness was on the stand describing another aspect of the Nov. 19, 1991, arrest of George McFarland in the robbery-killing of grocer Kenneth Kwan.
>
> When state District Judge Doug Shaver finally called a recess, Benn was asked if he truly had fallen asleep during a capital murder trial. "It's boring," the 72-year-old long-time Houston lawyer explained....

Court observers said Benn seems to have slept his way through virtually the entire trial. This sleeping did not violate the right to a lawyer guaranteed by the United States Constitution, the trial judge explained, because, "[t]he Constitution doesn't say the lawyer has to be awake." On appeal, the Texas Court of Criminal Appeals rejected McFarland's claim that he was denied his right to counsel over the dissent of two judges who pointed out that "[a] sleeping counsel is unprepared to present evidence, to cross-examine witnesses, and to present any coordinated effort to evaluate evidence and present a defense." Last year, the Court reaffirmed its opinion.

George McFarland was one of at least three people sentenced to death in Houston at trials where their lawyers slept. Two others were represented by Joe Frank Cannon. One of them, Carl Johnson, has been executed. Cannon was appointed by Houston judges for forty years to represent people accused of crimes in part because of his reputation for hurrying through trials like "greased lightening," and despite his tendency to doze off during trial.

Ten of Cannon's clients were sentenced to death, one of the largest numbers among Texas attorneys. Another notorious lawyer appointed to defend capital cases in Houston had 14 clients sentenced to death.

The list of lawyers eligible to handle capital cases in Tennessee in 2001, circulated to trial judges by the state Supreme Court, included a lawyer convicted of bank fraud, a lawyer convicted of perjury, and a lawyer whose failure to order a blood test let an innocent man languish in jail for four years on a rape charge. Courts in other states have upheld death sentences in cases in which lawyers were not aware of the governing law, were not sober, and failed to present any evidence regarding either guilt-innocence or penalty. One federal judge, in reluctantly upholding a death sentence, observed that the Constitution, as interpreted by the U.S. Supreme Court, "does not require that the accused, even in capital cases, be represented by able or effective counsel."

The Supreme Court has said that the death penalty should be imposed "with reasonable consistency, or not at all." That is simply not happening.

THE COURTS ARE FALLIBLE

Innocent people have been wrongfully convicted because of poor legal representation, mistaken identifications, the unreliable testimony of people who swap their testimony for lenient treatment, police and prosecutorial misconduct and other reasons. Unfortunately, DNA testing reveals only a few wrongful convictions. In most cases, there is no biological evidence that can be tested. In those cases, we must rely on a properly working adversary system— in which the defense lawyer scrutinizes the prosecution's case, consults with the client, conducts a thorough and independent investigation, consults with experts, and subjects the prosecution case to adversarial testing—to bring out all the facts and help the courts find the truth. But even with a properly working adversary system, there will still be convictions of the innocent. The best we can do is minimize the risk of wrongful convictions. And the most critical way to do that is to provide the accused with competent counsel and the resources needed to mount a defense.

The innocence of some of those condemned to die has been discovered by sheer happenstance and good luck. For example, Ray Krone, was convicted and sentenced to death in Arizona based on the testimony of an expert witness that his teeth matched bite marks on the victim. During the ten years that Krone spent on death row, scientists developed the ability to compare bio-logical evidence recovered at crime scenes with the DNA of suspects. DNA testing established that Krone was innocent.

The governor of Virginia commuted the death sentence of Earl Washington to life imprisonment without parole in 1994 because of questions regarding his guilt. Were it not for that, Washington would not have been alive six years later, when DNA evidence—not available at the time of Washington's trial or the commutation—established that Washington was innocent and he was released.

Poor legal representation led to a death sentence for Gary Drinkard, who spent five years on Alabama's death row for a crime he did not commit. At his trial, he was represented by one lawyer who did collections and commercial work and another who represented creditors in foreclosures and bankruptcy cases. The case was reversed on appeal for reasons having nothing to do with the quality of his representation. Our office joined with an experienced criminal defense lawyer from Birmingham and represented him at his retrial. After all the evidence was presented, including the testimony of the doctor, the jury acquitted Drinkard in less than two hours.

Evidence of innocence has surfaced at the last minute and only because of volunteers who found it. Anthony Porter, sentenced to death in Illinois, went through all of the appeals and review that are available for one sentenced to death. Every court upheld his conviction and sentence. As Illinois prepared to put him to death, a question arose as to whether Porter, who was brain damaged and mentally retarded, understood what was happening to him. Just two days before he was to be executed, a court stayed his execution for a mental examination.

After the stay was granted, a journalism class at Northwestern University and a private investigator examined the case and proved that Porter was innocent. They obtained a confession from the person who committed the crime. Porter was released, becoming the third person released from Illinois's death row after being proven innocent by a journalism class at Northwestern.

There has been some argument over how many innocent people have been sentenced to death and whether any have been executed. We do not know and we cannot know. If DNA evidence had not been available to prove Ray Krone's innocent, if Earl Washington had been executed instead of commuted to life, if Gary Drinkard had not received a new trial, and if Anthony Porter was not mentally impaired and the journalism class had not come to his rescue, all would have been executed and we would never know to this day of their innocence. Those who proclaim that no innocent person has ever been executed would continue to do so, secure in their ignorance.

With regard to the quibbling over how many people released from death rows have actually been innocent, even one innocent person being convicted of a crime and sentenced to death or a prison term is one too many. "Close enough for government work" is simply not acceptable when life and liberty are at stake. Regardless of how one counts and what one counts, we know that an unacceptable number of innocent people have been convicted in both capital and non-capital cases.

There is nothing wrong with looking at the system as it really is and with a little humility about what it is capable of. There are cases—many of them—in which the criminal courts have correctly determined that a person is guilty. There are others where it is clear the system was wrong because the innocence of those convicted has been conclusively established though DNA evidence or other compelling proof. There are also cases in which it is virtually impossible to tell for sure whether a person is guilty or innocent. There is no DNA evidence or other conclusive proof. The case depends upon which witness the jury believes. Or new facts come to light after the trial. It is impossible to know what the jury's verdict would have been if it had considered those facts. We want to believe that our judges and juries are capable of doing the impossible—determining the truth in every instance. And in most instances, they can determine the truth.

But cases that depend upon eyewitness identification, forensic evidence from a crime laboratory with shoddy practices like those that have come to light in Houston and Oklahoma City, the testimony of a co-defendant, who claims the defendant was the primary person, or the cellmate who claims the defendant admitted committing the crime to him, or there is inadequate defense for the accused, there is a serious possibility of an error. Just last week, a judge who presided over a capital case in California in which death was imposed wrote to the governor urging clemency for the defendant because the judge believes the sentence was based on false testimony from a jailhouse informant.

Often overlooked is the jury's verdict with regard to sentence—whether to condemn the person to die or sentence him to a long prison sentence—which is as important as its verdict on guilt. The decision of the legal system to bring about the deliberate, institutionalized taking of a person's life is surely a determination that the person is so beyond redemption that he or she should be eliminated from the human community. But that determination is quite often erroneous.

I have seen many people who were once condemned to die but are now useful and productive members of society. One of them, Shareef Cousin, works in our office. He was sentenced to death when he was 16 years old. However, it turned out that he was not guilty of the murder for which he was sentenced to death. We are tremendously impressed with him. He is a hard worker; someone we have found we can count on. He is applying to colleges. He is very serious about getting in to college and will be a very serious student.

But it is not just the innocent. William Neal Moore spent 16½ years on Georgia's death row for a murder he committed in the course of a robbery. He had eight execution dates and came within seven hours of execution on one occasion. His death sentence was commuted to life imprisonment in 1990 and a year later he was paroled. He comes to the law schools and speaks to my classes every year. He was very religious while in prison, and he is has remained every bit as religious in the 15 years he has been out. He met and married someone with two daughters and has been a good father. Both girls are in college. He has judgment and maturity now that he did not have when he committed the crime.

I can give you many more examples like these of people who were condemned to die but who have clearly demonstrated that they were more than the worst thing they ever did.

PEOPLE WHO KILL ARE NOT DETERRED

The scholars will address whether a punishment that is imposed in less than one percent of murder cases serves as a deterrent to murder. I offer no statistics, only a few observations from over 30 years of dealing with the people who are supposedly being deterred.

In my experience, these are not people who assess risks, plan ahead and make good judgments. They would not have committed their crimes if they thought they were going to be caught, regardless of the punishment. But they don't expect to get caught so they d don't even get to the question of what punishment will be inflicted. Why would anyone commit a crime—for example, murder and robbery to get money to buy drugs—if they thought that instead of enjoying the drugs in the free world they would be spending the rest of their life in prison or even years in prison?

Even if they get to the issue of punishment—I cannot imagine how they process the information. A large portion of the people who end up on death rows are people with very poor reading skills. They don't read the newspaper or watch the news or listen to public radio. When they are assessing the risk of getting executed, are they supposed to consider that nationally they have a one percent chance of getting the death penalty if they are caught and convicted? Or are they to consider whether they are in one of the 12 to 16 states that has carried out a death sentence in the last three years? How much of a deterrent can it be in the states that have two or three people on their death rows and have carried out one or two executions over 30 years? Are they deterred if they are in New Hampshire, which has a death penalty law but has never imposed it? How do they learn that New Hampshire has a death penalty law? Do states that have not carried out any executions or have carried out just a few need to carry out more in order to deter, or can they benefit from executions in other states?

The more routine executions become, the less media coverage they get. How are people supposed to find out about executions and be deterred if they are not getting any media coverage?

Beyond that, is the potential murderer going to take into account the likelihood of being assigned a bad court-appointed lawyer, of being tried before an all-white jury instead of a racially diverse jury, and other factors which will increase his chances of getting the death penalty?

The people I have encountered who committed murder do not have the information and many are not capable of going through a reasonable consideration of it if they had it. Many people who commit murder suffer from schizophrenia, bipolar disorder, major brain damage or other severe mental impairments. They may have a very distorted sense of reality or may not even be in touch with reality.

Finally, if death were a deterrent, it would surely deter gang members and drug dealers. They see death up close. Killings over turf and in retaliation for other killings make death very real. It is summary and there are no appeals. They see brothers and friends killed; go to funerals. They have much greater likelihood of getting death on the streets than in the courts. But, it does not change their behavior.

THE COST IS NOT JUSTIFIED

There is a growing recognition that it is just not worth it. A Florida prosecutor let a defendant plead guilty to killing five people because a sentence of life imprisonment without parole would bring finality. The Palm Beach Post observed "The State saves not only the cost of a trial; the victims' relatives—who supported the deal—do not have to relive the horror. The state will save more by avoiding years of appeals;…Most important, [the defendant] never again will threaten the public."

New York spent more than $170 million on its death penalty over a ten year period, from 1995 to 2005, before its Court of Appeals declared its death penalty law unconstitutional. During that time, the state did not carry out a single execution. Only seven persons have been sentenced to death—an average of less than one a year—and the first four of those sentences were struck down by the New York Court of Appeals on various grounds. The speaker of the state's assembly remarked, "I

have some doubt whether we need a death penalty.…We are spending tens of millions of dollars [that] may be better spent on educating children." He also pointed out that the state now has a statute providing for life imprisonment without parole that ensures those convicted of murder cannot go free. Similarly, Kansas did not carry out any executions between 1994, when it reinstated the death penalty, and 2004 when the state supreme court ruled it unconstitutional. Kansas had eight people under sentence of death, six from one county. New Jersey, which just declared a moratorium on executions, has spent $253 million on its death penalty since 1983. It has yet to carry out an execution and has only ten people on its death row. In other words, the state has spent a quarter of a billion dollars over 23 years and has not carried out a single execution. Michael Murphy, a former prosecutor for Morris County, remarked, "If you were to ask me how $11 million a year could best protect the people of New Jersey, I would tell you by giving the law enforcement community more resources. I'm not interested in hypotheticals or abstractions, I want the tools for law enforcement to do their job, and $11 million can buy a lot of tools."

These are states which made every effort to do it right. It is also possible to have death on the cheap. A number of states have done this. Capital cases may last as little as a day and a half. Georgia recently executed a man who was assigned a lawyer—a busy public defender—just 37 days before his trial and denied any funds for investigation or expert witnesses. But this completely undermines confidence in the courts and devalues life.

CONCLUSION

Supreme Court Justice Arthur Goldberg said that the deliberate institutionalized taking of human life by the state is the greatest degradation of the human personality imaginable. It is not just degrading to the individual who is tied down and put down. It is degrading to the society that carries it out. It coarsens the society, takes risks with the lives of the poor, and diminishes its respect for life and its belief in the possible redemption of every person. It is a relic of another era. Careful examination will show that the death penalty is not serving any purpose in our society and is not worth the cost.

The Death Penalty:
Defensible

JOHN MCADAMS

There are a huge number of issues that relate to the merits of the death penalty as a punishment, including deterrence, the moral justice of the punishment, the cost of the imposition of the sanction, and even (implausibly) what policies European nations have. But I'm going to concentrate, given the limited time I have, on two issues that I think are key: the issue of "innocents" convicted and sent to death row, and the issue of racial disparity in the application of the punishment.

HOW MANY INNOCENTS ON DEATH ROW?

One of the most compelling arguments against the death penalty, at least one that accepts the claims of the death penalty opponents at face value, is the claim that a great many innocent people have been convicted of murder and put on death row. Liberal Supreme Court Justice John Paul Stevens, just to pick one case out of hundreds, told the American Bar Association's Thurgood Marshall Award dinner that "That evidence is profoundly significant, not only because of its relevance to the debate about the wisdom of continuing to administer capital punishment, but also because it indicates that there must be serious flaws in our administration of criminal justice."

The most widely publicized list of "innocents" is that of the Death Penalty Information Center (DPIC). As of January 2003, it listed 122 people. That sounds like an appallingly large number, but even a casual examination of the list shows that many of the people on it got

off for reasons entirely unrelated to being innocent. Back in 2001, I analyzed the list when it had ninety-five people on it. By the admission of the Death Penalty Information Center, thirty-five inmates on their list got off on procedural grounds. Another fourteen got off because a higher court believed the evidence against them was insufficient. If the higher court was right, this would be an excellent reason to release them, but it's far from proof of innocence.

Interestingly, prosecutors retried thirty-two of the inmates designated as "innocent." Apparently prosecutors believed these thirty-two were guilty. But many whom prosecutors felt to be guilty were not tried again for a variety of reasons, including the fact that key evidence had been suppressed, witnesses had died, a plea bargain was thought to be a better use of scarce resources, or the person in question had been convicted and imprisoned under another charge.

More detailed assessments of the "Innocents List" have shown that it radically overstates the number of innocent people who have been on death row. For example, the state of Florida had put on death row 24 inmates claimed, as of August 5, 2002, to be innocent by the DPIC. The resulting publicity led to a thorough examination of the twenty-four cases by the Florida Commission on Capital Crimes, which concluded that in only four of the twenty-four cases was the factual guilt of these inmates in doubt.

Examinations of the entire list have been no more favorable. For example, [in

2002] a liberal federal district judge in New York ruled, in *United States v. Quinones*, that the federal death penalty is unconstitutional. In this case, the court admitted that the DPIC list "may be over-inclusive" and, following its own analysis, asserted that for thirty-two of the people on the list there was evidence of "factual innocence." This hardly represents a ringing endorsement of the work of the Death Penalty Information Center. In academia, being right about a third of the time will seldom result in a passing grade.

Other assessments have been equally negative. Ward A. Campbell, Supervising Deputy Attorney General of the State of California reviewed the list in detail, and concluded that:...it is arguable that at least 68 of the 102 defendants on the List should not be on the list at all—leaving only 34 released defendants with claims of actual innocence—less than ½ of 1% of the 6,930 defendants sentenced to death between 1973 and 2000.

There is, of course, a degree of subjectivity in all such assessments. The presence of "reasonable doubt" does not make a person factually innocent (although it's an excellent reason to acquit them), and circumstances might conspire to make a factually innocent person appear to even an objective observer to be guilty "beyond a reasonable doubt." The key thing to remember is that the numbers produced by DPIC are "outliers"—grossly inflated. Indeed, staffers of this very committee have pretty much dismantled the DPIC list. Taking at face value the claims of the activists is about as bad as taking at face value the claims of the National Rifle Association about the number of Americans who save themselves from bodily harm because they own and carry guns, or the claims of NARAL [National Abortion & Reproductive Rights Action League] about how many "back alley abor-

tions" would result from overturning *Roe v. Wade* [1973].

HAVE ANY INNOCENTS BEEN EXECUTED?

Worse than putting an innocent person on death row (only to have him later exonerated) would be to actually execute an innocent person. But death penalty opponents can't point to a single innocent person known to have been executed for the last 35 years. They do make claims, however.

In the 1980s, two academics who strongly opposed the death penalty (Hugo Adam Bedau and Michael Radelet) claimed that of 7,000 people executed in the United States in the 20th century, 23 were innocent. This doesn't seem like a large number, especially when we remember that most of the cases they claimed were from an era when defendants had many fewer due process rights than they do today, when police forces and prosecutors were much less well-trained and professional than they are today, and when the media was less inclined to take an "advocacy" role in claimed cases of injustice.

Indeed, Bedau and Radelet produced only one case since the early 1960s where they claimed an innocent man had been executed—that of one James Adams. But even this one case was quite weak. Steven J. Markman and Paul G. Cassell, in a *Stanford Law Review* article, took Bedau and Radelet to task for "disregard of the evidence," and for putting a spin on the evidence that supported their thesis of Adams' innocence. Markman and Cassell concluded that there is, "no persuasive evidence that any innocent person has been put to death in more than twenty-five years." In response, Bedau and Radelet admitted to the *Chronicle of Higher Education* that (in the words of the *Chronicle's* reporter) "some cases require subjective analysis simply because the evidence is incomplete or tainted." They admitted this was true of all 23 cases that they reported.

The most sober death penalty opponents have apparently given up claiming solid evidence of any innocent person executed in the modern era. Indeed Barry Scheck, cofounder of the Innocence Project, was featured speaker at the Wrongfully Convicted on Death Row Conference in Chicago (November 13–15, 1998), and was interviewed by the "Today Show."

Schenk was asked by Matt Lauer, "Since 1976, 486 people have been executed in this country. Any doubt in your mind that we've put to death innocent people?" Scheck responded "Well, you know, I—I think that we must have put to death innocent people, but if you're saying to me to prove it right now, I can't."

Nothing stops death penalty opponents from making all sorts of claims about innocent people being executed. But in the rare cases when their claims can actually be tested, they turn out to be false. Consider, for example, the case of Roger Keith Coleman, who was tried for a rape/murder, and finally executed by the State of Virginia in 1992. An essay still on the site of the Death Penalty Information Center discusses the case at considerable length, and clearly leaves the impression that Coleman must be innocent. After attacking all the evidence against Coleman, the essay claims that "official misconduct that has left the case against Roger Coleman in shreds" and goes on to claim:

> …there is dramatic evidence that another person, Donney Ramey, committed the murder. For one thing, a growing number of women in the neighborhood have reported being sexually assaulted by Ramey in ways strikingly similar to the attack on Wanda McCoy. For another, one of these rape victims, Teresa Horn,

has courageously signed an affidavit stating that Ramey told her he had killed Mrs. McCoy. He threatened to do the same to Ms. Horn.

Someone reading the Death Penalty Information Center website, and lacking due skepticism toward the assertions there, would doubtless conclude that Coleman was innocent. Unfortunately, the State of Virginia allowed DNA testing of key evidence in 2005, using technology unavailable in 1992, and proved decisively that Coleman was in fact guilty as charged. The credibility of anti-death penalty activists when making claims of innocence—whether for those on death row or those who have been executed—is tenuous at best.

HOW MANY INNOCENTS ON DEATH ROW ARE ACCEPTABLE?

At this point, death penalty opponents will argue that it doesn't matter if their numbers are inflated. Even if only 20 or 30 innocent people have been put on death row, they will say, that is "too many" and calls for the abolition of the death penalty. If even one innocent person is executed, they claim, that would make the death penalty morally unacceptable.

This kind of rhetoric allows the speaker to feel very self-righteous, but it's not the sort of thinking that underlies sound policy analysis. Most policies have some negative consequences, and indeed often these involve the death of innocent people—something that can't be shown to have happened with the death penalty in the modern era. Just wars kill a certain number of innocent noncombatants. When the FDA approves a new drug, some people will quite likely be killed by arcane and infrequent reactions. Indeed, the FDA kills people with its laggard drug approval process. The magnitude of these consequences matters.

Death penalty opponents usually implicitly assume (but don't say so, since it would be patently absurd) that we have a choice between a flawed death penalty and a perfect system of punishment where other sanctions are concerned.

Death penalty opponents might be asked why it's acceptable to imprison people, when innocent people most certainly have been imprisoned. They will often respond that wrongfully imprisoned people can be released, but wrongfully executed people cannot be brought back to life. Unfortunately, wrongfully imprisoned people cannot be given back the years of their life that were taken from them, even though they may walk out of prison.

Perhaps more importantly, its cold comfort to say that wrongfully imprisoned people can be released, when there isn't much likelihood that that will happen. Wrongful imprisonment receives vastly less attention than wrongful death sentences, but Barry Scheck's book Actual Innocence lists 10 supposedly innocent defendants, of whom only 3 were sent to death row.

Currently, the Innocence Project website lists 174 persons who have been exonerated on the basis of hard DNA evidence. But the vast majority was not sentenced to death. In fact, only 15 death row inmates have been exonerated due to DNA evidence.

There is every reason to believe that the rate of error is much lower for the death penalty than for imprisonment. There is much more extensive review by higher courts, much more intensive media scrutiny, cadres of activists trying to prove innocence, and better quality counsel at the appeals level (and increasingly at the trial level) if a case might result in execution.

Consider the following quote from an article about how prosecutors in Indiana are tending more and more to ask for life imprisonment and not the death penalty because of the cost of getting an execution:

> Criminal rules require a capital defendant to have two death penalty certified attorneys, which, if the defendant is indigent, are paid for on the public dime. Other costs that might be passed onto taxpayers are requirements that the accused have access to all the tools needed to mount a fair defense, including mitigation experts, investigators, and DNA experts. Because the stakes are so high in a death penalty case, the courts believe a defendant is entitled to a super due process. The cost of getting a death penalty is too high in some ways (seemingly endless appeals). But in other ways lesser penalties are too cheap (lacking good lawyers, DNA testing, etc.). The system, in fact, it quite unbalanced, with it being relatively cheap and easy to sentence someone to life imprisonment but excessively expensive to have them executed. But until some balance is restored, the death penalty will remain the fairest penalty we have.

Balance will be achieved by ending "dead weight loss" in administering the death penalty (further limiting the number of appeals), while working for more substantive justice where lesser sanctions are at issue.

Playing the Race Card Death penalty opponents tend to inhabit sectors of society where claiming "racial disparity" is an effective tactic for getting what you want. In academia, the media, the ranks of activist organizations, etc. claiming "racial disparity" is an excellent strategy for getting anybody who has qualms about what you are proposing to shut up, cave in, and get out of the way.

Unfortunately, this has created a hot-house culture where arguments thrive that carry little weight elsewhere in society, and carry little weight for good reasons.

Consider the notion that, because there is racial disparity in the administration of the death penalty, it must be abolished. Applying this principle in a consistent way would be unthinkable. Suppose we find that black robbers are treated more harshly than white robbers?

Does it follow that we want to stop punishing robbers? Or does it follow that we want to properly punish white robbers also? Nobody would argue that racial inequity in punishing robbers means we have to stop punishing robbers. Nobody would claim that, if we find that white neighborhoods have better police protection than black neighborhoods that we address the inequity by withdrawing police protection from all neighborhoods. Or that racial disparity in mortgage lending requires that mortgage lending be ended. Yet people make arguments exactly like this where capital punishment is concerned.

A further problem with the "racial disparity" argument—and one underlining the fundamental incoherence of the abolitionist's thinking—is the fact that there are two versions of it, both widely bandied around, and they are flatly contradictory. I have elsewhere described these as the "mass market" and the "specialist" versions of the racial disparity thesis.

The mass market version is the easiest to understand, since it relies on the notion that racist cops, racist prosecutors, racist judges, and racist juries will be particularly tough on black defendants. Jessie Jackson, never one to pass up an opportunity to nurse a racial grievance, has expressed this view as follows:

> Numerous researchers have shown conclusively that African

American defendants are far more likely to receive the death penalty than are white defendants charged with the same crime. For instance, African Americans make up 25 percent of Alabama's population, yet of Alabama's 117 death row inmates, 43 percent are black. Indeed, 71 percent of the people executed there since the resumption of capital punishment have been black.

In a more scholarly vein, Leigh B. Bienen [of Northwestern University Law School] has claimed:

> There is a whole other dimension with regard to arguments that the death penalty is "racist." The death penalty and the criminal justice system is an institutional system controlled by and dominated by whites, although the recipients of punishment, including the recipients of the death penalty, are disproportionately black. The death penalty is a symbol of state control and it is a symbol of white control over blacks, in fact and in its popular and sensationalist presentations. Black males who present a threatening personae and a defiant personae are the favorites of those administering the punishment, including the overwhelmingly middle-aged white male prosecutors who are running for election or retention or re-election and find nothing gets them more votes than demonizing young black men. By portraying themselves as punishers and avengers of whites who are the "victims" of blacks, prosecutors get a lot of political support.

Thus Bienen adds another element to the mix: a racist public whose bias is translated by those paragons of political incorrectness, middle-aged white males, into harsh punishments for blacks. The problems of this view are numerous, but I'll discuss only the most important one: it's empirically just flat wrong. A whole raft of relatively sophisticated studies of the death penalty have been done, and findings of bias against black defendants are rare. Indeed, they are so few that they seem to illustrate the point that if you run a huge number of statistical "coefficients," a few will turn up as "significant" when in fact nothing is there.

What the studies do show is a huge bias against black victims. Offenders who murder black people get off much more lightly than those who murder whites. Since the vast majority of murders are intraracial and not interracial, this translates into a system that lets black murderers off far more easily than white murderers.

This is clearly unjust, but it leaves open the question of whether the injustice should be remedied by executing nobody at all, or rather executing more offenders who have murdered black people.

Even more relevant is the question: would doing away with the death penalty improve the situation? Here, as elsewhere, death penalty opponents assume that the choices are a flawed death penalty and a pristine system of criminal justice for every other punishment. But the data don't support that.

Scholars who study the death penalty often study several decisions in the process that might theoretically lead to execution. What they almost invariably find is large-scale bias in these earlier decisions, including decisions that would continue to be made if the death penalty were abolished. One particularly interesting study (although pre-Furman)…dealt with 245 persons arrested for homicide in Philadelphia in 1970.

Of these, 170 were eventually convicted of some charge. Sixty-five percent of defendants who killed a white got either life imprisonment or a death sentence, while only 25 percent of those who killed a black did. Since these murders produced only three death sentences (all imposed on blacks who killed whites), most of the apparent racial unfairness involved life imprisonment, not execution. Blumstein, in a study of the racial disproportionality of prison populations, found that in 1991 blacks were underrepresented among prisoners convicted of murder. There were many limitations to Blumstein's study, including failure to control for aggravating circumstances, and a research design what leaves possible racial discrimination in arrests entirely out of account. But his results strongly imply that the system does for imprisonment what it does with regard to executions: under punish those who kill blacks.

William J. Bowers [also at Northwestern University]…found that defendants who killed whites were more likely to be indicted for first degree murder—rather than a lesser charge—and more likely to be convicted for first degree murder than defendants who killed blacks. Along similar lines…a study of indictments for murder in Florida found that 85 percent of the killers of white victims were indicted for first-degree murder, while only 53.6 percent of the killers of black victims were.

Leigh Bienen and her colleagues, in their study of New Jersey homicides examined the issue of whether a particular case is plea bargained, or whether it goes to trial. Cases involving white victims were found to go to trial more often than cases involving either black or Hispanic victims.

One particularly interesting study involved prosecutors' decisions to "upgrade" or "downgrade" a homicide. An "upgrade" involved a prosecutor making a charge of a felony connected with the homicide when no such felony was mentioned in the police report. On the other hand, cases were said to be "downgraded" when the police report indicated the commission of a felony, but the prosecutor's charge did not mention it. A statistical model which controlled for the circumstances of the crime and of the offender showed that white victim murders were more likely to be upgraded than black victim murders.

In sum, the system is relatively lenient toward those who kill blacks, and that leniency extends to decisions that would continue to advantage those defendants who have killed blacks even in the absence of the death penalty. All of this makes perfect sense. If the system is biased toward punishing those who murder whites, it is implausible indeed that decisions leading up to sentencing are made with strict racial fairness, and only the imposition of a death sentence is racially biased. If people want to punish those who murder whites more harshly than those who murder blacks, this is likely to be reflected in prosecutors' decisions to move ahead with a case, in decisions about whether to plea-bargain, in the allocation of staff to a particular case, in the decision to indict on more or less serious charges, and in jury verdicts. Even in sentencing, abolition of the death penalty only narrows the range of possible punishments, rather than eliminating it. While not all decision points have been studied equally well, theoretically the pervasive undervaluing of the lives of black victims ought to be reflected everywhere there is discretion.

CONCLUSION

It cannot be stressed too strongly that we do not face the choice of a defective system on capital punishment and a pristine system of imprisonment. Rather, nothing about the criminal justice system works perfectly. Death penalty opponents give the impression that the death penalty is uniquely flawed by the simple expedient of dwelling on the defects of capital punishment (real and imagined) and largely ignoring the defects in the way lesser punishments are meted out.

The death penalty meets the expectations we can reasonably place on any public policy. But it can't meet the absurdly inflated standards imposed by those who are culturally hostile to it. But then, no other policy can either.

THE CONTINUING DEBATE:
The Death Penalty

What Is New

Globally, almost two-thirds of the world's countries have abolished the death penalty, and most of those that retain it seldom use it. According to Amnesty International, there were 1,591 known legal executions (judicially imposed) in 25 countries in 2006. More than 90% of these occurred in just six countries. China had by far the most (1,101), followed by Iran (177), Pakistan (82), and Iraq and Sudan (65 each), and the United States (53). The number of death row inmates in U.S. prisons has grown from 692 in 1980, to 2,246 in 1990, to 3,350 in 2007. In another U.S. development, the Supreme Court ruled in *Roper v. Simmons* (2005) that executing prisoners for crimes committed as juveniles (under age 18) was unconstitutional. Whatever the arguments about the death penalty or the data may or may not indicate, Americans continue to strongly support capital punishment. A 2007 poll recorded 65% supporting executions, even though another recent poll found that 63% of its respondents thought it probable that at least one innocent person had been executed in the previous 5 years. People seem to see the death penalty more as punishment than a deterrent. When asked what would happen if capital punishment were abolished, with only 34% think the murder rate would increase.

Where to Find More

A pro-death penalty position is taken by Joshua Marquis, "The Myth of Innocence," *Journal of Criminal Law & Criminology* (Winter 2005), and the opposite view is taken by Eliza Steelwater, *The Hangman's Knot: Lynching, Legal Execution, and America's Struggle with the Death Penalty* (Westview Press, 2003). For a group on each side of the issue, visit the Web sites of Pro-Death Penalty.com at www.prodeathpenalty.com/ and the Death Penalty Information Center at www.deathpenaltyinfo.org/. A site worth visiting is that of the Texas Department of Criminal Justice at www.tdcj.state.tx.us/stat/deathrow.htm. You can hyperlink from the name of each of the more than 400 people executed since 1982 to a picture, personal information, a description of the crime each committed, and their last statement. It puts a "face" on the data about both those convicted of murders and the victims.

What More to Do

Discuss all the various permutations of the death penalty debate, including whether it is ever justified under any circumstances and, if so, under what circumstances; whether it is only justified by utilitarianism (it deters later murders) and/or as punishment per se, and whether the fact that executions are not proportionate among various demographic groups is evidence that capital punishment should be abolished. Also, get active. The federal government and 38 states have death penalty laws on the books; 12 states and the District of Columbia do not. Find out the law in your state and support or oppose it.

17 EDUCATION POLICY

ASSIGNING STUDENTS TO SCHOOLS BASED ON RACE:
Justified *or* Unacceptable?

JUSTIFIED

ADVOCATE: National Education Association, et al.

SOURCE: Amicus Curiae brief to the U.S. Supreme Court in *Parents Involved in Community Schools v. Seattle School District No. 1* (2007)

UNACCEPTABLE

ADVOCATE: Asian American Legal Foundation

SOURCE: Amicus Curiae brief to the U.S. Supreme Court in *Parents Involved in Community Schools v. Seattle School District No. 1* (2007)

The intersection between education and race has long sparked emotional. Prior to the Civil War it was uncommon and in some places illegal to educate children who were not white. The Fourteenth Amendment (1868) requiring equal protection of the law for all citizens made it illegal to overtly deny children of color an education or to give them an expressly inferior one. However, the changes were more cosmetic that substantive. In many places, Jim Crow laws legalized accommodations that were supposedly "separate but equal," but in reality were highly unequal. Blacks were the most numerous victims, but Asian Americans, Hispanics, and others also were relegated to second-class facilities and services. The Supreme Court upheld this fictitious equality in *Plessy v. Ferguson* (1896), a case that involved railroad car accommodations but also applied to schools and many other points of segregation.

That decision stood until the Supreme Court overturned it in *Brown v. Board of Education* (1954). Writing for the unanimous court, Chief Justice Earl Warren opined that in "public education the doctrine of 'separate but equal' has no place. Separate educational facilities are inherently unequal."

Over the years, the application *Brown v. Board of Education* slowly eliminated the overtly intentional school segregation, but, like the Fourteenth Amendment, there was a large gap between theoretical importance and practical impact. Two factors limited *Brown*. One was that some school districts build schools or drew district lines in ways that maintained or created schools that were de facto racially segregated. The second factor involved living patterns. Whites fled cities to the suburbs or sent their children to private schools to avoid racially integrated schools, and urban schools became more and more minority dominated. These population shifts also left cities with diminished tax bases, and the schools declined for want of adequate funding.

In response, the courts moved to a more proactive stance. In a case involving the region centered on Charlotte, North Carolina, where schools remained very segregated and the school board resisted moving to desegregate, a federal judge in 1965 found that the segregation was intentional, ordered that all 105 schools integrate, and specified that children be bussed between schools in necessary. The Supreme Court in

Swann v. Charlotte-Mecklenburg Board of Education (1971) unanimously backed the lower court. Bussing was soon adopted by school boards or ordered by judges in a number of other cities. However, just three years later in *Milliken v. Bradley* (1974), the Supreme Court ruled narrowly (5 to 4) that court-ordered bussing between Detroit and suburban towns to promote integration was not constitutional because racial imbalances existed based on population patterns and on town lines rather than government decisions. Bussing continued within towns and districts, but not across borders.

Some schools systems and other educational institutions moved voluntarily to integrate. They were sometimes met with suits by parents opposed to sending their children to more distant and/or more integrated schools or by applicants who felt they had been unfairly rejected by a school in favor of a minority student with weaker credentials. In such cases, as with the larger area of affirmative action, the Supreme Court has been less than crystal clear. In one case a white applicant who had been denied admission to the University of California-Davis Medical School filed suit claiming that 16 positions had been set aside for minority students and that he had a better record than some of those 16 students. In *Regents of the University of California v. Bakke* (1978), the court found for Bakke, saying quotas were unacceptable. But the court's opinion also noted that race could be a factor, although not the only factor, in admission decisions. The subtlety of this position again came to the fore in two decisions, both involving the University of Michigan. In *Grutter v. Bollinger* (2003) the court upheld the law school's affirmative action plan which set a goal of improving diversity but left the specific steps vague. On the same day in *Gratz v. Bollinger* (2003), however, the court rejected the university's undergraduate admission plan because it assigned a specific number of points to the application scores of minority students. The court said this approach was not "narrowly tailored" enough, leaving unsaid was exactly that meant.

These decisions set the stage for the debate here. In Seattle, Washington, all students apply to the school, from elementary up, that they wish to attend. If a school has more applicants than places, four criteria are used. The most important is whether a sibling goes to the school. Second is racial/ethnic balance; third is distance from home, and fourth is chance, with a lottery drawing use to determine any last placements. The parents of some students denied their first choice and sent to another school to achieve racial/ethnic balance sued the Seattle schools. The Washington State Supreme Court, the U.S. District Court, and the U.S. Court of Appeals for the Ninth Circuit all found for the school. The parents appealed to the Supreme Court, and it is from arguments in briefs to the court that the following debate is drawn.

POINTS TO PONDER

➤ If you were a Supreme Court justice, how would you rule in *Parents Involved in Community Schools v. Seattle School District No. 1*?
➤ Do you believe the government has a "compelling interest" in trying to achieve more integrated schools?
➤ If you agree that schools should be integrated, and disagree with Seattle's plan, what would you do?

Assigning Students to Schools Based on Race: Justified

National Education Association, et al.

The National Education Association (NEA) is a nationwide employee organization with more than 3.2 million members, the vast majority of whom are employed by public school districts, colleges, and universities. NEA operates through a network of affiliated organizations at the state and local levels, including the state and local education associations that have joined in this brief. One of NEA's core principles is that "great public schools are a basic right for every child." To implement this principle, the NEA Representative Assembly, which is NEA's highest governing body, has adopted a resolution declaring that a "racially diverse student population is essential for all elementary/secondary schools" because it "promote[s] racial acceptance, improve[s] academic performance, and foster[s] a robust exchange of ideas." These are likewise the views of the NEA affiliates that have joined in this brief.

The American Federation of Teachers (AFT) represents over 1.3 million members, the majority of whom work in our nation's urban public schools. Dating back to the Court's historic desegregation decision in *Brown v. Board of Education* (1954), in which the AFT filed an amicus curiae brief supporting the plaintiffs, the AFT has had an enduring commitment to educational equality for all, regardless of race. That interest continues in the present cases in which core questions of integration, and educational and economic opportunity are presented.

People For the American Way Foundation (People For) is a nonpartisan, education-oriented, citizens' organization established to promote and protect civil and constitutional rights. Founded in 1980 by a group of civic, religious, and educational leaders devoted to our nation's heritage of tolerance, pluralism, and liberty. For now has more than 700,000 members and supporters nationwide. People For continues to seek to combat discrimination and its effects and to promote quality public education, including classroom diversity, through educational programs and participation in important litigation such as these cases.

I. A SCHOOL DISTRICT'S EDUCATIONAL POLICY JUDGMENT THAT TAKING RACE INTO ACCOUNT IN MAKING STUDENT ASSIGNMENTS IN ORDER TO ACHIEVE RACIALLY INTEGRATED PUBLIC ELEMENTARY/SECONDARY SCHOOLS, WILL ALLOW IT TO FULFILL ITS MISSION, SHOULD BE ACCORDED JUDICIAL DEFERENCE.

As this Court repeatedly has recognized, public elementary/secondary schools serve as the critical foundation for our democratic society, providing students with the education necessary...to participate effectively and intelligently in our political system, and teaching them how to be self-reliant and self-sufficient participants in society. The public schools not only instill in the 49 million students who attend them the values on which our society rests, but they provide those students with the skills and knowledge necessary to realize their full potential.

If a school district concludes that it cannot accomplish these two important interrelated objectives without racially integrated public elementary/secondary schools, and that it cannot achieve such schools without taking race into account in making student assignments, the federal courts should defer to that educational policy judgment. Doing so would acknowledge that, under our federal system, the responsibility for providing public education rests primarily with states and school districts, and would accord with this Court's long-standing practice of giving deference to the educational policy judgment of school districts as to how best to fulfill their mission.

This Court's recognition [in *Swann v. Charlotte-Mecklenburg Board of Education* (1971)] that school districts have "broad power" "to formulate and implement educational policy"—including an educational policy that takes race into account in making student assignments in order to achieve racially integrated public elementary/secondary schools—rests on a firm foundation. Under our federal system, providing public education has always been primarily the responsibility of states and school districts—constituting "perhaps the most important function of state and local governments" [as this Court said in *Brown v. Board of Education* (1954)].

The educational systems that states and school districts have developed under this federal system are complex and varied. While every state constitution obligates the state legislature to provide a public education system, and state and local revenues provide the vast bulk of public education funding, the resulting state educational systems vary widely in their legal obligations, governance, and policies. State constitutions, for example, contain markedly different language regarding the type of public education that must be pro-

vided by the state, which has been interpreted to markedly different ends. Most to the point for present purposes, some states have interpreted their constitutional obligation to provide a public education system to encompass the duty to provide an integrated system by remedying not just de jure, but also de facto, racial segregation in the schools.

When states and school districts make the educational policy judgment that racially integrated public elementary/secondary schools are necessary for them to fulfill their mission, it is appropriate under our federal system for the federal courts to defer to that judgment. As this Court has advised, "federal courts should not ordinarily 'intervene in the resolution of conflicts which arise in the daily operation of school systems.'" Such matters generally fall within "the comprehensive authority of the States and of school officials…to prescribe and control conduct in the schools." Putting that presumption into practice, this Court has upheld various state and school district actions against constitutional challenges, even though the challenged conduct would have been unconstitutional if it had occurred outside the school context.

The same reasoning has led this Court to direct federal courts to terminate school desegregation decrees "at the earliest practicable date" in order to return schools "to the control of local authorities," and thereby "restore their true accountability in our governmental system." In doing so, this Court has made clear that the termination of such desegregation decrees does not mean "that the potential for discrimination and racial hostility" no longer exists, but that each state and school district should decide how to "ensure that such forces do not shape or control the policies of its school systems."

These precedents counsel that when states and school districts decide, as a matter of educational policy, that racially integrated schools are a key component of the education that they seek to provide, the federal courts should be reluctant to second-guess that decision. In the words of this Court [in *San Antonio Independent School District v. Rodriguez* (1973),] "Education…presents a myriad of 'intractable economic, social, and even philosophical problems.'" "The very complexity of the problems" involved "suggests that 'there will be more than one constitutionally permissible method of solving them.'"

In such circumstances, the judiciary is well advised to refrain from imposing on the States inflexible constitutional restraints that could circumscribe or handicap the continued research and experimentation so vital to finding even partial solutions to educational problems and to keeping abreast of ever-changing conditions.

II. A SUBSTANTIAL BODY OF EMPIRICAL EVIDENCE DEMONSTRATES THAT RACIALLY INTEGRATED PUBLIC ELEMENTARY/SECONDARY SCHOOLS SERVE A COMPELLING GOVERNMENTAL INTEREST BY PROVIDING SIGNIFICANT SOCIETAL AND EDUCATIONAL BENEFITS TO STUDENTS OF ALL RACES.

In concluding that they could not adequately fulfill their mission without racially integrated public elementary/secondary schools, respondent school districts were on very firm ground. A substantial body of empirical evidence demonstrates that such schools provide significant societal and educational benefits to students of all races—and, accordingly, serve a com-

pelling governmental interest. We survey that empirical evidence below.

A. The Societal Benefits of Racially Integrated Schools

Because public elementary/secondary schools are an important socializing institution, imparting those shared values through which social order and stability are maintained, racially integrated schools provide children of all races with the opportunity to interact with one another on equal terms. Such contact "teach[es] members of the racial majority 'to live in harmony and mutual respect' with children of minority heritage" and provides "minority children" with the opportunity to "learn to function in—and [be] fully accepted by—the larger community" [as this Court said in *Washington v. Seattle School District No. 1* (1982)].

In contrast, when children attend racially and ethnically isolated schools, these "shared values" are jeopardized. [As the New Jersey Supreme Court said in one case,] "If children of different races and economic and social groups have no opportunity to know each other and to live together in school, they cannot be expected to gain the understanding and mutual respect necessary for the cohesion of our society."

The commonsense assessment that interracial contact reduces racial stereotypes and prejudice, reflected in these decisions, is supported by substantial empirical evidence.

1. The theory that interracial contact reduces racial stereotypes and prejudice was articulated by Gordon W. Allport in his seminal work, *The Nature of Prejudice*. Allport posited that racial isolation breeds stereotypes and prejudice, and that "equal status contact between majority and minority groups in the pursuit of common goals" is a critical ingredient in improving relations between members of those groups, especially if such contact "is of a sort that leads to the perception of common interests and common humanity between members of the two groups."

Subsequent empirical research has repeatedly and consistently confirmed that interracial contact combats stereotypes and prejudice, and makes individuals more comfortable relating to members of other racial groups. This research makes plain, however, that the conditions of contact are critical to its impact.

In the first place, contact that occurs during key periods of personal development—most importantly during a child's formative years—and that frequently recurs, is far more effective at promoting tolerance and cross-racial understanding than intermittent contact among persons whose social beliefs and identities are fully formed. That is so because "[t]he early school years are crucial for the formation of the child's own racial identity as well as an understanding of prejudice and fairness." Once the destructive "habit" of "racial stereotyping" is learned, it is difficult to break, making it "more difficult to teach racial tolerance to college-age students" than to public elementary/secondary school students.

So too, contact with a number of different people of another race is more effective in breaking down racist attitudes than contact with just a few individuals of another race, because it forces people to "decategorize" those with whom they are dealing and to treat them as individuals rather than simply as members of a particular racial group. While there clearly is no "magic number" of students of each racial subgroup required, to realize the greatest benefits of contact a school's population should be within the range of the demographic breakdown of the school district as a whole, so as to prevent students in minority groups from becoming isolated and shut out of the school's mainstream.

Finally, contact must be among individuals of equal status—e.g., between friends, teammates or classmates—lest contact serve simply to reinforce rather than reduce racist attitudes and prejudices.

Given these findings, it is not surprising that interracial cooperative contact among students of different races in public elementary/secondary schools—our most powerful agency for promoting cohesion among a heterogeneous democratic people—has repeatedly been linked with increased levels of tolerance for children of other races, and increased likelihood that children of different races will become and remain friends.

The foregoing evidence reflects the reality that stereotypes do not as easily take hold of children who interact early and often with children of other racial and ethnic groups. The personal connections forged between students of disparate racial backgrounds challenge race-based assumptions they might otherwise develop about one another.

Illustrating that point in stark terms, three recent studies demonstrate a marked difference between the racial preconceptions of students educated in racially integrated schools versus those educated in racially homogenous schools. In each study, first and fourth graders were shown pictures of two children (one black and one white) in an ambiguous situation in which one could, but need not, attribute negative intentions to one of the children depicted (e.g., a child standing behind a swing could be viewed as having pushed the child in front of him to the ground or could be viewed as simply standing next to that child). The studies found that when white, black, Latino, and Asian children, who attended racially integrated schools, were asked what happened in these pictures their responses displayed no "implicit intergroup biases"; evidencing neither an "effect for the race of the transgressor" in the picture nor for the race of the study participant. In contrast, white students who attended schools in which over 85% of the students were white "displayed racial bias in their interpretations of [the same] ambiguous interracial encounters," and that bias increased with age.

The fact of the matter is that one-on-one contact has been found to be more effective in promoting racial tolerance and cross-race interaction than any other pedagogical method—including a multicultural curriculum—confirming the view that without meaningful social contact, talk of tolerance and cooperation is nothing but an abstraction. Where school districts are allowed to take the steps necessary to ensure that students of different races have a meaningful opportunity to interact in the schools, a remarkable transformation can take place, replacing racial stereotypes, hostility and tension with racial and ethnic tolerance and an emerging sense of community that crosses racial barriers. Such schools allow for the formation of "close, reciprocated [interracial] friendship choices, the kind of friendships that should be [the] most difficult to change," and which social scientists have long viewed "as one of most potent agents for ethnic change."

As the foregoing review of the empirical evidence indicates, cooperative interracial contact reduces racial stereotypes and prejudice by teaching students that individuals hold a multitude of different viewpoints, experiences and attitudes, which cannot be meaningfully captured by reducing individuals to racial categories. By providing students with the opportunity to individualize others with whom they interact, schools also provide students with the opportunity to identify the concerns they share in common with students of other races.

In the end, this process—far from resulting in the racial balkanization that petitioners evoke—leads to precisely the opposite result. As one researcher explained, cooperative interaction between different groups "induces the members [of different groups] to conceive of themselves as one (superordinate) group rather than as two separate groups, thereby transforming their categorized representations from us and them to a more inclusive we."

2. These consequences of racial diversity in our public elementary/secondary schools offer enduring benefits to our multiracial, democratic society and its citizens. "As adults [students who learn to interact with individuals of other races in elementary/secondary school] more frequently live in desegregated neighborhoods, have children who attend desegregated schools, and have close friends of the other race[s] than d[o] adults…who had attended segregated schools." They are also more likely as adults to interact and work with individuals of other races than are students educated in racially homogeneous schools.

Several comprehensive studies of the racial attitudes of high school students, who were educated in integrated schools, support these conclusions. These studies demonstrate that racially integrated schools and classrooms produce students who have very high levels of comfort in dealing and working with individuals of other races in later life—which they attribute in large part to their school experiences. For example, a survey of 242 high school graduates from the Class of 1980, reports that the graduates—even twenty years after the fact—viewed as "critically important" to their ability to interact cross-racially without fear or harmful preconceptions, their "daily exposure to people of other racial groups in their early years in K–12 education—at a time when they were forming their beliefs about the world."

In sum, students who attend racially integrated public elementary/secondary schools are far more likely in later life to function effectively in a variety of contexts—including as members of a racially diverse and non-discriminatory workforce. Racially integrated public elementary/secondary schools produce these long-range benefits because they break the cycle of segregation in neighborhoods, schools, social networks, and occupations. Equally to the point, this evidence demonstrates that by closing the door on racial diversity in the schools, we open the door to further racial prejudice and discrimination by perpetuating the racial isolation that breeds such prejudice and discrimination.

B. The Educational Benefits of Racially Integrated Schools

Teaching students to individualize the persons with whom they are dealing and identify common ground is of great consequence not only to the students' development as citizens in a multiracial democratic society, but also to their intellectual development and academic success.

1. Social scientists have reported that heterogeneous groups—including groups that differ only in the participants' races—are better at creative problem-solving than homogeneous groups, due to the benefits of interactions between individuals with different vantage points, skills, and/or values. That research reflects the fact that due to the continuing corrosive effect of racism in our society, people of different races often have very different life experiences and viewpoints. Reflecting that real-

ity, high school students who are asked whether or not racial integration has enhanced their educational experience respond in the affirmative in overwhelming numbers.

Other research provides further evidence of the cognitive benefits of interracial interactions in the educational context. For example, in one study, 250 high school students were asked to view a short film showing two boys (one black and one white) engaged in various activities—some positive, some negative and some ambiguous. The students were asked to describe what the boys had done and predict what each would do in various situations. White students who had had the opportunity for more interracial classroom contact

> (1) described [the boys] in ways that were more differentiated, more integrated, and more multivalent; (2) made prediction of the future behavior of [the boys] that were less absolute; (3) inferred the presence of attributes in [the boys] with less certainty; and (4) were less likely to perceive [the black boy] as submissive and [the white boy] as domin[a]nt.

The white students' greater ability to describe the film participants in meaningful, individualized ways applied not only to their description of the black boy but to their description of the white boy as well, "suggesting that interracial contact had a facilitating effect on the development of interpersonal cognitive skills in general."

These studies corroborate the evidence credited by the court below in the *Seattle School District No. 1* case, linking racial diversity in schools to "improved critical thinking skills—the ability to both understand and challenge views which are different from [one's] own."

2. Further support for the proposition that racial integration yields educational benefits is found in the voluminous social science literature analyzing the impact of school desegregation on student performance. Although not every study in this area has reached the same conclusion, once one accounts for methodological differences a broad consensus emerges that school desegregation has resulted in tangible and lasting improvements in black student academic achievement. As one of the definitive reviews of the literature concludes, desegregation has been positively linked to increases in black student achievement levels, generating gains on average of 0.3 of a grade year in student performance at the elementary/secondary school level, and gains on average of 0.57 of a grade year at the kindergarten level.

More recent studies also have demonstrated positive links between black students' test achievement and their schools' racial diversity, as well as between school desegregation and promotion and dropout rates, particularly for minority students. Additional evidence to the same effect is provided by school districts that have pursued voluntary integration efforts. In Lynn, Massachusetts, for example, the voluntary integration plan has resulted in "higher [school] attendance rates, declin-ing suspension rates, a safer environment, and improved standardized test scores."

There is also a small but robust group of studies linking black student enrollment in predominantly white schools to significant gains in those students' long-term educational achievement. Black students enrolled in predominantly white high schools are more likely than black students enrolled in predominantly black high schools to graduate, more likely than those students to go on to higher education, and more likely when they do so to pursue higher-paying occupations that traditionally have been dominated by whites.

The sum of the matter is this: because racially integrated public elementary/secondary schools provide significant societal and educational benefits, federal courts should allow school districts some room to consider race in making student assignments when those school districts determine that doing so is necessary to achieve and/or maintain such schools. This is not an illegitimate use of race, but is amply justified by the compelling governmental interest in educating all of our children to function effectively in a multiracial, democratic society and realize their full intellectual and academic potential.

Assigning Students to Schools Based on Race: Unacceptable

ASIAN AMERICAN LEGAL FOUNDATION

STATEMENT OF INTEREST

The Asian American Legal Foundation ("AALF"), based in San Francisco, California, was founded to protect and promote the civil rights of Asian Americans. Americans of Asian origin have a particular interest in use of race in K–12 school admissions. They have historically been, and continue to be, denied access to public schools due to overt racial and ethnic prejudice as well as ostensibly well-intentioned "diversity" programs. Despite the advances our society has made with respect to racial equality, discriminatory treatment of Asian Americans finds resurgence in the racial balancing schemes at issue here which, even if inadvertently, are used to exclude Asian Americans from public schools. Students of Asian American descent living in Seattle are subject to the school districts' racial balancing plans.

AALF's constituents have also suffered from similar racial classification in the San Francisco, California public school system. In *Ho v. San Francisco Unified School District* [before the 9th Circuit Court of Appeals, 1998]), San Francisco's schoolchildren of Chinese descent sued to end a consent decree that mandated racial and ethnic admissions quotas in the San Francisco public school system. After five years of litigation, and after the court found [that the school district] had almost no chance of prevailing, [it] agreed to modify the consent decree and to cease the use of race.

AALF members organized and supported the *Ho* litigation from the outset. Many of the same issues are presently before this Court in [this case]. As in *Ho*, the Seattle school districts is engaged in racial balancing to prevent "racial isolation." [It is] similarly denying schoolchildren access to public schools and programs solely because of their race.

Significantly, in the courts below, [Seattle has] relied on the Ninth Circuit Court of Appeals' rulings in *Ho* to argue that the racial assignment schemes at issue here are illegal. A decision by this Court upholding the use of race in the Seattle school district would have implications for schoolchildren in all of the nation's public schools. It would endanger the relief secured in *Ho* and could erase the judicial benchmark against K–12 racial balancing schemes established by the *Ho* litigation.

AALF submits that the long and tragic history of discrimination against Chinese Americans in this country, the Chinese American experience in the *Ho* case, and present, ongoing discrimination faced by members of this historically oppressed group, provide this Court with compelling reasons why it should not allow the equal protection rights of individuals, especially innocent schoolchildren, to be eroded in the name of diversity or social engineering.

ARGUMENT

I. USE OF RACE IS ODIOUS AND SHOULD BE RESERVED FOR SITUATIONS WHERE IT WILL VINDICATE, NOT TRAMMEL RIGHTS.

A. A decision allowing school officials to classify students by race would encourage renewed discrimination against San Francisco's Chinese American schoolchildren.

This Court has repeatedly warned [in various decisions], "Classifications of citizens solely on the basis of race are by their very nature odious to a free people whose institutions are founded upon the doctrine of equality" [and that] use of race "threatens to stigmatize individuals by reason of their membership in a racial group and to incite racial hostility."

The Seattle school district's use of race in admissions is dangerously unbounded by any remedial purpose, instead resting on the school officials' notion of proper racial balance. [Seattle school officials] argue the racial mix they seek will provide benefits that justify the sacrifices of those injured by their use of race. Whatever the benefits of this skin-deep diversity, it comes at too heavy a price. Any decision allowing K–12 school officials to classify students by race at their whim would have a far-reaching and chilling effect on individual rights in schools across the nation.

In particular, in a relevant case that AALF respectfully brings to the Court's attention, such a decision would likely result in San Francisco's schoolchildren of Chinese descent again facing race-based discrimination in the city's public school system.

In *Ho v. San Francisco Unified School District*, which began in 1994, San Francisco's Chinese American schoolchildren were forced to turn to the courts for redress of their rights, in order to halt the school district's policy of classifying and assigning them to the city's K–12 schools on the basis of their race.

Similar to the objectives of the Seattle plan, the San Francisco school district's plan sought "to eliminate racial/ethnic segregation or identifiability in any school, classroom, or program, and to achieve throughout the system the broadest practicable distribution of students from all the racial/ethnic groups comprising the gener-

al student population." This was supposed to produce "academic excellence."

Under the admissions program, nine ethnic groups were arbitrarily defined, including "Chinese." Members of at least four of the groups were required to be present at each school; and no one group could represent more than 45 percent of the student body at any regular school or 40 percent at any alternative school. The promotion of racial diversity, and not the remediation of past racial discrimination, was the only real purpose. As described by the district court, "This plan is designed to provide relief for all San Francisco school children; it does not address the needs of any particular racial or ethnic group."

By the time of the *Ho* challenge, the school district had enlarged the original nine arbitrary racial categories to thirteen equally arbitrary categories to take into account the growing prominence of additional racial groups in the district. Nevertheless, despite the numerous racial categories, no provision was made for the growing number of children of mixed race or for those children who preferred not to declare their race. They were not given the option of refusal [to choose a racial classification].

B. The experiences of the plaintiffs and class in *Ho* demonstrate that mandated diversity harms individuals, even members of groups that have historically suffered discrimination.

In *Ho*, as in the instant cases, the school district's racial balancing plan affected students of different races in different ways. However, as previously stated, in San Francisco, the burden fell heaviest on students identified as "Chinese." With a long history in San Francisco, over the years, Chinese Americans had come to constitute the city's largest identifiable ethnic group. See Levine, supra, at 55–56.

Accordingly, in the San Francisco school district's student assignment process, a child identified as Chinese was most likely to be "capped out"—that is, barred because the child's racial quota was exceeded—at desired schools and forced to attend a non-chosen school, often far from his or her neighborhood.

At Lowell High School, an academic "alternative" high school that admitted students from middle and junior high schools based on a numerical index derived from a combination of grades and standardized test results, the school district's mandated diversity was maintained by requiring Chinese applicants to achieve numerically higher index scores compared to applicants of all other racial or ethnic groups, including White, Japanese, and Korean, in order to gain admission. Also, even where preferences were not required to maintain the district's racial caps, the district nevertheless adopted a policy of granting preferences to applicants classified as "Hispanic" or "African American."

The parents of affected children and other concerned Chinese Americans, including officials of the Chinese American Democratic Club, sought relief from the school district, but the unlawful discrimination continued. Chinese American parents' frustration mounted as their children were turned away from schools for no other reason than that there were too many Chinese.

On July 11, 1994, the *Ho* class action was filed by three Chinese American schoolchildren denied admission to city schools because of their race, suing on behalf of themselves and all children of Chinese descent of school age who were current residents of San Francisco and who were eligible to attend public schools of the school district.

The named plaintiffs' situations amply illustrate the discrimination meted out to Chinese American schoolchildren by school officials:

- Brian *Ho* was five years old at the time the suit started. In 1994, he was turned away from his two neighborhood kindergartens because the schools had accepted the maximum allowed percentage of "Chinese" schoolchildren. He was assigned to a school in another neighborhood.

- Patrick Wong, then fourteen years old, applied for admission to Lowell High School in 1994. He was rejected because his index score was below the minimum required for Chinese American applicants. However, his score was high enough that he would have been admitted to Lowell had he been a member of any other racial or ethnic group recognized in the consent decree. He was rejected at two other high schools because such schools had also accepted the maximum number of schoolchildren of Chinese descent. When he tried to apply to a fourth high school, a newly established academic high school, his mother was told that all spaces for Chinese Americans were "filled" even though spaces for applicants of other racial or ethnic groups were still available.

- The family of Hillary Chen, then eight years old, moved from north of Golden Gate Park to a neighborhood south of the park in December 1993. Hilary was not allowed to transfer into any of three elementary schools near her new home because all three schools had accepted the maximum number of Chinese American schoolchildren.

C. A settlement ending racial balancing was reached in *Ho* only because the law was clear that the school district's goal of diversity could not justify its use of race.

After five years of vigorous litigation, the *Ho* case settled on the first day of trial with the defendants agreeing to (i) cease using race to assign students to the city's schools and (ii) end the mandatory requirement of self-classification by race on student enrollment forms.

Beyond question, settlement in *Ho* would never have been reached if the district court and the Ninth Circuit had not emphasized to [San Francisco] that (1) under this Court's decisions, the school district's goal of diversity did not justify its use of race in accepting students to K–12 schools, and (2) at trial the school district would have to prove a past constitutional violation tied to its present use of race—a burden defendants were extremely unlikely to carry.

Thus, key to the *Ho* plaintiffs' vindication of their constitutional rights was the recognition by the district court, and ultimately the school district, that, under the strict scrutiny required by this Court's precedents, racial balancing could not be used to justify the district's use of race, no matter how well-intentioned the district's goals.

If this Court, in deciding [this case], allows Seattle to continue to classify K–12 students by race, there is a very real danger that the San Francisco Unified School District will again try to implement a race-based student assignment program, in spite of the *Ho* settlement and in spite of a new state law prohibiting use of race. Indeed, San Francisco school officials have already announced they will move ahead with plans to reintroduce race as a factor in enrollments.

If the Seattle racial balancing scheme is upheld, it is likely that other school districts around the country will similarly subject millions of other schoolchildren to race-balancing programs. While racial balancing plans would victimize schoolchil-

dren of all races, their impact on the members of ethnic groups historically victimized by state-mandated discrimination would be a dark stain on American jurisprudence. If Seattle's policies are upheld, the doctrine of "different but equal" at the heart of Seattle's arguments will not be viewed by future generations any more favorably than is today the notion of "separate but equal" finally rejected by this Court in *Brown v. Board of Education* (1954).

II. Historically, the State's Discretionary Use of Race Has Never Been Justified by a Compelling Government Purpose.

A. The experience of Chinese Americans amply illustrates that, whatever the excuse of the times, history will find that it was wrong to treat individuals as faceless members of a "race."

The experience of Chinese Americans in this country illustrates that, whatever the justification given by state officials at the time, history will in the end find that group identity should never be elevated above individual rights. The struggle by Chinese American schoolchildren in *Ho* against race-based treatment was particularly ironic in that, for much of the preceding century and a half, Americans of Chinese descent had struggled against racial discrimination, particularly in San Francisco.

Throughout their history in this country, individuals of Chinese descent have sought to participate in and contribute to American society but have often faced significant barriers solely because of their race. Time and again, Chinese Americans received equal treatment only after appealing to the federal judiciary for the protections guaranteed individuals by the United States Constitution.

For example, in 1879 a district court invalidated San Francisco's infamous "Queue Ordinance" on equal protection grounds. In 1880, the court declared unconstitutional a provision of California's 1879 constitution that forbade corporations and municipalities from hiring Chinese. [And in 1886], this Court ruled that Chinese were "persons" under the Fourteenth Amendment and could not be singled out for unequal burden under a San Francisco laundry licensing ordinance.

Chinese American schoolchildren were long denied access to the public schools. In 1885, [a federal district] court had to order San Francisco public schools to admit a Chinese American girl who was denied entry because, as stated by the State Superintendent of Public Instruction, public schools were not open to "Mongolian" children. In response, the California legislature authorized separate "Chinese" schools to which Chinese American schoolchildren were restricted by law until well into the twentieth century. [Thus,] even though it is not widely known, Chinese American schoolchildren were some of the earliest victims of "separate but equal" jurisprudence as it related to education.

In all the historical instances in which the state used race to classify Chinese Americans, the state officials articulated reasons—exactly as they do here—why such use of race was necessary or advanced legitimate societal goals. In every instance, the racial classification scheme was later acknowledged to have been wrong and an impermissible infringement of individual rights.

B. Seattle's classification of schoolchildren by race is unlikely to produce benefits but is certain to cause harm.

The school district's classification of children by race teaches them precisely the wrong lessons, and can only cause harm.

As this Court has explained, "One of the principal reasons race is treated as a forbidden classification is that it demeans the dignity and worth of a person to be judged by ancestry instead of his or her own merit and essential qualities."

In *Ho*, as here, the school officials claimed that classifying students by race saved them from "racial isolation," and would bring them educational benefits. The decree's two goals were to "eliminate racial or ethnic segregation" and to "achieve academic excellence" throughout the school district, by which it meant "raising the academic performance of black and Hispanic students."

After the filing of the *Ho* case, however, even proponents of San Francisco's racial balancing scheme were forced to admit that no discernable benefits had been produced. One of the more telling indictments was issued by a grand jury convened to investigate the success of the program. After extensive investigation, including analysis of collected data and reports by Professor Gary Orfield, a court-appointed education expert, the grand fury concluded that racial balancing had achieved nothing but racial balancing. [The grand jury found,] "Fourteen years of experience [with the city's school plan] have established that while it has met its goal of de facto desegregation, it has been a failure at accomplishing its primary purpose of achieving academic excellence for all ethnic groups." The grand jury in particular found that racial balancing had not worked for Hispanic and African American students, whose academic scores were "lower than those of comparable students around the country [and, therefore the program] is not working, at least for the substantial African American and Hispanic groups."

The grand jury found that what was needed was, not more racial diversity, but rather more family involvement. The grand jury's findings are consistent with the long-standing consensus of experts on the subject: "The legendary Coleman Report of the 1960s found that after the influence of the family, the socioeconomic status of a school is the single most important determinant of a student's academic success."

While mandated racial balancing in San Francisco's schools did not produce discernable benefits, it caused obvious harm. San Francisco schoolchildren were stigmatized by the school district's use of race. Newspapers widely reported the stigmatization felt by children targeted by the racial quotas. As stated by the parent of one "Chinese" youth turned away because of his ethnicity, "He was depressed and angry that he was rejected because of his race. Can you imagine, as a parent, seeing your son's hopes denied in this way at the age of 14?"

Many Chinese American children have internalized their anger and pain, confused about why they are treated differently from their non-Chinese friends. Often they become ashamed of their ethnic heritage after concluding that their unfair denial is a form of punishment for doing something wrong. Thus, in San Francisco, mandated diversity in K–12 schools produced no educational benefits. Instead, it taught schoolchildren that they were categorized and limited by their race. There is no reason to suppose that in Seattle the result could be any less damaging.

C. The argument that students are not really burdened because their "race" is already "overrepresented" and they are placed in school somewhere is a modern-day perversion of the "separate but equal" doctrine.

There is no merit to the suggestion that students in Seattle are somehow not really burdened because their "race" is "overrepresented" in their chosen school and, in the end, they are assigned to a comparable school somewhere in the district.

First, the record shows that the schools at issue are not equal, but vary widely in desirability. [Second,] underlying the arguments of those who favor racial balancing is the mistaken assumption that it is moral to turn away an individual because that person's "group" is already "overrepresented." This kind of thinking invariably is used to oppress individuals, diminishing them as persons in proportion to the perceived numbers of their "group." It also invariably insures that the burden will fall heaviest on the poorer or weaker members of the disfavored group.

In one cautionary example from higher education, in the 1920s, Harvard College and other prominent universities reacted to the perceived "over-representation" of Jews in their student bodies by setting up informal quotas that persisted through the 1950s.

These institutions argued that their diversity schemes brought benefits to all and would lessen ethnic tension. "Harvard initiated its diversity discretion program to decrease the number of Jewish students; President Lowell of Harvard called it a 'benign' cap, which would help the University get beyond race." In *Ho*, a similar sentiment was voiced—that Chinese schoolchildren already had "enough" places in the cities' schools, and that individuals who were turned away had no right to complain.

Unfortunately, the same arguments are again used today to condone turning away Asian American individuals from the nation's universities. [One news report indicated] that former President Clinton commented favorably on race-based admissions, saying that otherwise, "there are universities in California that could fill their entire freshman classes with nothing but Asian Americans."

As history shows, artificial attempts to mandate a racially diverse student body invariably lead to oppression. Here, as in *Ho*, the Seattle school district oppresses individuals by requiring them to be viewed and treated only as faceless members of the racial groups into which they are classified. Such classification of school-children by definition causes injury.

D. Particularly suspect are declarations by experts and other luminaries that social agendas or national necessity require classifying citizens by race.

The Court should be wary of Seattle's attempt to do an end run around its need for a compelling state interest to justify use of race by proffering statements by government officials, experts and other luminaries that classification by race is necessary to advance societal and other goals. Where such self-serving statements have in the past been accepted by courts, they have consistently failed to pass the test of time.

In *Plessy v. Ferguson* (1896) the Court accepted the view of society that, even though all persons were equal before the law, the public good allowed the use of "distinctions based upon color." The lone dissenter, Justice John Harlan, wrote: "Our Constitution is color-blind, and neither knows nor tolerates classes among citizens."

In *Brown v. Board of Education* (1954), this Court properly rejected arguments by state officials that black and white children learned better in a single-race environment, and for societal purposes could be kept separate by state mandate. Expressly rejecting any contrary findings regarding "psychological knowledge" made in *Plessy v. Ferguson*, the Court found that use of race produces a "sense of inferiority." "We conclude that, in the field of public education, the doctrine of 'separate but equal' has no place."

Today, it is universally acknowledged that the [President Franklin D.] Roosevelt administration and military authorities infringed the constitutional rights of Japanese Americans when, during World War II, the government placed them under curfew, then removed them from their West Coast homes and placed them in internment camps. Yet, at the time, when the affected citizens pled with the courts to uphold their constitutional rights, the courts passively accepted statements by administration and military officials that such use of race was necessary in the national interest. [For example,] in *Korematsu v. United States* (1944), this Court upheld the conviction of an American citizen of Japanese descent, who had violated an exclusion order by remaining in his San Leandro, California home, rather than go to an internment camp. The courts at all levels deferred to declarations by military authorities that such discrimination by race was necessary to advance compelling government interests.

Much later, of course, it was discovered that government and military figures had misled the courts; and that the government had known that there was no national necessity requiring the use of race. The 1980 [U.S.] Commission on Wartime Relocation and Internment of Civilians found that the curfew and exclusion orders had been motivated by "racism" and "hysteria" and not "military necessity."

Here, also, this Court should be wary of the attempts by Seattle and those who defend it—no matter how illustrious their credentials or purportedly noble their goals—to manufacture a compelling state interest to excuse the use of race. If history teaches any lessons, it is that generally, proffered justifications for the state's use of race will, in the end, be found to be hollow.

E. Seattle schools impermissibly use race as the sole determinant of "diversity"

Seattle's admissions programs are unconstitutional because they use race as the sole measure of diversity, and thus cannot be narrowly tailored. As this Court's precedents teach, race-neutral alternatives must be used, if available. As Justice Lewis F. Powell stated in *Regents of the University of California v. Bakke* (1978), "Preferring members of any one group for no reason other than race or ethnic origin is discrimination for its own sake. This the Constitution forbids." As this Court explained in *Grutter v. Bollinger* 2003), if an admissions plan assures some specified percentage of a particular group merely because of its race, that "would amount to outright racial balancing, which is patently unconstitutional."

There are many sound reasons for foregoing the uneasy proxy of race in determining diversity. Even where generalizations can be made for a group—always a dangerous practice—common sense tells us they are never true of all individuals in the group. Race-conscious programs foster unfortunate stereotypes, detrimental even to members of those ethnic groups favored by the program.

In *Grutter*, this Court held that an institution using race must demonstrate operation of an admission program that evaluates an applicant as "an individual," without race as the "defining" feature. This Court found the Michigan law school plan constitutional only because, rather than considering race alone in evaluating "diversity," the law school "engages in a highly individualized, holistic review of each applicant's file, giving serious consideration to all the ways an applicant might contribute to a diverse educational environment." Applying that rule in *Gratz v. Bollinger* (2003), the Court found the college admission plan at issue there

unconstitutional because, instead of considering the totality of the diversity the applicant had to offer, it assigned automatic points for race.

The Seattle [schools] have failed to show that they review applicants holistically. Instead, they openly use race as the sole criterion of diversity. [Seattle officials] completely ignore all other measures of diversity they could have used. Exactly as did the San Francisco school district in *Ho*, Seattle blindly seeks nothing more than racial "percentages" reflecting their view of diversity. Thus, because Seattle schools classify students by race but have failed to implement programs that consider the totality of the person and not just race, the admission programs at issue cannot be narrowly tailored, and are unconstitutional.

CONCLUSION

The Seattle school district's use of race is merely the latest chapter in the long history of state attempts to use race in the public school system. Until recently, many states did not allow "Black" and "Yellow" schoolchildren to attend "White" schools. In the 19th century, children of Chinese descent were denied access to San Francisco's schools. A hundred years later, in the *Ho* case, Chinese Americans were again singled out for unequal treatment. Now, school officials in Seattle and Jefferson County seek to turn the clock back so that, once again, schoolchildren will be denied access to educational opportunities solely because of their race or ethnicity.

If nothing else, these experiences demonstrate the continuing danger of allowing the state to use race except in the most limited circumstances. There simply can be no compelling interest present in K–12 schools—schools that American children are compelled by law to attend—

to justify the use of racial classifications. The desire for a "diverse" student body cannot provide such a compelling interest—and certainly not when, as here, diversity is measured only by race.

Any discretionary use of race by K–12 school officials inevitably results, as in *Ho* and the instant cases, in the stigmatization of children. And, as such use of race is unbounded by any fixed, remedial goal with respect to scope and time, it will, if permitted, continue without end, to the detriment of our society.

Therefore, Seattle's race-conscious admissions programs further no compelling government interest, are not narrowly tailored, and should be found to violate the petitioners' Fourteenth Amendment right to the equal protection of the laws.

THE CONTINUING DEBATE:
Assigning Students to Schools Based on Race

What Is New

In 2007, the Supreme Court overturned the decision of the district and appeals courts and rule against Seattle's plan by a narrow 5 to 4 vote. When asked whether they agreed with the court's decision, 71% of Americans said that they did. Although the decision was a blow to those who believe that it is vital to achieve racially integrated schools whatever the cause of imbalances may be. Nevertheless, the court's decision almost certainly did not end the controversy because while 5 justices found against Seattle, only four joined Chief Justice John Roberts opinion that Seattle had failed to show that achieving racial diversity in its schools was a compelling interest. Four other justices dissented that it was a compelling interest, while the fifth and deciding judge, Anthony Kennedy, voted against the Seattle plan as too mechanistic. He also rejected the chief justice's opinion as "an all-too-unyielding insistence that race cannot be a factor in instances when, in my view, it may be taken into account." Kennedy went on to write, "To the extent the [chief justice's] opinion suggests the Constitution mandates that state and local school authorities must accept the status quo of racial isolation in schools, it is, in my view, profoundly mistaken." The implication is that a different approach to diversity might win Kennedy's vote and shift the 5 to 4 vote in the opposite direction.

Where to Find More

A good source of data is the National Center of Education Statistics at nces.ed.gov. Gary Orfield, a professor of education and social policy at Harvard University is mentioned in the readings as an expert in the field. More on him and his work can be found at www.researchmatters.harvard.edu/people.php?people_id=134. Among other works, consult Orfield's and Chungmei Lee's, *Why Segregation Matters: Poverty and Educational Inequality* (Civil Right Project, Harvard University, 2005). For a study suggesting that school integration alone is likely to have only a limited impact on student achievement is Russell Rumberger and Gregory J. Palardy, "Does Segregation Still Matter? The Impact of Student Composition on Academic Achievement in High School," *The Teachers College Record* (2005).

What More to Do

Start with data from the National Center of Education Statistics that indicate that about one-third of all pubic schools are "minority-majority," those in which minority students account for more than 50% of enrollment. These schools include 70% of black students and 37% of Latino students. The percentages are growing. Moreover, half all minority students go to schools considered poor, where as only 18% of white students go to these schools. Debate whether this pattern is acceptable and what, if anything, to do about it.

18 BUDGETARY POLICY

A LINE-ITEM VETO FOR THE PRESIDENT:
Prudent Way to Restrain Spending *or* Unwise Grant of Power?

PRUDENT WAY TO RESTRAIN SPENDING

ADVOCATE: Paul Ryan, U.S. Representative (R-WI)

SOURCE: Testimony during hearings on "The Constitution and the Line-Item Veto," U.S. House of Representatives, Committee on the Judiciary, Subcommittee on the Constitution, April 27, 2006

UNWISE GRANT OF POWER

ADVOCATE: Cristina Martin Firvida, Senior Counsel, National Women's Law Center

SOURCE: Testimony during hearings on "The Constitution and the Line-Item Veto," U.S. House of Representatives, Judiciary Committee, Subcommittee on the Constitution, April 27, 2006

"Take it or leave it" is a familiar phrase most of us have used, and it is also implicitly the reality of every bill passed by Congress and sent to the president. Once a bill arrives in the Oval Office, the president has three options: (1) Sign it into law. (2) Veto the bill by returning it to Congress. In this case it requires a two-thirds vote in both houses to override the veto and to make the measure law. (3) Do nothing, figuratively put the measure in his pocket, in which case there are two possible outcomes. If Congress has adjourned, then the bill dies after 10 days by what is called a pocket veto. If, however, Congress remains in session, then after 10 days the bill becomes law in what might be called a pocket passage. What presidents cannot do is "line out" specific provisions of a measure presented to them. They must accept or reject it as a whole.

The president's ability to reject legislation gives him considerable influence in the legislative process. By threatening to veto an act, presidents gain leverage to have it shaped at least in part according to their wishes. But Congress also has it ways and means of avoiding vetoes. One is to build provisions that a president might dislike into important legislation that the president would be reluctant to veto. If, for instance, a member manages to get a provision to build a veterans hospital slipped into the Defense Department budget, the president can either accept a hospital he had not wanted or veto the entire defense appropriations act. Sometimes, especially in the Senate, such unwanted provisions are attached to bills that are not related. These are called riders and would apply to a veterans hospital inserted into a bill about food stamps.

From the very beginnings of the Republic, presidents have been frustrated with their take-it-or-leave-it position. "From the nature of the Constitution," George Washington grumbled, "I must approve all the parts of a bill, or reject it in toto." And as far back as Ulysses S. Grant, presidents of both parties have sought the authority to line-item veto. In a literal sense the term line-item veto could apply to any provision of any legislation, but in practice it has come to apply mostly to spending and taxation measures. Advocates of a line-item veto argue it is particularly important to combat "pork barrel" provisions, or just "pork," a designation that stems from the pre–Civil War practice of providing barrels of salt pork to be divided among slaves. These are expenditures like the hypothetical veterans hospital above, which benefit the district of a member of Congress and which are added on to spending bills because of a member's power, to secure a member's vote, or to help a member get reelected.

The pressure to give the president a line-item veto has increased in recent years, and is very much related to budget deficits that the federal government has had during all but three years since 1970. This line-item veto drive reached its high point when in 1996 the Republican-dominated Congress and Democratic President Bill Clinton found it was something they could agree on. From the Republicans' perspective, the Line Item Veto Act seemed to be a way to restrain spending. From the president's point of view, it added to his powers. The act permitted the president to line out specific spending provisions and those taxing provisions that affected fewer than 100 taxpayers before signing the legislation. Any lined out provision had to be sent back to Congress, which could once again approve the item by a majority in each house. In this case, the re-approved provisions went back to the president, who could sign or reject them, subject to the normal override procedures.

During the first two years after the Line Item Veto act became law, President Clinton lined out very few items, a record that can be reviewed in the section Where to Find More that follows. Then, however, the act was ruled unconstitutional by a 6 to 3 vote in the Supreme Court case of *Clinton v. City of New York* (1998). The court found that eliminating some items created a law different from the one passed by Congress. In the majority opinion, Justice John Paul Stevens wrote, "If the Line Item Veto Act were valid, it would authorize the President to create a different law—one whose text was not voted on by either House of Congress or presented to the President for signature. [Such a law] may or may not be desirable, but it is surely not [valid] pursuant to the procedures designed by the Framers of…the Constitution." The Court's decision led to proposals in Congress to amend the Constitution to permit a line-item veto and others to try to craft a line-item veto that would pass the Court's scrutiny. It was during those hearings on such a proposal that the two advocates in this debate gave testimony.

POINTS TO PONDER

➤ Notice that like many debates in this volume, the controversy over the line-item veto has ramifications beyond the immediate issue. In this case, giving the new authority to the president would enhance the power of the presidency relative to Congress.

➤ Consider whether it would be better for Congress to control its own pork barrel spending rather than give a new grant of power to the president.

➤ Think about whether the budget does or should reflect the interests of the whole versus the disaggregated interests of the many. Since every budget inherently collect revenue and distributes benefits, what is the line between what is laudable and what is pork?

A Line-Item Veto for the President: Prudent Way to Restrain Spending

Paul Ryan

[I am here] to testify…on H.R. 4890, the Legislative Line-Item Veto Act of 2006. This legislation would help the President and Congress work together to reduce our budget deficit by providing the President with the authority to single out wasteful spending items and narrow special-interest tax breaks included in legislation that he signs into law and send these specific items back to Congress for a timely vote. Unlike the line-item veto authority provided to President [Bill] Clinton in 1996, H.R. 4890 is constitutional because it requires an up-or-down vote in both chambers of Congress under an expedited process in order to effectuate the President's proposed rescissions. It is important that Congress act now to give the President this tool to bring greater transparency, accountability and a dose of common sense to the federal budget process.

THE PROBLEM

The amount of pork-barrel spending included in the federal budget continues to increase every year. According to Citizens Against Government Waste (CAGW), the federal government spent $29 billion on 9,963 pork-barrel projects in Fiscal Year 2006 (FY 2006), an increase of 6.3% from 2005, and an increase of over 900% since 1991. [Pork barrel spending refers to budget allocations favored by one or another member of Congress but are of questionable national concern.] Overall, the federal government has spent $241 billion on pork-barrel projects between 1991 and 2005, an amount greater than two-thirds of our entire

deficit in FY 2005. This includes irresponsible spending on items such as the $50 million Rain Forest Museum in Iowa; $13.5 million to pay for a program that helped finance the World Toilet Summit; and $1 million for the Waterfree Urinal Conservation Initiative.

Many of these pork-barrel spending projects are quietly inserted into the conference reports of appropriations bills where Congress is unable to eliminate them using the amendment process. In fact, the only time that Congress actually votes on these items is during an up-or-down vote on the entire conference report, which includes spending for many essential government programs in addition to the pork-barrel earmarks. In this situation, it is very difficult for any member to vote against an appropriations bill that, as an overall package, may be quite meritorious, despite the inclusion of wasteful spending items.

Unfortunately, the current tools at the President's disposal do not enable him to easily combat these wasteful spending items either. Even if the President identifies numerous pork-barrel projects in an appropriations bill, he is unlikely to use his veto power because it must be applied to the bill as a whole and cannot be used to target individual items. This places the President in the same dilemma as members of Congress. Does he veto an entire spending bill because of a few items of pork when this action may jeopardize funding for our troops, for our homeland security or for the education of our children?

The President's ability to propose the rescission of wasteful spending items under the Impoundment Control Act of 1974 has been equally ineffective at eliminating wasteful spending items. The problem with the current authority is that it does not include any mechanism to guarantee congressional consideration of a rescission request and many Presidential rescissions are ignored by the Congress. In fact, during the 1980's, Congress routinely ignored President Reagan's rescission requests, failing to act on over $25 billion in requests that were made by the administration. The historic ineffectiveness of this tool has deterred Presidents from using it with any regularity.

SUMMARY OF H.R. 4890, THE LEGISLATIVE LINE-ITEM VETO ACT OF 2006

I introduced H.R. 4890, the Legislative Line-Item Veto Act of 2006, on March 7, 2006. This legislation, which currently has the support of 101 bipartisan cosponsors in the House, is based on the administration's proposal to provide line-item veto authority to the President and is the product of discussions that I and my congressional colleagues have had with the White House since the President announced his intent to seek line-item veto authority in the State of the Union Address on January 31, 2006.

The Legislative Line-Item Veto Act is very similar to an expedited rescissions amendment that I offered during the consideration of H.R. 4663 on June 24, 2004, with my former colleague Representative Charlie Stenholm, a Democrat from Texas. Like H.R. 4890, this amendment would also have allowed the President to propose the elimination of wasteful spending items subject to congressional approval under an expedited process. Although this amendment failed to pass the House, it attracted the support of 174 members of Congress, including 45 Democrats. A similar provision is also included in Section 311 of the

Family Budget Protection Act, legislation that I introduced along with Congressman Jeb Hensarling of Texas [R], Congressman Chris Chocola of Indiana [R], and former Congressman Christopher Cox of California [R] during 2004 and again in 2005.

If passed, H.R. 4890 would give the President the ability to put on hold wasteful discretionary spending, wasteful new mandatory spending, or new special-interest tax breaks (those that affect less than 100 beneficiaries) after signing a bill into law. The President could then ask Congress to rescind these specific items. The requirement that both the House and Senate approve all proposed rescissions means that Congress will continue to control the power of the purse and will have the final word when it comes to spending matters. However, unlike the current rescission authority vested in the President under the Impoundment Control Act of 1974, the bill also includes a mechanism that would virtually guarantee congressional action in an expedited time frame.

Using the Legislative Line-Item Veto, the President and Congress will be able to work together to combat wasteful spending and add transparency and accountability to the budget process. This tool will shed light on the earmarking process and allow Congress to vote up or down on the merits of specific projects added to legislation or to conference reports. Not only will this allow the President and Congress to eliminate wasteful pork-barrel projects, but it will also act as a strong deterrent to the addition of questionable projects in the first place. On the other hand, members who make legitimate appropriations requests should have no problem defending them in front of their colleagues if they are targeted by the President. With H.R. 4890, we can help protect the American taxpayer from being forced to finance wasteful pork-barrel spending and ensure that taxpayer dollars are only directed toward projects of the highest merit.

The process under H.R. 4890 would begin with the President identifying an item of wasteful spending or a special-interest tax break in legislation that is being signed into law. The President would then submit a special message to Congress, asking for Congress to rescind this wasteful item or items. House and Senate leadership would have the opportunity to introduce the President's rescission requests within two days following receipt of the President's message. After that time period, any member of Congress would be able to introduce the President's rescission proposal, virtually guaranteeing congressional action. Once the bill is introduced, it would be referred to the appropriate committee, which would then have five days to report the bill without substantive revision. If the committee fails to act within that time period, the bill would be automatically discharged to the floor. The bill would have to be voted on by the full House and Senate within 10 legislative days of its introduction, with a simple majority required for passage.

Since introducing H.R. 4890, I have received substantial feedback from interested Members of Congress on ways to improve the legislation to ensure that it best meets its intent of controlling federal spending while keeping the power of the purse squarely in the legislative branch. Among the changes that I think may improve the legislation are the following: limiting the time period available to the President to make a rescission request after signing a bill into law; limiting the number of rescission requests that can be made for each piece of legislation signed into law; allowing for the bundling of rescission requests; explicitly prohibiting duplicative requests; and tightening the

language that allows the administration to defer spending while a rescission request is being considered by Congress. These changes will strengthen the bill and better ensure that the legislative branch retains all of the powers delegated to it by our founding fathers. I am committed to continuing to work with my colleagues in Congress and the administration throughout the legislative process to make sure that H.R. 4890 is narrowly drafted in order to best achieve its goals.

CONSTITUTIONAL ISSUES

H.R. 4890 passes constitutional muster because it requires both the House and Senate to pass rescission legislation and send it to the President for his signature before the rescissions become law. In *Clinton v. City of New York* [1998], the U.S. Supreme Court held that the line-item veto authority provided to President Clinton in 1996 violated the Presentment Clause of the U.S. Constitution (Article I, Section 7, Clause 2), which requires that "every bill which shall have passed the House of Representatives and the Senate, shall, before it become a Law, be presented to the President of the United States." The problem with this version of the line-item veto was that the President's requested rescissions would become law by default if either the House or Senate failed to enact a motion of disapproval to stop them from taking effect. The lower court in *Clinton v. City of New York* also held that this version of the line-item veto upset the balance of power between the executive and legislative branches. Unlike the 1996 line-item veto legislation, H.R. 4890 leaves Congress in the middle of the process where it belongs and follows the procedure and balance of power outlined in our Constitution.

H.R. 4890 also withstands constitutional scrutiny under the U.S. Supreme

Court's holding in *I.N.S. v. Chadha* [1983]. In *I.N.S. v. Chadha*, the Supreme Court invalidated part of the Immigration and Nationality Act that allowed a single house of Congress to override immigration decisions made by the Attorney General. The Legislative Line-Item Veto Act of 2006 is consistent with this holding because the President's authority to defer funds would not explicitly be terminated by the disapproval of a proposed rescission by one of the houses of Congress.

I agree with the Supreme Court's rulings in *Clinton v. City of New York* and *I.N.S. v. Chadha*. It is extremely important that Congress does not cede its law-making power to the President. I believe that this violates the Separation of Powers in addition to the Presentment Clause. In contrast, H.R. 4890 would withstand constitutional scrutiny because it requires both houses of Congress to act on any rescission request and for this legislation to be sent back to the President for his signature.

CONCLUSION

In 2006, the federal government will once again rack up an annual budget deficit of over $300 billion, and our debt is expected to surpass $9 trillion. Meanwhile, the retirement of the baby boom generation looms on the horizon, threatening to severely exacerbate this problem. Given these dire circumstances, it is essential that we act now to give the President all of the necessary tools to help us get our fiscal house in order. By providing the President with the scalpel he needs to pinpoint and propose the elimination of wasteful spending, H.R. 4890 takes an important first step toward achieving this goal.

A Line-Item Veto for the President: Unwise Grant of Power

Cristina Martin Firvida

[I am here] to testify on behalf of the National Women's Law Center on H.R. 4890, the Legislative Line Item Veto Act of 2006. The bill would dramatically expand the powers of the President in relation to Congress, presenting serious policy and constitutional questions while doing little, if anything, to control growing deficits.

The bill has sometimes been described as a means of eliminating unnecessary earmarks, but its scope is far broader. H.R. 4890 would give the President unprecedented power to suspend, and effectively cancel, provisions of law enacted by Congress, even after Congress has rejected the President's rescission proposal. The expanded rescission power would apply not only to appropriations, currently subject to a more limited rescission authority, but also to direct spending for programs upon which millions of Americans rely, and, on its face, some targeted tax benefits. In addition, the bill would enable the President to control the legislative agenda of Congress, because the President would have the ability to control the timing and number of rescission bills sent to Congress, and the expedited rescission process would require that Congress respond. These sweeping new provisions raise significant policy issues and effectively confer upon the President the power to amend or repeal duly enacted legislation, in violation of the separation of powers doctrine and the presentment and bicameralism clauses of Article I, Section 7 of the Constitution of the United States.

In addition, empirical evidence suggests that the proposed Legislative Line Item Veto Act would not result in substantial savings that would reduce our nation's record deficits. Indeed, the potential for Congress to agree to fund the President's priorities in exchange for the President's promise not to exercise the veto suggests that spending may increase as a result of this legislation.

H.R. 4890 GRANTS THE PRESIDENT SWEEPING POWERS TO SUSPEND— AND EFFECTIVELY CANCEL— COVERED SPENDING AND TAX PROVISIONS

This bill would give the President the unilateral power to suspend, and in some cases, effectively cancel, spending and tax provisions enacted by Congress. This Presidential power to essentially amend or repeal duly enacted legislation is bad public policy and presents the clearest constitutional violation in H.R. 4890.

H.R. 4890 would give the President sweeping new authority to suspend covered spending and tax provisions even after Congress had rejected the proposed rescission. The bill would allow the President to suspend funding for a period of 180 days (and possibly more) after sending a special message to Congress seeking legislative approval of the rescission, even if Congress explicitly rejects it. This is a dramatic departure from current rescission authority. Current law gives the President authority to withhold appropriated funds for up to 45 session days while Congress considers a proposed rescission, but explicitly requires that the President's suspension of funding immediately end if one legislative house rejects the President's rescission request (or at the end of the 45-day period if no action is taken) and that budget authority be made available for obligation immediately. The Line Item Veto Act of 1996 likewise required the President to immediately reinstate canceled funding if Congress adopted a joint resolution of disapproval. Giving the President the power to ignore the expressed will of Congress as H.R. 4890 would do is unprecedented.

In addition, H.R. 4890 grants the President extremely broad discretion to determine when, in what fashion, and how often to rescind covered provisions of law. While H.R. 4890 requires Congress to act upon a rescission request sent by the President within 13 session days, the bill permits the President to send his proposed rescissions to Congress up to one year after enacting a spending or tax bill. In addition, the bill allows the President to send rescissions from one spending or tax law in numerous rescission bills to Congress, or to send rescissions from several spending or tax laws in one rescission bill. Finally, in contrast to current law, the bill does not appear to prohibit the President from resubmitting the rejected rescission in a different rescission request, and continuing to suspend the operation of the provision.

The powers granted to the President under H.R. 4890, taken together, would effectively grant the President the ability not merely to delay, but to cancel provisions of law unilaterally. For example, the President could submit a package of rescissions to Congress in the spring and withhold funding until the end of the fiscal year, when spending authority would cease for many items, terminating the program even if Congress explicitly rejected the rescission. As a result of the broad new powers granted to the President in H.R. 4890, federal agencies, state and local governments, and individuals who administer or receive federal funding through a variety of programs and benefits, would be unable to rely on funding approved by Congress.

H.R. 4890 WOULD ALLOW THE PRESIDENT TO RESCIND DIRECT SPENDING AS WELL AS APPROPRIATIONS, BUT DO LITTLE TO CONTROL SPECIAL INTEREST TAX BREAKS

The breadth of the cancellation power granted to the President under H.R. 4890 is matched by the breadth of the spending items to which it can apply, compounding the constitutional and policy concerns raised by the new power. Despite the fact that H.R. 4890 has been justified as a mechanism for controlling earmarks and tax benefits for powerful special interests, the bill also would apply to broad-based items of direct spending, and render low-income recipients of mandatory spending programs especially vulnerable to program cuts.

The expanded rescission powers authorized by H.R. 4890 would apply not only to appropriations, to which more limited rescission authority currently applies, but also to new items of mandatory spending, allowing the President to override individual entitlements enacted into law. The expansion of the President's rescission authority to apply to direct spending items is especially troubling because the broad definition of "direct spending" in the bill may be claimed to allow the cancellation of existing entitlement spending in reauthorizations, rather than only new spending. For example, if H.R. 4890 were to be enacted, it is possible that a significant number of provisions in the reauthorizations next year of the State Children's Health Insurance Program and the Farm Bill (which authorizes Food Stamps) could be subject to rescission even if those provisions were not new and did not add to the costs of the legislation.

Conversely, the definition of targeted tax benefit in the bill is so narrowly constructed as to virtually guarantee that no carefully drafted tax benefit will be subject to the new cancellation power. The definition used in the bill would apply to tax provisions that benefit 100 or fewer beneficiaries, except that it would not apply if the provision treats all persons engaged in the same industry or activity or owning the same type of property similarly. The Joint Committee on Taxation [of Congress] analyzed this definition (which was included as part of the Line Item Veto Act of 1996), and concluded that the exceptions were vague and poorly defined. As a result, this creates the potential to altogether exempt tax breaks from the line item veto. For example, had the Legislative Line Item Veto Act of 2006 been in effect when the 2004 corporate tax bill was passed, the President might have been powerless to cancel special interest tax breaks for ceiling fan importers and tackle-box manufacturers, among others, which were criticized by many observers as pork, and which presumably would be the type of targeted tax benefit H.R. 4890 is supposed to eliminate.

While some justify limiting the definition of "targeted tax benefits" to ensure that only special interest tax breaks and not broad-based tax policies are subject to cancellation, no similar limitation exists to ensure that broad-based direct spending policies are also not subject to cancellation. In fact, the only broad-based tax policies that may be subject to the Legislative Line Item Veto are those that include items of direct spending. The two most prominent tax credits that trigger direct spending are the Earned Income Credit and the Additional Child Tax Credit. Both of these credits assist low-income families. Should H.R. 4890 be adopted, the President may be authorized to cancel portions of these credits should Congress, for example, vote to extend improvements to the credits passed in 2001 and 2003. There is no justification for giving the President the authority to suspend tax provisions that help millions of poor children but not tax provisions that benefit a few thousand multi-millionaires.

H.R. 4890 ALLOWS THE PRESIDENT TO CONTROL THE CONGRESSIONAL AGENDA

The process for Congress to respond to the President's proposed rescissions set forth by H.R. 4890 creates the potential for the President to exercise considerable control over the congressional schedule and agenda, above and beyond budget and spending bills. This ability to reorder congressional legislative priorities in and of itself will result in a bad policy outcome, and when combined with the broad authority to cancel spending granted by H.R. 4890, exacerbates the constitutional breach contained in this proposal.

Under current law, if Congress fails to approve the President's rescission proposal within 45 session days, including by inaction, spending authority must be restored. Given that Congress has the power of the purse under our constitutional structure of separation of powers, it is appropriate to leave to Congress the discretion to act on the President's suggested rescissions, to act instead on its own package of rescissions, or to do nothing at all. However, H.R. 4890 would strip Congress of this discretion and would amend House and Senate rules to provide for fast-track consideration of presidential rescission messages.

Under the new fast-track rules in H.R. 4890, a bill encompassing the President's rescission package must be introduced by congressional leadership no later than two session days after the President sends a special message to Congress proposing the rescissions. If no bill is introduced by the second session day, any member may introduce the bill thereafter. Once the rescission bill is introduced, the appropriate committees are required to approve the bill without any change no later than the fifth session day, or, if the appropriate committees fail to do so by that day, the bill is automatically discharged from the committees. Both the House and Senate must have an up or down vote on the rescission bill, without amendment, by the end of the tenth session day after introduction of the bill. In summary, if the procedures are adhered to and are not waived by rule or otherwise ignored, Congress would be compelled to complete action on the President's rescissions within 13 session days of the President's sending the proposal to Congress.

In combination with the broad discretionary authority granted to the President to send rescission messages at any time and in any manner that the President sees fit, these fast-track procedures are an invitation to allow the President to control the entire Congressional legislative agenda. For example, a President could exercise the rescission authority as a parliamentary tool to tie up the Congressional schedule indefinitely or until the President receives the concessions he or she seeks. The President could send over a series of bills that rescind spending items from bills that were passed and signed at different times, bundling the rescission of spending items that are popular in Congress with those that are unpopular with the public, in order to compel Congress to turn away from other work and dispose of the rescissions. This would enable the President to control the timing of votes in Congress on other pending legislation. If deployed during the second half of a second session of any given Congress, the tactic could run out the clock on other pending legislation. It is important to note that H.R. 4890 could affect consideration of all pending legislation in this way, not just legislation related to spending items.

THE EXPANSIVE POWERS GRANTED TO THE PRESIDENT BY H.R. 4890 RAISE SERIOUS CONSTITUTIONAL PROBLEMS

The extraordinary new powers that H.R. 4890 would confer upon the President raise serious constitutional problems under the separation of powers doctrine, as well as the presentment and bicameralism requirements of Article 1, section 7 of the Constitution of the United States.

The separation of powers is a fundamental feature of our Constitution and our system of government. It was designed to and does play a crucial role in safeguarding the liberties and freedoms that the Constitution created and which the founding fathers endeavored to protect. As Justice [Anthony M.] Kennedy so succinctly put it in his concurrence in *Clinton v. City of New York* [1998]:

> Liberty is always at stake when one or more of the branches seek to transgress the separation of powers. Separation of powers was designed to implement a fundamental insight: Concentration of power in the hands of a single branch is a threat to liberty. The Federalist states the axiom in these explicit terms: "The accumulation of all powers, legislative, executive, and judiciary, in the same hands...may justly be pronounced the very definition of tyranny."

The Supreme Court has historically taken a strict approach to analyzing potential violations of the separation of powers doctrine. A long line of cases demonstrates that the Court is extremely skeptical of any encroachment on the power of each branch and consequently will apply a strict formal analysis frequently resulting in the invalidation of the Congressional act. As the court stated in *Mistretta v. United States* [1989]:

> Accordingly, we have not hesitated to strike down provisions of law that either accrete to a single Branch powers more appropriately diffused among separate Branches or that undermine the authority and independence of one or another coordinate Branch. For example, just as the Framers recognized the particular danger of the Legislative Branch's accreting to itself judicial or executive power, so too have we invalidated attempts by Congress to exercise the responsibilities of other Branches or to reassign powers vested by the Constitution in either the Judicial Branch or Executive Branch.

In *Clinton v. City of New York*, the Court emphasized that while some lawmaking responsibilities are assigned to the President in Articles I and II of the Constitution, "there is no provision in the Constitution that authorizes the President to enact, to amend, or to repeal statutes." In addition, the lack of a constitutional provision assigning the President such a role was interpreted to be the equivalent of an express prohibition. The Court ruled in Clinton that allowing the President to cancel spending unilaterally amounted to an impermissible exercise of the power to amend or repeal statutes, a power that is explicitly reserved for the Congress under the Constitution.

Like the power to cancel items of spending struck down by the Court in Clinton, the powers granted to the President by H.R. 4890 constitute an amendment or repeal of a statute by the President. Under H.R. 4890, the President can suspend the operation of provisions of law for 180 days even if Congress rejects the proposed rescission. H.R. 4890 gives the President the power to decide when to submit a rescission request, and, depending when the rescission is submitted, the "suspension" could result in the permanent elimination of spending authority. H.R. 4890 also would allow the President to resubmit proposed rescissions that Congress had previously rejected, which likewise could effectively terminate spending authority. Because the broad powers granted to the President by H.R. 4890 could end, as a practical matter, programs funded by discretionary spending, direct spending programs, or tax benefits previously approved by Congress, "[i]n both legal and practical effect, the President [would have] amended...Acts of Congress by repealing a portion of each." As the Congressional Research Service concluded, these provisions may reach "far enough to be considered an effective grant of authority to cancel provisions of law...," and that was proscribed by the Supreme Court in *Clinton v. City of New York*.

In addition, because the cancellation authority the President is granted by H.R. 4890 is legislative in nature, it also violates the provisions of Article I, Section 7 of the Constitution of the United States, namely, the presentment and bicameralism clauses. These clauses provide that no law can take effect without the approval of both Houses of Congress and that all legislation must be presented to the President before becoming law. As *INS v. Chadha* [1983] makes clear, the amendment and repeal of statutes, no less than their enactment, must conform with Article I. Pursuant to H.R. 4890, the President would have the ability to create a different law from one duly enacted by Congress and signed by the President, temporarily and possibly permanently, without Congressional approval and despite Congressional disapproval.

The fact that Congress is considering granting the President such extraordinary power does not resolve the constitutional issues. The Constitution does not authorize Congress to cede to the executive that power which is properly its own. As Justice Kennedy stated in his concurrence in Clinton:

> That a congressional cession of power is voluntary does not make it innocuous. The Constitution is a compact enduring for more than our time, and one Congress cannot yield up its own powers, much less those of other Congresses to follow. …Abdication of responsibility is not part of the constitutional design.

H.R. 4890 IS UNLIKELY TO REDUCE AND COULD EVEN INCREASE SPENDING

The experience with line item vetoes at the federal and state level does not suggest that enacting H.R. 4890 will significantly reduce the deficit. Moreover, by significantly increasing the President's ability to negotiate for the Administration's own budget priorities, the line item veto may actually increase spending. While no amount of savings or deficit reduction could justify a violation of the Constitution, the very poor track record of the line item veto as a tool to control spending should alone be grounds to reject the proposal.

The President's current rescission authority has not produced significant savings over time. In fact, the current administration (in contrast to other administrations) has never used current rescission authority (nor the constitutional veto power) to curtail spending.

Nonetheless, frustration with current rescission authority has suggested to some that a line item veto is needed to give the President the power to control spending.

However, the evidence on the effect of a more aggressive—and unconstitutional—rescission authority, the Line Item Veto Act of 1996, shows minimal impact on budget savings. According to the Congressional Research Service, the implementation of the 1996 Act produced modest savings. In one year, the President successfully vetoed $355 million in spending out of a $1.7 trillion budget. The total savings produced by President Clinton's line item vetoes amounted to less than $600 million over five years. The savings would have been greater had Congress approved all of the President's request to cancel funding—but even if each and every cancellation had been accepted, the amount would still have come to well under $1 billion over five years.

The picture from the states also provides little evidence that the line item veto is an effective means of controlling spending. Currently, 43 states have line item veto authority for their governors. State budget practices are fundamentally different from federal budgeting practices, in part because the constitutions of most states provide very explicit details on how budgets are to be enacted, and most give the executive branch of government a much stronger role in budgeting than is constitutionally permissible at the federal level. However, even governors with significant line item veto power are unable to secure significant savings through it. Douglas Holtz-Eakin, former director of the Congressional Budget Office [CBO], in a survey of evidence from the states concluded "that long run budgetary behavior is not significantly affected by the power of an item veto." In testimony last month before the House Rules Committee, the CBO renewed the observation that in some states the line item veto has not decreased spending, as the result of governors and legislatures negotiating to include a governor's spending priorities in a state's budget in exchange for a promise that the governor will not exercise line item veto authority. The CBO expressed concern that a similar dynamic at the federal level would result in higher spending.

Indeed, the concerns expressed by the CBO have been echoed and expanded upon by other observers. George Will, in an insightful column examining the line item veto, stated that, "knowing the president can veto line items, legislators might feel even freer to pack them into legislation, thereby earning constituents' gratitude for at least trying to deliver." He went on to describe how the President could buy the support of members of Congress on his legislative priorities in exchange for a promise that he would not veto the spending priorities of the members. The Congressional Research Service came to a similar conclusion in a 2005 report. Warning that savings would be very limited under a line item veto, the Congressional Research Service went on to state, "Under some circumstances, the availability of an item of veto could increase spending. The Administration might agree to withhold the use of an item veto for a particular program if Members of Congress agreed to support a spending program initiated by the President." The concern that the Legislative Line Item Veto will not only fail to decrease spending but may exacerbate the record deficits that we face is one that must be taken seriously.

CONCLUSION

The separation of powers is fundamental to our Constitution and system of government. Our Constitution does not authorize the President to enact, amend, or repeal statutes. Granting the President that authority—as H.R. 4890 would effectively do—would be unwise as well as unconstitutional.

THE CONTINUING DEBATE:
A Line-Item Veto for the President

What Is New

The bill discussed in this debate, H.R. 4890 passed the House of Representatives by a vote of 247 to 172, with most Republicans voting yes and most Democrats voting no. However, the bill died in the Senate without ever coming to a vote. Meanwhile, Congress spent $29 billion for almost 10,000 pork barrel projects, also called "earmarks" in 2006. When the Democrats captured Congress in the 2006 elections, Speaker-elect Nancy Pelosi pledged, "We will bring transparency and openness to the budget process and to the use of earmarks." Action did not follow the rhetoric. As CNN reported in mid 2007, "Despite [Pelosi's] promise of 'openness and transparency' in the budget process, a CNN survey of the House found it nearly impossible to get information on lawmakers' pet projects." CNN went on to report that less than 10% of House members agreed to list the earmarks they were seeking. Indeed, earmark requests increased, with the chairman of the House Appropriations Committee putting the number at about 32,000 and rising. Among other requests in the House, Kathy Castor (D-FL) was seeking $2,000,000 for streetcars in Tampa, and Louie Gohmert (R-TX) was asking for $1,675,000 million for the Big Cypress Bayou Fish and Wildlife Habitat Restoration project in Jefferson. In the Senate, Barack Obama (D-IL) was hoping for $500,000 to widen Miller Road in McHenry County.

Where to Find More

A group favoring a line-item veto is the Citizens Against Government Waste at www.cagw.org/. Among other things, you will find a hyperlink to the annual *Pig Book* detailing pork barrel legislation. How the Line Item Veto Act of 1996 was used before it was ruled unconstitutional is at the National Archives and Records Administration, "History of Line Item Veto Notices," at www.access.gpo.gov/nara/nara004.html. More information can be found in a Congressional Research Service report, "Item Veto and Expanded Impoundment Proposals," September 15, 2000 at: www.senate.gov/~budget/democratic/crsbackground/itemveto.pdf. The National Conference of State Legislatures reviews the use of line-item veto authority in the states in, "Gubernatorial Veto Authority with Respect to Major Budget Bill(s)" at www.ncsl.org/programs/fiscal/lbptabls/lbpc6t3.htm.

What More to Do

What to some is outrageously wasteful spending is to others a prudent allocation of budget dollars. One way to evaluate this is to go the Web site of Citizens Against Government Waste and to the last annual *Pig Book*, which lists the spending that group considers pork barrel appropriations. Think about the items. Do you agree all are wasteful? You can even divide the class up. One person or a team could be the "pork prosecutors" indicting these spending items. Others in the class could be senators from the states receiving the alleged pork. They would defend the appropriations for their state. The rest of the class could be the collective president, assuming you have a line-item veto and lining out or leaving in each item presented by the pork prosecutors and defended by the senators.

CREDITS

Adler, Jonathan H. "How Conservative Is This Court?" Copyright © 2007 by National Review Online, www.nationalreview.com. Reprinted by permission.

Amicus Curiae brief to the U.S. Court of Appeals, District of Columbia Circuit in *Parker v. District of Columbia* (2006).

Amicus Curiae brief to the U.S. Supreme Court in *Morse v. Frederick* (2007).

Amicus Curiae brief to the U.S. Supreme Court in *Parents Involved in Community Schools v. Seattle School District No. 1* (2007).

Berenson, Bradford. Testimony during hearings on "Exercising Congress's Constitutional Power to End a War" before the U.S. Senate, Committee on the Judiciary, January 30, 2007.

Berman, Douglas A. Testimony during hearings on "Use and Misuse of Presidential Clemency Power for Executive Branch Officials" before the U.S. House of Representatives, Committee on the Judiciary, July 11, 2007.

Best, Judith A. Testimony during hearings on "Proposals for Electoral College Reform: H.J. Res. 28 and H.J. Res. 43" before the U.S. House of Representatives Committee on the Judiciary, Subcommittee on the Constitution, September 4, 1997.

Blumenthal, Richard. Testimony during hearings on "Prices at the Pump: Market Failure and the Oil Industry" before the U.S. House of Representatives, Committee on the Judiciary, Antitrust Task Force, May 16, 2007.

Brief for the Plaintiff to the U.S. Supreme Court in *Scott v. Harris* (2007).

Brief for the Respondent to the U.S. Supreme Court in *Scott v. Harris* (2007).

Bright, Stephen B. Testimony during hearings on "An Examination of the Death Penalty in the United States" before the U.S. Senate, Committee on the Judiciary, Subcommittee on the Constitution, February 1, 2006.

Cain, Becky. Testimony during hearings on "Proposals for Electoral College Reform: H.J. Res. 28 and H.J. Res. 43" before the U.S. House of Representatives Committee on the Judiciary, Subcommittee on the Constitution, September 4, 1997.

Cannon, Carl. "She Can Win the White House," *The Washington Monthly*, July/August 2005. Reprinted with permission from *The Washington Monthly*. Copyright © by Washington Monthly Publishing, LLC, 733 15th St. NW, Suite 520, Washington, DC 20005. 202-393-5155. Web site: www.washingtonmonthly.com.

Felmy, John. Testimony during hearings on "Prices at the Pump: Market Failure and the Oil Industry" before the U.S. House of Representatives, Committee on the Judiciary, Antitrust Task Force, May 16, 2007.

Firvida, Cristina Martin. Testimony during hearings on "The Constitution and the Line Item Veto," U.S. House of Representatives, Committee on the Judiciary, Subcommittee on the Constitution, April 27, 2006.

Fisher, Louis. Testimony during hearings on "Exercising Congress's Constitutional Power to End a War" before the U.S. Senate, Committee on the Judiciary, January 30, 2007.

Fonte, John. Testimony during hearings on "Comprehensive Immigration Reform: Becoming Americans—U.S. Immigrant Integration," U.S. House of Representatives, Committee on the Judiciary, Subcommittee on Immigration Citizenship, Refugees, Border Security, and International Law, May 16, 2007.

Hansen, James E. Testimony during hearings on "Political Interference with Government Climate Change Science" before the U.S. House of Representatives, Committee on Oversight and Government Reform, March 19, 2007.

Kunkel, Dale. Testimony during hearings on "The Effects of Television Violence on Children" before the U.S. Senate, Committee on Commerce, Science, and Transportation, June 26, 2007.

Laycock, Douglas. From a discussion of the topic "Under God? Pledge of Allegiance Constitutionality," sponsored by the Pew Forum on Religion & Public Life, March 19, 2004. Reprinted with the permission of the Pew Forum on Religion & Public Life. For more information on this issue, please visit www.pewforum.org. Copyright © 2006 Pew Research Center.

Levy, Robert A. Testimony during hearings on "Oversight hearing on the District of Columbia's Gun Control Laws" before the U.S. House of Representatives, Committee on Government Reform, June 28, 2005.

Lincoln, Jeff. "Supreme Court Term Marks Shift to the Right," *World Socialist Web Site*, July 14, 2007 (www.wsws.org). Reprinted with permission.

McAdams, John. Testimony during hearings on "An Examination of the Death Penalty in the United States" before the U.S. Senate, Committee on the Judiciary, Subcommittee on the Constitution, February 1, 2006.

McDonald, Forrest. Testimony during hearings on "Constitutional Amendment to Allow Foreign-Born Citizens to Be President" before the U.S. House of Representatives, Committee on the Judiciary, Subcommittee on the Constitution, July 24, 2000.

O'Connor, Sandra Day. Opinion in *Gonzales v. Raich*, U.S. Supreme Court, June 6, 2005.

Rivkin, David B. Jr. Testimony during hearings on "Use and Misuse of Presidential Clemency Power for Executive Branch Officials" before the U.S. House of Representatives, Committee on the Judiciary, July 11, 2007.

Ryan, Paul. Testimony during hearings on "The Constitution and the Line-Item Veto," U.S. House of Representatives, Committee on the Judiciary, Subcommittee on the Constitution, April 27, 2006.

Sekulow, Jay Alan. From a discussion of the topic "Under God? Pledge of Allegiance Constitutionality," sponsored by the Pew Forum on Religion & Public Life, March 19, 2004. Reprinted with the permission of the Pew Forum on Religion & Public Life. For more information on this issue, please visit www.pewforum.org. Copyright © 2006 Pew Research Center.

Spencer, Roy W. Testimony during hearings on "Political Interference with Government Climate Change Science" before the U.S. House of Representatives, Committee on Oversight and Government Reform, March 19, 2007.

Stahlman, James. Testimony during hearings on "Comprehensive Immigration Reform: Becoming Americans—U.S. Immigrant Integration," U.S. House of Representatives, Committee on the Judiciary, Subcommittee on Immigration Citizenship, Refugees, Border Security, and International Law, May 16, 2007.

Stevens, John Paul III. Opinion in *Gonzales V. Raich,* U.S. Supreme Court, June 6, 2005.

Sullivan, Amy. "Hillary in 2008? Not So Fast," *The Washington Monthly*, July/August 2005. Reprinted with permission from *The Washington Monthly.* Copyright © Washington Monthly Publishing, LLC, 733 15th St. NW, Suite 520, Washington, DC 20005. 202-393-5155. Web site: www.washingtonmonthly.com.

Tribe, Laurence H. Testimony during hearings on "The Effects of Television Violence on Children" before the U.S. Senate, Committee on Commerce, Science, and Transportation, June 26, 2007.

Yinger, John. Testimony during hearings on "Constitutional Amendment to Allow Foreign-Born Citizens to Be President" before the U.S. House of Representatives, Committee on the Judiciary, Subcommittee on the Constitution, July 24, 2000.